MILLARD FILLMORE
Biography of a President

Millard Fillmore

Biography of a President

By

ROBERT J. RAYBACK

Published by American Political Biography Press

Newtown, CT

Published by
AMERICAN POLITICAL BIOGRAPHY PRESS

Library of Congress Catalog Card Number 91-78015
ISBN Number 0-945707-04-5

The dust jacket photo is from the Library of Congress
(Number Z62-8229)

AMERICAN POLITICAL BIOGRAPHY PRESS
39 Boggs Hill
Newtown, Connecticut
06470-1971
Tel: (203) 270-9777 * Fax: (203) 270-0091

This is the seventh printing of the First Edition

Preface

S I BEGAN my research for this book, I expected to find that Millard Fillmore was a weak and pompous President, for tradition had painted that portrait of him. When, instead, my investigations revealed that he possessed extraordinary strength of character and an enviable tenacity of purpose — as well as an admirable personality — I was startled.

For a while this discrepancy between the man I had encountered and his historical image caused me no end of concern. Eventually it became clear that until now the picture of Fillmore which is found in most history books was a product of the reports of his enemies, just as Hamilton's and Hoover's were of theirs.

What was disparagingly reported as Fillmore's overweening, personal ambition, upon investigation, turned into self-sacrifice; his fatal vanity, moreover, became simple dignity. True, he was not a clever politician or an inspiring orator. But, more important, if promotion and preservation of the nation are the criteria, he was a statesman with only a handful of White House rivals. Even after retiring from a lifetime of public service, his actions for civic improvement at the local level were nearly boundless, and his personal life was impeccable. Instead of a self-serving politician, the person who emerged from the sources was a quiet, almost modest, man who had no desire for power and who wanted to do good and make good according to the best conventions of the day. And he succeeded.

*   *   *   *   *

Since knowing the genesis of a book is an aid to the reader, I must admit that curiosity about the Whig party, rather than admiration for Fillmore, started me on the research that led to this biography. Early in the century, a few scholars had begun to re-examine the Whig party. Their probings had given promise of a fundamental reappraisal of Whig actions. Unfortunately, their research stopped short of a full exposition, and I was never satisfied with the resulting explanation of the Whig role in America's development.

Generally, to this day, histories continue to describe the Whig party as an illegitimate union of anti-Jackson capitalists who occasionally won wide support by spurious means but failed when the moral force of the antislavery movement undid their union. Nor have biographies of leading Whigs modified this theme, for the authors have found it a convenient matrix for their work. Viewed broadly, the interpretation contains elements of truth, but known facts make it too evasive a generalization. For me it became even more suspect after I learned that only a handful of qualified writers had ever done basic research into the role of this party in the nation's history.

My own probing soon suggested that a biography of Millard Fillmore could be used to continue the re-examination of the Whig party. He had participated in nearly every significant deed of the group from its birth — even conception — to its death. Moreover, his "life" offered an opportunity to review all Whig activity from a fresh vantage point. Instead of standing on one of the provincial hills (North or South) or one of the determinists' hills (economic, racist, geographic, moralistic) to watch the passing parade, I would be looking at these events from a hill no one had claimed or used. The changed focus might provide new insight into the period. That Fillmore was a little-known President who "needed to be done" made the prospect of a biography even more attractive.

At the outset I had no idea that Fillmore's contribution to America's development was any greater than convention had reported and did not anticipate any startling discoveries. Rather, I expected to use the "man-and-his-times" technique as a form of presentation in order to achieve the goal within the framework of a biography. Digging into the literature of the period, however, soon showed that almost all that anybody knew about Fillmore was what his bitterest political enemy had written nearly ten years after the President's death.[1] Thereafter, for nearly three-quarters of a century, many of those who have written about the period have been repeating this enemy's opinions. Occasionally an adjective is altered, but the President always emerges as a man of limited ability and doubtful integrity. Not many years ago a biographer of a famous Whig captioned a picture of Fillmore with the phrase: "A Vain and Handsome Mediocrity."[2] Sweeping judgments of this kind were made despite the modest amount of investigation that had been made into his life.

To a student of the era, such cavalier treatment is understandable. Probably no period in American political history is more complicated than the 1840's and 1850's — the period of Fillmore's greatest activity and influence. To be able to dismiss safely, i.e. without fear of contradiction, one of the major figures of the era relieves the investigator of a great number of problems. With this I can sympathize, even if I cannot condone the action.

One factor (and there are many others) that encouraged writers to repeat the unfavorable opinions of Fillmore, to the point that they became clichés, was the lack of any literature that would support a contrary position. Only two campaign biographies existed, and until 1907 no one had collected Fill-

[1] Weed, Harriet A., ed., *Autobiography of Thurlow Weed*, 584-588.
[2] Van Deusen, Glyndon G., *Thurlow Weed, Wizard of the Lobby*, opposite 150.

more's known correspondence and addresses. In that year the Buffalo Historical Society published two volumes of his papers. Even then it contained precious little private correspondence. At the time it was thought that the son had destroyed all his father's personal papers. Fortunately this was not wholly true. Four years later a body of approximately 8,500 pieces — mostly incoming correspondence during the Presidential years — were discovered in a Buffalo attic. Considering the care with which these letters had been organized, mounted, and indexed, the absence of any comparable body of his outgoing letters is all the more striking. An unending search by the Buffalo Historical Society has added only a comparatively few letters written by Fillmore. The fate that had saved part of the papers did not have all-embracing power.

Since the original discovery in 1911, a few authors have mined the collection for the correspondence of others. For example, a significant group of Webster's letters were found in the collection. No one, however, used them for a realistic appraisal of Fillmore himself. Either the clichés had discouraged another look at this man, or the effort necessary to see him through his correspondents and the current newspapers seemed too exhausting. So the old picture remained unchanged.

After digging into the materials, I discovered that the task of re-creating the real Fillmore was not impossible, even though the challenge seemed great. Reading the sources against the conditions of the times brought into being a political figure of considerable stature and ability — one who served his nation and community with courage and devotion.

Under the circumstances, the need to write a more orthodox biography became evident, and the re-examination of the Whig party, while not discarded, slipped into the background of Fillmore's story. Consequently the findings about the Whigs may be less obvious, and possibly, it might be argued, less valid. Certainly there is no pretense that this is "the" or even "a" history of the Whigs. Yet in it there is a sizeable piece of their story, and it is not presented in the tradition of conformity. Those readers who need guidance should be alert to at least these areas where departure from the norm exists: i.e., the assessment of the purpose of the political antislavery movement after the mid-forties; the nature of the structure, as distinct from the composition, of the ante-bellum parties; the techniques and processes by which the old Whig party and Fillmore prevented disunion; and the altered dimension of the Know-Nothing party.

*   *   *   *   *

Without the support and aid of others, this work would never have been possible. In my own case the passage of time has deepened my realization that more people than I can name participated in the production of this book.

The bibliography attests to the dependence I have had on others who have plowed the ground before me. A bibliography, however, cannot give credit to those silent partners on whom I leaned heavily — the librarians and caretakers of the memorabilia that became the sources of information. I would have been hopelessly mired without the aid of the staffs of the public libraries of Buffalo, Rochester, and New York; the university libraries of Wisconsin, Rochester, and Syracuse; the State Education Library at Albany, the Library of Congress, and the historical societies of Wisconsin, Ohio, and the Western Reserve. A note of special appreciation is due to the staff of the Buffalo Historical Society and particularly to its librarian, Miss Alice Pickup.

My gratitude also goes out to my colleagues at Syracuse University who took over some of my duties in order to provide me with time to write; to the Maxwell School of Citizenship for helping to defray the cost of research at a critical moment; to Glyndon Van Deusen and Holman Hamilton, historians, who opened my eyes to unrecognized truths; to the late William H. Seward, who permitted me to use his grandfather's papers while they were still in the family home in Auburn, New York; to Arthur C. Cole, who started all this when I was an undergraduate at Western Reserve University; and to Professor John T. Horton of the University of Buffalo for his critical reading of the manuscript.

I save to the end the acknowledgment of my indebtedness to William B. Hesseltine, of the University of Wisconsin, who undertook the monumental task of trying to teach me to be a literate historian and whose advice and help enter more directly into the final results of the book than any other single individual; and to Wilbur H. Glover, Director, and Julian Park, President, of the Buffalo Historical Society, whose unflagging encouragement and blue pencil made a manuscript into a book. And finally I am anxious to admit that this project was feasible only because of the patience, understanding, and faith of my wife, Marguerite Leadrach Rayback, who served throughout as typist, secretary, grammarian, critic, breadwinner, and companion.

Contents

CHAPTER   PAGE

1 "If thee has an ambition for distinction . . . . "   1

2 The Trojan Horse   16

3 Buffalonian   40

4 A New Departure   60

5 Antimason into Whig   69

6 Nascent Rebellion   91

7 At the Altar of Mammon   115

8 Nativism and Defeat   137

9 The Comptrollership: Marking Time   160

10 The Road Back to Washington   173

11 "We could put up a cow . . . . "   192

12 Toward the Compromise of 1850   207

Contents — Continued

13 President Fillmore Wrecks the Omnibus 238

14 Warfare: The Bolt of the "Silver Greys" 254

15 The Great Silence 268

16 The Lure of the East 293

17 Fillmore Obstructs Manifest Destiny 318

18 Self-Sacrifice: "The Hopes of Good Men" 333

19 Webster and the Baltimore Convention 349

20 Retirement to Grief 364

21 National Whigs Find a Host 375

22 Candidate of the Know-Nothings 394

23 Spectator 415

24 First Citizen of Buffalo 431

Bibliography 447

Index 458

Illustrations

Pictures to be found between pages 116-117

Portrait of the youthful Fillmore — Sully

Fillmore's law office

Fillmore's first wife

Fillmore's second wife

Fillmore's daughter

Fillmore's son

Vice-President Fillmore

"Grand National, American Banner"

"Champion of the Light Weights" (Cartoon)

Fillmore's home

Fillmore's home (Interior)

Fillmore of the Union Continentals

Fillmore about 1870

Fillmore, Statue of — Bryant Baker

Home of Buffalo Historical Society

Chapter 1

"If thee has an ambition for distinction . . ."

A STRIKINGLY handsome young man in his late twenties swung his big frame down from the stagecoach platform to the wooden sidewalk before Albany's famed Delevan House. A wet December gust threatened his hat, and as his hand instinctively clutched for the "stove-pipe," his eyes wandered over the hotel's white, classical columns. Momentarily they reminded him of Buffalo's Eagle Tavern, but a quick glance at the swinging sign above the doorway assured him that this, indeed, was a "Temperance Hotel."

Curiosity drew his gaze up and down the unpaved road and, by contrast, revived his memory of Buffalo. Instead of its flimsy, wooden construction and open fields, he saw a row of brick and stone buildings shoved together in European style which gave the impression of sturdiness and density. Twenty thousand citizens crowded their businesses and residences into the Hudson River's narrow west-bank valley.

The traveler shook off an impulse to gawk at New York's second largest city, stepped into the hotel, sought out the proprietor, and with a suavity becoming his appearance, made himself known as Millard Fillmore — recently elected state assemblyman from Erie County.

A few years had wrought a magnificent change in Fillmore's social station. Only recently he had stepped out of the role of a cheerful country bumpkin into the garb of a public servant fingering a walking stick and glowing pink and blond above the intense whiteness of his winged collar. This smart-looking, dignified young man could not see into the future, yet in less time than had passed since his birth, he would be President of the United States, deciding the fate of twenty-three million people.

Only a few years before his birth, his father and mother, Nathaniel and Phoebe Fillmore, had been in the vanguard of a great westward migration. They had been only two among the hopeful thousands who had crossed the Appalachian Mountains, east of which the nation had huddled for nearly two centuries. They had added their day-to-day activities to those of others to make the great central plateau and valley of the continent burgeon with homemaking, lumbering, farming, road and canal building, cotton growing, and moral and political reform.

Later generations were to look with awe and wonder at their ancestors' tremendous re-creation of civilization. Yet the Fillmores, like other pioneers, had not sought heroism. Rather a combination of slick salesmanship and personal frustration had tricked them into abandoning their native New England for a fresh start in a region only recently freed of bloody Indian wars. The Fillmores were more prone to curse than celebrate the events that had pushed them into this wilderness.

During the Revolution, New York had set aside nearly one and one-half million acres of land in central New York to pay bonuses promised its war veterans. Few qualified veterans ever settled in the reserved area. Like the remainder of New York's vast twelve-million-acre public domain, this Military Tract, too, had passed quickly into the hands of real estate promoters. The process was common throughout the nation, and the salesmen of these land promoters traveled the globe for customers. Farmer Nathaniel Fillmore, whose stone-strewn lands near Bennington, Vermont, gave little hope for the future, fell easy prey to a land agent's glowing picture of the fertility of central New York's Military Tract. In 1799 he and his brother Calvin purchased, sight unseen, a farm in Locke township, Cayuga County.[1]

Expectations of a better life had warmed them to the back-breaking tasks of clearing fields and raising a cabin while their wives filled the chinks between the logs. Yet their anticipations were ill-founded. Instead of fertile loam, the Fillmore brothers found unyielding clay. Instead of prosperity, they found poverty.[2]

Here in this wilderness cabin, separated from its nearest neighbor by four miles of forest and snow-covered underbrush, on the morning of January 7, 1800, there was born the first son of Nathaniel and Phoebe Fillmore. While the initial delight of having a son prevailed, the proud mother and father forgot their straitened condition and lost themselves in the joy of selecting a name for the boy. They searched for one which would express their faith in each other and finally bestowed upon the child the mother's maiden name, Millard.[3]

For Nathaniel the birth of Millard was a brief distraction from mounting misfortunes. To his woes of poor crops, poor weather, and a crowded cabin was added a defective land title — a common frontier ailment that was peculiarly vicious in the Military Tract. Faulty surveys, claim-jumping, ignorance, and downright chicanery had so confused the region's legal titles that the state sent a team of commissioners to review and settle all land titles in the area. The Fillmore brothers, unable to defend their ownership against the commissioners' findings, packed their families and few belongings on the farm wagon and moved a

---

[1] Frank H. Severance, ed., *Millard Fillmore Papers*, 2 vols. (*Publications of the Buffalo Historical Society*, vols. 10, 11) 2:469. Hereinafter this work will be cited as *Fillmore Papers*. See also, *ibid.*, 1:3. This latter reference is to "Fillmore's Autobiography of His Earlier Years" which may also be found in *Publications of the Buffalo Historical Society*, vol. 2. James Grant Wilson, "Traits of Mr. Fillmore," *The Home Journal*, June, 1874; James Grant Wilson, *Presidents of the United States*, 246.

[2] *Fillmore Papers*, 1:3; [Ivory Chamberlain] *Biography of Millard Fillmore*, 25.

[3] *Fillmore Papers*, 2:469, 1:21.

few miles north to Sempronius.[4] This time, instead of settling on their own land, they took a perpetual lease on a 130-acre farm and condemned themselves to tenantry.[5]

On the edge of civilization in the forest country of New York (in a later generation to become the highly prized recreation area of the Finger Lakes) Millard passed his childhood. Necessity had forced hard labor upon his father, and as Millard grew older, the chores around the farm demanded even his small hands. Occasionally he stole away into the forest glens with a borrowed rifle or relaxed on the shores of Lake Skaneateles with a fishing pole balanced lightly in his fingers, but on every occasion Nathaniel lectured him on the evils of such idleness. "No man," he had cautioned with leaden certainty, "ever prospered from wasting his time in sporting." Fishing and hunting were fit employment only for Indians and their white counterparts. Civilized life was a serious matter.[6]

Early, Millard learned to hoe corn, mow hay, and reap wheat. As he grew older, the wooden plow became a familiar implement in his hand. During the long winter months, he supplied the logs for the cavernous fireplace. When the need for these activities slackened, he cleared, burned, and stumped new crop fields. By the time he had reached the age of fifteen he had mastered most of the primitive, frontier farming skills.[7]

Bystanders at Delevan's could hardly have guessed that the young gentleman, now twenty-nine, who had just come into the hotel had not been born to gracious living. He looked so poised and comfortable in his finery, and handled his cane with such grace, that only the most perspicacious could have seen signs of his humble, bucolic background. It was easy, however, for even the most casual listener to guess that he had come to Albany for the opening of the state legislature. He was a rare political specimen — an Antimason — and not many of the breed had been seen in the capital. Albany abounded with Democrats and Na-

[4]Now called Niles and located about one mile west of Lake Skaneateles and 15 minute walk from the little hamlet of New Hope.
[5]*Fillmore Papers*, 1: 4, 5.   [6]*Ibid.*, 2:471, 1:4.   [7]*Ibid.*, 1:5.

tional Republicans — even an occasional unreconstructed Federalist — but for the first time in America's history men who called themselves "Antimasons" had been elected to offices. Their number was small, but their ardor was high, and they all came from the western part of the state. From what they had said during the campaign they seemingly were intent upon destroying the Masonic lodge. If the truth were known, however, their objectives were much broader, and the future would reveal that they were in the forefront of a major change in New York's and the nation's political life.

For the moment Millard Fillmore was less concerned with Antimasonry than with his own welfare. His transformation from farmer's son to legislator, though gradual, had been accomplished with almost no training or preparation. As a boy he had dreamed of fame, and as a result he had found farm labor chafing, less from the physical exertion — for he was a brawny lad — than from his own pride. Work he was willing to do, but the degradation of menial labor wounded his spirit. He had lamented his father's poverty, and the few opportunities of his own position. If it were humanly possible, he had promised himself, he would rise above that position.[8] He was now on his way, but little in his background justified the air of quiet confidence that surrounded him. It was stage presence rather than natural composure.

*　　*　　*　　*　　*

The change in Millard Fillmore's station in life arose as much from his father's blunders as from his own ambition. Nathaniel's experience with farming was unhappy. His tenant farm also proved to be clay-condemned, and, still rankled by the loss of his original homestead, he damned farming as the meanest of occupations. Certainly he would not urge it upon any of his five sons. He lacked the money to aid them in learning a profession, but they could learn trades without cost, and not be farmers. To start, he apprenticed his fourteen-year-old son, Millard, to a cloth-dresser. The master mechanic, however, fell

[8]Fillmore to William Scott, June 28, 1860, *ibid.*, 2:387-8.

short of being the ideal teacher and employer, and four months later a tearful and terrorized Millard returned home. Nathaniel lost little time in putting Millard in the care of the owners of another carding and cloth-dressing mill. Here, as the years passed, Millard grew from boy to man.[9]

During the months of attending the mill machines, he became painfully aware of his ignorance. In previous years he had taken all the schooling the surrounding country could offer, but this had given him only a slight exposure to the three "R's." He could read, to be sure, but almost nothing except the Bible and a few spelling and reading books were available. Years later he described the family library as "a Bible, a hymn book, and an almanac." His enlightenment began at seventeen when neighbors organized a circulating library and he bought a share in it. Voraciously he attacked the books. No method plotted the course of his reading; it was aimless, but extensive. Immediately one lesson emerged. He recognized the woeful limitations of his vocabulary. He purchased a dictionary, and, determined to learn the meaning of every unknown word, he set up his own school on a desk in the shop. In a spare moment as he passed between the wooden mill-machines, he looked up a word, and fixed its meaning in his memory while changing rolls.[10]

Soon the village of New Hope, not far from the mill, whirled in the eddy of another cultural stream — an enterprising pedagogue had established an academy. Though a pale replica of eastern models, the school surpassed anything Fillmore had known. Taking advantage of the slack season at the mill, Fillmore enrolled in the new academy. He gloried in the experience. For the first time he heard a sentence parsed, for the first time he saw a map, and for the first time he began to experience the pleasures of female society.[11]

[9]*Ibid.*, 2:382, 383, 388, 384, 1:5-9; Lockwood L. Doty, *History of Livingston County*, 251. Fillmore's first employer, Benjamin Hungerford, was a former neighbor and cloth-dresser who had moved to Sparta, N. Y. His second position was with Zaccheus Cheney and Alvan Kellogg in New Hope.
[10]*Fillmore Papers*, 1:4, 5, 9; Fillmore to Scott, June 28, 1860, *ibid.*, 2:383.
[11]*Ibid.*, 1:11.

Abigail Powers was twenty-one; he, nineteen. She was the youngest daughter of Reverend Lemuel Powers of Moravia, and the sister of a local judge. He was the oldest son of a dirt farmer. Her education aimed at polish; his at building a ladder out of the cellar. But the social gap that separated them was too small to discourage their friendship. Their studies cast them into intimate association, and both were young. Her long, black hair drawn tight to her head and her large, dark eyes appealed to him; her rapt interest in his progress flattered him, and her gentle nature consoled him. In turn, his six feet of sturdy manhood aroused her admiration, while his dignified bearing forecast a promising future. He was an unusual specimen on the frontier; she was a superior type, of honored lineage.[12] They sought each other's company constantly in the winter months of 1819, and what time Millard lost from his studies was compensated by the spur she applied to his ambitions. They fell in love, but for a while the progress of that love marked time while Millard endeavored to forge the better life he promised both her and himself.[13]

Once again Nathaniel moved with providential force in his son's life. While Millard courted Abigail at New Hope, his father plotted a new career for him. Seventeen years of struggling with clay soil finally persuaded Nathaniel to sell his tenancy at Sempronius. He and his family moved a dozen miles southwestward, over a range of hills, to Montville, where he became a tenant of County Judge Walter Wood. Septuagenarian Wood possessed more wealth than any other person in the region. His law office thrived on the land title litigations that plagued the Military Tract, and he attended to business with the same scrupulous punctuality as he attended the Quaker meeting. Seeing an opportunity, Old Nat visited his landlord, and with inspired salesmanship persuaded the judge to try out Millard for two months as a clerk in his law office.[14]

Millard knew nothing about the arrangements until his return home. The first evening at the dinner table his proud

---

[12]Chamberlain, *Fillmore*, 31.   [13]*Fillmore Papers*, 1:11.   [14]*Ibid.*, 1:11-12.

mother suddenly and unexpectedly announced the news. It fell with the force of judgment day. In spite of himself, overpowered with joy, Millard burst out crying. He left the table, mortified by his weakness.[15]

Early the next morning he called at Judge Wood's office. The wrinkled, old man greeted him briefly, shoved the first volume of Blackstone's *Commentaries* into his hand, and directed: "Thee will please turn thy attention to this."[16]

In June, after the two trial months had passed, Millard gathered together his few belongings and prepared to go back to New Hope, the mill, and his apprenticeship. The day was sad. Although he had spent only two months reading English law — a phenomenon he did not understand and the source of much agony—he had grown to like his new post. But more important, the law profession appealed to him: it promised money, position, and security. By contrast, wool-carding looked mean and hateful.[17]

Yet Millard had little reason to believe that he would be encouraged to continue. Sour-faced Squire Wood had seldom commented on his work. As the saddened young man took his leave, the judge in characteristic style remarked, "If thee has an ambition for distinction, and can sacrifice everything else to success, the law is the road that leads to honors; and if thee can get rid of thy engagement to serve as an apprentice, I would advise thee to come back again and study law."[18]

Instead of elation, black despair showed on Millard's face. Custom required seven years of clerkship before a candidate was admitted to the bar. Crestfallen, he informed the judge, "I have no means of paying my way." Generously, the Quaker came to his aid. "I can give thee some employment in attending to my business in the country," he encouraged, "and if necessary I will advance thee some money and thee can repay it when thee gets into practice."[19]

---

[15]*Ibid.*, 1:12.   [16]*Ibid.*   [17]*Ibid.*, 1:11, 12.
[18]*Ibid.*, 1:12.   [19]*Ibid.*, 1:12, 13.

Thus the opportunity for a distinguished career burst providentially upon Millard. Quickly he proved that his "ambition for distinction" could overcome his first obstacle. For three months, he taught elementary school at Sempronius (New York's undernourished common school system had finally reached Fillmore's home town) and earned enough money to buy the remaining time of his apprenticeship. Freed at last to pursue an honorable profession, he returned to Judge Wood's office and settled down to the task of learning law. He discarded his cowhide boots for a new pair of shoes, donned a new suit of homespun, and began to wear white collars. He bought a cane. No longer was he Millard, the apprentice — but Mr. Fillmore.[20]

But the course to a lawyer's career did not run smooth. Judge Wood owned a great number of farms, and his tenants were scattered over several counties of the Military Tract. As a clerk, Fillmore helped his employer administer his holdings, and Fillmore became thoroughly familiar with the business methods of the judge. They were cold and methodical, and not a small amount of his personal activity revolved around the eviction of tenants.[21] Before eighteen months of his clerkship had passed, Fillmore, himself, became a victim of the calculating judge.

A farmer with suit before a justice of the peace in the adjoining town offered Fillmore three dollars to pettifog for him. Anxious to have a few dollars that he did not borrow from the judge, Fillmore accepted. Fortunately he concealed his ignorance of law by settling the suit out of court. But Judge Wood soon heard of the incident and indignantly reprimanded his charge. He was not to practice before a justice of the peace again. It would ruin him by corrupting his language with the slang of justice-of-the-peace cases. Fillmore pleaded poverty and the need of earning money. The judge was inexorable

---

[20]*Ibid.*, 1: 9, 10, 13; *Homer Post* (Homer, N. Y.) May 17, 1935, a clipping in the Millard Fillmore Manuscripts; see also teaching certificates, October 8, 1819, June 3, 1820, and Fillmore to William Slade, August 7, 1821, Fillmore Mss.

[21]*Fillmore Papers*, 1:11.

and demanded his promise not to do it again. If he did, they must separate.[22]

To Fillmore, in the heat of an exchange of words, the image of the judge's grasping hand suddenly appeared, and it was reaching out to ensnare his own life. He is "more anxious to keep me in a state of dependence and use me as a drudge in his business," Fillmore thought, "than to make a lawyer of me."[23] A touch of righteousness colored his personality. In the years to come, the trait would be a source of both his strength and his undoing. Yet, even at this time, a spark of idealism smouldered in his mind. Because his whole training had been aimed toward making or improving his livelihood, nothing could ever ignite the spark that would place him in that class of complete idealists who steadfastly cling to their visions no matter how inimical to their interests. But the trait was there, seldom dominating, yet always helping to shape his values. To its urgent call he often responded even if it meant personal sacrifice. Now as he faced the irate judge, Fillmore felt justice was being violated. His employer's greed was repulsive to him. An older person, or one who had more experience with the sordid qualities of men, might have shrugged his shoulders and conformed to the judge's demand, but Fillmore quit the office forever and left his I.O.U. for sixty-five dollars.[24]

It was a time of despair. Saddened by what seemed to be the death of his career, Fillmore joined his father on the farm. Old Nat, meanwhile, had become convinced that central New York was not the ideal farming country and had uprooted the family and moved westward to the township of Aurora, New York, eighteen miles from Buffalo. As he settled down in his parents' house, Fillmore, now almost twenty-one years old, saw the future stretching emptily into time. That winter of 1822 he handled a few justice-of-the-peace cases for his relatives and neighbors, and took a school in East Aurora, but he "was

[22]*Homer Post*, May 17, 1935, Fillmore Mss.; *Fillmore Papers*, 1:13, 14.
[23]*Ibid.*, 1:14.   [24]*Ibid.*

very much discouraged." All he could do was hope, "like Micawber, that something would turn up."[25]

Unwittingly, however, by moving to a community near Buffalo, Nathaniel again created a favorable climate for his son's ambition. At first Millard hardly appreciated that his future lay in Buffalo, for, as he remembered the village, its prospects were not promising. The summer he had been seventeen and the slack season had closed the mill, he had shouldered a knapsack and walked 140 miles to Buffalo "to visit some relatives," in nearby Wales, "and see the country." He had seen Buffalo in May of 1818, four and one-half years after the British had burned it during the War of 1812 in retaliation for the American destruction of York and Newark. The village "then presented a straggling appearance," he reported.

> It was just rising from the ashes and there were many cellars and chimneys without houses, showing that its destruction by the British had been complete. My feet had become blistered, and I was sore in every joint and muscle; and I suffered intensely. I crossed the . . . Indian reservation to Aurora, and recollect a long rotten causeway of logs extending across the low ground from Seneca Street nearly to the creek [Buffalo River?] over which I paddled myself in a canoe. I staid [sic] all night at a kind of Indian Tavern about six miles from Buffalo. . . . A number of drunken Indians and white men kept up a row during most of the night. Next day I went through the woods alone to . . . Wales.[26]

By 1822, in the few years since his visit, Buffalo had changed radically. Its residents had repaired the damage of the British torch and were caught up in a building boom that would continue far into the future. The guarantee of future prosperity was close at hand. During the previous five years the construction gangs of the Erie Canal had inched their way westward across the state. At Rochester advance units had built an aqueduct to carry the canal across the Genesee River, and shortly the pick and shovel gangs arrived in Buffalo. The basins for harboring canal boats had been begun, and off-shore barges

[25]*Ibid.*   [26]*Ibid.*, 1:5, 10-11.

ladened with great stones plied the waters of Lake Erie toward a breakwall that was slowly emerging to make a basin for Great Lakes ships. Already Buffalo possessed over 300 buildings, and its population bordered on 4,000.[27] Speculators scrambled for land, building sites, hydraulic power, harbor construction contracts, and future shipyards; the hum of Buffalo's busy life was almost unrivaled in all of the great West.

Fillmore's lack of appreciation for Buffalo's possibilities was short-lived. In the spring of 1822 he took a teaching post there, and undoubtedly gazed with amazement at the activity all about him. Never before had he seen so many people living together. All his life he had rubbed shoulders with farmers and farmers' sons and the sight of merchants, stage owners, hotel keepers, lake captains, and canal workers gave him a new outlook on life. Unlike sophisticated travelers from abroad who visited the growing West and complained about its uncouth, boisterous, mad scramble for wealth, Fillmore avidly absorbed the town's atmosphere and tried to become part of it.

His move to Buffalo was well calculated. Already a dozen law firms were transacting the legal business of the village and its surrounding Erie County. Getting a clerkship in one of them proved far less difficult than he had anticipated. Early in the summer of 1822 he entered the law firm of Asa Rice and Joseph Clary as a clerk.[28] By agreement he continued to teach school in season and devote all his spare time and free months to law. The arrangements were ideal. Teaching paid his expenses and the clerkship permitted him to consort with Buffalo's leaders.[29] Bit by bit he impressed himself on the community. Modulated speech, meticulous dress, serious attitude, carefully selected words, orthodox opinions, decorous bearing, correct manners, temperate habits — all gained the approval of his associates. He excelled in all the qualities they saluted.

[27]Julius Winden, *The Influence of the Erie Canal upon the Population along its Course*, 38; *Buffalo Republican*, June 21, 1828.
[28]*Fillmore Papers*, 1:14.
[29]*Ibid.*; A. H. Denis, October 29, 1820, William Fuller *et al*, April 20, 1821, certificate to teach in Buffalo, March 23, 1822, Fillmore Mss.

In and out of the law office, his associates were impressed by his industry. He attended to the details of law with even greater concern than to the social graces, and Buffalonians found him sound and steady. A common saying, "If Millard Fillmore goes for it, so do I," eventually developed in Buffalo and attested to his judgment. Even at this early day his solid qualities were evident, and within a year of entering the firm of Rice and Clary, several older members of the bar who recognized the mettle of young Fillmore persuaded the Court of Common Pleas to admit him to practice.[30] He was overjoyed. At last the coveted goal to which chance and ambition had beckoned him was his.

Yet for all his joy a note of anxiety troubled his mind. Beneath his suavity was a quality which few of his contemporaries ever saw. He was essentially a modest man. Success never boosted his self-esteem to pretentiousness. At best it gave him courage to overcome the inertia of modesty. In future years a good deal of his sound judgment and cautious action would arise out of his inability to develop an overweening confidence. Some of his greatest triumphs, and worst failures, too, would stem from this modesty.

Now, even as he was admitted to practice, he could think less of what he had done than of what he had not done. His training for law had been confined to twenty-seven months instead of the usual seven years. Gaping holes existed in his legal knowledge. To be admitted to the bar after so short a preparation made him timorous. Almost immediately he had an offer to join his former mentor, Joseph Clary, in a law partnership in Buffalo. Instead of seizing the opportunity he returned to lawyerless East Aurora, opened a small office, and there monopolized the petty legal business. It hardly appeared to be a wise move. Fifty years later, when old age had mellowed his pride, Fillmore explained his decision. " . . . Not having sufficient confidence in myself to enter into competition with

[30] *Fillmore Papers,* 1:15.

the older members of the Bar . . . I opened an office at East Aurora."[31]

At East Aurora most of his professional work revolved around land titles, mortgages, and debt collections. His fees were small but adequate. Rapidly the same qualities that had distinguished him in Buffalo aided him in East Aurora. Young as he was, he became the hamlet's leading citizen and helped set the town's social and political tone. Because of his familiarity with law, he early obtained the appointment of commissioner of deeds for the region.[32] In an area where speculators and settlers sold and resold their holdings with heated haste, the fees for recording deeds increased his income substantially. It was his first public office, but there was little in it to forecast a great career.

After two years of practice, he felt sufficiently certain that he could make a comfortable enough living to recapture a dream and to fulfill the promise he had made six years before to Abigail Powers. They had not seen each other since his admission to the bar. Previous to that another long period of separation had marked their relations. But their affections had survived the ordeal. This time Fillmore abandoned foot-travel and like a successful man arrived in Abigail's home town by stagecoach. The reunion in Moravia was as joyous as both had anticipated, and on February 5, 1826, Reverend Orsanius H. Smith joined the couple in matrimony. Immediately the bride and groom returned to East Aurora.[33]

As in 1819, when Abigail's love had spurred him on to higher ambitions, so now her faith and his responsibility stirred him to greater activity. The feeling of inadequacy which had guided him into a backwoods village had diminished but it still troubled him. He resolved to dispel it by learning his profession thoroughly. He purchased volume after volume of law texts and religiously applied himself to mastering them. Within

[31]*Ibid.*, 2:100-101.
[32]Fillmore to Philander Bennett, May 7, 1828, Fillmore Mss.
[33]*Fillmore Papers*, 1:15; William E. Griffis, *Millard Fillmore*, 4.

a year, he had progressed far enough to be admitted as an attorney, and then counselor, to the state Supreme Court, which brought the higher court business in East Aurora to his office. His reputation spread, and clients from distant Cattaraugus and Genesee counties brought their cases to him. Exhausted by expanding business, Fillmore looked for clerical help. At this juncture, gangling, youthful Nathan K. Hall, a family friend from Wales, presented himself for a student-clerkship, and the overworked lawyer took him in. The event excited Fillmore for it meant that he had arrived. He was a teacher again, to be sure, but this time it was in his own profession.[34]

Buffalo lawyers heard of Fillmore's enlarged activities. They saw him at Supreme Court and Court of Appeals sessions. Some envied, others congratulated him. One Philander Bennett, a Buffalo lawyer, prominent Jacksonian and soon to be judge, bid for Fillmore's business friendship and suggested a partnership. Before rejecting it, Fillmore toyed with the idea. For the present the Aurora practice was too comfortable.[35] But he would not be able to resist for long. The strong attraction of Buffalo drew him gradually toward his future.

[34]Fillmore to William Gould and Co., April 16, 1827, Fillmore to Bennett, May 7, 1828, Fillmore Mss.; *Fillmore Papers*, 1:15; Crisfield Johnson, *Centennial History of Erie County, N. Y.*, 331.
[35]Fillmore to Bennett, May 7, 1828, Fillmore Mss.

Chapter 2

The Trojan Horse

N the night of December 31, 1828, other residents of Albany had already begun to welcome in the New Year, but instead of joining the revelry Millard Fillmore and a score of sober-faced men groped through the corridors of New York's capitol. Flickering oil lamps dimly lit their way as their voices echoed off the granite walls. A number of them had never been inside their state capitol, and those who knew the building shepherded the rest toward a committee room. The small band constituted the legislative caucus of the Antimasonic party, and it had gathered to plan for the coming session of the state legislature.[1]

Three years before not one of the group had dreamed of such a party; and like Fillmore, most of those assembled around the caucus table had had no connection with politics. Now their party controlled one-eighth of the seats in New York State's legislature. In some ways this did not accurately represent their strength, for they really dominated the political life of the state's western counties. Already a score of newspapers

[1]*Fillmore Papers*, 1:43; *New York State Assembly Journal, 1829*, 35.

were supporting their cause, and their movement was spreading into neighboring states.[2]

* * * * *

Fillmore himself had been buried in law tomes preparing for admission to higher court practice when the antimasonic movement began. It started on September 12, 1826, when the citizens of the farming community of Batavia, New York, first missed their hard-drinking stonemason. They shrugged their shoulders and assumed that the charge of petty thievery on which the sheriff had arrested him was true. For several days village gossips clucked over the virtues of honesty, but when they later learned the court had discharged William Morgan, they began to wonder why he did not return home. His wife and worried local creditors decided to investigate; a citizens' committee journeyed to the scene of the trial at Canandaigua, fifty miles away. There officials knew only of Morgan's release; what became of him after that no one could say. Friends of Morgan, suspecting foul play, raised the hue and cry.

William Morgan was a stonemason by trade and a Royal Arch Mason by avocation. He was frequently in debt, and his business suffered from his intemperate habits. To increase his depleted funds, he had prepared a book divulging the secrets of the ancient Masonic Order. Rumors of his planned treachery reached several lodges of western New York, and apprehensive members secured his arrest, first as a thief and then as a debtor. Neither charge held and the court restored the stonemason to freedom. Thereafter Morgan was never seen, but rumor soon wove an elaborate account of his strange adventures. As he stepped from the prison, ran the tale, unknown men fell upon him, bound his arms and legs, forced a gag into his mouth and thrust him violently into a covered carriage. His captors, said these rumors, drove fast, with horses and men in relays, over a circuitous route to Fort Niagara. There they locked him

[2]The Antimasons boasted of 32 of the 211 papers in New York State by their own count. See the Report on Newspapers to the State Convention of March 6, 1830, in *Buffalo Journal*, March 10, 1830. For a convenient check list to Antimasonic papers see Milton W. Hamilton, "Anti-Masonic Newspapers, 1826-1834," in Bibliographic Society of America, *Papers*, 32:(1938).

in the fort's magazine, and no one outside the inner circle of Masonry knew the exact nature of his violent and untimely death.

Unsuspectingly, Morgan's kidnappers touched off a political bonfire. His friends demanded his return, and before long public meetings all over western New York were organizing committees to search out and seize the stonemason's abductors. Little success attended the investigators' efforts. Difficulties obstructed their inquiries; their questions fell upon deaf ears. No man could give the lie to Dame Rumor's loquacious murmurings, and the excitement grew in intensity.

While indignation was high, Morgan's book exposing Masonry came from the press. Eagerly the curious fell upon it, seeking therein the key to their fellow citizen's disappearance. They found — whether the key or no — the solemn oaths of Free Masonry. Literally accepted — if practiced — these oaths indicated a total disrespect for law and the established authorities. Pulpits rang with denunciations of Masonry, and editorials in the local press demanded the dissolution of the Order. Soon great numbers of New Yorkers were reasonably certain that Masons, in the name of loyalty to the Order, had engineered Morgan's abduction. Possibly the hierarchy itself had directed the operation. Catching the hysteria, the governor offered a reward for the discovery of the culprits, the legislature selected able lawyers to investigate the crime, and county sheriffs arrested numerous suspects. William L. Marcy and Samuel Nelson, justices of the state Supreme Court, held special circuits which tried the accused and found many guilty of participating in the kidnapping. Even then the excitement did not abate.

By early spring, 1827, New Yorkers were beginning to suspect that something more evil than the complicity of the Masonic Order lurked behind Morgan's disappearance. In spite of all the arrests and trials, public officials seemed incapable of finding out what happened to Morgan after he was locked in Fort Niagara's powder room. With increasing frequency, newspapers asked why it was impossible to penetrate the curtain of ignorance. Suspicion turned upon state officials when probing revealed that some of them were Masons, too. The conclusion seemed inescapable. The Ancient Order of Masons was an invisible empire, whose adherents had infiltrated the government of New York and probably that of other states and the United States as well. They controlled key offices and used their official authority to promote the goals of the Order. Now when one of its members had sought to reveal its secrets, so ran the conclusion, this empire of oath-bound men had done away with him, and, because they controlled the officials, were capable of obstructing and quashing the whole investigation. If good and just government were to be restored all Masons must be purged from public office.[3]

*   *   *   *   *

Fillmore's East Auroran neighbors liked to collect in his office — a remodeled outbuilding, a few yards from his home — to pass the time of day. Almost any evening they could find him dressed in a black, quilted robe and seated at his large desk. They enjoyed their evening chats around his fireplace as much for what he had to say as for escape from a boring family circle. His greetings were always cheerful; he usually had news from Buffalo and other circuit towns like Canandaigua, Mayville, and Batavia, and willingly he would lean back in his chair, slip a green eyeshade to the top of his head, and relax for an hour or two in neighborly conversation.[4]

Frequently the office rang with heated arguments. Politics, and now in 1827 antimasonry, inspired these outbursts. Aurorans could not ignore the issue. Every newspaper that found its way into the hamlet aligned itself on one or the other side. Every visitor brought in more rumors of the great Free Mason conspiracy.

[3]The literature concerned with Morgan's abduction is voluminous. This account is based primarily upon: Thomas A. Knight, *The Strange Disappearance of William Morgan;* Thurlow Weed, "Morgan, the Man the Masons Killed," a letter written on September 9, 1882, and appearing in the *Buffalo Express,* November 27, 1882; John C. Spencer, "Report to the Baltimore Convention," in Rochester *Antimasonic Enquirer,* May 6, 1832; *Report on Morgan's Abduction submitted by the Special Counsel,* reprinted in *ibid.,* January 16, 1830; Thurlow Weed, *Autobiography of Thurlow Weed,* edited by Harriet A. Weed, 210-335.

[4]*Fillmore Papers,* 2:499.

Aurorans might have been less concerned — or certainly less indignant — had they known what lay behind the movement. To the unwary observer it all appeared to arise from natural causes. Resentful men, outraged by flagrant injustice, were reminded of their duties as citizens and were rising spontaneously to drive the rascals out. In the beginning appearances were correct. Yet sixty miles away at a desk in a two-room newspaper plant in Rochester, calm, gray-eyed editor Thurlow Weed knew better. He, too, watched the progress of the agitation.

Daily he picked up the reports and learned where public demonstrations were being made: Canandaigua, Geneseo, Le Roy, Batavia, Lockport, East Aurora, Buffalo. Throughout western New York his aides were prodding the local citizenry to action, suggesting to leading men the possibility that Morgan's abductors might have passed through that very town. Maybe, the agents hinted, some trusted men in the community had loaned their horses for one of the relays. It would be wise to ferret out the evildoers. Organize a meeting! they suggested. Once public alarm had turned to demonstrations, Weed's organizers were on hand to speak or offer resolutions. The following week the stories would appear in his own newspaper, the Rochester *Anti-Masonic Enquirer*.[5]

Thurlow Weed[6] promoted antimasonry and edited his newspaper for one purpose. By fair means or foul he was striving to re-elect John Q. Adams as President of the United States. His methods were devious, but training had prepared him for the task, and he believed the goal justified his method.

[5]Weed, *Autobiography,* 242, 100, 230, 301, 310, 316, 336; Rochester *Antimasonic Enquirer,* 1828, *passim; Rochester Telegraph,* 1827, *passim;* Glyndon G. Van Deusen, "Thurlow Weed in Rochester," *Rochester History* (April, 1940); *Buffalo Republican,* July 19, 1828; *Albany Argus,* July 21, 1828; Albany *Evening Journal,* April 3, 1830; William H. Seward to Weed, February 28, March 19, March 25, 1828, Seward Papers. In later years Weed boasted that all antimasonic movements "whether of a judicial or legislative character, emanated" from Rochester, *Autobiography,* 300.
[6]This sketch based upon Van Deusen's "Weed in Rochester," and his biography *Thurlow Weed: Wizard of the Lobby;* also Weed, *Autobiography,* 56-139.

In that era of American politics all newspapers were party organs and their editors were party hacks. Only rarely did an editor attain high political stature. Weed was among the rarities. At thirty he was about to become a powerful political boss.

Born in the foothills of the Catskill Mountains in 1797, Weed had spent his youth learning the savage law of tooth and claw of both the frontier and political journalism. By 1815 he was working full time as a journeyman printer on an old-line Federalist paper in Albany. Here he had become fascinated with New York's politics. Two years later he had taken charge of the composing room of the Albany *Register*. Thanks to the indulgence of the editor, Weed had written much of the paper direct from his typesetting box. Soon he had developed a vituperative style that had stung the party's enemies with telling effect. This had attracted the lieutenants of New York's foremost politician, DeWitt Clinton, and the nation's leading statesman, John Quincy Adams. They had taken young Weed under wing, and from them and following a natural propensity for politics, he had learned the politician's arts. He had learned all but their chanting, pulpit-like oratory. Seemingly shy and unaggressive, he had shown himself a weak platform speaker, but he wrote with a pen dipped in venom. Journalism would continue to make his bread and butter, and a deep understanding of human emotions would make him a political success.

When in 1818 DeWitt Clinton's managers had needed support in Norwich, New York, they had bought a newspaper and had sent Weed there as its editor. A few years later he had moved to Rochester as a junior editor of the *Telegraph*. With this organ, in 1824, he had carried Monroe County for both Governor Clinton and President Adams, and had won a seat in the New York assembly for himself. In the legislature Weed's fabulous ability at undercover politicking had come forward. By backroom dealings, he had manipulated the legislators into giving New York's electoral vote to John Q. Adams.[7]

7*Ibid.*, 123-28; Jabez D. Hammond, *History of the Political Parties in the State of New York*, 3 vols., 2:152-53.

With this maneuver, he had raised himself high on the list of party leaders.

After the spring of 1825, however, all had not gone well for either Weed's favorites or his own future. Governor Clinton died in office, and his death threw state politics into disorder.[8] Meanwhile, in his bid for re-election in 1828, President Adams faced wise and crafty opponents in the managers of Andrew Jackson's Presidential campaign. Ever since the election of 1824, Jackson's managers had been laboring valiantly to identify their candidate with the underdogs of American life. Everywhere politicians could sense the tug that such an appeal exerted on their constituents. Against its attraction Adams seemed powerless and his chances for re-election were fading.

With Clinton gone and Adams going, Weed could see his own world crumbling about him. With it would go his momentary flight into stardom. Yet Weed was a man of imagination and action. He recognized New York's need for a vigorous boss to replace Clinton, and he could see that the state might still be saved for Adams if someone could come forward with a real vote-getting issue. He saw salvation in the antimasonic commotion. If this excitement could be whipped into a political party, the means of success would be at hand. To the public an Antimasonic party would seem a third force between Jacksonians and Adamsites. Behind the scenes, however, through political trading and the electoral college, the party would support the election of Adams in the nation and an anti-Jackson government in the state. An Antimasonic party could become the balance of power in both state and nation, and if successful in either area, Weed's career would be saved. With his strategy determined, Weed left the *Telegraph,* created the Rochester *Anti-Masonic Enquirer,* and sounded the drums for the rally.[9]   *   *   *   *   *

[8]This story is probably best told in DeAlva S. Alexander, *Political History of the State of New York,* 1: chaps. 18, 19, 22, 23.

[9]*Ibid.,* 1:287-290, 326, 344-356; *Albany Argus,* April 5, 12, July 4, 28, September 5, October 1, 5, 15, 21, 27, November 15, 1827, February 3, 1828; Charles Francis Adams, ed., *Memoirs of John Quincy Adams,* 8:441; Weed, *Autobiography,* 242; *Buffalo Journal* reviews the story of Antimasonry, May 26, 1830.

Fillmore and his Auroran neighbors heard the drumroll. Unlike their friends in bordering counties, they hesitated to respond. All about them during 1827 the antimasonic excitement was being directed into political channels. But Erie County politicians mistrusted Weed's strategy for Adams' re-election. They would not move until antimasonic sentiment proved itself capable of winning local elections. When it did, early in the spring of 1828, General Peter B. Porter, Secretary of War in Adams' cabinet and Buffalo's leading public servant, gave the signal, and the entire Adams following of Erie County gave antimasonry its blessing but retained its National Republican organization.[10]

Up to now Fillmore had associated only casually with the National Republican cause. In 1824, he had voted for Adams supporters and had cooperated with their Erie County corresponding committee. At the time, however, politics had been a minor concern for him. Now, suddenly, he appeared as a county delegate at the first state-wide Antimasonic convention, whose purpose was to organize the party, township by township.[11] Fillmore never explained his move into politics, but undoubtedly a mixture of motives guided him. For a young lawyer with "an ambition for distinction" politics held out tempting promises. Antimasonry's high-sounding cant about purifying government, moreover, could easily have appealed to his idealism. Certainly, since antimasonry had won the endorsement of National Republicans in Buffalo, it could only improve the cause of the business world with which Fillmore was coming to identify himself.

Whatever his motives, Fillmore was now, in the spring of 1828, in the thick of politics: within two months he was a

---

[10]Peter B. Porter to Henry Clay, February 20, 1828, Porter Papers; *Buffalo Republican*, October 10, 1828.

[11]*Buffalo Journal*, September 17, 1828; *Buffalo Republican*, December 5, 1827, March 18, 1828; Weed, *Autobiography*, 256; "Proceedings of the Delegates at LeRoy," in *Albany Argus*, May 17, 1828. The first convention was held at LeRoy, N. Y., March 6, 1828. Fillmore's name appears as "Willard Filmore."

delegate to Erie County's National Republican convention which endorsed John Quincy Adams for the Presidency; in July and again in August he attended state Antimasonic conventions. In these months he discovered that he was in the midst of a very sticky political fight. No man had ever chosen to enter politics at a less auspicious time. If he had been unacquainted with the complexities and uncertainties of New York politics, he now received memorable lessons at these conventions.

Weed had consistently planned that the Antimasons, while pretending to be a third force between the Democrats and National Republicans, would rally at the critical hour behind the National Republican candidates. His scheme called for the Antimasonic conventions to endorse National Republican tickets made acceptable by including Antimasons. But so persuasively had Weed and his agents presented their charges against Masons that a strong and strange fanaticism gripped large numbers of the party. When the time came to endorse National Republican candidates, the fanatics among the Antimasons revolted. They accepted Adams but demanded and got an independent state ticket. Weed's scheme collapsed. Eventually the election returns showed that this convention revolt cost the Antimasonic-National Republican alliance a state victory.[12]

At the convention Fillmore never once failed to support Weed.[13] When the show ended he returned home saddened, half expecting to discover that the Erie County organization was torn with strife. To his relief he found no split between the fanatics and the calculating politicians at home. Though bitter over the convention result, leaders of the Erie County machine were grateful for Fillmore's staunch support of Weed's

[12]*Buffalo Republican*, May 31, 1828; July 19, August 9, 1828; Albany *Daily Advertiser*, April 5, 1828; *Buffalo Journal*, May 1, 1828; June 2, 1830; *Albany Argus*, May 7, July 14, August 6, 11, 20, September 30, October 11, 1828; Weed, *Autobiography*, 43, 46, 86, 110, 302, 305, 306; Alexander, *Political History of N. Y.* 1: 154, 191-194, 239, 319, 320, 361, 363, 365; Thurlow Weed Barnes, *Memoir of Thurlow Weed*, 5; Proceedings of the convention of August 4 in Rochester *Antimasonic Enquirer*, August 9, 1828; William E. Griffis, *Millard Fillmore*, 10; Hammond, *N. Y. Parties*, 2:285-287.

[13]*Buffalo Journal*, July 8, 15, 22, 29, September 5, 12, October 3, 10, 17, 24, 1828.

plans. Instead of reprimanding him, they made him their candidate for the state assembly.[14]

The times were not propitious for either Antimasons or National Republicans. Democrats had placed the greatest vote-getter of the nineteenth century, Andrew Jackson, at the head of their ticket. As their candidate for governor, they offered Martin Van Buren, for whom history would have trouble in finding a challenger for the title of the most astute politician of his time, and even if he faltered, the split in the ranks of his opponents guaranteed him a victory. Democratic office seekers, riding on the coat-tails of Jackson and Van Buren, reveled in their opportunity. Against them Fillmore's campaign for state assembly appeared doomed. Yet, when the results were counted and Jackson, Van Buren, and the Democratic state ticket had won, here and there enclaves of strong opposition stood out. Western New York, with Erie County at its hub, had spurned the Democrats. The local coalition tickets of Antimasons and National Republicans had swept into office. Fillmore had no need to apologize for his showing, for he received more votes in Erie County than any other candidate.[15]

*   *   *   *   *

When Fillmore was growing into manhood the modern political party did not exist. No tightly organized hierarchy of authority from the national central committee down to the precinct leader directed the thinking of rank and file. No one acquired a party at birth. Unheard of was the idea that a political party would go on indefinitely through the generations, like a great living organism, with a life apart from its members. The idea that loyalty and fealty were owed to a political party just as a citizen owes them to a nation was unknown. Later

[14]*Buffalo Patriot*, September 3, 1828; Peter B. Porter to Jabez Smith, September 12, 1828, Porter Papers.

[15]Weed, *Autobiography*, 307; *Albany Argus*, November 18, 24, 27, 1828, Hammond, N. Y. *Parties*, 2:289; *Buffalo Republican*, November 14, 1828. Fillmore received 2731 votes and his running mate, Edward Hall, obtained 2437. B. F. Fox to the Buffalo Historical Society, April 4, 1899 in Fillmore Mss.

generations of Americans would expect their national parties
to "stand for something," even though the principles were only
vaguely expressed. Twentieth-century political scientists could
even talk of the thoughtful citizen who could choose between
the principles of the parties. Had such a thoughtful citizen lived
in the pre-Jackson era he would have searched endlessly, and
in vain, for the principles of the national parties.

In the 1820's Americans conducted their politics in ways
which were as closely related to Old World palace intrigues as
they were to organized twentieth-century political action. Innumerable small factions made up the parties. Seldom were
these factions as large as a state and rarely did they cross state
borders. Usually each consisted of one man's personal followers. What he desired, so did they; and his desires might
change from year to year. For state elections factional leaders
would confer together informally and form a loose agglomeration of their groups. If their combination won, they would
keep it together for a couple of years; if it failed, the leaders
would dissolve it and seek new alliances. For national elections,
a number of state-wide combinations would federate, without
losing their separate identities, into a temporary national party.
But like the state parties, these national groupings were fragile
and their participants fickle. The circumstances did not dictate
a two-party system; three could function just as well, and one
was sufficient. Allies of one year were frequently enemies the
next. By the 1820's they had changed partners so often that
almost every major New York politician had been both friend
and foe of every other leader. If any political principles existed
in this milieu, they were held at the level of the faction, not
the agglomeration. The bulwark of the whole procedure —
that which made it possible — was the limitation on the number
of voters and a system of indirect elections and executive appointments.

Around 1815, however, a new faith in the goodness of
common men began to cut away state restrictions on the right

to vote and the nation's electorate started to expand. New Yorkers, themselves, in 1821 reappraised humanity and removed their property qualifications for the voting franchise.[16] Indirect elections and executive appointments were less easily changed, but during the quarter-century following 1821, New Yorkers gradually extended democracy. Whereas formerly they could vote for only three officials, by 1846 every state, county, city, village, and town office was filled by direct election.

As the bulwarks of trade-and-barter-politics weakened, the ways of politicians changed. Factional leaders could no longer determine election results through their personal tie with a few voters, nor could they control officeholders through appointments. To meet the challenge of the new democracy, the old leaders experimented, in a fumbling manner, with new techniques rather than give up. Eventually they were to find two new tools — control of party nominations and clever propaganda that plucked at the heartstrings of constituents — which were excellent substitutes for the devices of old. The task of using the new tools was arduous and required extraordinary talents which one man seldom possessed. For the most part only co-ordinated teamwork of vast numbers could undertake the job. Gradually the factional leaders were to disappear, to be replaced by party functionaries in a hierarchy of authority. The process was slow and was not completed until the Civil War had come and gone. But as the old system gave way the base of American politics shifted to a new foundation.

Looking backwards, a later generation could see that the vast transformation occurring in America's public life both created and victimized the Antimasonic party as it partook of both the old and the new. Its righteous appeal to masses of voters, its highly organized committee system topped by a state central committee, its state-wide conventions and prompt in-auguration of a national nominating convention (the first in America's history), its conscious effort at propaganda — all represented the new departure. But Antimasonry's grand strategy

[16]Except Negroes.

in 1828 — trade and bargain with National Republicans — had been borrowed from the past.

*   *   *   *   *

After the election of 1828, the caucusing Antimasons at the state capitol recognized that their party strategy had gone astray. Their candidate for President had suffered a staggering defeat, and they were without influence in the national government. They had failed to capture New York and some of their National Republican allies were even beginning to regret the association. Indeed, the grave men of the caucus had little occasion for joy. Exactly what their course for the future should be was the question which ran through their minds. If despair alone had prevailed, they would have dissolved their party. But their answer came from their hopes, not their failures, for any analysis of New York's politics indicated that opportunities still existed for them.

In 1829, besides their own party, Antimasons saw New York's factions arrayed into three other groups. Of these the largest and most successful was the Democratic party. Partisans sometimes called it the "Jacksonian" party, but later contemptuously referred to the "Locofocos." Whatever its name, it was a composite of divergent groups. The hard core of the party — its key faction — was New York's Tammany Hall. Other groups were to come and go, but Tammany Hall was almost permanent. If anyone had the leadership of this party, it was Martin Van Buren, the resourceful, paunchy, elegant, and eloquent chief of the "Bucktails." He had just been elected governor, but was about to resign to become Secretary of State in Jackson's cabinet. Actually, the Democratic coalition of New York was in the hands of a dozen closely allied, well-drilled leaders (two of whom, William Marcy and Silas Wright, became governor) whom their opponents dubbed the "Regency." The factions that the Regency brought together represented the entire state, but it had no legislative program. What was advocated one day, expediency might change the next. Nor was the Regency motivated by any common political philosophy or economic program. Some of their protagonists tried to identify the Regency with the labels "liberal" and "progressive." These labels implied that the Democratic party took a more sincere interest than their opponents in the needs of the less fortunate members of society; but the description fitted them no better than others. Even in the matter of extending political democracy, New York's so-called "Democracy" was frequently arrayed against an advance. Long before other political leaders, however, the Regency had seen the meaning of the expanding number of voters. To attract them, it had begun to adjust its tactics. It campaigned to identify itself with the underprivileged. In reality New York's Democratic party had its due proportion of "aristocrats," "squires," bankers, and commercial magnates, and as a party was not notably antagonistic toward the business world or the specially privileged.[17]

Like their Democratic opponents, Antimasons had recognized the need for mass appeal. Already they had tried to associate themselves with a righteous cause in order to acquire the aura of liberality which came from siding with the oppressed against the tyrannical, and their victories in western New York gave them hope that they might be as successful in challenging Democrats in other parts of the state. Should this come to pass, they might be able to attract whole factions of the Democratic coalition to their own party, for they had already proved that neither tradition nor interest made the bonds of the Democratic party unbreakable.

In New York City, meanwhile, a movement was occurring that might give Antimasonic strategists a chance to claim that their party was the champion of the underprivileged. In the large cities by the late 1820's, manufacturing had advanced sufficiently far to have created a class of industrial laborers and craftsmen. These workers had grievances which they thought could be solved by state legislation. Consequently they organized a Working Man's party, first in Philadelphia, and now in 1829, in New York City. If experience in Philadelphia were a guide,

[17]Alexander, *Political History of N. Y.*, 1:231-344.

Antimasons were glad to spy an opportunity to make the "Workies" their ally, even though they were a small group. The strategists at Albany set their caps to attract them.[18]

New York's third grouping was the National Republican party. Its leaders had no greater attachment to principles and goals than their opponents, but they were less gifted at politicking. Many who had once been National Republicans, but who were most sensitive to the new age or most impatient for success, had deserted to either the Democrats or the Antimasons. The leaders that were left were solid, stable, and competent men. Historians of later years, however, could run down a list of their names — Mathew L. Davis, Elisha Williams, Peter B. Porter, Esra Gross, Smith Thompson, Philip Hone, Henry Wheaton, Jesse Buel, Gamaliel Barstow, Joseph Hoxie, Ambrose Spencer, Hiram Ketchum, J. L. Lawrence, D. B. Ogden — and have difficulties identifying them. Few were to write their names indelibly on the pages of time. None among them had that natural flair for politics that guided Van Buren or Thurlow Weed. None had the charismatic qualities of previous New Yorkers like George Clinton, DeWitt Clinton, or Aaron Burr. Rather, National Republican leaders were rational, reasonable men who appreciated traditional practices; probably the period's ablest lawyers and judges were numbered among them. But, lacking versatility, they became plodders in politics. They did not have the agility to recover a position once lost although they possessed the tenacity to hold on to what they had. Consequently they continued to look for support from the older enfranchised classes — men of property. In a general way these men of property were those who were entrenched in their own business fields, but few were really rich even by the standards of that day. Established merchants in both foreign and domestic trade, older manufacturers, pedigreed estate holders, rather than the bumptious capitalists on the make, tended to put their trust in the staid National Republican leadership. In personality, these politicians

[18]F. T. Carlton, "The Workingmen's Party of New York," *Political Science Quarterly*, 22:401-415.

and businessmen were cast from the same mold. National Republicans were most heavily concentrated in New York City. Westward from Gotham their numbers declined almost in direct proportion to the newness of an area. Their tendency to focus in New York City was even more pronounced after their alliance with Antimasons.[19]

To the more astute leaders of Antimasonry, as they looked back on the events of 1828, the election proved that their public campaign of simple opposition to a secret order was too slim a base on which to build a successful party. Nine-day wonders lose their appeal, and Morgan's murder could not sustain their party indefinitely. If their organization was to continue, its leaders must broaden its base. The need was obvious and the leaders were spiritually capable of meeting the need.

Most of Antimasonry's experienced leaders had only a slight attachment to the avowed purpose of their party, and its top brass had records rich in opportunism. No one ever accused Weed of letting consistency stand in the way of success. A product of the same school was lean, red-haired Albert H. Tracy of Buffalo, who was smugly conscious of a close physical resemblance to Thomas Jefferson. At the moment, Tracy stood at the helm of Erie County Antimasonry. He had had the advantage of being well born and well educated. In 1819, at the age of twenty-six, he had entered Congress, where he was neither brilliant nor distinguished. Yet he was a skillful advocate, easy and natural, and so dextrously did he straddle camps in the interparty fight between Clinton and Van Buren that by 1825 rumor had him going to the United States Senate. The rumor died stillborn, and he was without office. But Tracy was inordinately ambitious for public life. At first he eyed Antimasonry with suspicion, but

[19] *Albany Argus*, October 3, 8, 18, 27, 1828, February 26, March 3, 1829, lists a number of Federalists, too, including the sons of Alexander Hamilton and John Jay, and Stephen Van Rensselaer; *Buffalo Republican*, January 20, March 15, 1827, January 3, February 7, April 18, 25, July 2, August 8, 1828; Horace Greeley, *Recollections of a Busy Life*, 215; Claude M. Fuess, *Daniel Webster*, 1:409; Charles Francis Adams, Jr., *Charles Francis Adams*, 84. Belle L. Hamlin, ed., "Selections from the Follett Papers," *Quarterly Publications of the Historical and Philosophical Society of Ohio*, 5 (1910); 9 (1914), *passim*.

after it proved itself in western New York, he stepped into its local leadership. In spite of this he turned in 1829 to New York City National Republicans for help in obtaining the presidency of the Buffalo branch of the Bank of the United States. The position slipped through his fingers, and he appeared hat in hand before the Democratic governor, Enos Throop, begging for a judgeship. That, too, he was denied. But a few days later Antimasons nominated him for the New York senate from the western district.[20]

No less ambitious, but considerably more genteel, was Francis Granger. Then just thirty-seven years old, he was a model of grace and manhood. As a legislator he had been the idol of the ladies' gallery. He had youth, enthusiasm, and resourcefulness. Even a critical contemporary saw him as a "gallant and fashionable man" who was "honest, honourable, and just first and beyond comparison with other politicians of the day." From youth he had been constantly associated with statesmen and politicians. His father, Gideon Granger, had headed the Jeffersonian forces in Connecticut, and as a reward, Thomas Jefferson had appointed him Postmaster-General. For eight years Francis had lived amid the political embroilments of Washington. Upon his father's death, Granger had inherited a small fortune and had moved to a spacious estate in the pleasant valley of Canandaigua, New York. In 1817 he had married into the fabulous Van Rensselaer fortune. At first he had refrained from politics but in 1825 he had joined the Clintonians, just as they were becoming pro-Jackson, and had won a seat in the state assembly. There he had remained for three years but gradually drifted to the National Republican side. Though he had formed a fast friendship with Weed in those three years, Granger had been slow to move into Antimasonry. It had mattered not that William Morgan's abductors had seized the hapless mason in September of 1826 almost at Granger's front door in Canandaigua. In July of 1828 he had accepted the nomination for lieutenant-governor from the National Republicans and

[20] Alexander, *Political History of N. Y.*, 1:372-373; Weed, *Autobiography*, 340.

had hoped for an endorsement from the Antimasons, even though he had not openly identified himself with them. His hopes were realized when the fanatics split away from the rest of the Antimasons; Weed's group endorsed Granger. Less than two months later he was sitting with the Antimasonic caucus, next to Weed, second in command in the hierarchy of Antimasonry.[21]

It came as no surprise, therefore, that Antimasons in 1829 launched themselves upon a campaign to become all things to all men. Their strategy in 1828 had failed, but they could reorganize for another fight. From the caucus emerged a plan of action. First, Antimasons must continue to cooperate with National Republican leaders while ingratiating themselves with National Republican voters. Second, they must win the support of the underprivileged by championing their cause. Third, they must reduce the Democratic vote by identifying Democrats with rascality in every phase of public life. Fourth, they must continue to raise the hue and cry about Masonry's misdeeds in order to keep those already converted voting the Antimasonic ticket.

Antimasons could not foresee the future, but for four years they were going to belabor this strategy, and in the end abandon it as hopeless.

*   *   *   *   *

Fillmore left no clear record of his reaction to the caucus meeting or the strategy devised there. Whether or not he understood the full implications of the strategy — use of Antimasonry as a Trojan Horse — was hard to say. That strong strain of idealism that frequently guided his actions might have repelled him from the masquerade of Antimasonry. But the stronger strain of practicality might have let him believe that just goals could best be achieved by artful means. Certainly, the current political fashions were not instilling in him or anyone else the value of forthright political behavior. Nowhere were political parties living by the code of a later generation. That probity was used

21Albany *Evening Journal*, December 21, 1830; for belittling sketches see *Buffalo Express*, April 11, 1829, and Frederick W. Seward, ed., *Life of William H. Seward*, 1:171.

only as a veneer caused little alarm. It was a raw age, boisterous and greedy, and its society accepted and even honored cunning practices. In all probability Fillmore acceded to the craftiness of his colleagues without much reflection.

In his first year in the assembly, rather than being concerned with the propriety of Antimasonic methods, he was more interested in learning parliamentary procedures and protecting himself against ridicule because of his inexperience. At first the strangeness of the assembly floor made him seek a haven where he could view the whole legislative procedure without exposing himself to its dangers. As he had hidden away in East Aurora until his self-training bolstered his confidence, so in his first year in the assembly he sheltered his ego beneath a cloak of inconspicuousness. During the entire 1829 session he spoke little and accomplished less. The house speaker assigned him to the minor committee on bills, where he functioned without influence. As chairman of several special committees, he handled two insignificant matters concerning East Aurora's old schoolhouse and bridges.[22]

But Millard Fillmore had an acquisitive mind and no parliamentary trick escaped his notice. The session was barren of results for the Antimasonic cause, but for Fillmore it was an education. When he returned the following year, after a triumphant re-election, he was prepared to take an active part in his party's future.

In the legislative session of 1830, he began to grow in confidence and stature. He shed his protective cocoon of anonymity and with increasing frequency took the floor of the assembly. If in the previous session his attitude was obscure, it now became clear that he favored broadening the base of his party. As could be expected from an Antimason, he called for the abolition of the Grand Chapter of the Masonic Order. He also helped his colleagues figuratively drag William Morgan's body before the assembly and, while shielding themselves from the horror,

[22]*Fillmore Papers*, 1: 43, 44-46; *New York State Assembly Journal, 1829*, 35, 403-404, 409-410.

charge the Democrats with sabotaging the investigations that would bring Morgan's murderers before the bar. While he beat the drums of Antimasonry, he also turned to the business world with words and deeds of sympathy. He urged the building of branch canals from the main line of the Erie. He helped defeat a transfer of taxes from bank deposits to bank stock. He fought the state-wide banking monopoly of the friends of the Regency. A small business man, Lyman B. Spaulding of Lockport, found himself facing a hostile government because he refused to turn over a valuable water power site to members of the Regency; he appealed for help and Fillmore and the other Antimasonic assemblymen fought hard to save Spaulding's property from Democratic rapacity. Everywhere Antimasons dramatized the Spaulding case as proof that Democrats were scoundrels and Antimasons were the friends of mistreated businessmen. In that same legislative session Fillmore had a chance to try to extend a mechanic's lien law beyond New York City. The Working Men's party favored the measure but it had run into strong opposition from National Republicans and some Democrats. Fillmore's effort failed. Yet it could be pointed out to laborers that they had the sympathy of Antimasons. In the fall, Antimasons courted the "Workies" more openly. They nominated a "Workie," Samuel Stevens, for lieutenant-governor. Some die-hard Antimasons objected and bolted the nominating convention. By this time, Fillmore, as a delegate from Erie County, not only toed the party line but was helping to make it.[23]

In 1830 Fillmore was heading for the leadership of his party in western New York. It was no small task to move into a spot already occupied by so opportunistic a man as Albert Tracy and

[23]*Fillmore Papers*, 1:47; *Buffalo Republican*, January 16, February 6, 1830; *Albany Argus*, January 20, 21, 25, February 8, 10, 11, 13, 19, 23, March 5, 8, 14, 27, August 18, 1830; see letters of John Crary and Solomon Southwick in *ibid.*, August 24, October 16, 1830; Rochester *Antimasonic Enquirer*, May 18, 1830; Albany *Evening Journal*, February 13, 19, March 9, 10, 11, 17, 18, 20, April 2, May 5, 6, 1830, April 8, 15, 16, 1831, April 19, 1832; *Buffalo Journal*, February 2, 1831, January 28, 1832, March 3, 1830; Hammond, *N. Y. Parties*, 2:327, 328; *New York State Assembly Journal, 1830*, 273, 353; Carlton, "N. Y. Workingmen's Party," 401-415; Seward, *Autobiography*, 78; Weed, *Autobiography*, 367; *National Observer*, August 21, 1830.

so experienced a campaigner as Peter B. Porter. Yet Fillmore
was on his way. Thurlow Weed was not himself a contender;
the previous spring he had left Rochester and had settled permanently in Albany where he could guide the fortunes of his
party with greater facility. There he had created the Albany
Evening Journal which was to be his forum for the next thirty-
three years.[24]

As Fillmore began to appear before the public, the kind
of performer he would be for the rest of his life became clear.
He spoke slowly, almost deliberately. The low pitch and mas-
culine timbre of his voice seemed to be in keeping with his hulk-
ing frame and jovial eye. Usually he chose common household
words to express himself, and these he arranged in short, direct
sentences. Except for careful inflections, little that was precious
clung to his speech and his audiences gained the impression of
good-natured, simple sincerity. In a later age of electronics, a
coach might have been able to train him into an accomplished,
maybe even great, public speaker, for both his manner and his
thinking were precise and unembellished. In his own day, however, no one ever credited him with great oratorical ability. He
was at his best in private conversations and small groups. He
lacked the elegant language and the turgid figures of speech which
the nineteenth century usually associated with masterful orators.
In situations where accepted elocution required impassioned
utterances that fused thought and feeling, he resorted to logic,
simple exposition, and called for reasonableness. He neither
timed his quips, measured his cadence, nor felt out the whims of
his audience. He was not a showman, but rather a citizen-in-
office, and about him was always an aura of dignity.[25]

During his third term as an assemblyman, in 1831, his colleagues suspected that the peak of their party's popularity had
already passed. They pecked away only halfheartedly at their
program. Democrats, meanwhile, controlled the state govern-

[24]*Fillmore Papers*, 2:293; Weed, *Autobiography*, 1:8, 360-362; Rochester *Antimasonic
    Enquirer*, June 1, 1830; Albany *Evening Journal*, March 22, 1830.
[25]*Ibid.*, March 10, 11, May 6, 1830; *Buffalo Journal*, February 2, 1831.

ment and were content to sit quiet. With one exception the four-month session was dull and produced no glorious legislative gains. The one bright spot resulted from Fillmore's actions.

Since colonial days a harsh law had plagued American debtors. If they defaulted, their creditors could put them in jail. For years various groups had been urging the abolition of the practice. Taxpayers who built and supported jails, debtors who hovered on the brink of disaster, and humanitarians whose hearts bled for the unfortunate, constantly denounced the law. Their outcries had gone unheeded. The law's beneficiaries would not relinquish so simple and effective a system of social and economic control.

The practice continued in every state in the Union until two things happened. The Working Men's party demanded its abolition, so that for the first time the ideal had an organization behind it. Simultaneously it got support in the business world when speculative capitalists realized that imprisoning debtors hobbled their own freedom of enterprise. Many fanciful business ideas had chilled and died in the cold shadow of a jail. The death in debtor's prison of William Duer — revolutionary leader, land speculator, and onetime assistant to Alexander Hamilton in the United States Treasury — was still fresh in the memory of many New Yorkers. These businessmen, however, desired more than the simple elimination of imprisonment for defaulting debtors. They wanted a bankruptcy law that would abolish the debt itself, as well as imprisonment. With such a law, old misjudgments would not plague their future; indeed, it might unleash creative, if risky, enterprise.[26]

The coincidence of the workingmen's demands and the business community's needs matched the Antimasonic program. Fillmore immediately saw a way of sponsoring a law that would satisfy almost everyone, including creditors. He maneuvered himself into the chairmanship of a special legislative committee

---

[26]Carlton, "N. Y. Workingmen's Party," 406; Albany *Daily Advertiser*, January 23, February 5, 19, March 3, 5, 17, 22, 30, April 15, May 5, 1831; Moses H. Grinnel to Weed, March 7, 1831, Weed Papers.

to consider the measure. There, in a thorough, workman-like fashion, he prepared for the successful passage of the bill. First he sounded out the opinions of leaders of all parties. Next he crammed himself full of factual information. Then he interviewed the lobbyists on both sides of the issue. Filled with facts and biases, he set himself to framing a law satisfactory to everyone. The task required painstaking treatment of details. Feeling insecure in his grasp of all the legal ramifications, he called in his fellow partyman, State Senator John C. Spencer, to write the sections dealing with court procedures. Spencer's wide experience as a judge fitted him for the job. The rest of the act Fillmore could claim as his own.[27]

Once the measure was framed Fillmore and Spencer introduced it into both houses. For a while the job of procuring its passage looked impossible, for the Democratic opposition held a three-to-one majority. Fillmore knew, however, that some Democrats favored the bill. To bring them into open support of the measure, he resorted to a little-tried legislative technique. He persuaded Democrats to accept the law as nonpartisan. Thus he divorced the fate of the bill from pure partisan hostility and held out to the Democrats the chance to claim, later, that they were responsible for the measure. It meant, unfortunately, that Fillmore had to bargain away personal glory for Democratic cooperation. He willingly accepted inconspicuousness. As a result, a few days before adjournment the measure passed with strong Democratic support.[28]

The artistry of the actor and demand for the limelight seldom guided Fillmore's behavior but his understanding of the role of public officials frequently did. The American scene required harmonization of its discordant groups, and responsibility for the task belonged to the practitioners of politics. Twenty years later, when he truly became a statesman, few men understood better than he this highest purpose of politics. Yet

[27]Chamberlain, *Fillmore*, 50; Albany *Evening Journal*, January 20, February 16, March 3, May 8, 1831; *Fillmore Papers*, 2:54.
[28]*Albany Argus*, April 4, 1831; Albany *Evening Journal*, April 4, 1831.

even here in his last term in the assembly, in the youth of his career, he was beginning to appreciate and accept the role.

To the mechanics Fillmore gave freedom from debt imprisonment and also freed the debtors who were then in jail. To the rising new business world, he gave a state bankruptcy law that unshackled its talented and ambitious members. To creditors he gave protection by making fraudulent bankruptcy a crime against society, punishable by imprisonment.[29]

Diligently the Democratic press tried to claim credit for the act. But it was the Antimasons who leaned back to enjoy the profits of the measure. Fillmore's stature in his party grew. When he returned home, the politician of three winters took his rightful place among other party leaders.[30]

[29]*Laws of New York State,* 1831, Chapter 300.
[30]*Albany Argus,* April 27, May 3, 1831; Griffis, *Fillmore,* 5.

Chapter 3

Buffalonian

N THE spring of 1830, the Fillmores moved to Buffalo.

Joseph Clary had prepared the way by asking his former law student to join him in a partnership. Unknowingly, he had touched a tender spot in Fillmore's heart. Ever since his earlier residence there, Buffalo had had an irresistible attraction for the young lawyer. And now, evidently purged of his former fears of incompetency by two terms in the assembly, Fillmore eagerly accepted the offer. No fanfare accompanied the change, but in many ways it heralded a new life for him and his family.[1]

They purchased a six-room, frame house two blocks from the main street[2] and about three-eighths of a mile north of the village's physical center.[3] It was a simple, two-story, clapboard house with five bays and a center hall. It had been designed in the delicate Federal style that antedated Greek Revival. Soon a white picket fence framed the yard as Fillmore tried to keep the passers-by and animals from wandering onto his narrow front lawn as they skirted the mudholes in the street.

[1]*Fillmore Papers*, 2:101.
[2]Original address was 114 Franklin street, now 180 Franklin street. See picture in Frank H. Severance, ed., *The Picture Book of Earlier Buffalo, Buffalo Historical Society Publications*, 16:384.
[3]Approximately present day Shelton Square.

Buffalo in 1830 was a booming village of about 8,000 people. Most of its hustle and bustle was taking place less than a mile south of Fillmore's home at a place called "The Dock." This was a portion of the right bank of Buffalo Creek. It had been wharfed and platformed for a thousand yards inland from its mouth on Lake Erie. In the past few years, along this dock, Buffalonians had dredged out the creek to a depth of eight feet and widened it to a hundred. Thus they had created a harbor without state or federal aid, and they were proud of their work.[4] The Erie Canal entered this elongated harbor at right angles and drew from it the waters of Lake Erie which then flowed eastward through the canal's entire length.

There was little in the appearance of the dock to satisfy aesthetic cravings. Rather it was repulsive in appearance and odor. Yet the livelihood of almost all villagers was dependent upon it. Here boatloads of people and merchandise were collected from the east and transferred to lake vessels going west. Not until the end of the decade did the flow of traffic reverse itself. When Fillmore arrived in Buffalo, the Great Lakes area, except for Lake Erie's shore to Cleveland, was nearly empty. Eventually the wheat trade from the Great Lakes region would transform Buffalo into the nation's milling center and the Erie Canal into the mid-century's wheat carrier par excellence. Yet before that trade could begin, the wheat-producing areas of northern Ohio, Indiana and Illinois, and of Michigan and Wisconsin, had to be peopled. For at least the first fifteen years of its life as the canal terminal, Buffalo's primary function was to funnel thousands upon thousands of immigrants into the Old West and follow them up with tons of the artifacts of civilization.[5] From this trade the young village mushroomed into a rich and fat city. By 1840 her population was pushed beyond 18,000 and within another ten years had passed 40,000.

*   *   *   *   *

From his home on the higher lands away from the harbor,

[4]John C. Lord, "Samuel Wilkeson," *Buffalo Historical Society Publications*, 4:71-85.
[5]Marvin Rapp, *Rise of the Port of Buffalo*, Duke University, 28.

Fillmore could see only the mast tops of the ships at anchor. The hodgepodge of misshapen buildings, weathered and unpainted, and the spume and refuse in the back eddies of the wharves were out of sight. Instead he caught glimpses, through the tall trees, of the sunlit lake beyond. Yet even on his higher ground he was surrounded by a raw community with apparently little elegance or civic pride. Indians from the nearby reservation walked the streets in "blankets and moccasins;" cows grazed at the roadsides, and "pigs roamed at their own sweet will." Except for a few hundred feet on Main Street, none of the village roads were paved. Even sidewalks were lacking in the greater portion of the town.[6]

Appearance, however, did not tell the whole story. A feeling for gentility coursed through the rough exterior of this pioneering community. A few homes like those of Philander Bennett, Orlando Allen, and the stately columned Goodrich house pointed to what became common when the dock paid off. The numerous cellar holes and partially completed structures, momentarily scarring the landscape, soon became tasteful homes built to the high standards of the Marshalls, the Townsends, the Pratts, the Andrews, and the Wilkesons. Before another ten years had passed, elaborate churches complemented the quiet repose of the First Presbyterian and St. Paul's Episcopal. Benjamin Rathbun added a long two-story Greek Revival wing to his Eagle Tavern, and next to it a six-story hotel.[7] Next, Buffalonians flagstoned their sidewalks along Main Street, graveled their most traveled roads, and even began a community water system.

The civility of these early Buffalonians went beyond mere physical improvements and polish. They were highly sociable and given to formal entertaining in their homes. For eight months each year they attended to business, and then, as ice closed in on navigation, they gave over the four winter months

[6]Martha Fitch Poole, "Social Life in Buffalo in the '30's and '40's," *Buffalo Historical Society Publications*, 8:443; J. N. Larned, *A History of Buffalo . . . .*, 1:137-43.
[7]Severance, *Buffalo Picture Book, passim.*

to a gay social season. It had to be provincial in scope but not
in taste. "We were literally ice-bound," explained a hostess, and
"everybody stayed at home, contributing to the general pleasure.
Buffalo was at this time pre-eminently a social center."[8]

The Fillmores were quickly accepted into this society.
Never before had they experienced anything quite like it. In
their youth hard work and hamlet life had limited their social
outlook. After marriage, Abigail's teaching, Fillmore's law texts,
then child care and Fillmore's absence in Albany had contributed
little to raising their social activities above the simple levels of
their youth. Now, however, a bright and undiscovered world
had become theirs. Formal dinners, chamber recitals, dances,
visiting lecturers, celebrities, plays — all crowded into their lives.
The naive, impressionable couple became enthusiastic devotees
of this new world, and throughout the rest of their lives they
made its standards and patterns their own.

They contributed more than material adventures to the
pleasures of their group. Both had always placed great faith in
books and yearned for knowledge. This might have resulted
either from their teaching experiences or a source deeper in their
personalities. Whatever the cause, both were avid readers.
Fillmore haunted bookstores wherever he found them. Never
was he to return from New York City without a few books
under his arm, and he "was often followed or preceded by a
package sent by express." After many years their library reached
4,000 volumes, and each time it grew beyond its bounds, Abigail
would happily call in a carpenter to extend the bookcases. To
collectors of rare books the Fillmore library was undistinguished.
Its books were more valuable for reference than resale, and it
reflected the interests of its owners.[9]

The aesthetic tastes of the Fillmores were relatively unde-
veloped, and only the smaller part of their library was given
over to belles-lettres and works that breathed of beauty and

[8]Poole, "Social Life in Buffalo . . .", 443-444.
[9]*Fillmore Papers*, 2:596.

spirit.[10] Yet Abigail cultivated a flower garden that had few
rivals, and their daughter was to become an accomplished musi-
cian. Sensitive students of poetry would have been aghast to hear
Fillmore declaim that Shakespeare was overrated. They would
have had an insight into the nature of this man, however, had
they known that he admired Alexander Pope's *An Essay on Man*.
A century, an ocean, and a civilization separated Fillmore from
Pope. Yet the two had something in common. The poet's
demand for greater simplicity in verse — the neat, measured,
exact, regular heroic couplet — found a kindred spirit in Fillmore's simple, untortured exposition. Their kinship went beyond
style. Both were didactic, and, more significantly, taught by
precept rather than by imagery. Both, though seemingly opti-
mistic, perceived the injurious pride of man — his vaunting
ambitions — in contrast to his inadequate abilities. Correct or
not, Fillmore and his wife talked easily, and with knowledge,
upon a wide variety of subjects, including contemporary authors.
In Buffalo's social gatherings they were conversational gems.

The teacher in Fillmore, or possibly the idealist, could not
be confined to hearth and friends. His temperament destined
him forever to promote libraries, learning, and knowledge. Even
before he moved to the village he helped form the Buffalo High
School Association, which opened its doors to students in January
of 1828 and offered academy work for the first time to the
youths of the area. When he settled in Buffalo he joined the
Lyceum and soon became one of its vice-presidents. This club
had come into existence only a few months before in response
to a nation-wide craze for self-improvement. The movement
eventually created thousands of local study groups, called
Lyceums, all aiming to educate adults through self-help. Buffalo's
Lyceum was no exception. It scheduled lectures on any con-
ceivable subject, encouraged formal debates, conducted simple
experiments in chemistry and physics, collected rocks and plants,
agitated for better public schools, and maintained a library and

[10]A catalog of the library in 1847 in Fillmore Mss. See also "Lars G. Sellstedt's
   Tribute to Fillmore," *Fillmore Papers*, 2:493; Laura Langford, *Ladies in the White
   House*, 467; *Fillmore Papers*, 2:506.

reading room. In a few years the local club collapsed but the spirit behind it was still virile. In 1837 the Young Men's Association took up Buffalo's leadership in a new experiment in the cult of self-improvement and acquired the library of the defunct Lyceum, thus beginning a career that did not end until the Buffalo Public Library replaced it in 1897. From the first Fillmore associated himself with the Young Men's Association and to it he gave not only time and money, but great chunks of his own private library.[11]

Whether because of their eagerness for social acceptance or no, the Fillmores joined the Unitarian church.[12] They never explained why they chose this sect or this particular time for their decision. Nothing in either of their religious backgrounds guided them toward Unitarianism. Up to now, Fillmore himself had been without a church. Even though a King James version of the Bible was always in the home of his father, his acquaintance with it was not equal to the standards of the day. In all probability he had never been baptized.[13]

In his family there was at least one minister of the Methodist church — his cousin, the Reverend Glezen Fillmore. While a circuit rider, this same cousin, as coincidence would have it, had organized the first Methodist congregation in Buffalo, built the village's first church, and was its pastor when the Fillmores moved into town. Yet the young couple avoided Methodism. In contrast, Abigail's father had been a minister of the Baptist church, and though he had died in her infancy, she had been raised in his faith. Twenty-five years later, however, it had been an Episcopalian minister who had united Abigail and Millard in

[11]*Ibid.*, 1:53, fn. 1; Larned, *Buffalo*, 2:157-164; *Fillmore Papers,* 1:xxxiii.
[12]The *Buffalo Republican* connects them with the church as early as November, 1831.
[13]The author could find no evidence that Fillmore was ever a churchgoer before he and Abigail settled in Buffalo. That he had not been a Unitarian previous to 1831 rests on the fact that no Unitarian churches or societies existed near any of his residences prior to 1831. Fillmore, moreover, almost never, in his extant writings, quotes, cites, or alludes to the Bible. Considering that literary and political fashion almost demanded Biblical allusions, this implies that Fillmore was either poorly trained in its content or he was a conscious literary and oratorical rebel. The latter is hard to believe.

marriage, albeit in the home of Abigail's brother rather than a church.[14] When the couple arrived in Buffalo, they made no effort to join either congregation. Rather, within a year, the Fillmores became charter members of the first Unitarian society and rejoiced when it built its permanent home a few hundred feet down the street from their front door.[15]

Whatever else might have persuaded the Fillmores into becoming church-goers, reason probably played the key role in choosing the denomination. As yet it was less noticeable than it would become later, but Fillmore was prone to accept the judgment of his mind rather than his heart. He permitted reason, rather than emotion, to define the boundaries of his behavior. Unitarianism showed a similar proclivity in its practices. It played down the role of faith in the church, encouraging its members to settle any questions of dogma for themselves, thus magnifying the part reason was to play in their association with the church. To a man of Fillmore's temperament, the Unitarian rejection of the Trinity was of less significance than its rejection of all dogma that offended reason. When, in conformity to this, the Unitarians replaced the angry God of the Calvinists with a benevolent one and a sinful mankind with a virtuous one, and thereby embraced the idea of progress, they magnified the attraction of their church for Fillmore. Once he and his wife entered, they became faithful, life-long supporters of all its goals even after the local pastor in later years displayed an implacable hatred for Fillmore's politics.[16]

The steady flow of immigrants, on whose dollars Buffalonians were building their churches and staging their dinner parties, brought trials as well as joys to the community. In the summer months of 1832, their coming caused epidemic and death. The Fillmores, who had every reason to be happier than usual that year, were torn by anxiety. Their son, Millard Powers,

[14]Langford, *Ladies of the White House,* 4:58-71.
[15]In 1834, Larned, *Buffalo,* 2:34. This building is still standing.
[16]James K. Hosmer to Andrew Langdon, December 7, 1898, *Fillmore Papers,* 2:508-509.

was now five years old. When their daughter, Mary Abigail, arrived in early spring, their parental pride was boundless. That same May, English immigrants landing in Quebec brought with them the dreaded Asiatic cholera. Buffalo's newspapers kept track of the disease as it spread up the St. Lawrence Valley, and anxious Buffalonians wondered how long it would be before this terrifying killer — they knew nothing about its cause or cure — would take to get to Buffalo. In June it was reported along the shores of Lake Ontario. By the end of the month it was taking victims along the Niagara River. Then in July it struck Buffalo.[17] A number of Buffalo residents fled to the country, and the Fillmores took their children to the home of their grandparents in East Aurora. All through the hot dog-days of July and August, the disease ravaged the town, and before it had spent itself, it had claimed nearly 200 victims. The Fillmores breathed more easily as fall approached, for cooler weather seemed to temper and then dissipate the epidemic. They happily brought their children back to their own fireside, and "Abby," as they came to call their little girl, soon established herself as the adored mistress of the household.

* * * * *

Buffalo found a loyal champion in Fillmore. America's public men — especially elected officeholders — have found it politically rewarding to serve their constituents' special desires. In Fillmore's day the practice was imperfectly developed, but already it had sufficient force to lead him to aid his friends and acquaintances with their problems in Albany. In the state legislature he helped Erie County people obtain charters for turnpike companies, ferries, banks; he tried to get a charter for the Buffalo Female Academy; he protected a local school district before the state superintendent of public instruction; he procured for Clark Hilton the right to build a dam on Tonawanda creek.[18]

[17]Lewis F. Allen, "The Cholera in Buffalo in 1832," in *Buffalo Historical Society Publications*, 4:245-256.
[18]*Fillmore Papers*, 1:viii, 43-53; *Buffalo Journal*, March 3, 1830; *New York State Assembly Journal*, 1830, 273, 353.

Such action might have suggested that he could easily have become the tool of invidious special interests. On the contrary, unscrupulous self-seekers were as repugnant to him in manhood as they had been in his youth. Fillmore's aim was to help people with legitimate ends operate in a system which required special laws for almost any activity. Fully appraised, he appeared to be a promoter of civic improvement.

By 1832 his adopted home town had outgrown its village government of five unpaid trustees. Its inhabitants began to demand incorporation as a city which, at the time, was a rare form of government in New York. He joined the movement. Since he had not run for re-election, he could not promote the cause in Albany. But when the time came to draw up the city charter, he sat at the composing table.[19]

One feature of the new city government reflected Fillmore's civic consciousness. The previous year he had shepherded a bill through the assembly which improved Buffalo's ability to fight fires. He obtained for the community the privilege of raising an extra three thousand dollars to dig wells, build four reservoirs, and buy fire engines.[20] Seventy years later the reservoirs were still a part of the city's fire protection system. His association with this measure made him aware of fire hazards, and he conveyed his caution to the city charter commission. For the new government, he raised fire-fighting to a new dignity by giving the common council power to eliminate fire hazards.[21] His participation was not the idle theorizing of a bystander. He punctuated his views with deeds. As he turned from charter writing, he joined with a number of his townsmen in forming the Buffalo Mutual Fire Insurance Company, of which he became a director. A year later, in respect for his position, the Fulton Street Volunteer Company renamed itself the Fillmore Company.[22]

[19]His influence was felt largely through his law partner, Clary, who was president of the village board of trustees at the time the city charter was written. *Fillmore Papers*, 2:101; *Buffalo Journal*, February 15, 1832.
[20]*Fillmore Papers*, 1:51-52.   [21]Larned, *Buffalo*, 1:162.
[22]*Fillmore Papers*, 1:51-52.

There was no doubt about his intimate connection with the growing city. His townsmen began to recognize him as a person of unassailable integrity.[23] His law practice, meanwhile, developed in him marked financial abilities, and the city fathers, eyeing these qualities, saw him as the person to handle testy situations. When someone was needed to carry out the delicate task of assessing special taxes for street improvements in the heart of the business district, they turned to him again and again.[24] And in no case did Fillmore lose friends or arouse ire.

The enterprise in Buffalo that naturally elicited the most concern was the canal. Without it the city might have been just another village on the lake, and the dock a picturesque fishing pier. Understandably the people of the dock looked after the canal with a possessive spirit, and once Fillmore had come to appreciate its role, he, too, willingly did battle for its welfare.

As a state-owned and operated project, the canal's fortunes swayed with the whims of the government. In practice this meant with the whims of the canal commissioners. They had received from the state legislature broad discretionary powers to manage the project. Almost as soon as the canal was done, the commissioners had correctly decided that it was too small. Buffalonians agreed with them and had no cause to battle over this decision. By the mid-thirties the rest of the state also agreed. As a result, in 1835 the legislature authorized the commissioners to proceed with an enlargement program. Its exact nature was left to the judgment of the commissioners. In proper bureaucratic manner they sent engineers to every section of the canal to gather pertinent information. In each community the arrival of the investigators was the signal for local interests to make their special pleas.[25]

At this time what Buffalo wanted most was an enlargement of the canal's terminal facilities — more slips, basins, and canal frontage for wharves and warehouses. To persuade the com-

[23]*Ibid.*, 1:xi.   [24]*Ibid.*, 1:ix.
[25]*New York State Laws, 1835*, Chapter 274; Report of the Canal Commissioner for 1835, N. Y. State *Assembly Documents*, no. 99 (1836).

missioners that these needs were pressing, the people of the dock got up a spirited public meeting that passed resolutions and set up a "committee of correspondence" — an early-nineteenth-century euphemism for "lobbyists." On the committee was the "Hon. Millard Fillmore," now a United States Congressman from Buffalo. Three months later rumor had the commissioners reviving Buffalo's old rival, Black Rock, as a canal terminal. Fear that this might happen jolted Fillmore's committee into increased activity. Another public meeting, another set of resolutions, another committee of correspondence, and once again Fillmore was conspicuous in the action.[26]

The difference between the canal and the harbor at Buffalo sometimes confused strangers who looked out upon it from a nearby height of land called the "Terrace." But there was at least one distinction, not apparent to the eye, of which the people of the dock were painfully aware. The canal belonged to the state, but the harbor fell under federal jurisdiction. Already booming traffic was making the harbor pitifully small. Unless the Buffalonians wanted to assume the costs of improving it themselves, it was the federal government's responsibility. Naturally they turned their eyes toward Washington. Here, also, Fillmore did his best. All through his first term in Congress he badgered the House committee on canals and roads to improve his hometown's harbor.[27]

At this point his efforts to persuade either the state or the federal government were unsuccessful. He had, however, made himself the champion of Buffalo's most vital resource.

*   *   *   *   *

Every morning except Sunday, which he kept inviolate as a day of rest, Fillmore walked the short distance to his office on Main Street. Even after he and Clary ended their partner-

[26]*Fillmore Papers*, 1:ix; Buffalo *Commercial Advertiser*, October 1, 1835, December, 1835, *passim*.
[27]*Fillmore Papers*, 1:vii; Samuel A. Bigelow, "The Harbor-Makers of Buffalo: Reminiscences of Judge Samuel Wilkeson," *Buffalo Historical Society Publications*, 4:225.

ship the routine did not change. With or without Clary, once Fillmore moved to Buffalo, Main Street between Eagle and Court would always contain his place of business, and he and the shopkeepers along the way established a ritual of morning greetings that rarely varied.[28]

The parting with Clary was amicable. It came in November, 1832, after Fillmore won election to Congress. For a number of years Clary had been a justice-of-the-peace, and his attention to the firm's business had to be limited. Now with Fillmore expecting to be away in Washington for months at a time, new arrangements for handling their clients were necessary. They separated, and to solve his own problems Fillmore formed a partnership with his law student, Nathan K. Hall, who had just been admitted to the bar.[29] It was apparent to Fillmore that Hall, the lad of sixteen who had wandered into Fillmore's East Aurora law office and asked for a clerkship six years before, was now not only a competent lawyer but an admirable person clearly foreshadowing the pure, incorruptible, great-hearted man Hall would become.

From the beginning they had almost been neighbors. Nathan Hall had been born only a dozen miles from Fillmore's boyhood home.[30] Hall's father, like Fillmore's, had struggled constantly to make a living. He was a shoemaker who at the time of his son's birth supplemented his income by working as a farm hand. Shortly after Nathan's birth his mother died, but Ira Hall had stayed on with his employers, the Kelseys, who took care of the child.[31] Then in 1818, Ira married again and struck out on his own, setting up a shoe shop on a small farm near East Aurora. Nathan, however, had stayed behind with the Kelseys. In those years his education had been the meager fare of the district school, but it had been the best the neighbor-

---

[28]*Fillmore Papers*, 2:499.
[29]*Ibid.*, 2:101 and note.
[30]In present-day Skaneateles.
[31]Hall's middle name was Kelsey which might mean that his benefactors were his relatives or that he used this name legally until he went to live with his father and then added "Hall" to "Nathan Kelsey."

hood offered. At the age of fifteen, needing to prepare for his future, Nathan rejoined his father and, while helping with the farm, tried to learn his father's trade. In later years Hall laughed at his effort. "I can boast of no great success as a son of St. Crispin. . . . " The day "I left the shop," to clerk for Fillmore, he quipped, "there was no very serious violation of the good old adage, 'Let the shoemaker stick to his last.' " From that day onward a bond developed between Fillmore and Hall which held them together as intimate friends for the rest of their lives. At this point it made them partners.[32]

Creating the firm of Fillmore & Hall linked together two lawyers of a famous legal triumvirate. Three years later the third member joined them. This was Solomon G. Haven, whose ready wit and bright intellect would soon mark him for distinction. Only a few months earlier he had arrived in Buffalo fresh and enthusiastic from Chenango County, where he had read law after first trying medicine. Tall, bony, dark-skinned, he looked a good deal like Daniel Webster before that statesman permitted corpulence to overwhelm him. Haven's youth was slightly less influenced by poverty than those of his partners, and possibly because of this he was less circumspect. His carefree moods — even his impish tongue — provided good balance to the stern, tensely serious demeanor of Nathan Hall. Even Fillmore's good humor and zest for life — occasionally they encroached upon his dignity — were leavened by Haven's lively quips.[33]

Here were three young men whom chance had brought together. None had had the help that family position or wealth or formal education presumably gave to success. None had been trained in an eminent law office nor inherited, by seniority, a going firm. Yet in western New York, and possibly in a broader area, they had no peers, and their professional colleagues readily admitted this.

[32]James O. Putnam, "Nathan Kelsey Hall," *Buffalo Historical Society Publications,* 4:286-287.
[33]*Ibid.*, 289-290.

Long after Haven's death, an astute member of the Buffalo bar looked back through the years and appraised the scene. Haven "was the prince of jury lawyers. . . , " he said, "and I have never seen his equal in this department . . . at this or any other Bar."[34] To still another colleague Haven was "unquestionably" the "most rarely endowed" jury lawyer "we have ever had among us."[35] Contrarily, Hall was almost graceless in expression and had none of Haven's genius for fascinating a jury. Rather Hall was an ideal office lawyer and a safe counselor. His clear analytical mind — uncreative and unencumbered with fervid fancy — penetrated readily to the core of a legal problem. He was an admirable commercial lawyer, but he had a delicate sense of justice and loved the broad principles of equity which governed all just dealings between men. These made him a specialist in equity jurisprudence — a field in which he achieved acclaim. No one, apparently, could match his industry or his enormous power of concentration. "If pressed for time," noted a fellow lawyer, he "could do more work in an hour and do it well, than most others could do in a day."[36]

Between these two partners Fillmore stood as a balance. He was the well-rounded member of the triumvirate — the one who eventually moved with ease in many branches of law. He never quit studying, and to the problems of the firm he brought great learning. Also he had a quality that was rare even among lawyers — excellent common sense. The same observer who could become ecstatic over Haven's courtroom abilities assessed fifty years of the Buffalo bar to conclude, "I have not known . . . [Fillmore's] . . . superior, upon the whole, as a professional man."[37]

For a team of men who acquired high professional stature these three partners gave over an extraordinary share of their lives to public affairs. Each year one or more engaged in a

[34]E. Carleton Sprague in Larned, *Buffalo,* 1:203, in 1876.
[35]Putnam, "Hall," 289.
[36]T. J. Sizer in Larned, *Buffalo,* 1:203.
[37]Sprague in *ibid.,* 1:203.

political campaign or held an office. Hall's experiences were
widely varied — clerk of the board of supervisors, city attorney,
alderman, master of chancery, common pleas judge, assemblyman, Congressman, United States Postmaster-General, United
States District Judge. Haven, after being county commissioner
of deeds, had a greater attraction for elective posts than Hall.
He served as district attorney, mayor of Buffalo, and Congressman for three terms. Fillmore, himself, before he became Vice-
President and then President of the United States, served four
terms in Congress, was New York's first elected comptroller,
and had run for governor.

Like Fillmore the partners frequently responded to the call
of their civic consciences to perform lesser duties. In this Hall
was exceptional, and the results of his work in education would
live forever. The common, or district, schools which he and
his partners had attended — the public school system of New
York — were not free. The state subsidized each school, and
the difference between the state aid and the actual cost of maintaining an elementary school was made up by the local community. Usually each district procured this difference by
charging students tuition or by taxing (rating) the parents who
had children in attendance. Some progress had been made until
the panic of 1837, but the subsequent depression dealt these
common schools a fearful blow. In Buffalo alone, because parents
could not or would not pay the tuition charges, more than half
of the children were receiving no education. Where the schools
stayed open, it became common for the district boards to hire
a teacher who would take the school for the smallest charge for
the length of time needed to collect the state aid. Some boards
went so far as to pay the teacher the state aid and let him collect the tuition himself, if he could. The obvious decay of
education alarmed some citizens, and after a series of widely
attended public meetings, they set up a fact-finding committee.
Nathan K. Hall served on this committee and carried on his
shoulders the burden of most of its work. It spent months surveying the whole problem, district by district, and then sub-

mitted to the common council not only its findings but a recommendation that the city levy a general tax on all property to raise enough money to make all their elementary schools free. In 1839 the common council accepted the recommended policy, and as a result Buffalo claimed the distinction of being the state's first community to establish free, tax-supported elementary schools.[38]

The extraprofessional work of the partners strained the working mechanism of the firm, but not the relations between the members. Through all their professional and political activity neither jealousy nor dissatisfaction ever marred their friendship. For over a third of a century, Buffalonians habitually linked them name to name. Because of this, even old-timers were struck with wonderment when Fillmore and Hall passed away within a few days of each other. When the two were laid to rest next to Haven, the same old-timers nodded their approval of a befitting symbol.

If the ties of trust were unbreakable, those of business were not. The partnership could not endure the demands that public office made on its members. When Hall was appointed master in chancery — a full-time judicial position — he felt he could no longer carry his weight and withdrew from the firm. Fillmore and Haven continued until the end of 1847 when Fillmore, himself elected to a position which would take him out of Buffalo, felt impelled to give up his private practice. Though the old firm was gone, its spirit lived on in more than memory. Better than a score of students could trace their training back to the Main Street office, and these in turn trained others. One firm — Rogers, Bowen & Rogers — could even trace a direct descent, for in 1842 Hall had formed a partnership with Dennis Bowen, one of the students of Fillmore, Hall & Haven. In turn, when one of its students, Grover Cleveland, took his oath of office as President of the United States, its proud members needed

38Oliver G. Steele, "The Buffalo Common Schools," in *Buffalo Historical Society Publications*, 1:405-432.

no legerdemain to establish the fact that their law office had the unique distinction of giving the nation two of its Presidents.[39]

For most of its life the firm was located in a suite of rooms on the second floor of the American Block. Steep wooden steps rose from the street directly into a large room. Here Haven held forth and was surrounded by student-clerks. Beyond was another room of the same size, about thirty feet square, which Fillmore and Hall used together until Hall left. A small consulting room where client and counsel might have privacy led off each of the larger offices. All was bare of elegance. Two cast-iron, wood-burning stoves heated the rooms. The walls of Fillmore's office were covered with books, and on his desk, since he frequently worked late into the night, were two sperm-oil lamps and a green eyeshade. Hanging on a clothes-tree in the corner were two long, black working gowns; one was padded for cold mornings and the other was of ordinary weight.[40]

Always four to six student-clerks were at hand, and for these the senior partner took the major responsibility. Looking over his career, modern psychologists would probably suggest that Fillmore had a compulsion to teach. Once a week he gathered together his charges in an evening session to examine them on the week's studies. He enjoyed these gatherings and his normally happy face would glow with pleasure as a session got under way. He would lean back in his swivel chair — two lamps burning behind him and the students sitting in a half circle before him — and begin by asking a student what he had been reading. A few leading questions would follow, then explanations and discussions. Occasionally he would talk at length on a principle of law. His sense of humor was keen, and he studded these informal lectures with anecdotes. Almost always they were told to make a point rather than to amuse, for he was not a garrulous entertainer even though he had a large fund of stories. Before the evening had passed each student had been questioned and drilled, examined and re-examined — all

[39] Allan Nevins, *Grover Cleveland, A Study in Courage*, 36.
[40] *Fillmore Papers*, 2:499.

in an atmosphere of cordiality. A newcomer, experiencing a session for the first time, was surprised that he had "had a most agreeable evening." And, he continued, "I learned more law than I had acquired during all the time I had been reading."[41]

Fillmore was tenderly alive to the individual progress of these students. It was not unusual for him to come into the office in the morning and lay a book on the table before one of the students. He had just finished reading the book the night before, he would remark, and it was the ablest and best work on the subject that he had ever read. The student should drop everything else until he had finished reading it, too. The welfare of the students concerned him as well as their knowledge of law. No notable person went through Buffalo without meeting his students if it could be arranged. One of the consultation rooms was always available to house a needy student, and credits on the firm's books were easily attainable.[42]

Instruction did not end with lessons in law. It was not unusual for Fillmore to fix a stern glare on a student, as he did one spring morning to Hiram C. Day, and remark: "Last evening as I was taking a ride with Mrs. Fillmore, we saw you and Powers walking out on Main Street and going as though you were walking on a wager; that is undignified and unprofessional."[43]

[41]*Ibid.*, 2:500.   [42]*Ibid.*   [43]*Ibid.*

Chapter 4

A New Departure

Y 1831 Fillmore's Antimasonic party was in a dying state.

The party's original purpose had been to elect John Quincy Adams to the Presidency yet it had failed to get him even one electoral vote. Then its leaders had tried to broaden the party's appeal. The years that followed tested their effort and, once again, pointed toward failure. By 1831 the New York party — the hub of the movement — had faltered. That year it was less successful at the polls than previously and its decline had begun.[1]

Beyond New York's borders[2] the trend was confused, but ominous. In Vermont success seemingly beckoned. Antimasons there had captured both the governor's chair and control of the legislature. In Massachusetts, also, their numbers in the legislature had increased six-fold. Closer analysis, however,

---

[1] Of 160 legislative seats, the Antimasons had won 21 in 1828, 30 in 1829, 37 in 1830, and only 28 in 1831. Charles McCarthy, *The Antimasonic Party: A Study of Political Antimasonry in the United States, 1827-1840*, 362, 511; Weed, *Autobiography*, 339, 341; *Buffalo Republican*, November 14, 1829; January 16, 1830; *Civil List of New York* (1887), 171; Seward, *Autobiography*, 75, 78; *Albany Argus*, November 11, 1830; *Buffalo Journal*, November 11, 1830; Hammond, *N. Y. Politics*, 1:397.

[2] The best single source for this study is in McCarthy, *Antimasonic Party*: for Vermont see 506-509; Massachusetts, 519; Pennsylvania, 437-441; Rhode Island, 551-553; Michigan, 558; Ohio, 526-30; New Jersey, 555; Connecticut, 556.

showed the Massachusetts situation to be less encouraging than it would appear. A bitter fight with National Republicans darkened the future. Even at that, Vermont and Massachusetts were the only bright spots in the Antimasonic picture.

Elsewhere gloom prevailed. In seventeen states of the Union, Antimasons had no places on the ballot. Pennsylvania's party was tiny and woefully weak, showing none of the strength it would have in a few years; Rhode Island Antimasons had gone berserk and supported Democrats; Michigan's party had died in 1830; and leaders in Ohio, New Jersey, and Connecticut could not make headway. Thus by 1831 if Antimasons had had any success it could not be measured by election results.

The panic which they had caused among Masons may have consoled Antimasons for their failure at the polls. Thousands of rank and file Masons had deserted their lodges, and many local chapters had disappeared. But the consolation was without foundation. The Order survived and the charters granted by the states remained untouched.

Driving Masons out of public office, moreover, had proved more difficult than driving them out of their lodges. As if in symbolic defiance of five years of Antimasonic campaigning, a thirty-two-degree Mason was still President of the United States and was a candidate to succeed himself. To make the Antimasonic despair for success even more desperate, the other leading contender for the Presidency, Henry Clay, ridiculed Antimasons and steadfastly clung to his own Masonic membership.

The cause of the Antimasons' failure was plain. They had, in the first place, a formidable foe in Andrew Jackson. Against his clarion call to the common man their indirect appeals — made from the eccentric position of objection to the special power of a secret fraternity — sounded weak. The new voter understandably preferred Jackson.

The failure to compete at this level left Antimasons the alternative of allying with — or absorbing — the National

Republicans. This, too, failed, for only in New York and Vermont was a working arrangement reached between the two parties. Even here the union was fraught with trouble. Jealous of sharing power, many National Republicans resented the need to cooperate with Antimasons. Others felt that Antimasons were opportunists, in particular mistrusting Thurlow Weed, whom they thought unprincipled and deceitful.[3]

Among the National Republicans, moreover, were a number of leaders in New York City whose pride in their work made acceptance of Antimasons more difficult.[4] The capable editors of the *Commercial Advertiser* and the *American;* David B. Ogden, an eminent constitutional lawyer;[5] Philip Hone, a society figure and former mayor, who was an invaluable link between politicians and businessmen; Hone's friend Hiram Ketchum, wholesale merchant and *bon vivant;* Gulian C. Verplanck, a man of literary talent who preferred an alliance with Tammany to an Antimason alliance;[6] Joseph Hoxie and W. B. Lawrence, party leaders, all condemned cooperation with, as Lawrence expressed it, "this demon of Anti-Masonry."[7] Theirs was no evanescent leadership; a quarter-century later they were still giving their city its political direction. Now they were perfecting a central committee system to give new life to the National Republican party.[8]

Elsewhere in the state, other leaders infected with values picked up in the world of business could not bring themselves to accept Antimasonry and dream of creating a new party.

[3]S. R. Gammon, *The Presidential Campaign of 1832,* 55-60.
[4]Albany *Evening Journal,* December 15, 1830, lists about fifteen of the outstanding Clay politicians of New York City; see also Oran Follett to Joseph Hoxie, February 2, 1832, in Belle L. Hamlin, ed., "Selections from the Follett Papers," Ohio Historical and Philosophical Society, *Quarterly Publication,* 5:53-54; Bayard Tuckerman, ed., *The Diary of Philip Hone, 1828-1851,* 1:27-70, *passim. National Intelligencer,* February 29, 1832.
[5]Cohens v. Virginia, Ogden v. Saunders, Gibbons v. Ogden; *Dictionary of American Biography,* 13:638-639; Weed, *Autobiography,* 1:408.
[6]Tuckerman, *Hone,* 1:97-99; *Albany Argus,* April 23, 1834.
[7]Lawrence to Clay, November 8, 1830 quoted in E. Malcolm Carroll, *Origins of the Whig Party,* 49.
[8]Gammon, *Campaign of 1832,* 60 ff.

They had found palace-intrigue politics tiresome and recognized that the swelling of the electorate demanded something more stable if the needs of society were to be met. Among them were the sanctimonious and long-winded Daniel Dewey Barnard of Rochester;[9] future Governor John Young in the Genesee country;[10] John Spencer of Binghamton, who from being special investigator of the Morgan affair had shifted to outright hostility to the Antimasons;[11] and former Secretary of War Peter B. Porter and his Buffalo associates, Reuben B. Heacock and Sheldon Smith.[12]

Oran Follett, editor of the *Buffalo Journal*, despaired of Antimasonry. He called it a "hoax."[13] But Follett was among the most perspicacious of National Republicans. As early as 1829 he told his colleagues that they would find success only by creating a new party. A party built upon principles instead of personalities was his formula for stemming the growing popularity of Jackson. The principles he preferred were Hamiltonian: sound currency, protection for manufacturers, improvement of canals and harbors, and encouragement of railroads. The aim of government, he urged, should be to aid the groups who could make the nation prosperous.[14]

If his advice had fallen on deaf ears in 1829, now, four years later, it began to attract attention.

Most Antimasons were less perceptive than Follett and refused to accept the lessons of these years. They drew confidence from the little progress they had made rather than vigilance from their shortcomings. The Presidential year of 1832 merely aroused their hopes that the right candidate would set

---

9*Dictionary of American Biography*, 1:617; Edward Everett, *Orations and Speeches*, 4:339-44.
10*Dictionary of American Biography*, 20:628-629.
11*Dictionary of American Biography*, 17:449-450.
12Albany *Evening Journal*, December 15, 1830, contains a list of about ten outstanding Clay politicians in Buffalo; see also Hamlin, "Follett Papers," 5: *passim*; *Buffalo Journal*, April 4, May 25, September 9, 16, October 7, 14, 21, November 4, 1831.
13*Buffalo Journal*, October 10, 1829.
14Follett to Clay, March 21, to Hoxie, April 1, to H. Maxwell, April 19, 1829, in Hamlin, "Follett Papers," 5:219-220; 222-223; 230-232.

all to rights. They proposed to nominate a man who could draw large groups away from the Democratic coalition and, at the same time, unite all the factions already anti-Jackson. As usual the Antimasons were satisfied to ramble along opportunistically, expecting that the right man would turn up. There was, however, a fatal reservation forced upon them by their extremists: the candidate must give at least lip service to the Antimasonic creed. This seemed to exclude but one possibility — Henry Clay.

As fate would have it, Henry Clay was the only man the Antimasons could nominate that the National Republican extremists would have. Clay was a perennial seeker of the Presidency. He had run well in 1824 and again in 1828. He was an orator who moved men to action, and his friends remained unswervingly loyal in the face of charges that he was a demagogue with pronounced weaknesses for gambling and drinking. If he was also an opportunist he refused to evince the weakness at this time. He would make no statement or gesture of concession to the Antimasons.[15]

When the Antimasons met in their first national nominating convention in October, 1831, they waited until the last moment, and in vain, for Clay to make it possible for them to put him at the head of their ticket. He remained silent. In near desperation they then turned to John McLean, who had recently been appointed to the Supreme Court by Jackson as a reward for his support in the election of 1828. He was acceptable to most Antimasons and National Republicans and might have united them and drawn Democratic votes, too. But he demanded a clear field against Jackson and this the National Republican leaders refused to assure him.[16] He withdrew and the rebuffed convention nominated William Wirt of Maryland, formerly Attorney-General in John Quincy Adams' cabinet.[17]

[15]George W. Bungay, *Off-hand Takings; or, Crayon Sketches of the Notable-Men of our Age*, 43. H. W. Hilliard, *Politics and Pen Pictures*, 83; Adams, *Memoirs*, 5:325; Harriet Martineau, *Retrospect of Western Travel*, 1:242, 275, 290.

[16]Gammon, *Campaign of 1832*, 45.

[17]J. P. Kennedy, *Memoirs of the Life of William Wirt*, 2:317.

There was still a faint hope of union. The National Republicans met at the end of December. They might have persuaded Wirt to withdraw by nominating McLean. Instead they unanimously chose Clay and the die was cast.

During the following months moderates among both Antimasons and National Republicans tried to merge their tickets and were partially successful.[18] Infidelity to the coalition arrangements soon appeared. In New York extremists in both factions deserted the other candidates.[19] John Crary, former Antimasonic candidate for lieutenant-governor, openly denounced the coalition ticket[20] and Francis Granger, the candidate for governor, was defeated by a margin so small that a change in 1.5 per cent of the vote would have brought him victory. Refusal to accept the coalition arrangement guaranteed defeat to both Antimasons and National Republicans.

Defeat in 1832 at last convinced both factions that they were on the wrong track. Oran Follett's advice was now taken more seriously; James Watson Webb of the New York *Courier and Enquirer,* newly converted from the Democratic party,[21] harshly and loudly demonstrated that National Republicanism needed "remaking."[22] Thurlow Weed was quieter, indeed his Albany *Evening Journal* was ominously quiet about politics; the master behind-the-scenes performer was working for a transformation.[23] Manifold difficulties quickly became apparent, but the significant political event following the Presi-

[18]Carroll, *Whig Origins,* 51, 52; Weed, *Autobiography,* 839; George Rawlings Poage, *Henry Clay and the Whig Party,* 9; before the nominating conventions, Weed tried to get Clay to abandon his opposition to Antimasonry and abjure his Masonic oaths, but the Ashlander proved adamant; Albany *Evening Journal* June 1, 6, October 1, 3, 11, 1831, June 28, July 31, 1832; *Buffalo Journal* July 18, October 5, 12, 1831, June 8, December 2, 1832; Rochester *Antimasonic Enquirer,* June 26, 1832, *Albany Argus,* June 30, 1831; McCarthy, *Antimasonic Party,* 410, 415, 416, 446, 528-30, 510, 518, 551, 555.

[19]*Ibid.,* 417-418.

[20]*Albany Argus,* August 14, 1832.

[21]*Dictionary of American Biography,* 19:575.

[22]See his newspaper the *Courier and Enquirer* during 1832-1833, *passim.*

[23]Van Deusen, *Weed,* 65.

dential election of 1832 was the decision of many Antimasonic and National Republican leaders to create a new party.

*   *   *   *   *

As Millard Fillmore approached the outskirts of Washington, in late November of 1833, excitement showed on his face. He leaned forward on his cane, poked his long nose out of the carriage window and gazed curiously at the nation's capital. It looked oddly similar to the open country he had just come through from Baltimore. Along the roadside, and occasionally in the road, cows stopped momentarily to watch the carriage pass. Here and there clumps of houses broke the plains. Only as he drew closer to the center of the capital could he realize that there was more to Washington than these scattered shacks. The number of dwellings increased. But as the coach rounded a corner and clattered into Pennsylvania Avenue, "the buildings were standing with wide spaces between, like the teeth of some superannuated crone."[24]

Once on Pennsylvania Avenue, Fillmore caught his first full view of the national capitol. Majestically it dominated the wastelands and the few miserable shack-like boarding houses that lay at its feet. The President's mansion was surrounded by the plain red brick buildings of the State, Treasury, War and Navy departments. Scattered amid these, a few pretentious houses vainly denied the city's dowdiness. As Washington impressed its image on Fillmore's eye, possibly he recalled that Buffalo's original surveyor, Joseph Ellicott, had also helped lay out the nation's capital after President Washington had dismissed Major L'Enfant.[25]

As the carriage rattled down the avenue, Fillmore directed the coachman to drop him at Gadsby's. Travelers reckoned it Washington's most popular and comfortable hostelry. There,

[24]Nathan Sargent, *Public Men and Events*, 1:54, 57 for quotations; Thomas Hamilton, *Men and Manners in America*, 14; Martineau, *Retrospect*, 1:143; W. A. Butler, *Retrospect of Forty Years, 1825-1865*, 47.
[25]N. P. Willis, *American Scenery*, 2:55; Sargent, *Public Men and Events*, 1:55; Frederick Marryat, *A Diary of America*, 1:163.

previous visitors had assured him, he could find not only a clean bed, but excellent service and a hospitable host.[26] Congress would meet in a few days, on December 2, and he had a number of things to do before he took up his responsibilities there. No longer was he the uninitiated legislator who years earlier had stopped before Albany's "Temperance House," hardly knowing what he would do in the coming months. Nor was he troubled by the indecision that had preoccupied him in April, 1831, when he had finished his third term in New York's assembly. Then he had been uncertain what course to follow for the future. Now he had no doubts. He was working, with clear vision, within an inner circle of Antimasons and National Republicans to create a new party.

Personal objectives had little to do with his new goal, for he was only slightly concerned with his own success in politics. To be sure, he had sought and would continue to seek public office, but to satisfy his own desires he did not need a better political organization than he already had. The old alliance had provided him with all the personal satisfaction he wanted from the game of politics: a place in the local limelight. It had given him nearly seventy per cent of the vote in three successive elections and, in all likelihood, he would continue to get that kind of support for any office in western New York. Yet, just as that alliance reached its apogee, in the spring of 1831, he had begun to turn away from it. Something above personal ambition had taken hold of him. Possibly he had now caught a glimpse of the role of a statesman. Whatever it was within eighteen months after leaving Albany, he was deeply involved in making a new party.

Unwittingly, he had made his spiritual break with Antimasonry while still at Albany, one that was noticed by the faithful to his discredit. It occurred over religious oaths in New York's courts. Oddly enough, the man who one day would be derisively called an arch conservative had taken an advanced position to promote democracy. In his day, according to New

[26]Sargent, *Public Men and Events*, 1:53-54.

York law, no witness was qualified to speak in a New York court who did not swear to belief in God and a hereafter. Fillmore had taken exception to this test oath and sponsored a bill to eliminate it from the courts. It was an "absurd" law, he had charged, and "the narrow feeling of prejudice and bigotry" behind it must give "way to more enlightened and liberal views."[27] This from a man who had just joined a church, even though it was the Unitarian. He was in step, however, with young, democratic America's march toward complete separation of church and state.

But his action had denied the spirit of Antimasonry. In the last analysis, Thurlow Weed's party had only been possible because of deep religiosity among the rank and file. Whatever the motives of the leaders, great numbers had voted the ticket only because they had considered Masons to be unchristian.[28] In the society of the day religious tests were common criteria for judgments. For Fillmore to divorce God from justice, as they saw it, had separated him from true Antimasonic feelings.[29]

[27]*Fillmore Papers*, 1:73-78.

[28]McCarthy, *Antimasonic Party*, 540-541; Weed, *Autobiography*, 289; *Albany Argus*, July 18, September 25, 1829, January 5, June 10, September 10, 1831, November 24, 1832. *Proceedings of the Genesee Synod, September 30, 1829; Proceedings of the Oneida Synod of February 1820;* Kennedy, *Wirt*, 2:314; for a typical Antimasonic document by a Presbyterian preacher see, *Masonry Proved to be a Work of Darkness Repugnant to the Christian Religion and Inimical to Republican Government by Lebeus Armstrong . . . of New York.* See also, Proceedings of the Pittsburg Annual Conference of the Methodist Episcopal Church, Resolutions of the Annual Conference of the Methodist Ministers held at Perry, N. Y., the resolutions of the Annual Methodist Conference in Rochester, the Report on the General Synod of the Dutch Reformed Church in the Rochester *Antimasonic Enquirer*, September 24, 1830, July 29, 1829, June 28, 1829, September 21, 1831. Antimasons made a concerted effort to identify themselves with this religious spirit. See report of committee "to consider nature, principles, and tendency of Freemasonry as regards its effects on the Christian religion" in the proceedings of the National Convention of 1830, Albany *Evening Journal*, September 22, 1830.

[29]*Buffalo Journal*, February 2, 1831; New York State, *House Journal*, January 27, 1831. That Fillmore had joined the Unitarian church was an indication that he and Antimasonry were parting company. The Unitarians and Universalists condemned the Antimasonic excitement and refused to take part in it, an action which ranked them with the Masons in the eyes of Antimasons. See Boston *Christian Register* (Unitarian), September 12, 1829, December 19, 1829. See also quotations from the Universalist magazine, the *Olive Branch*, of New York, in *American Masonic Register*, September 21, 1829.

His proposal never emerged from the legislative committee. His attachment to the cause, however, had been no passing fancy. That winter, back in Buffalo, he had addressed a series of four letters under the pseudonym "Juridicus" to Hezekiah A. Salisbury, editor of the *Buffalo Patriot*. Once again Fillmore had voiced his arguments against the religious test. Then in October of 1832, just as he had sought election to Congress — and as if in defiance of the extreme Antimasonic element in his party — he had republished the series as a pamphlet. Though not openly announced as the author, he had acknowledged, and few had doubted, his authorship.[30]

Other Buffalo leaders likewise shifted away from their old alliance. They, however, were mostly National Republicans and had displayed their changing attitudes in other deeds. Ever since 1828 Buffalo's National Republicans had played the supporting role to the local Antimasons, but by 1832 they had begun to recover their identity.

For this they had drawn inspiration from New York City. There the reviving National Republican leaders had created a Committee of Seventy to supervise the renovation of National Republicanism.[31] This city committee had transcended its boundaries and had sought to set up a strong central committee in each New York county to revitalize the old party. It had made funds available for its friends in other locations.[32]

In Buffalo Oran Follett and Peter B. Porter had been quick to respond.[33] Though they had done nothing to upset their existing relations with the Antimasons, they were restless for a new departure. Fillmore, who in September, 1831, had withheld his name from nomination for a fourth term in the legislature (possibly because Abigail was expecting their second child in early March, when, if elected, Fillmore would be in Albany) had

30For pamphlet and evidence of Fillmore's authorship see *Fillmore Papers*, 1:68-82.
31*Niles Weekly Register*, 39:303.
32*National Intelligencer*, January 4, February 17, 1831.
33Follett to Hoxie, February 6, Hiram Ketchum to the State Committee in Buffalo, August 10, John Youngs to National Republican Corresponding Committee in Buffalo, September 19, 1832, all in Hamlin, "Follett Papers," 5:53, 54, 66, 67, 71.

given his sympathy to the National Republican revival.[34] Yet, like the others, he had refrained from openly disavowing the existing alliance.

In the months since those days of indecision, however, a change had occurred. He was in Washington, now, nominally an Antimason, but dedicated to the founding of a new party. And one thing was quickly apparent from his actions. If any segment of the old alliance would have to be sacrificed, he was willing that it be the extreme Antimasons. Time had proved to him that they alienated more votes than they provided.[35]

---

[34]*Buffalo Journal*, November 22, 1831.

[35]As a vital cog in the Antimasonic political machine, Fillmore had the responsibility of keeping Western New York in the proper column. In 1833 he belonged to the central committee of the eighth senatorial district. Rochester *Antimasonic Enquirer*, September 10, 1833. The Antimasonic control of this district had been so effective, that it was universally known as the "infected district." For four years the Antimasons had carried the eighth district by majorities ranging from twelve to fifteen thousand. *Ibid.*, November 26, 1833. But in the election of 1833, the Democrats almost cured the region of its Antimasonic infection. Only Erie County, Fillmore's responsibility, upheld the tradition, and Albert Tracy squeezed through a victory with a bare 600 majority. The results in the rest of the state were as discouraging to Antimasons as the election in the eighth. Only nine Antimasonic assemblymen were elected. *Albany Argus*, November 16, 30, 1833.

Chapter 5

Antimason Into Whig

IKE most Congressional freshmen, Fillmore spent the first few days in the nation's capital getting acquainted with his new surroundings. He met many future colleagues, caught glimpses of some of the famous personages who gathered in Gadsby's dining room and chatted with a few of the national figures.

He had the good fortune to dine in the company of Senator Daniel Webster who was enjoying, temporarily, high popularity both for his defense of Jackson in the nullification crisis and his conciliatory, yet anti-Jackson, position in the great issue of the day: the Bank of the United States.[1] For Fillmore, at the moment, Webster's political attitudes meant less than the Senator's great warmhearted nature. Just away from pleading a case before the Supreme Court, he showed an interest in young Fillmore's law career, and within a month he took the new Congressman around to the Supreme Court chambers. There the great constitutional lawyer arranged Fillmore's admission to practice before the highest court in the land.[2] Fillmore never forgot Webster's kind gesture, and in later years if he himself

[1]Claude M. Fuess, *Daniel Webster*, 2:20-26; Carroll, *Whig Origins*, 71-117.
[2]*National Intelligencer*, January 21, 1834.

was able to boost a fellow lawyer's career through his influence
with the Supreme Court he never failed to do so.[3]

Sight-seeing and making the acquaintance of the nabobs of
American politics were pleasant occupations for Fillmore, but
his conscience quickly recalled him to the serious work at hand.
Most Congressional novices tended to let their first session pass
in inaction, but not he. The old timidity was gone, and hardly
had he arrived in Washington than he was slushing through its
muddy streets, buttonholing Congressmen from all over the
nation for the grand cause.[4]

In the formation of a new party he would eventually perform a number of useful tasks, but at this moment his dreams
were racing ahead of him. He sought the man who could take
the existing chaos and from it magically create a winning national
party. Only a Presidential candidate with unique qualities could
fill this role, and the hopeful Congressman thought he had discovered this candidate: Justice John McLean.

"Sir," he addressed himself to the Supreme Court jurist,
"Although I have not the honor of a personal acquaintance, yet
I take the liberty of . . . suggesting . . . [that] on the subject of
the next presidential election . . . I am satisfied that a great
majority . . . of electors . . . [would] prefer you to any other
candidate. . . ."[5]

The problem was how best to launch McLean's candidacy.
Even though the election of 1836 was three years away, common
gossip had Martin Van Buren running as Jackson's successor.
Factions within the Democratic party, however, thought ill of
Van Buren, and Fillmore saw a chance of profiting from this
dissent. To him Pennsylvania, even more than New York, had
been the axis on which the previous two elections had turned,
and there Democrats were dissastisfied with Van Buren. These
"Jackson Anti-Van Buren" people, Fillmore speculated for

[3] *Fillmore Papers*, 2:498.
[4] Fillmore to McLean, December 9, 1833, in *ibid.*, 1:153.
[5] *Ibid.*, 1:152.

McLean, "might be induced immediately to come out and make . . . [your] nomination."

"It strikes me," continued Fillmore with keen insight into the politics of the day,

> this would be good policy. It would present you as the democratic candidate of the Jackson party of that state, around whom all of that party opposed to Van B. might rally without being charged with having joined the nationals or opposition; and the nationals and antimasons would fall in of course. This course would insure to you the state of Penna. and I am satisfied that the moment that state is safe against Van B. and the electors of New York are satisfied of the fact, that we can also carry New York against him."[6]

But the would-be President-maker was premature. His strategy was excellent, but he had chosen the wrong man. Instead, two years later his party nominated its most popular candidate, William Henry Harrison, in the manner Fillmore had prescribed for McLean.

*   *   *   *   *

Other work, meanwhile, called him. Washington crackled with political static. Few Congresses have earned distinctive names, but the first session of the Twenty-third Congress, which met on December 2, 1833, went down in history as the "Panic Session."[7]

The name was apt. The nation was experiencing a financial panic and Congressmen gave it their attention as they tried to place the blame for it on either President Jackson or his mortal enemy, the president of the Bank of the United States, Nicholas Biddle. For some time the two sides had been lunging at each other over the bank issue. Now Jackson's enemies controlled the Senate; his friends, the House; and against the background of economic distress they squared off and did battle throughout the session.

The controversy went back to the spring of 1832. At that time Henry Clay and Daniel Webster saw a way of embarrassing

[6]*Ibid.*, 1:153.　　[7]Fuess, *Webster*, 2:22.

Jackson by making the national bank a campaign issue.[8] They had prodded Biddle into requesting a renewal of his bank's charter, due to expire in 1836. Congress had complied, but Jackson, recognizing the political tricks of his opponents, had blasted the renewal with a scorching veto. With what Biddle called "the fury of the unchained panther, biting the bars of his cage," Jackson's veto message had aroused the passions of class consciousness in the humble members of society.[9]

Some of Jackson's enemies — and not all of these were sincere friends of the bank — had used the issue against him in the campaign of 1832. They had lost, but their tactics had swelled Jackson's hatred for the bank to phobic proportions. He and his advisers had decided to hasten its end by removing millions of dollars of government deposits from the bank. During the summer and fall of 1833 his Secretary of Treasury had worked feverishly to complete the design, and in those few months he had drained twelve million dollars from Biddle's bank. It writhed in agony while forty-nine recipient state bankers — the "pets" — divided the spoils.[10]

Nicholas Biddle, however, had no intention of abandoning his fight. Three years of life remained in the bank's charter. Possibly in that time Jackson's whole program could be discredited and the bank rechartered. His strategy called for a financial panic. "Nothing but evidence of suffering," he confided to a friend, "will produce any effect on Congress."[11] He used the resources of his bank to rig the nation's credit structure, and the business world began to suffer from deflation. By December,

---

[8]Carroll, *Whig Origins*, fn. 109; Martin Van Buren, *Autobiography*, J. C. Fitzpatrick, ed., 663, 664; Webster to Biddle, December 21, 1833, R. C. McGrane, ed., *Correspondence of Nicholas Biddle, Dealing with National Affairs, 1807-1844*, 218.
[9]R. C. H. Catterall, *The Second Bank of the United States*, 243.
[10]Amos Kendall, *Autobiography*, 376; James A. Hamilton, *Reminiscences*, 258; Van Buren, *Autobiography*, 601-604, 607; correspondence between Jackson and Van Buren, August-September, 1833, Andrew Jackson, *Correspondence*, J. J. Bassett, ed., in vol. 5; W. J. Duane, *Narrative and Correspondence Concerning the Removal of Deposits*.
[11]Biddle to William Appleton, January 27, 1834, in McGrane, *Biddle Correspondence*, 219.

1833, a panic had broken, and as Congressmen poured into Washington the complaints of the nation followed. For seven months the work of Congress swirled around the issue.

The Senate, especially, was in an angry mood. It turned out of office the bank directors who had carried tales to Jackson; it passed resolutions demanding information from the President; it demanded that the deposits be returned to the bank, and it entertained measures for rechartering the bank. It even censured the President for assuming "authority and power not conferred by the Constitution and laws but in derogation of both."

Fillmore watched this show with some misgivings. He was chary, in part, because Henry Clay directed it. He never had had much respect for Clay's position, and even after another year of observing the Kentuckian at first hand his opinion would persist. Clay's "ambition is as insatiable as that of Julius Caesar," he explained to Thurlow Weed. "It has . . . swallowed up judgment and reason, and I think I may say PATRIOTISM. . . ."[12]

Fillmore's wariness also arose from a source deeper than distaste for Clay. In 1829 a branch had been established in Buffalo, and at the time Buffalonians had welcomed it. The mushrooming village needed capital and banking services, for the two banks which had been serving the community were shaky and inadequate.[13] As Fillmore recalled, "No murmur, no complaint was heard from the people" in Buffalo about the bank's operation in his own town.[14]

Rather it was the state banking system as controlled by the Albany Regency — Martin Van Buren's Democratic machine in New York — that had disquieted Fillmore. For years the Regency had heaped favors on the Farmers and Mechanics Bank at Albany and used it as the state's central financial institution. The bank's life-time president, Benjamin Knower, was closely affiliated with

[12]*Fillmore Papers*, 1:156.
[13]*Buffalo Republican*, April 9, August 8, 1829, August 21, 1833; *Buffalo Journal*, March 3, 1830; *Directory of the City of Buffalo for 1830*.
[14]*Fillmore Papers*, 1:127.

the Democratic party. He and the other bank officers controlled most of the credit in the state. No bank could obtain a charter without their approval, and when new bank stock went on sale, they always managed to buy a controlling interest. If investors oversubscribed an issue, the bank commissioners allowed the Regency's bid over all others. Through the Regency's control of the Democratic party, these banking monopolists framed legislation to enhance their profits. The Safety Fund System, designed to set up an insurance system against bank failures, permitted the New York banks to raise interest rates from 6 to 7 per cent. They contributed one-half of 1 per cent to the fund. Thus the Regency, by installing an insurance system, gave their banking friends an extra one-half per cent interest. The state, moreover, always had surplus revenues which sometimes ran into millions. The Regency banks captured the whole amount, including the entire canal fund. On this they paid the state 3 or 4 per cent interest and reloaned it at 7 per cent. By acting as safety deposit boxes for the state, the Regency banks made several hundred thousands of dollars each year.[15]

Fillmore had joined his Antimasonic colleagues in condemning the bank practices in his state. In every election after 1829 his party had charged the Democrats with maintaining a vicious financial monopoly.[16] They had so repeatedly shouted "down with monopoly" that they had become thoroughly enamored with the sentiment.

Now, as Fillmore watched the drama of the Panic Session unfold, memories of the New York banking fight were refreshed. He could remember how the whole anti-Biddle movement in his state had been created by Regency bankers — "birds of ill-omen" who had been seeking to consolidate their control of the state's financial institutions. "It was a Shylock feeling of avarice and revenge," he charged, an attempt to destroy "a hated rival that

[15]Weed, *Autobiography*, 336; Albany *Evening Journal,* April 3, 1830; William H. Seward to Weed, February 28, March 19, March 25, 1828, William H. Seward Papers.
[16]Weed, *Autobiography*, 100, 230, 310, 316, 336.

kept [the state banks] in check and loaned at 6 per cent" rather than 7.[17]

His knowledge of and distaste for the anti-Biddle movement in New York, however, did not make him a friend or defender of either Biddle or his bank. Instead, it made Fillmore suspicious that Biddle's side of the issue was tainted with the same stain. Later he would confirm his suspicions. Meanwhile he harbored a guarded disdain toward both sides.[18]

Exactly what he wanted as a banking system he either did not know or would not say. Though the Panic Session was filled with opportunities to speak out in favor of a national bank — even one divorced from Biddle — he never said one word in its favor or disfavor. Reluctance to express himself as a freshman Congressman did not keep him silent, for in this session he was more garrulous than usual. In the next session, however, when bank debate was resumed, he broke his silence and openly revealed his position. He "regretted extremely . . . to see this controversy . . . renewed . . .," but he willingly admitted the right of the government to use state banks as its fiscal agents.[19]

Eventually he became one of the nation's experts on public economy and had a clear and penetrating view of what was needed for a banking system. But for the time being he appeared to have had a vague repulsion against one aimed primarily at promoting the interests of favorites and politicians to the detriment of the people who used the bank's facilities.[20]

Even if Fillmore could not accept the Bank of the United States, he agreed with the major purpose of all the yammering about it: the creation of a strong national party to replace the inadequate alliance of Antimasons and National Republicans.

[17]*Fillmore Papers*, 1:127-128, 126.
[18]*Ibid.*   [19]*Ibid.*, 2:101, 102.
[20]Buffalo *Patriot*, March 12, 1832, January 8, July 6, September 30, 1833. Fillmore's attitude toward the Bank of the United States may be revealed in the fact that when the Democratic controlled House set up a committee to investigate the political activities of the bank for corruption, he voted for the investigation, *National Intelligencer*, April 8, 1834.

He was practical enough to see that the party a-borning would be made up of diverse groups, some of which might be at odds. Consequently, he was able to overlook the fact that many of the men whom he expected to be leaders in the new party were pro-bank.[21]

To build a party required discrediting its opponents, and in this he could cooperate. His best forensic effort, on April 17, 1834, was occasioned by the general appropriation bill. He chose to demonstrate that the Jacksonian officeholders were profiteering at the expense of their constituents. ". . . Salaries paid by . . . government" officials to themselves "were too high," he badgered. "It . . . seemed to be conceded on all hands," that Jacksonian policies were responsible for the depressed state of business. As a result, most incomes had fallen 25 per cent and the people generally "were suffering by the act of the Government." He "deemed it no more than right and just that the legislators themselves, and all public officers from the President down, should . . . be put upon an equality" with the rest of the nation. He saw "no injustice to public servants" in reducing their salaries by one-fourth, too. It would be just retribution.[22]

But he aimed deeper than retribution. His logic was better calculated to drive an emotional wedge between some voters and their representatives. It was part of the grand maneuver to win support for the new party.

Probably only by coincidence, as Fillmore spoke the core of the new party underwent its first election test in New York City.

*   *   *   *   *

New York City had always been a Democratic stronghold. For years it had been giving Democratic candidates majorities of 5,000 votes or better. Yet the city also contained a large and aggressive group of National Republicans who had been seeking to reverse their fortunes. Until Jackson's war on the bank, they

---

[21]*Ibid.*; Rochester *Antimasonic Enquirer*, November 26, 1833.
[22]*Fillmore Papers*, 1:89-99; *Congressional Globe*, 23 cong., 1 sess., 107-110.

had appeared almost helpless. Jackson's veto message, however, brought both men and journals to their support. Jackson may have won every battle with Nick Biddle, but his war was creating what would become for twenty years the Democratic party's nemesis: the Whig party.

Unknowingly, the city's bankers gave the fillip to the creation of the Whigs. Among them none loved Biddle or shed any tears when he failed to get a renewal of his charter. Even when the withdrawal of deposits began, these city bankers felt no need to protest. Actually they awaited the event with happy expectations, for tax officers in New York City, already the great import market of America, collected at least 50 per cent of the federal income.[23] And it was evident that a great share of the government's deposits would be placed in their own banks. This would increase their own wealth and opportunities to lend money.[24]

Their expectations, however, went awry. In late fall of 1833, when Biddle's bank began to curtail credit sharply, the city's businessmen grew alarmed. Their demand for specie and Biddle's squeeze made the precious metals scarce. The deflationary process quickly spun the economy into a downward spiral. Fear that specie payment would cease gripped the entire business world.

Northward in Albany, meanwhile, the Regency's own pet Farmers and Mechanics Bank was experiencing the first pangs of bankruptcy. It had grossly overissued its notes, and its assets were burdened with "character" loans to its political benefactors. It was an easy target for Biddle's reprisal action. In despair, Ben Knower resigned as president, and Charles E. Dudley assumed the task of forestalling receivership. Quickly supplications were heard at party headquarters.

The state Democratic banking commissioner came to the rescue. Over one-half million dollars of state funds were in New York City banks. The bank commissioner had made these

[23]R. G. Albion, *The Rise of the Port of New York*, 181.
[24]Hammond, *N. Y. Parties*, 2:435; *Albany Argus*, May-July, 1832, *passim*.

deposits earlier to quash complaints against the Regency monopoly. But with the Farmers and Mechanics Bank facing ruin, the
banking commissioner withdrew the state's money from New
York City and transferred it to the Albany bank. For the
moment he saved his pet but he had made the city bankers' plight
more intolerable.[25]

For relief, the city bankers called upon the Chamber of
Commerce and the Board of Trade — Democrats and National
Republicans, alike. Their officers got up a mass meeting of the
two groups and sent a committee to Washington to lobby before
Congress and the President. The lobbyists memorialized Congress[26] and called upon the President in person to urge him to
give up his war and return the deposits to Biddle's bank. In no
uncertain terms, Jackson told them that he would never return
the deposits, that he would never advocate the creation of another
national bank, and that if the pet bank system failed, then some
means independent of banks would be devised to keep government funds.[27]

The report shocked a number of influential New Yorkers
into parting company with Jackson. The Chamber of Commerce and the Board of Trade, meanwhile, organized into a
general pressure group to give the "great mercantile community
its just and proper influence." As its agent, it created the Union
Committee — a permanent lobby — and charged it with bringing the bankers of the state together as a pressure group.[28]
Eventually the committee persuaded the state to make six million
dollars of its credit available to New York banks which
proved sufficient to save them.[29] But politically the damage
had been done.

New York City National Republicans saw their chance
to use the Union Committee politically. Philip Hone, one of

[25]Three hundred thousand dollars were withdrawn from New York City banks and
    transferred to Albany. *Albany Argus,* March 31, February 5, 1834.
[26]*National Intelligencer,* February 15, 1834, contains the report of the delegation to
    another meeting of the merchants and traders of New York City.
[27]*Ibid.*   [28]*Ibid.*
[29]Catterall, *Second Bank of U. S.,* 343-344.

their prime movers, was a member, and he directed it smoothly into the right political channels. Theoretically, the committee was bipartisan, or nonpartisan; this suited the National Republicans, for it facilitated the conversion of Democrats to their side.[30]

By early March, 1834, the Union Committeemen had set the stage. They had decided that the national administration must be chastised and purged. Normally city elections had only small national significance, but one was at hand in New York — at that time local elections were held in spring — and the Union Committee decided to use it as a challenge to Democratic policy. Ignoring local issues they deliberately made the bank their cause and nominated for mayor Gulian C. Verplank, a former Democrat and a stockholder in the bank who was filled with the enthusiasm of a recent convert.[31] Two days later the Democrats nominated C. W. Lawrence, who was equally vehement in his support of Jackson.

James Watson Webb, editor of the *Courier and Inquirer,* recruited to the cause at the time of Jackson's veto, suggested that the opponents of Jackson should be known as the Whig party and it was adopted.[32] "It is a petty conceit," sneered a Jackson newspaper. "The Whigs of England had fought the battles of the people against the usurpation of the throne, and the Whigs of America are fighting the usurpations of Jackson."[33]

A spirited campaign followed, and it attracted nation-wide interest.[34] The newly formed Whig party won control of the City Council, but its candidate for mayor lost by 213 votes.[35] Nevertheless, Whigs were jubilant. They held a great celebration at Castle Garden and the faithful poured forth by the thousands. Learning that Webster was the guest of a lady at her house, they moved thence en masse and there the orator, who had declined to appear among the beer kegs in the Garden, presented himself

[30]Tuckerman, *Hone,* 1:91-97.
[31]*Ibid.,* 1:97-99; *Albany Argus,* April 23, 1834.
[32]New York *Courier and Inquirer,* February 2, 1834.
[33]*Albany Argus,* April 23, 1834.
[34]*National Intelligencer,* April 5, 1834; *Niles' Weekly Register,* 46:82.
[35]Hammond, *N. Y. Parties,* 2:442.

at the window and proudly announced he was happy to be numbered among them.[36]

Throughout the state and beyond, the anti-Jackson elements insisted on interpreting the defeat of Verplanck as a victory. Philadelphians held "a grand celebration at Pawelton on the Schuylkill." At New York's capital one hundred guns were fired in honor of Verplanck. In Fillmore's home town "a great affair" was made of it "with guns and illumination." At Portsmouth, Webster's men received the news with one hundred guns and "had a town meeting and made speeches."[37]

What was being celebrated was the discovery of a way to victory. The normal Democratic 5,000-vote margin was gone in New York City and would vanish more easily elsewhere. Rejoicing, Weed received Union Committeemen, and in a few days more the remnants of the Antimasonic legislative delegation met in caucus, not to compose their usual annual address, but to consider the future. Without debate they resolved to disband their party and read the last rites over the "blessed Spirit."[38]

In one city after another the Whig ticket faced the Democrats unopposed and in Albany a bitter struggle brought them victory. Everywhere the Union Committee was active in this lusty birth of the Whig party. Fate and the politicians had cast the Union Committee in the role of Pegasus.[39]

Through the summer the union movement swept westward, into the Ohio Valley and as far southwestward as Louisiana. Occasionally an Antimasonic voice cried out in anguish: "We will not be killed off."[40] In Pennsylvania the Whig movement

[36]Tuckerman, *Hone*, 1:101; Albany *Evening Journal*, April 17, 1834; *National Intelligencer*, April 19, 1834.

[37]Tuckerman, *Hone*, 1:103.

[38]Granger to Weed, April 16, 1834, Granger Papers; Johnathan Goodhue, et al. to Weed, April 16, 1834, Weed Papers; Albany *Evening Journal*, April 12, 13, 17, 1834.

[39]*Albany Argus*, March 21, May 4, June 13, September 2, 1834. On May 4 Editor Croswell charged that Weed was completely subservient to the Whigs, and Weed, who usually denied all charges, true and untrue, made by "Miss Croswell," kept beneficently silent. See also Albany *Evening Journal*, May 5, 7, 1834.

[40]Lockport (N. Y.) *Courier* in *Albany Argus*, June 13, 1834.

looked like one of Biddle's schemes and the state's German population, which had begun to move to the Antimasonic party, and which hated Philadelphia's pretensions, could not be forced into an alliance with Banker Biddle. Antimasonic boss Thad Stevens had no choice but to avoid a premature juncture with the Whigs.[41]

In Vermont and Massachusetts a hard core of religious orthodoxy preserved Antimasonic strength and posed a deadly problem to the Whigs, one that they never truly solved. The Antimasons were the majority party in Vermont and as such condescendingly accepted National Republican and Whig cooperation. In Massachusetts, J. Q. Adams and Edward Everett had captured leadership of the Antimasons, but at this point they also failed to bring the group into the new coalition.[42]

One voice that had cried out "We will not be killed off," had come from Lockport, Buffalo's neighbor. The cry should have been a special warning to Fillmore for it sounded an ominous note of dissent in his home territory. Almost everywhere else in New York the merger was taking place without undue friction, and by September it was evident to all that Antimasons planned to have no distinctive state ticket.[43] Ever since Fillmore's election in 1828, however, Erie County had been Antimasonry's largest and strongest bailiwick. Until it cooperated and joined the Whigs, unanimity would be blocked and amalgamation fruitless. Already Erie's National Republicans had adopted the Whig name[44] but their allies held back.

Fillmore thought he was prepared for this moment. During his first year in Congress he had bent every effort toward blending National Republicans and Antimasons of his "infected dis-

---

[41]McCarthy, *Antimasonic Party,* 461.

[42]*Ibid.,* 523-524; *Niles' Weekly Register,* 48:238; Adams, *Memoirs,* 9:65, 170.

[43]Almost all the opposition county conventions meet under the Whig label. Albany *Evening Journal,* August 9, 1834. Even the Antimasonic state convention called by the legislative caucus for September 10 at Utica merged into a Whig conclave which met simultaneously. *Ibid.,* May 7, September 10, 12, 13, 1834; *Albany Argus,* September 4, 1834.

[44]*Buffalo Journal,* May 3, 1834.

trict" into a new party.[45] Now as a member of the central committee for the eighth senatorial district and a possible candidate
for re-election, he felt he could guide his friends into the merger.
Here he miscalculated. For years he had followed a course in
Albany, in Buffalo, in Washington, and in private life that identified him more with urban and commercial Buffalo than with
rural western New York, the Antimasonic stronghold. He had
lost some of his influence with Antimasons. They still admired
him and were willing to vote for him, but the rock-ribbed refused
to follow him into Whiggery. They split into two groups, and
throughout spring and summer of 1834 the two factions bick-
ered. Fillmore diligently tried to draw them into a compromise.
By midsummer disgust and despair overwhelmed him. He resigned as committeeman, refused to let his name be used by the
Antimasonic party, and openly threw in his lot with the Whigs.[46]

He also refused a Whig nomination to Congress, and
shrewdly advised Whigs not to nominate a Congressional candidate, but rather to endorse the county Antimasonic ticket. The
Whig committee saw the wisdom of avoiding a division of
strength and with an eye to the future urged all to follow Fillmore's advice.[47]

*   *   *   *   *

The election in November disappointed New York Whigs.

Though the new party had been born in their state, its
successes came elsewhere. In part the nature of its birth explained
its failure, for the bank panic had fathered the New York party
and it had been thoroughly identified with Biddle's bank. In other
states, however, the panic and New York City's spring election
had been a signal to act rather than a statement of goals.

Between spring and autumn, moreover, federal deposits in
the state banks counteracted Biddle's contraction of loans and

[45]See his relations with Follett and Peter B. Porter, Fillmore to Follett, February 26,
1834, Oran Follett Collection.
[46]*Buffalo Journal,* June 20, July 12, August 4, 9, September 19, 1834; Buffalo *Commercial Advertiser,* July 2, 9, 15, September 18, 23, 1834.
[47]Albany *Evening Journal,* October 8, 1834.

stopped the downward spiral. Prices recovered, the flow of money quickened, and by midyear the nation's economy regained its vigor. Jacksonian newspapers, meanwhile, pressed home their claim that Biddle had intentionally caused the panic, and by late August the bank issue was more of a hindrance than a help to Whigs. Already Clay and Webster had cast it aside, and others hurriedly tried to purge themselves of Biddle's mark. The panic was no longer an ally.[48]

As they read the signs of the times, New York party leaders tried to shift their tactics. Their favorite for governor — Gulian Verplanck — was now unthinkable. But they had no other strong man who was not thoroughly identifiied with the past. Unfortunately for their cause, this was an ideal situation for Thurlow Weed to employ his talents and satisfy his ambitions. Though earnestly sympathizing with the Whigs, he had played only a secondary role in the emergence of the party. He had no intentions, however, of remaining an observer.

In spring, when the Union Committee had approached him for help, he had driven a hard bargain and obtained the right of naming the candidate for lieutenant-governor. The man he had in mind was William Henry Seward. Seward had not earned the post, nor had he yet shown the ability that would one day make him a contender for the Presidency. The hatchet-nosed, stubby-legged Seward, from Auburn, New York, had been elected in 1830 as an Antimason to the state legislature. Twice

[48]*Albany Argus,* August 31, 1834. In the Senate, the hopelessness of recovering government funds for Biddle revealed the extent to which the bank was a political carrier. Biddle fell victim to political expediency and Clay actually turned perfidious. At one point in the Congressional melee, Webster in agreement with Democratic leaders had prepared a measure which would have given the Bank of United States seven years of extended life. But the Sage of Ashland had other plans. Though he directed the foray for Biddle, he actually was using the agitation for political ends. He welcomed the panic as a means of casting mud at the Administration; he encouraged the reception of the petitions that pointed with alarm at the consequences of the removal policy as a means of organizing opposition at home and as an aid in the smear campaign. Because Anti-Jacksonians controlled the Senate, Clay forced through a resolution censuring Jackson's "executive usurpation." It was a preliminary to contemplated impeachment proceedings in the House. Not wanting to harm this campaign by removing its *casus belli,* Clay quashed the reprieve for Biddle's bank that Webster had contrived.

before he had sought office, but each time his audiences laughed at his red hair and his ridiculous, sawed-off figure. On the third attempt they quit smiling and elected him; in 1834, as the Whig party came into being, he was serving in the state senate.

Weed watched Seward's campaigning with deepening interest, for he perceived redeeming qualities in the youthful lawyer. Seward was an indefatigable worker and nothing Weed asked him to do — no matter how disagreeable — was shirked. His rasping voice and colloquial style dulled his rhetoric, but he could judge men. Even in his youth he understood that within most men was a spark of idealism, and he fanned that spark whenever he could. He was, moreover, unconscionably ambitious, but still capable of seeing that he lacked Weed's talents for politicking. In his long career he would grow to understand Weed thoroughly, and with each passing year he would tie himself more closely to Weed's star. At the moment he was sending interminable, detailed political reports couched in flattery to his boss. Weed was pleased and the two men began to talk of joint land speculations; between them, a fast friendship grew.[49]

Now, however, in the fall of 1834, Weed saw his chance to do more for Seward than name him as the Whig candidate for lieutenant-governor. Antimasons who accepted Whiggery had not championed the bank as Verplanck had done, nor were they associated in the voter's eye with New York City. A young former Antimason as candidate for governor, Weed argued, would correct the impression being made by the Whig party. With this point he won the nomination for Seward.[50]

The selection was a mistake. The inexperienced Seward was not prepared to lead the Whigs in their first state-wide campaign against a thoroughly organized Democracy headed by Governor William Marcy, a veteran of proven power, and supported from

[49]Seward, *Autobiography*, 50, 76, 238, 257-258; see also Seward's letters to Weed from 1830 to 1834 in Weed Papers and Seward Papers as revealing this relationship.
[50]*Albany Argus*, June 9, August 30, September 2, 4, 19; Albany *Evening Journal*, September 12, 13, 1834.

Washington by Vice-President Martin Van Buren, the heir-apparent of the Democratic party. Seward went down to ignominious defeat.[51]

The Whigs of New York might well have asked themselves if they were not duplicating the record of their predecessors, except that the hinterlands glowed bright with victories and promise. Connecticut, Rhode Island, Ohio, Indiana, and Illinois in the North returned Whig governors. In the South, Maryland, Virginia, North Carolina, Kentucky, and Louisiana deserted the Jacksonian fold. The Whig party was in the making, but New Yorkers still had a large task before them.[52]

* * * * *

In early December, "lame-duck" Fillmore returned to Washington. On his way he stopped in Albany to talk with Weed and plan for the future. In the past seven years these two men had been thrown together a great deal. Though they had not become close personal friends they were partners in politics. Generally Fillmore regarded the Albany editor as the senior member of the firm and sought his advice on tactics. He found Weed disconsolate over the election results and in no mood for planning. So discouraged had he become that he told Fillmore he would be glad to give up politics if he had some means of support. Fillmore was distraught to see Weed in this state of mind and offered his help. Knowing Weed's penchant for land speculation, Fillmore asked his law partner, Nathan Hall, to investigate the possibility of western New York lands. Later Hall informed Weed that he could get fifteen to fifty thousand acres of land in western New York that would "give quick results." He added: "If you feel disposed to try for improved and articled lands, any assistance Mr. Fillmore or myself can render you shall be at your service."[53]

Though nothing came of it, concern over Weed's troubled soul need not have lasted long. The political game at Albany

[51]*Ibid.*, November 19, 1834.
[52]*Ibid.*, October 20, November 19, 1834; Seward to Weed, November 12, 17, 1834, Seward Papers.
[53]N. K. Hall to Weed, February 17, 1835, Weed Papers.

and Washington was too appealing to the inveterate politician. He would rather play politics than eat, and was soon making plans for the Presidential election of 1836.

Neither had Fillmore any intentions of giving up. Once at the capital he quickly became involved in President-making. That he would soon be without an office whetted rather than dulled his appetite, and he used the lame-duck session to strengthen the Whig organization. Everyone expected Van Buren to succeed Jackson, and everywhere among the Whigs Van Buren's name evoked criticism. They dug deep into the records in search of material to discredit the "Old Fox." Having heard that Van Buren had behaved somewhat traitorously as far back as Madison's election in 1812, Fillmore sent a hurried request to Weed: "Either collect and publish the records and evidence of these facts or forward them to me."[54]

If the Whigs knew the man they would oppose in 1836, they were far from agreement on their own Presidential candidate. In any discussion Clay's friends always insinuated his name, Webster's partisans carried a torch for their hero, friends in the South speculated on the strength of Hugh Lawson White (a former Jacksonian from Tennessee) and Northerners mooted the chances of William Henry Harrison.

Fillmore's own predilections had changed. A year before he had been working for Judge John McLean's nomination, but now he would accept any man who could whip Van Buren. Fillmore was convinced that Henry Clay would surely lose, but feared that Clay's friends would insist upon his nomination and destroy the chance of a Whig victory. He fervently hoped that Clay would withdraw from the race before it was too late. "I find that Clay and his friends," he informed Weed, "cling to the last hope." They are

> doing everything to keep him on the course. It is not for you or me to calculate the extent of this pernicious influence. We regard him as a hackneyed politician, possessed of talent . . .

[54]Fillmore to Weed, December 10, 1834, *Fillmore Papers*, 2:155.

but so strongly suspected of a want of integrity that he might be regarded as a dead weight. . . . But here we are — no help for us. I think after all Clay will not decline.

Fillmore regarded Webster's candidacy "as the most extreme folly." To Weed he reported: ". . . I have not conversed with any member from any quarter of the Union who would say that he thought . . . Webster stood any change of success. . . ." As for White, Fillmore doubted that the Tennessean could win the North if he ran. If White "is distinctly the *Southern* candidate against Van B. [uren] as the *Northern* ought we to, or can we, support him? . . . I am informed that . . . [he] is not a Mason and never has been. *Tell this to our friends.*"[55] Almost by default he had moved to Harrison.

*   *   *   *   *

Fillmore exerted himself unremittingly to improve the party's position.[56] His major concern was to complete the transition of western New York to the Whig column. The troubles of 1834 still rankled, and once Congress adjourned he returned home to swing a heavy cudgel in his own and his party's behalf.

Buffalo needed a strong Whig paper. Up to this point Fillmore had depended on the *Patriot,* owned and edited by Hezekiah A. Salisbury. Long a weekly, the *Patriot* had in early 1834 changed its name to the *Commercial Advertiser* and appeared daily. But it lacked punch and aggressiveness. Oran Follett's *Journal,* meanwhile, had carried the cause of the new party with force and vigor. At the critical point in 1834, however, Follett had moved to Sandusky, Ohio, and the voice of Buffalo Whiggery, thereafter, only whispered.

Fillmore acted to repair the damage. After private negotiations with publisher Salisbury, he arranged for the *Commercial*

55*Ibid.,* Fillmore to Weed, December 28, 1834, *ibid.,* 2:157.
56Fillmore to H. B. Potter and G. Babcock, January 20, 1835, *ibid.,* 2:158-159; ". . . my duty to the hardy mariners of our lakes . . . induced me . . . to enter into an investigation . . . for the erection of a MARINE HOSPITAL . . ." Fillmore to Hezekiah A. Salisbury, January 21, 1835, *ibid.,* 2:159-61, Fillmore to Salisbury, February 11, 1835, *ibid.,* 2:161-162.

Advertiser to take on a new editor. He was Dr. Thomas M. Foote, a young physician with a bent for journalism. Only twenty-four years old, Foote was a native of East Aurora, where Fillmore's parents still lived and where Fillmore frequently visited. Fillmore had watched Foote grow into manhood, and the two had respect for each other's abilities. Within a half-year, Foote bought a one-third interest in the *Commercial Advertiser* and for twenty years remained at his editorial post as the staunch supporter of the Whig party and his warm patron and friend, Fillmore.[57]

With a newspaper behind him, Fillmore turned to other phases of his political task. On one occasion he promoted Whig prestige among the rural communities where the Antimasonic sentiment still lingered. Earlier in the decade, two out-of-state speculators, Jacob LeRoy and Heman J. Redfield had bought large tracts of land in western New York, where they developed a harsh landlord system. From their mortgagees and tenants they exacted fees and charges beyond the terms of their contracts. Usually the victims had the choice of paying or suffering eviction. Gradually their resentment rose to hatred. The speculators, meanwhile, had their own troubles. A state law in 1832 had placed a tax on payments of debts to nonresident creditors. LeRoy and Redfield had endeavored to have the tax repealed. They failed and then tried to pass the expense of the tax on to their tenants and mortgagees. In the spring of 1836, the victims rebelled.[58]

Quickly Fillmore joined the fracas. In a peculiar way he felt almost responsible for the affair. During his last year at Albany, he had introduced a tax bill similar to the one that was irritating the speculators. The ways and means committee had reported it too late for action, but the next year the bill became law. Now Fillmore defended both the law and the settlers. With a group of public-spirited men, he called for a delegate meeting

[57]See editor's note, *ibid.*, 1:71; 2:223-224.

[58]As the excitement which covered seven western counties began to abate, Seward became an agent for the Land Company. His account in his *Autobiography*, 301-14, is colorful, albeit prejudiced and self-centered.

of settlers to "resist the unjust oppression of the late purchasers of the Holland Purchase. . . ."[59]

From twenty-five towns in Erie, Chautauqua, Genesee and Niagara counties, representatives of the farmers came to Buffalo, and Fillmore himself attended the meetings as one of Buffalo's delegates. The wrathful assemblage adopted a long series of resolutions and a memorial to the legislature. One resolution demanded that the nonresident tax never be repealed.

Faced with this rebellion, LeRoy and Redfield succumbed to the settlers' demands for fairer treatment. The tax remained, and for his part, Fillmore earned the enduring gratitude of many harassed settlers in western New York.[60]

With this triumph fresh Fillmore returned to the task of consolidating Whig power. Wiping out the last vestiges of Antimasonic resistance in the rural communities was impossible. For years die-hards would resent the betrayal of their cause. But in the fall of 1835 he succeeded in persuading Antimasons to dissolve their county organization, and their supporters had almost no choice but to accept the Whig party.[61]

*   *   *   *   *

For a while in late 1835 the goals toward which Fillmore had been working for four years appeared in sight. In his own region where his responsibility was great, his efforts had drawn together a greater number of groups than the old National Republican-Antimasonic alliance had ever done. So well was he satisfied with his work that in the fall of 1836 he accepted the Whig nomination for Congress with complete confidence of victory.[62]

Throughout the nation, moreover, hope rode high among Whigs, for they believed they had created an organization capable

[59]Buffalo *Commercial Advertiser*, March 6, 31, 1836; *Fillmore Papers*, 1:x-xi.
[60]*Ibid.*
[61]Buffalo *Commercial Advertiser*, September 22, October 2, 15, 18, November 3, 4, 1835.
[62]*Ibid.*, August 12, 19, 30, September 2, 17, 20, October 14, 1836.

of winning the Presidential election. To be sure a variety of regional groups, and state and local machines — some quite inharmonious — made up the party, but at the end of 1835 this did not cause Whig leaders undue anxiety. Homogeneity could not be expected and, indeed, it was not essential. In late 1835 the party's prospects had been brightened immeasurably when both McLean and Henry Clay withdrew from the Presidential canvass. Unanimity of action, if not principle, appeared to be near. In December of 1835 a Pennsylvania convention nominated William Henry Harrison, rapidly followed by most of the border, northern, and New England states. In February, Fillmore traveled to Albany to a state convention to cast one of Erie County's nominating votes for Harrison.[63]

But the high point of hope in the Presidential campaign had been reached. From here on the Whigs blundered. Webster and White, already nominated by their state conventions, would not quit the race, and no central authority existed in the party to force their withdrawal. In desperation, Whigs resorted to the ill-starred strategy of trying to arrange a disputed election that would go to the House of Representatives. Eventually South Carolina cast its votes for Willie P. Mangum to add another name to the list of Van Buren's opponents. The election became a free-for-all.

In the final reckoning in November of 1836, the Whig strategy failed. The blow stunned the New York leaders. Here at their party's birthplace they had gone down to the worst defeat the Regency had inflicted on its opponents in sixteen years. Only western New York — where Fillmore's work and candidacy carried the day — stood out as an exception.[64] Had others been as successful as Fillmore in other parts of the state, they might have reversed the national result, for New York's vote stood between Van Buren and defeat. Yet what had once been hope was now despair, and the query: "will we ever be successful?" was in the minds of many baffled Whigs.[65]

[63]*Buffalo Commercial Advertiser*, February 2, 9, 14, 15, 26, 1836.
[64]*Ibid.*, November 6, 7, 9, 11, 1836.
[65]*Ibid.*, December 2, 1836.

Chapter 6

Nascent Rebellion

IGHTEEN - THIRTY - SIX gave resplendent prosperity to every part of the nation. Buffalo, too, enjoyed the boom for eight months of that year, when suddenly catastrophe struck. The fantastic business empire of Benjamin Rathbun collapsed, and with it went the golden glow that had hung over the Lake Erie port.

Benjamin Rathbun was Buffalo's king of speculators. He had arrived in town in the early twenties as the landlord of Eagle Tavern. From this he went on to enterprises that had no limit. He "exhibited a Napoleonic grasp of mind in business affairs," Fillmore noted later, "and he . . . managed to engross and control" most of the construction business in the burgeoning town. By 1836 he had 2,500 workmen in his employment, and his real estate was valued at two and a quarter million dollars. One of his boldest building projects, begun in 1836, was a city exchange. "It was to be a vast colonnaded building, with a tower 220 feet high." As work began, however, the sheriff arrested Rathbun. He had been staving off his creditors and paying his workmen by recklessly and daringly forging the names of many Buffalo businessmen to his notes. Exposure came, panic followed, and Buffalo's prosperity evaporated.[1]

[1] *Fillmore Papers*, 2:103, 104, 1:ix; Guy H. Salisbury, "The Speculative Craze of 1832," Buffalo Historical Society, *Publications*, 4:317-338.

In jail, awaiting trial, Rathbun assigned all his property for liquidation to Hiram Pratt, president of the Bank of Buffalo, Lewis F. Allen (Fillmore's colleague at the Whig state convention), Joseph Clary (Fillmore's former law partner), Thomas C. Love, and Fillmore himself. All the assignees, except Fillmore, were victims of Rathbun's forgeries. The case dragged on for six years, and long before its conclusion Fillmore withdrew as an assignee. But from it, Fillmore's already abundant knowledge of the problems of the business community reached the saturation point and his heart was sick with the community's miseries.[2]

Six months after Rathbun's failure the rest of the country felt the impact of the crashing empires of other entrepreneurs. From the fall of 1834 onward, the nation's economy had gradually fevered into a speculative spree. Surplus federal funds were fed into the orgy by Jackson's pet banks. These banks were stable enough, but there had sprouted in addition to them scores of spurious banks designed to traffic in the speculation. They issued bushels of worthless currency and the Secretary of the Treasury, alarmed at the character of the money the government was receiving, prodded Jackson into requiring all moneys paid to the government to be gold and silver. This "Specie Circular" made the worthlessness of the "wildcat" currency apparent, a rush for specie followed, and a nation-wide panic broke a few weeks after Jackson left office. Hundreds of banks refused to honor their currency, hundreds more closed their doors. Soon the New York safety fund system failed and specie payment ceased.

The combination of Rathbun's failure, the panic, and its subsequent depression gave Fillmore his fill of hard times. One of his principal sources of income as a lawyer had been to represent out-of-city business houses in their dealings with Buffalo clients. For years he had been reporting on the credit and character of his fellow townsmen and, when the need arose, suing them for debts due his own clients. His collection service charges

[2]*Ibid.; Fillmore Papers*, 2:104; 1:x.

usually ran to 5 per cent of the debt. A flood of business now deluged him. It was lucrative, but discouraging.[3]

Hardly a business failure occurred in Buffalo in which Fillmore was not involved. With each passing month his gloom deepened. Discount rates soared. Loans could be had only at 5 per cent for fifteen days. "No business can be done under these conditions," commented Fillmore. "Lawyers may perhaps make money in such times, but to them they are unpleasant when they see the ruin of business men from whom they derive their patronage."[4]

Griffin & Wheaton, a large New York City credit-rating and collection agency, planned to delve deeper into the misfortunes of others and proposed to enlarge its facilities. It canvassed its agents, offered to create a partnership with them, divide the "spoils" and create a monopoly in their line. Fillmore rejected the offer. He was not interested in becoming a partner in what was becoming to him a hateful collection business.[5]

The disorder in the financial world grew beyond reason. Uncertainty ruled everywhere. From one day to the next, no one knew which bank would fail or which currency would become unredeemable. By the summer of 1837, Fillmore, unable to draw a draft on his account in the Bank of Buffalo, was sending currency to New York City clients, letting the creditors worry about its "currency" or "uncurrency." Soon the Bank of Buffalo closed its doors. Hiram Pratt, its president, knowing of Fillmore's connection with New York's financial circle, called upon him for help. Although ill, Fillmore traveled to New York City, but it was only a mission of relief and he could not solve the problems that were not the bank's making.[6]

[3]Fillmore, Haven and Hall to Griffin and Wheaton, September 21, 1837, Letterbook of the firm of Fillmore, Haven and Hall for 1836-1837.
[4]Salisbury, "The Speculative Craze," 398; Fillmore to. Stans and Hoffman, April 8, 1837, Letterbook.
[5]Fillmore, Haven and Hall to Griffin and Wheaton, March 29, April 1, June 19, July 25, 1837; to Stans and Hoffman, January 24, 1837, *ibid*.
[6]Commission to Fillmore dated May 10, 1837, signed by Hiram Pratt as president of bank in possession of James Babcock of Buffalo; Fillmore to W. S. Worden, May 29, 1837; Fillmore, Haven and Hall to Griffin and Wheaton, May 15, June 19, 1837, Letterbook.

In the midst of these shambles, President Van Buren called a special session of Congress, and Fillmore journeyed to Washington filled with hatred for the government whose policies he was convinced had brought down upon the nation this unprecedented ruin.

*   *   *   *   *

Fillmore found Washington a sharp contrast to his memory of it. The city's physical appearance remained the same but its opulence and gaiety had disappeared. The depression had ensnared even the capital in its all-embracing grasp.

Believing that his government had the right to protect only itself, but not the people, from economic ravages, Van Buren confined his recommendation for fighting the depression to two measures. First he asked Congress to replace the pet bank system with a group of local depositories owned and operated by the Treasury. None of these branch treasuries would ever engage in banking, nor would private individuals have the use of government funds. A treasurer in charge of each depository, rather than a banker, would collect government revenues and pay out government expenditures in his locality. The plan was known as the "Independent" or the "Sub-treasury System," and Van Buren designed it to divorce the government from the insecurities of private banking.

His second proposal was to shore up the government's income. During the boom of 1835-1836, federal revenues had far exceeded expenditures and, having no use for the surplus money, Congress had decided to lend it to the state governments. It had directed that thirty-seven of the forty-two million dollars of surplus funds be distributed, in the form of loans, to those states willing to receive it. Distribution was scheduled in four installments, and by the time the special session of Congress convened, three payments had been made.

Meanwhile, the depression had sharply curtailed the government's income, and it was quite obvious that there was no longer a surplus with which to meet the fourth installment. Van Buren called upon Congress to make it lawful for the Treasury not to honor its promise to the states.

With these two proposals Fillmore wrestled in the special session of Congress. Since his experience with the panic had convinced him that political interference with banking had caused the nation's distress, he frowned on both measures. His conviction went back to Jackson's fight with Biddle. ". . . This war against the United States bank," he charged was

> got up for political effect, regardless of the peace of society or the interests of the country. . . . The more intelligent of the middle class never engaged in it. . . . It was really a war of the State banks against the United States bank got up by artful politicians. . . .

The result, he continued, has been "all the evils of overbanking, overtrading . . . ruinous gambling . . . and the final . . . derangement of the currency, and the bankruptcy of the government. . . ." Now, Van Buren proposed to repeat, in principle, what Jackson had done. The same politicians who had debased the state banks with their pet bank system had a scheme to destroy both state and pet banks with the Independent Treasury. To Fillmore it was a "noxious pill" and another politician's trick. The retributive justice of seeing the pet banks destroyed by their very creators caused Fillmore to be favorably disposed toward the new bill for a moment. But the vengeful emotion passed.[7]

He could see nothing but evil from Van Buren's proposals. The government would hoard the nation's supply of specie in its vaults and leave almost nothing to support the nation's currency and credit, which, after all, was issued by private banks. New York's twenty-five-million-dollar credit structure, for example, would be supported by a mere two million in specie held by a monopoly of banks that belonged to the safety fund system. The rest might easily become "wildcat" issues.

[7] *Fillmore Papers,* 1:126.

What Fillmore wanted was a "free-banking system" — not a national bank, or pet banks, or an Independent Treasury, but state banks unmolested by politics. He urged Congress, to

> purge [our banking system] of its corruptions and abuses, and strip it of its odious monopoly, and open the privilege of banking to all who comply with such prescribed rules of the legislature as secure the bill-holder and public generally from fraud and imposition. I . . . hope to see the day when . . . the moral pestilence of political banks and banking shall be unknown.[8]

His own state would have to wait until his party won office before this goal was reached.

Less vituperative, but equally strong, was Fillmore's opposition to Van Buren's efforts to annul "distribution." At the beginning of 1837, when New York had accepted its share of the surplus, it loaned almost the entire amount to institutions and communities in distress. The rigors of the depression were thus softened. The state, moreover, had loaned the money at 7 per cent, netting over $350,000 in interest each year and pledged this income to support the common schools. Decreasing state revenues were bolstered and the great source of state income — the canal revenues — was preserved for canal enlargement. The state, however, had loaned all it had contracted to receive in four payments. If the federal government refused to fulfill its contract, the state must either repudiate its obligation on one-quarter of the promised aid, or get the money elsewhere. If the latter were the choice, the canal fund would be the most logical reserve to raid. Such a move would indefinitely defer canal

---

[8]*Ibid.*, 1:127, 129. When misrepresented by the *Globe* as favoring the Bank of the United States, Fillmore chided its editors. ". . . Passing over some evident misapprehensions of your reporter to the purport of my remarks generally, I wish to say that he is entirely and most singularly mistaken in saying that I made a lengthy argument in favor of a United States Bank. I made no argument in favor of the United States Bank, nor of a United States Bank; but, on the contrary, expressly disclaimed ever having been the particular friend of the United States Bank, and expressed my sincere doubts whether the incorporation of a new United States Bank, at this time, would relieve the present embarrassments of the community. Will you do me the justice to correct the mistake?" Fillmore to Blair and Rives, September 27, 1837, Fillmore Mss.

enlargement and, in either case, the common schools would suffer.[9]

In spite of his opposition, and that of Whigs and a growing body of anti-Van Buren Democrats, both measures passed. But Fillmore had not said his last word on either subject.

*   *   *   *   *

While Fillmore fulminated against the Administration's bank policy, the depression reaped a harvest of votes for the Whigs. In the local elections of 1837, state after state turned to the new party. Surprisingly, after their staggering defeat the previous year, New York's own Whigs captured control of the state assembly. Pundits had to go back eleven years to discover a time when the Van Buren machine had not controlled all branches of New York's government. The successes began to make Fillmore feel both the tug and the comfort of a possible major party victory. Yet it did not seem right after all the labor and planning that he and his colleagues had done for the last nine years that they were moving into office by default rather than design. Whether just or no, Whig politicians glowed with anticipation as they looked forward to the gubernatorial and Congressional year of 1838.

The Democrats began to carp at each other. Some of their bankers had grown alarmed at Van Buren's subtreasury scheme. It meant they would not only lose the pet bank deposits but would be squeezed by a shortage of specie. They squealed, and Nathaniel P. Tallmadge, one of New York's Senators, took up the leadership of the Democratic opposition. Espying the change occurring in his state, and needing support from Whigs for his own re-election, Tallmadge called a convention of dissident Democrats for September, 1837, at Syracuse. There they denounced Van Buren, repudiated his most influential New York henchman, Governor William L. Marcy, and endorsed William H. Seward, a Whig, for governor in 1838. Pet bank stockholders

[9] *Fillmore Papers*, 1:109-134.

applauded Tallmadge's break and liberally paid for fireworks and shouters to usher in this Democratic schism.[10]

Although revolting Democrats selected Seward for governor, Whigs had not yet agreed on their candidate. Three men stood out: Seward, Francis Granger, and Luther Bradish. Weed favored his protégé, Seward. Luther Bradish's support came from the old National Republican elements in the party and a growing body of men who disliked Weed, especially in New York City. Granger drew his strength from central New York and the Chenango Valley region, where he stood out as the champion of that area's special interests. Actually, little hostility existed among the candidates, but at the level of their supporters the air was charged with recriminations.

The question placed Fillmore in a ticklish position. Until now he had never doubted the wisdom of Weed's political gyrations. Yet in 1838, Fillmore thought Granger the wisest choice. The nomination of Seward threatened to embarrass him. Seward had taken a job with the hated western New York landlords, LeRoy and Redfield, and in the eyes of rural New Yorkers he was tainted with oppression. He also enjoyed the applause of New York City supporters of Henry Clay, which made western New Yorkers disdainful. A faint note of jealousy also crept into Fillmore's dislike of Seward. The two men had begun their political careers simultaneously, but despite Fillmore's valiant work and unequaled success in keeping his portion of the state in the Antimasonic and Whig columns, Seward was receiving favored treatment from Weed. Seward's candidacy, moreover, would not serve what possibly was Fillmore's guarded aspiration. With a Senatorship falling vacant, the job might be his, but the Weed-Tallmadge entente darkened Fillmore's hopes.

Instead of broadcasting his preference for Granger, Fillmore played a cautious game. To Weed he wrote that he was willing to support anyone who could win. To Seward and Granger he

[10]Alexander, *Political History of N. Y.*, 2:24-25; *Albany Argus*, September 12, 21, 1837, January 21, 1838; Albany *Evening Journal*, September 19, 20, 23, 1837.

said nothing. But when the time came for the state convention to decide, Fillmore was on hand to urge Granger's nomination.[11]

As the convention deliberated, Weed hung back. He had no desire to show his hand unnecessarily. To maintain peace within the party, he preferred to let the convention appear to be independent.[12]

The first ballot gave Seward 52 votes to Granger's 39 and Bradish's 29. Preconvention prophets supposed this was Granger's greatest limit. But on the second ballot, Bradish's friends transferred 13 to Granger and a few to Seward. The count stood Seward 60, Granger 52, Bradish 10. The third ballot brought an even greater surprise. Seward fell to 59, Granger rose to 60, and Bradish dropped to 8. During each ballot, Fillmore stayed with Granger. The situation was serious. If the remaining 8 fell to Granger, Seward would collapse. Weed abandoned his caution. A long intermission followed the third ballot.[13]

Weed canvassed the Bradish delegates and the Granger delegates one by one. "Weed," said one of them, "tell me to do anything else; tell me to jump out of the window and break my neck and I will do it to oblige you; but don't ask me to desert Granger." With quiet good nature, Weed continued to talk to the delegates. On the fourth ballot, Weed's intervention showed results. Eight votes switched to Seward and the favorite was in, with Bradish as his running mate.[14]

Deeply disappointed, Granger's friends reproached Weed for his favoritism. But Granger stoically accepted defeat and

---

11Fillmore to Weed, June 4, 1838, *Fillmore Papers*, 2: 169-172; Alexander, *Political History of N. Y.*, 2:18; Weed, *Autobiography*, 451-452; see use made by Democrats of Seward's association with the successors of the Holland Land Company in *Albany Argus*, September, *passim*; Albany *Evening Journal*, October 1, 1838.

12Weed, *Autobiography*, 451-452.

13Albany *Evening Journal*, September 13, 14, 20, 29, 1838; Buffalo *Commercial Advertiser*, September 13, 1838.

14*Albany Argus*, September 14, 1838; New York *Express*, September 13, 1838; Seward, *Autobiography*, 373.

zealously supported the ticket.[15] Heartsick, Fillmore turned to the task of selling Seward to western New York.

*   *   *   *   *

The Buffalo Congressman made stupendous campaign efforts in the fall of 1838. No stump in five counties was too small for him to mount. He personally escorted Seward through his bailiwick,[16] though the task became doubly arduous one month after the state convention.

Albert H. Tracy, on whom formerly a good share of party work had rested, took umbrage at Seward's nomination, retired to a sickbed, and sulked. Meanwhile Fillmore obtained without difficulty another nomination to Congress, but the entire work of keeping western New York in line now rested on his shoulders.[17]

During the year another development increased Fillmore's fears regarding Seward's candidacy. In 1837 and 1838 the forces of antislavery were gathering. Already they were beginning to sway political action and it proved to be an acceptable substitute for many former Antimasons. Zealous antislavery workers began to plague the Whigs. To Seward they put many questions, but the Whig candidate flatly refused to make any pre-election pledges.[18]

Four days after his own nomination for Congress, Fillmore picked up his morning mail to find the local antislavery society in hot pursuit of his own opinions.

"Do you believe that petitions to congress on . . . slavery and the slave trade, ought to be received . . . and . . . considered . . . ?"

[15]*Ibid.*, 374; Granger to Weed, September 18, 1838, Weed Papers.
[16]Fillmore to Weed, October 2, 1838, *Fillmore Papers*, 2:172.
[17]Fillmore to Weed, October 28, 1838, *ibid.*, 2:175; Buffalo *Commercial Advertiser*, September 26, 29, October 5, 1838.
[18]Ralph V. Harlow, *Gerrit Smith: Philanthropist and Reformer*, 136-144.

"Are you opposed to the annexation of Texas . . . ?"

"Are you in favor of congress . . . [abolishing] the . . . slave trade between the states?"

"Are you in favor of immediate . . . abolition of slavery in the District of Columbia?"

Fillmore threw down the letter with disgust and shouted, "The Philistines are upon us."

After two days of mulling over the questions, Fillmore buried his despair. He answered a simple "yes" to all. But he refused to give any pledges that would tie his hands.[19]

As similar inquiring epistles reached all Whig candidates party leaders grew panicky. Francis Granger estimated that abolitionists would control 20,000 votes. And "before the grand contest of 1840 they will control one-fourth of the votes of the state," he predicted. "They are engaged in it with the same honest purpose that governed the great mass of Antimasons." Seward feared the state was lost.[20]

None of the Whigs, however, correctly judged the forces in action. In the eyes of the ordinary voters, the depression over-whelmed all other considerations. Harassed by hard times, the great mass of voters turned upon the party in power and "voted the rascals out." Throughout the nation Whigs fell heir to power. When the final count was in, they had even gained a narrow control of the House of Representatives.

In New York State years of unrewarded labor had finally brought results: Democrats were inundated. Seward won by 10,000 votes; both branches fell to the Whigs. As Fillmore sur-veyed the election returns he could compliment himself on his own success and his original judgment that Seward would be

[19]Fillmore to W. Mills, October 17, 1838, Fillmore to Weed, October 15, 1838, *Fillmore Papers*, 2:174, 173.
[20]Granger to Weed, October 12, 1838, Weed Papers; Seward, *Autobiography*, 376.

weak in western New York. In his own Congressional district
he had polled five votes to every three for Seward.[21]

* * * * *

After the election Whigs enjoyed a honeymoon. The gen-
eration-old grip of the Regency on the state had been broken.
Weed, who had fought it for sixteen years without success, could
hardly contain his joy. Never before in New York had this
younger generation of politicians controlled the state. For the
first time Whig leaders began to taste both the sweets and acids
of victory. Hordes of office seekers descended upon Albany to
badger the governor who held thousands of jobs in his hands.
But Seward turned the patronage over to Thurlow Weed.

Weed followed a policy that could not avoid alienation and
disappointment. Looking toward the future, he used the patronage to woo the fence-sitters. The faithful, who had remained
at his side for sixteen years, moaned, and the honeymoon atmosphere quickly disappeared.

Instantly Fillmore felt the impact of Weed's policy. Many
disappointed westerners, who had loyally followed the party's
tortuous course, beat a path to Fillmore's door to voice their
complaints. Usually they accused Seward of coquetting with
Clay. They were ready to "swear" that former "Antimasons are
to be cut off."[22] Even before the administration took office, the
region was "rife with this apprehension." An inner voice whispered to Fillmore that this was retribution for his actions at the
nominating convention.[23]

Though Fillmore stifled his distrust of Seward, others were
less magnanimous. Albert Tracy had had a falling-out with the
newly elected governor, and there were others. John C. Spencer
felt that Seward had been unduly elevated;[24] Francis Granger,
too, could find reason for grumbling.

[21]Albany *Evening Journal,* December 3, 1838; *Civil List of New York,* 166. Where
Fillmore had drawn 5,400 votes, Seward could only obtain 3,448.
[22]Fillmore to Weed, December 26, 1838, *Fillmore Papers,* 2:180.
[23]Fillmore to Weed, April 10, 1839, *ibid.,* 2:188-189.
[24]Fillmore to Weed, January 1, 1839, *ibid.,* 2:181.

Of the political offices open to appointment, that of the comptroller was most desirable. In some respects, because of his supervisory power over the economy of the state, the comptroller wielded more power than the governor. Now the job became a bone of contention among the disappointed. Weed wanted to see the comptrollership in trusted hands, and he considered Fillmore.

Approached, Fillmore quickly decided it was not the kind of job he wanted. Ten years before, he had taken up politics as a springboard to a better social and financial position. He had made up his mind when he first coquetted with Antimasonry "never to go so far as to feel for a moment that" he "depended upon any office or any popular favor for a livelihood." "He is miserable whose happiness 'hangs on a Prince's favors,'" he soliloquized. "But he is not only wretched, but infinitely degraded whose means of support depends on the wild caprice of the everchanging multitude."[25] All of his previous posts had been part-time offices. They gave him ample opportunity to pursue his profession, and he had prospered. But the comptrollership would occupy every available minute.

Weed, however, was insistent. Both Spencer and Tracy were organizing cliques to win the post, and Weed could trust neither. He pressed Fillmore further. One of the first measures the Whig administration had scheduled for passage was a free banking system to supplement the safety fund and political monopoly of the Regency. The new banking system would need a "high, unbending moral firmness" to guide it "safely through the breakers and quicksands of attempted frauds and knavish impositions."[26] Fillmore's ever increasing experience with financial matters recommended him for the office. Flattered, he temporarily stifled his distaste for the "capricious multitude" and re-canvassed his law partners' opinions. Still the answer was no.[27]

---

[25]Fillmore to Weed, December 6, 1838, *ibid.*, 2:176-177.
[26]Fillmore to Weed, December 23, 1838, *ibid.*, 2:179.
[27]*Ibid.*, 2:178; Fillmore to Thaddeus Joy, December 8, 1838, *ibid.*

When one of his progeny crossed him, Weed bristled. This was the first time Fillmore had ever denied Weed a whim. Already irked, Weed grew more bitter when one of his confidential letters to Fillmore, confessing the plot against Spencer, fell into Spencer's hands. Fillmore had inadvertently let it pass to Tracy and Tracy had shown it to Spencer. Instantly, Weed accused Fillmore of conspiring against him. Fillmore emphatically proclaimed his innocence.[28]

Doggedly he tried to placate the irate editor and finally devised a solution. After canvassing the New York Whig representatives in Washington for their suggestions, he persuaded Weed to take Bates Cook for comptroller.[29] But the foundations of a long-standing friendship had quivered.

A few months later Fillmore received confirmation that his misbehavior at the nominating convention and his uncooperative attitude on the comptrollership had exposed him to reprimand. The true situation dawned upon him over the appointment of a vice-chancellor for New York. It was a judicial position of great eminence. For years it had been located in Rochester and Lockport, and prideful Buffalonians hoped to capture it for their city. The Erie County bar petitioned the governor and offered Fillmore as the strongest man for the post. Fillmore had consented to be a candidate with "unfeigned reluctance." When so notified, Seward flatly stated he would name his and Weed's old Antimasonic crony, Frederick Whittlesey of Rochester, to the job.

Without showing the courtesy of considering Fillmore, Seward sent in Whittlesey's nomination to the senate. There was a chance that the senate would reject him and force Seward to make a new nomination. When Fillmore's friends brought this possibility to Seward's attention, the governor again asserted he would not nominate Fillmore, denied that Buffalo had any peculiar claim to the office, and asserted that he meant "to take the best man in the district." Sarcastically Fillmore remarked:

[28]Fillmore to Weed, January 3, 1839, *ibid.*, 2:181-183.
[29]Fillmore to Weed, January 11, 1839, *ibid.*, 2:183.

"I have not the vanity to suppose that I am 'the best man in the district,' and certainly shall be the last one to complain if I am passed over for the sake of arriving at so desirable and praiseworthy a result." But belying his denial of vanity, he had to "confess" that he felt "not a little mortified at the *Cavalier* manner" in which Seward treated him.[30]

When the senate finally confirmed Whittlesey, Fillmore drew his conclusion: "It has satisfied my friends, of what they seemed reluctant to believe, that I am no favorite with the powers that control this administration. . . . I believe no one appointment has been made in this county that I had the honor to recommend." Dourly, he added: "I regret it not. It has no power to grant what I have any desire to receive."[31]

* * * * *

With signs of growing Whig strength everywhere, Whigs began to prepare for the Presidential election; and candidates, smelling victory, appeared in public for admiration. The everready Henry Clay insinuated himself into the arena by the simple expedient of writing to his ubiquitous lieutenants. Simultaneously, off in Boston, friends of "the God-like" Daniel Webster flashed green eyes at Clay's pretensions. Encouraged by their patron, they pushed Webster into the ring. Others would have neither Webster nor Clay. In 1836 they had seen the vote-getting power of aged William Henry Harrison, hero of many Indian battles, erstwhile military and territorial governor of Indiana and Michigan, and they boomed his candidacy.

In the Presidential decision, New York held a critical role, Although Fillmore knew that Seward and Weed had been spiteful toward him, he curbed his feelings. He was too conscious of the need for harmony in his state. Whatever western New York said on the Presidency might determine the next President.

Setting aside personal complaints, Fillmore threw himself into President-making. From his observation post in Washing-

[30]Fillmore to Weed, April 10, April 23, 1839, *ibid.*, 2:188-189, 189-190.
[31]*Ibid.*

ton he kept a weather eye on the straws that indicated the direction of the prevailing wind. With the other eye he watched New York. Periodically, and always with bitter disgust, he reported his observations on Clay's candidacy. To Fillmore nothing that the Sage of Ashland had done commended him for political favor. Yet he would accept Clay if he must. His initial dislike for Clay began under Antimasonry, when Clay had refused to placate that spirit. The ghost of Antimasonry still stalked in western New York, and Fillmore believed in the power of ghosts in politics. Moreover, financial ruins stood as hollow reminders of the bank fight "got up for political effect." The patron of Biddle was as little in favor as the patron of the Albany Regency. Early in 1839 Fillmore heard former Antimasons roundly condemn Seward's administration for acting as if it wanted to be "stuck in the Clay."[32]

If Masonry and the bank were not enough to condemn Clay's candidacy in Fillmore's eyes, the rising strength of the abolitionist movement was. Fillmore lived in the heart of a region that had picked up the new standard. From the election of 1838 onward he knew and felt the force of abolitionism first hand, and he knew how it would react against Clay, a slave-holder.

If Fillmore's attitude toward Clay was negative, he was no happier with his favorite, Webster. After watching the political wheel of fortune turn, he early realized that Webster was "out of the question." What guided his judgment was his wish to find "the *Strong* and *safe* man for the Empire state." To a friend he presented the main problem in selecting a candidate.

> It must be recollected that we have got to cement the fragments of many parties and it is therefore very important that we get a substance to which all can adhere, or at least that presents as few repellent qualities as possible. Into what crucible can we throw this heterogeneous mass of old national republicans, and revolting Jackson men; masons and anti-masons; abolitionists, and pro-slavery men; bank men and

[32]Fillmore to Patterson, February 6, 1839, to Weed, May 1, June 5, June 16, 1839, *ibid.*, 2:183-187, 191, 191-192, 193.

anti-bank men with all the lesser fragments that have been, from time to time, thrown off from the great political wheel in its violent revolutions, so as to melt them down into one mass of pure Whigs of undoubted good mettle?[33]

In February, Fillmore was still speculating on possible candidates. He dismissed the strategy of 1836, declaring, "Our only chance . . . is in having one candidate who will obtain a majority of electoral votes." By this time he had narrowed the field to Harrison and Clay. With cold calculation he drew up a chart and discovered that both were certain of carrying 69 votes against 76 for Van Buren. That left 149 votes doubtful. Of these he reasoned that 87 were more likely to go for Harrison and 62 more certain for Clay. Adding these to the safe votes, Harrison would poll a majority — while Clay would fall short of victory by 17 votes.[34]

All through 1839 Harrison men used every sort of argument, subterfuge, and ruse to persuade Clay to withdraw. As part of the strategy, Clay's enemies looked around for a compromise candidate — someone popular, who could help save Clay's face by avoiding Harrison. Out in western New York, fortune and astute politics developed such a man. He was another old military hero, Winfield Scott.

In 1837 Canadian nationalists had led a revolt against Britain, and perhaps feeling too sober because of the depression, many Americans had seized upon it for emotional release. The British had easily subdued the uprising everywhere except on the Niagara frontier. There a number of insurgents held out on Navy Island.

A group of gun runners from Buffalo, in cooperation with British-hating Irish-Americans, supplied the rebels in their island fortress. Daily they made trips from the American side of the Niagara River to the British island. Between the island and the shore ran the international boundary line. Determined to wipe out this pocket of resistance, the British commander-in-chief set

[33]Fillmore to Patterson, February 6, 1839, *ibid.*, 2:185.
[34]*Ibid.*, 2:186.

out one night to capture the supply ship, the American-owned *Caroline*. Crossing to the American side he and his men boarded the anchored ship, set her afire, and turned her adrift down the Niagara River.

The indignant cries for reparation and retaliation that went up from the American shore almost drowned out the roar of Niagara and augured war. In the fore of the movement urging preparations for defense stood Fillmore. No warmonger, but a realist, he insisted on thorough defenses. The War Department assigned the old War of 1812 hero, Winfield Scott, to the scene. He directed a stern voice toward the British and won the hearts of Buffalonians, who had once seen their little village put to the British torch. Calculating politicians, looking beyond the brass of General Scott's uniform, saw Presidential material.[35]

By late spring of 1839, a full-blown boom to nominate Scott over Harrison and Clay gripped western New York politicians. Little of the sentiment was genuine; most of it grew out of the desire to use Scott as a stalking horse.[36] Fillmore saw the opportunity and urged it upon Weed. The Albany boss toyed with the idea and further questioned Fillmore. Fillmore assured him that in western New York "Scott would be supported with great enthusiasm." But he cautioned about the method of bringing Scott into the arena.

> . . . Should the west move first in this matter, there is great danger that it will create a jealousy among Clay's friends [in the] East that will be fatal. It will be at once said that this is the factious spirit of Antimasonry that seeks to bring forward Scott, not to advance the Whig cause, but to oppose and defeat Clay. Now it must be apparent to all, that unless both the Clay and Harrison men can, generally, yield their preferences and unite cordially in support of Scott, it is worse than idle to make any effort in his favor. . . . We, here, have no assurance that those of our brethren East who prefer Clay are equally willing with ourselves to yield their personal

[35]*Congressional Globe*, 25 cong. 2 sess., 110, 568, 943-944, 3 sess., 663; Buffalo *Commercial Advertiser*, August 12, September 15, 17, October 8, 1838.
[36]Fillmore to Weed, May 1, 1839, *Fillmore Papers*, 2:191.

preferences and go for Gen'l Scott. Give us that assurance, and we will make the welkin ring with his name. . . .[37]

Weed liked the advice, seasoned it with the salt of his own desires, and informed Webster, who was busily organizing New England sentiment, that New York was going to choose a Scott delegation to keep the state away from Clay, and that it looked to him as though Harrison would be the nominee.[38] Weed was prepared to swing finally to either Harrison or Scott on the ground of availability. By the end of July the Albany *Evening Journal* broke the ground for Scott's nomination.

Strategy called for eliminating Clay without alienating his supporters. For that maneuver the best means would be to have Clay withdraw voluntarily. But the Old Chief wanted the office. He realized, however, that success depended upon New York, and he urged his friends to prod the New York legislative caucus into an endorsement. Conscious that western New York was responsible for New York's hostility, he asked worried questions of his Buffalo henchmen. Fillmore and other New York Congressmen, he lamented, "while they are free to avow their own preference for me, profess to be apprehensive about my election." "How was western New York?"[39]

So worried did Clay become that by midsummer of 1839 he abandoned feigned reluctance to stump the country and invaded enemy territory. While he toured New York Seward refused to see him, and while he watered at Saratoga Springs Weed approached him directly to ask his withdrawal. But the chieftain, accepting the encouragement of Fillmore's neighbor, Peter B. Porter, and the kowtowing of some New York figures, refused to budge. Inwardly, however, his confidence faltered. The first hint that he might succumb to pressure came when he reached Buffalo from the east. Overcome by what he had seen in New York, he promised a Buffalo audience to withdraw, if necessary, in the interest of harmony and success.[40]

[37]Fillmore to Weed, June 5, 1839, *ibid.*, 2:192.
[38]Barnes, *Memoir of Weed*, 76.
[39]Clay to Porter, December 27, 1838, Porter Papers.
[40]Glyndon G. Van Deusen, *Henry Clay*, 329.

As the pace of Scott's campaign quickened, Clay's worries increased. By fall Democratic victories staggered him. But it was not until December that Clay accepted his fate. The *coup de grace* was delivered in Washington.

On Sunday evening, December 1, only a few days before the national convention, an informal meeting of the entire Whig delegation of New York discussed the coming election. In a final effort to show Clay that his situation was hopeless in New York, every member assembled, except three, stated that Clay could not win New York state.[41] Fillmore stood by and counted the vote. Charles Francis Mitchell, last-ditch supporter of Clay, saw that the last ditch had been passed, threw his weight to the anti-Clay men, and carried the opinion of the caucus to Clay. With outward calm and inward bitterness, Clay accepted the action.[42] *"We have done our duty here,"* shouted Fillmore on receipt of Mitchell's news. Now "If the convention . . . does its duty, all will be well."[43]

The convention performed its duty. On the third day of balloting, three Scott delegations switched to Harrison and sealed his nomination. Fillmore, remaining in Washington during the convention, received the news with pleasure.[44]

Then followed ten months of the most bizarre Presidential campaigning the nation had ever seen. All over the country the log cabin, the coonskin, the barrel of hard cider, and simple farmer Harrison formed the major part of the campaign. The log cabin became the symbol of a spurious Whig democracy.

*   *   *   *   *

During the Congressional session that followed Harrison's nomination, Fillmore used every opportunity to forward the

[41]The three were Seth M. Gates, Rufus Palm, and D. D. Barnard.
[42]Clay to Porter, December 4, 1839, Porter Papers.
[43]Fillmore to Weed, December 2, 1839, *Fillmore Papers*, 2:194; Granger to Weed, [November, 1839] Granger Papers; Curtis to Weed, December 2, 1839, Weed Papers.
[44]Fillmore to Weed, December 23, 1839, *Fillmore Papers*, 2:195.

Whig cause by smearing Democrats. He had gained a seat on the Committee on Elections, which for his purposes was the session's most important committee.

By a precarious margin, the failing Democrats had lost control of the House that met in December, 1839. So, at least, the first election returns had indicated. Ignoring this, Democrats devised a plan to defeat the election returns. Five of New Jersey's six Whig Congressmen appeared in Congress carrying certificates of election from their Whig governor. Behind them trailed five Democrats, who charged that fraud and violence had cheated them of rightful seats. Here were five contested seats that could return the House to Democratic control.

Moving rapidly, the Democratic quorum majority denied the New Jersey representatives their seats until the House, once organized, could review the dispute. Quickly Whigs spotted the trap. If the House were organized without the New Jersey Congressmen, Democrats would control the committees and pack the Election Committee to favor the Democratic claimants.

Fillmore stood in the van of the moves to avoid the snare. For a month the House was a scene of chaos and anarchy with nothing achieved, with no committees, and with only a skeleton organization.[45] Finally a two-party caucus reached a compromise. For the right to organize the House, Democrats traded a clear instruction to the Committee on Elections that would return the Whigs. The committee was to go beyond the commission of the New Jersey governor in search of the legality of the votes. To this committee Fillmore was appointed, confident of eventual victory for his five unseated colleagues.[46]

In keeping with instructions, the committee reviewed the testimony it had on hand, found it inadequate, and sent the ten claimants back to New Jersey to get evidence that they had been elected. With the claimants away, however, Democrats in the House unrolled a second plot. On an innocent proposal to

[45]*Congressional Globe* 26 cong., 2 sess., 5-114, *passim.*
[46]*Madisonian*, December 21, 1839, March 7, 14, 1840.

print pertinent documents the seed of the scheme took root. The proposal furnished the pretext for an instruction from the House to report immediately which of the parties had received the majority of votes. Though outnumbered, Whigs under Fillmore's prodding were able to modify the instruction to: "the majority of lawful votes."[47]

Back in committee the Democratic majority, still having learned nothing new on the election, declared all the votes "lawful." They justified their act on the ground that they had been instructed so to interpret the votes, since the House required them to report immediately. Fillmore vigorously protested the action in committee, demanded that the committee's evidence be examined and that he be given a chance to protest to the House. But the Democratic majority prepared its report, and couched it in a title to give the impression that the votes were "lawful." The body of the report, however, labored to excuse the committee for failing to ascertain whether the votes were lawful or unlawful.[48]

When the majority reported to the House, their whips had the Democratic members well primed. Fillmore obtained the floor and began to explain what the committee had done. He offered a resolution to force reconsideration. The entire sessions of March 5 and 6 were spent in points of order to stifle Fillmore. Someone protested his right to the floor. The Speaker decided in Fillmore's favor. But the well-greased Democratic machinery appealed the decision of the chair to the House. A reversed decision thereafter gagged Fillmore and all other protests by moving the previous question.[49]

Caught in the meshes of parliamentary procedure, Fillmore tried to use his rank. Rising as a member of the Election Com-

---

[47]Resolution to report "forthwith" February 28, 1840; Fillmore's resolution, March 5, 1840. See *Congressional Globe*, 26 cong., 2 sess., 218, 416; *Fillmore Papers*, 1:148-149; *Madisonian*, March 14, 1840.

[48]Fillmore, *Address and Suppressed Report of the Minority of the Committee on Elections on the New Jersey Case. . . .* , 4-5.

[49]*Congressional Globe*, 26 cong., 2 sess., 422, 446.

mittee, he claimed the right to submit the minority report. But the gag held. For a week, in a House chaotic with points of order, Fillmore used every parliamentary maneuver to avoid the previous question and present more of the minority view. He fought for the right to speak with a tenacity and ability that previously he had not displayed. The chair finally instructed him that he could submit a minority report only by permission of the House.[50]

"I speak by right, and not by permission," retorted Fillmore. "I will never tamely . . . submit to yield a right . . . guaranteed by the Constitution. . . . I would as willingly be the slave of one master as of a thousand."[51] But the House thought otherwise. Puffing with indignation, Fillmore sat down.

In a fit of fury, the calm, dignified Fillmore had lost his composure. But from his colleagues he gained new admiration. His tenacity in fighting for the party and his ability to stand up against a hostile House pointed a finger toward an even more fruitful leadership.

Unable to have the minority report printed as a government document, Fillmore and his colleagues issued it privately in pamphlet form. The various state central committees distributed it far and wide over the breadth of the nation. On the same subject, Fillmore independently addressed his constituents. Through the columns of the *Commercial Advertiser* he used the New Jersey election case to urge his state to forsake the party that "trampled underfoot" the sovereign state of New Jersey and that "desecrated" the "sacred principles" of the freedom of speech.[52] The session-long effort to save five Whigs from doom had made many lurid newspaper columns that not only advertised Fillmore but added one more black mark to the Democratic record. It was part of his own campaign to "keep the steam up" in the vital election year of 1840.[53]

[50]See debates, *Congressional Globe*, 26 cong., 2 sess., 417-472, *passim*.
[51]*Fillmore Papers*, 1:149-150; *Madisonian*, April 4, 1840.
[52]Fillmore's letter to his constituents, *Fillmore Papers*, 2:197-207.
[53]Fillmore to Weed, April 4, 1840, *ibid.*, 2:209.

Before parting from Washington, Fillmore made one last contribution to the party cause. Fearful that lassitude might overtake Whigs in the closing months of the campaign, and apprehensive over an "unearthly effort" of the foe that was "active, vigilant and unprincipled," he worked behind the scenes to replace the national party newspaper, the *Intelligencer*, with an invigorated *Madisonian*. "The *Intelligencer*," he explained to Weed, "is no partisan paper. It is good in its sphere but worth nothing to meet the vile slander and base fabrication of the *Globe*." To remedy this, "We are making arrangements to give a little more efficiency to the *Madisonian*."[54]

With that accomplished, Fillmore returned home to direct the fortunes of his own and the Harrison campaigns in western New York. Confident of a local victory for himself and the entire Whig ticket, only the urge to equal or better the 1838 majority spurred him into an active campaign.

In this election other areas almost duplicated Erie's previous feat. The Whig party swept the country for its first national triumph. The Presidency, both houses of Congress, and twelve governorships fell into the hands of power-starved Whigs. As expected, Fillmore's local machine retained its unblemished record. Again western New York laid claim to being the country's strongest Whig region. For the first time in his twelve-year-old career, Fillmore belonged to the nation's ruling clique.

[54]Fillmore to Weed, June 1, 1840, *ibid.*, 2:210; see also Fillmore to Haven, January 7, 1840, Fillmore Manuscripts, for early interest in giving life to the *Madisonian*.

Chapter 7

At the Altar of Mammon

S THEY prepared to pass the scepter of leadership to their Whig opponents, the Democrats felt, mingled with their regrets, a sense of gratitude at being relieved of the responsibilities that bedeviled the government. Treasury revenues had tumbled to a new low. Millions in suspended appropriations, unsettled claims, and bad debts had plagued Secretary of the Treasury, Levi Woodbury. In the last months of Van Buren's administration, conservative estimates placed the liability of the government at upwards of forty million dollars, whereas only five years before a surplus had existed. Soon the operations of the compromise tariff of 1833 would cut another five million from the annual revenue.

The woe at the capital found miserable company in the country at large. Through four years of lingering depression, businessmen had seen their volume of business dwindle. In a last desperate attempt to restore the country to financial health, Van Buren's administration had abolished all currency except hard cash. The measure cured nothing, but induced timid bankers to suspend specie payment for the third time in as many years. Previous suspensions and bank failures had erased 100 million dollars of banking capital. Merchants, manufacturers, bankers, investors, and capitalists of every variety writhed in anguish as they saw their fellow men go down in bankruptcy, public bonds sink in value, and some states repudiate their debts. Even the fountains of European credit dried up. A pall of disaster settled on trade and commerce.

The Wetmores, the Howes, the Cromwells, and the Lawrences throughout the nation clamored for relief. Hopefully they turned to the incoming Administration, for Whigs felt responsibile to these distressed interests, and amid the ferment of organizing the government they were shaping a program of relief. Measures of aid and reform were to fill the next few years. But before the victors in Washington could help their friends, the politicians had to settle their own weighty problems.[1]

*   *   *   *   *

A question of leadership agitated Whigs. Everyone conceded that Harrison was only a vote-getter and that the party had come into power without a recognized national head. Seeing an opportunity to capture the leadership, Clay formulated a program of economic relief for the nation and called for a special session of Congress to enact it immediately into law. He hoped, by leading the legislative program, to promote himself to the party's headship. But Webster, whom Harrison had selected to lead his cabinet, also had plans. If he could control the Administration through its cabinet, he would be able to use the party for his own purposes.[2]

Each eager contestant strove to embarrass the other. Webster opposed a special session of Congress as unnecessary, and Clay sought to influence the cabinet appointments. Into this struggle, politics inevitably drew the lesser figures.

[1] For an extended contemporary description of the plight of the country and the effects of the depression on the business community, see the Washington *Madisonian*, February 13, 1841.
[2] Poage, *Clay*, 19-21; Harrison to Webster December 1, 27, 1840, Webster to Harrison, December 11, 1840, Daniel Webster, *Writings and Speeches*, 13:90-97; Henry A. Wise, *Seven Decades of the Union*, 180.

Portrait of the youthful Fillmore, by Thomas Sully (1783-1872).

Fillmore's law office in East Aurora, N. Y., burned shortly after the picture was made.

Abigail Powers Fillmore, Millard Fillmore's first wife, born March 13, 1798, died March 30, 1853.

Caroline Carmichael McIntosh Fillmore (October 21, 1813-August 11, 1881), second wife of Millard Fillmore.

Mary Abigail Fillmore, born March 27, 1832, died July 27, 1854.

Millard Powers Fillmore, born April 25, 1828, died November 15, 1889, Fillmore's only son.

Henry Clay addressing the Senate on the Compromise of 1850, with Vice-President Fillmore in the Chair.

The "Grand National, American Banner" lithographed by N. Currier for the unfortunate 1856 campaign.

THE CHAMPION OF THE LIGHT WEIGHTS ON HIS GUARD.

M—l—d F—l——e (having shied his castor over the ropes, and followed it up himself).—BRING ON YOUR MAN, AND PUT HIM WHICH SIDE OF THE LINE YOU LIKE. *Cartoon published in "Young America" in 1856, emphasizing Fillmore's national position.*

MASON & DIXON'S LINE

Fillmore home, 52 Niagara Square, Buffalo, N.Y. (now the site of the Statler-Hilton Hotel), built 1850, purchased by Fillmore 1858.

Interior of 52 Niagara Square: the drawing room after the house became the Castle Inn.

*Fillmore as Captain of the Union
Continentals, September 1862.*

*Statue of Fillmore at southeast corner of the Buffalo City Hall.
Bryant Baker, sculptor.*

The home 1873-1887 of The Buffalo Historical Society, of which Fillmore was first President. Now home of the Western Savings Bank at Main and Court Streets, Buffalo, N. Y.

New York deserved a cabinet position but New Yorkers quarreled among themselves for the post. The New York City wing settled on its old favorite, Gulian Verplanck, the upstate Whigs urged Francis Granger upon Harrison, while Seward and Weed maneuvered for position. In Seward's bid for re-election, he had run 4,000 votes behind Harrison and had lost a half of his own 1838 majority. Weed, probing for the cause, had discovered some defections in the city. He now thought to assuage that wing by supporting Verplanck over Granger. But Fillmore, who led the New York caucus at Washington, was of a different opinion. He would have nothing to do with a political deal that would alienate western New York or again mistreat Granger. Without hesitation, Fillmore assembled the New York Whig caucus and put it on record in favor of his old friend, Granger. By the time Harrison arrived in Washington, Granger was assured of becoming Postmaster-General.[3]

Granger's appointment was also a victory for Webster over Clay, and the rest of the cabinet selections gave Webster the leverage he sought. Webster's success, however, did not deflect Clay from his purpose. He induced the President to call a special session of Congress, the *sine qua non* of Clay's campaign.

From the beginning, Fillmore had advised against a special session, and when he learned of Clay's maneuvers he resolutely set about to obstruct them. As Congressmen filed into Washington, Fillmore proselytized among them. He planned to capture the machinery of the House. If the Speakership could be kept beyond Clay's control, Clay's influence could be lessened. On the eve of the formal opening of Congress, Fillmore sallied into the Whig caucus which met to divide the fishes and the loaves. Behind him he had arrayed almost all of New York's many Congressmen, and he was prepared to accept the Speakership himself. After several ballots, however, Clay's candidate,

---

[3] Lyon G. Tyler, *Letters and Times of the Tylers*, 2:10 f.n.; *Madisonian*, February 13, 1841; Fillmore to Weed, December 27, 1840, *Fillmore Papers*, 2:216. In his re-election, Seward had run behind Harrison in every New York county. Albany *Evening Journal*, November 17, 30, December 9.

John White of Tennessee, was in the lead, and Fillmore judiciously retired from the running. Clay had won that tilt, and had divided the honors with Webster in the struggle for primacy.[4]

*   *   *   *   *

Scarcely had they compromised their major family problem and freed themselves for legislative action, when Whigs were beset by the tragedy of Harrison's death. His successor, John Tyler, was a Virginia aristocrat who had long been known as stubbornly independent and doctrinaire. He had repeatedly gone on record as uncompromisingly opposed to a national bank, protective tariffs, and federally financed internal improvements. He had ardently defended states' rights, slavery, and nullification. He was testy and vain, which made it extremely difficult for him to compromise. Of all the men in the Whig party, Tyler was least fitted to play either the figurehead role for which his predecessor had been cast or to give the Whig coalition common goals as Jackson, a dozen years before, had done for Democrats. Though faced with this changed character of the Administration, Clay persisted in his purpose to drive the executive before him.

During the depression years, Whigs as individuals, rather than as a party, had proposed many cures for hard times. Now they grouped these proposals into a comprehensive program designed to relieve two patients: the business community and the federal government. All of the suggested measures — a new national bank, elimination of the subtreasuries, distribution of the revenue from the sale of public lands to the states, a national bankruptcy law, a federal loan, and a protective tariff — carried within them restoratives for both sufferers.

Clay anticipated little difficulty in enacting the program. As yet the animosity that was to develop between President Tyler and himself had not emerged. After due consultation with businessmen in New York City, Clay placed at the head of the pro-

[4]*Madisonian*, June 5, 1841.

gram elimination of the subtreasury system and the creation of a uniform and flexible currency. If business were to prosper, Whigs unanimously agreed, they would have to free specie from the treadmill of circulation that the Van Buren program had established, and use it to support a sound and uniform currency. This could be done by re-establishing a national bank. That day's financial geniuses seemed unable or unwilling to conceive of a uniform currency and a sound credit system outside the limits of a privately owned national bank. This time they called it a "fiscal bank."

But here the friends of the bank ran into the hardheadedness of their new President. Before the session, Tyler had indicated a willingness to establish a national bank that would have branching rights only with the consent of the states it entered. In the eyes of Clay and the business community such a bank would be almost worthless. As Clay's own proposal came from committee, the fiscal bank was to be established in the District of Columbia with the right of setting up branches where it willed. In truth, Clay's measure tried to revive the old "Biddle bank" under a new name. As a Congressman, Tyler had incessantly denied the legality of the Second Bank of the United States, and now, as President, he could hardly be expected to abandon his principles. Yet even in the face of Tyler's known objections, Clay bludgeoned his measure through Congress. Tyler promptly vetoed it, and party harmony dissolved.[5]

The skein of Clay's personal ambition now began to unravel. The night before Tyler sent his veto message to Congress, the Whigs met in caucus. Here, under Clay's guidance, the Whigs decided to receive the veto without a word, lay it on the table, and immediately pass another bank bill to which the President and his cabinet had earlier given their approval. Clay and his confreres believed, however, that Tyler's veto of the first bank bill would force him to veto the second one. When that happened, they planned for the cabinet to resign, thus breaking

[5]Oliver P. Chitwood, *John Tyler: Champion of the Old South*, 219-236.

Tyler as a potential standard bearer of the party.[6] As this plan unfolded, the Webster-dominated cabinet members showed reluctance to assume their Clay-assigned role. It meant disarrangement of their personal plans, a surrender of honors and influence, and even considerable financial loss. From their reluctance emerged a plan to forestall Clay.[7]

At this point Fillmore entered the picture. When the bank bill first appeared, Fillmore had regarded it wryly. Only his partisan spirit and the crying need of business for a dependable currency had kept him in line with his party. During the three-month debate, his silence bespoke his distaste for the bill. Now with cabinet resignations next on Clay's agenda, Fillmore grew less cooperative. Clay's Presidential ambitions nauseated Fillmore, and he objected to a loss of his influence in the cabinet by the operation of the disruption scheme. So when Granger, Thomas Ewing, and John Bell cast about for a way to foil Clay's designs, Fillmore joined with these cabinet members in a counterplot.

The schemers searched for a way to commit Tyler to a bank bill that would save face for him and the Whig party. Fillmore found the key. He persuaded James A. Pearce of Maryland, one of his closest Congressional intimates, to bring Alexander H. H. Stuart, a fellow Virginian in the President's confidence, into the plan. Pearce urged Stuart to approach Tyler in regard to a new bill. At length Stuart yielded to Pearce's insistence and secured an interview with the President. Informed of the action of the caucus and aware of his danger, Tyler eagerly seized upon Stuart's proposition. After some discussion they agreed upon the provisions of a new bill. That evening Stuart reported to a joint committee of eminent Whigs from both houses. There an excited debate ensued. At its close the

---

[6]If Tyler did accept this new bank bill, the conspirators expected the plan to prove unworkable through failure of the stock subscription, which would force Tyler to agree to modifications they wanted. In either event, accept or reject, Tyler would be charged with inconsistency. Tyler, *Letters and Times*, 2:81 f.n. A. H. H. Stuart, "Statement" in Thomas H. Benton, *Thirty Years' View*, 2:344-47.

[7]Poage, *Clay*, 79 f.n.

group decided to postpone the previous decision of the caucus and recommend that the Whigs accept the new bill. Later a full Whig caucus endorsed the decision, and Clay's effort to break Tyler had snagged.[8]

All might have gone well with the plan to stop Clay except that during the next few days Tyler's ardor for Stuart's bank bill cooled. The more the President reflected, the more certain he became that the latest moves were only parts of the general caucus plot. Clay's old crony, Nathan Sargent, had taken charge of the new bill; the Whig press continued to hound the President for his previous veto; and even on the very day the bill came into Congress, a final insulting letter, known as the "coffeehouse letter," written by the boorish John Minor Botts, appeared in the *Madisonian*[9] Accusing Tyler of trying to "set himself up with the Democrats," Botts vowed that the President would "be headed yet," and that a bank bill would be passed which would "serve only to fasten him." This letter redoubled Tyler's suspicion, and confirmed his resolve to repudiate the bill.

The President's veto of the second bank bill did not surprise Whigs. Most of them knew that he had changed his mind.[10] As John M. Berrien and Sargent hurried the measure through Congress, Clay, who knew of Tyler's attitude, smirked with satisfaction. The plan in which Fillmore had participated to save the party from Clay's hands had failed.

The day after Tyler's second bank veto, part of the cabinet met in secret session to discuss their position. Granger, uncertain of the course to follow, consulted New York's Congressmen, and Fillmore had to take a stand on cabinet resignations. He had little choice but to follow the party, for Tyler was now thoroughly discredited. The New York Congressional group adopted a resolution calling upon Granger to resign. Fillmore could justify his desertion of Tyler only on the basis of New York

[8]*Ibid.*, 81; Benton, *Thirty Years' View*, 2:344, 347.
[9]Botts's letter dated August 16, 1841, in *Madisonian*, August 21; Tyler, *Letters and Times*, 2:112 f.n.
[10]Chitwood, *Tyler*, 247.

politics: not to go along with Clay at this point would split New York Whiggery and return the state to the Democrats.[11]

Three days later, as Congress adjourned, some fifty Whigs issued an address to the people of the United States. In this pronouncement, the party pundits repudiated Tyler and all his works and declared that the alliance between the President and Whigs was at an end. Tyler's expulsion was now formal and complete. Henceforth he was a President without a party.[12]

*   *   *   *   *

Although Henry Clay's personality tended to obscure the fact, the fundamental problem before the special Whig session was the depression. While Clay's antics spotlighted the intra-party struggle, other less spectacular Whig leaders worked to achieve the Whig program of relief. Among these was Fillmore.

Although he had lost the Speakership, his opportunity to shape the destiny of party and nation did not disappear. By long custom, the "runner up" in the Speakership race fell heir to the powerful Ways and Means Committee, and so Fillmore acquired the post. Critical times made the chairmanship doubly important. At least three-quarters of the relief program would pass through his hands. The young man, who fifteen years before had found it necessary to count his pennies in order to survive as a lawyer's apprentice, was now directing the finances of a nation. Gallantly, if not with Clay's theatrical genius, Fillmore steered two emergency measures through the House of Representatives.

The first bill authorized the President to borrow twelve million dollars. This emergency act aimed at filling a depleted

---

[11]Publically as his reason for resigning, Granger said it was his dissatisfaction with Tyler's policy on patronage rather than his bank policy, New York *Express,* September 15, 22, 1841; *National Intelligencer,* September 16, 1841; Fillmore to Weed, September 23, 1841, *Fillmore Papers,* 2:225; letter of Christopher Morgan to New York *Courier* in *Madisonian,* September 25, 1841.
[12]*National Intelligencer,* September 16, 1841.

federal treasury.[13] The second measure, although colored with urgency, forecast a fundamental Whig policy. Less than a month after Congress convened, Fillmore placed before the House what he called a "revenue bill." He demonstrated that the government had lost or would soon lose some highly remunerative sources of revenue. Within a year, because the final reductions of the compromise tariff of 1833 would go into operation, all import duties would decline to 20 per cent or lower, and revenues would fall. Moreover, a pending act to give all federal income from the sale of public lands to the states would further cut revenues. He reminded his colleagues that sources peculiar to the Van Buren administration — accumulated surpluses, loans to the states, and the sale of the United States Government's nine-million-dollar claim on the Bank of the United States — had also disappeared.

If the Administration were to avoid a deficit in each of the coming four years, some action, Fillmore prophesied, must be taken to increase revenues. Only three means lay at the disposal of the government — borrowing, direct and excise taxes, and increased duties on imports. Borrowing was not increasing the government's income; taxes, he attested, from long experience, were obnoxious. Hence only through higher duties, concluded Fillmore, could the government permanently enhance its income. To avoid collision with the compromise tariff, he advised that increases be kept within the 20 per cent level. Pleading with the freetraders that his proposal should be regarded as a revenue measure, not as protection for industry, he promised the antiprotectionists ample opportunity to defend their principles in the regular session when the Whigs would endeavor to overhaul the entire structure of the compromise tariff. For the present, he recommended the passage of his revenue bill, which raised all import duties, with few exceptions, to the 20 per cent level. A well-organized Whig party fell in behind Fillmore's proposal, and with hardly a murmur of dissent, enacted the bill into law.[14]

[13]*Fillmore Papers*, 1:167, 168.
[14]*Ibid.*, 1:170-189; *Madisonian*, July 31, 1841; Albany *Evening Journal*, August 2, 3, 1841.

Two other measures gave Fillmore opportunity to aid the merchants, investors, manufacturers, and bankers everywhere. Businessmen claimed old debts dampened their enthusiasm for new ventures and delayed recovery. If slates were wiped clean, the revered spirit of free enterprise would nurture a paupered nation back to prosperity. What business needed, declared businessmen, was a national bankruptcy act to free them of the shackles of past poor judgment. Agreeing, the Whig party passed a bankruptcy act, and Fillmore, who had sponsored a similar measure ten years earlier in New York, willingly endorsed this action.[15]

He showed even greater enthusiasm for the new distribution bill, calling for the proportional distribution to the states of the entire future federal income from the sale of the public domain. Every hard-pressed state administration, every holder of state bonds, every interest that hoped to cut the melon of public works which the fund would start, flocked to this "pork barrel" proposal.[16] While Fillmore pleaded the cause of a twelve-million-dollar loan to fill the empty coffers of the government, he and his party voted away an annual five to twenty million dollars. With unconscious irony, he rationalized his inconsistency. The objects which distribution would achieve, he solemnly noted, were "far above any temporary inconvenience that might arise to the treasury." The "great conservation measure" preserved a "rich patrimony for the people to whom it belongs" and prevented "its being squandered and gambled away by trading politicians and reckless demagogues." Federal surplus from land sales "was fast becoming a great corruption fund" and needed to be guarded from the "corrupt temptations of avarice, and the still more baneful and dangerous influences of inordinate and time-serving ambition."[17]

Land speculators, large and small, freetraders and dreamers of free homesteads arose to protest. If the public domain became a vested interest of the states, how could the railroad promoters

[15]*Fillmore Papers*, 1:191-192; *Madisonian*, June 20, 1840, July 31, 1841.
[16]Albany *Evening Journal*, March 23, 1842.
[17]*Fillmore Papers*, 1:180.

ever expect to get extensive grants, or the settler his free homestead? The most vocal enemies of distribution were the freetraders. From the beginning, they correctly suspected that Whigs were promoting the measure first to empty the national till, then to ask for increased duties on imports, which would give industry protection in disguise. Earlier Fillmore admitted that aim. The suspicious freetraders demanded a watch dog on Whig integrity. They appended a clause to the distribution act providing that if import duties ever rose above 20 per cent, distribution would cease.[18]

* * * * *

Ever since the days when Alexander Hamilton, dazzled by British mercantilism, urged protective tariffs upon the nation, tariff policy had troubled Washington lawmakers. For a half-century, the manufacturers, a weak minority in the nation's political economy, fought unsuccessfully for their cause. The western wilderness, beckoning the country's manhood to labor in the field, arrayed against the manufacturers a philosophy that glorified the simple rural life and deprecated an industrial economy. Though agrarians and planters occupied the national tribunal, manufacturers fought on for special privileges.

By chance and by default, rather than design, during the first fifty years of the nation's life, embryonic manufactories grew healthy and robust. Natural advantages assisted some industries; others profited by wars, embargoes, transportation difficulties, and depressions. After the War of 1812, as the nation knit into a closer union, industry found spokesmen and economic philosophers. By 1828, friends of industry had gathered together at Philadelphia to chart a route that would lead the nation to their way of thinking. Eastern politicians took cognizance of this gathering, linked its purpose with their own fortunes, and devised and passed a protectionist "tariff of abominations." In the ensuing scuffle over its "abomination," the country resounded with oratory, political war, and threats of disunion. In 1833 the politicians, the Hamiltonian philosophers, and the protected

[18]*Madisonian*, July 24, 1841.

groups compromised with the old agrarian philosophers and their own special interest group. By terms of this truce, the protectionists promised to retire slowly from the advanced position they had won in 1828 and 1832 by giving up one-tenth of their gains immediately, and one-tenth each succeeding two years until 1842. Then, in that year of reckoning, the two-thirds territory still occupied would be turned back to the agricultural freetraders. But hope lived on in the breasts of protectionists that before that eventful day a new and more advantageous treaty could be signed.

In 1841 the industrial forces had reassembled their strength in the Whig party. For the first time in a generation they had the political power to brave the issue. While merchants and investors marched forward during the special session, manufacturing interests marked time, awaiting the opening of the regular session. To lead them into battle against the compromise tariff and on to new conquests, they had chosen the chairman of the Ways and Means Committee, Millard Fillmore.

*   *   *   *   *

When Fillmore assumed the task of placing the protective tariff capstone on the Whig financial structure, he was espousing a cause dear to his heart and admirably suited to his intellect. Seldom did Fillmore's eyes gleam with the visions of a dreamer— never did he spin abstractions into full-blown systems. He observed what lay before him and let his judgment find order amid the facts that crowded in about him. Idealists could make him see their goal, but he also saw the pitfalls that pocked the road to Utopia. "If all the restrictive systems were done away with in every country," he sighed, "if we could confidently rely on continued peace, that would be a most prosperous and happy state." Each could then sell in the highest and buy in the cheapest market. But that beautiful "political millennium" would never evolve, warned Fillmore. "Wars will occur until man changes his nature; and duties [would be] imposed until man ceases to be selfish." The answer to the problems of national economy, he concluded, could thus be found only in the "collisions of interest and intellect." Given this formula, encouragement and protection of industry and commerce was the logical conclusion. Fillmore himself had nothing to gain but prestige among the Philistines.[19]

The moment was propitious for action. From every side forces were pressing Fillmore toward success. As if by magic there appeared in the North the "Home League," and in the South a wind filled the atmosphere with protariff propaganda. The wand wavers had gained their mystical force at a tariff convention in New York City on April 3, 1842. From this convention sprang the Home League, with a battle cry of encouragement to industry. Through hastily organized protectionist clubs the League spread its influence far and wide.[20]

Since the compromise of 1833 interests had arisen in the antitariff South to modify the South's attitude toward protection and made Fillmore's task easier. Enterprising citizens had constructed cotton mills in every Atlantic seaboard state. North Carolina boasted of several manufacturing centers, and to a lesser extent, Virginia, Georgia, South Carolina, and the Gulf states began to modify their purely agricultural economy. "The views of the southern people have been much changed in late years," declared the Savannah *Republican*, "and they do not view protective duties with quite so distempered an eye, for their own factories are already growing up."[21] Another southern Whig editor, inspired by the New York convention revelations, said: "We might as well confess that our free trade notions are looked upon at this time as vagaries of an unduly excited imagination."[22] Soon a host of southern spokesmen propagated the protectionist point of view. Former spellbinding nullifiers of 1832 like Robert

---

[19]For a complete summary of Fillmore's justification for his protectionist attitude see his tariff speech of June 9, 1842, *Fillmore Papers*, 1:196-236, particularly 215-224; for quotes see 2:216, 218.

[20]Albany *Evening Journal*, March 30, May 25, 1842.

[21]Quoted in Arthur C. Cole, *The Whig Party in the South*, 94.

[22]Quoted in *ibid.*, 95

Toombs, John M. Berrien, and T. Butler King arose in public meetings to announce their conversion.[23]

Ironically the abolitionist fringe arose to offer its hand to the protectionists. After their national convention in May, 1841, abolitionists repeatedly used the propagandist plea that slaveholders, by their free-trade policy, were preventing a return of prosperity for the northern laboring men.[24] These antislavery men helped to shape a popular northern attitude that through the tariff revenge could be worked on the slaveholders who were maliciously sacrificing the welfare of the North.

As Fillmore looked about him he saw other forces coming to his aid. Victims of a depression, Northerners were willing to seize upon any experiment that offered a return to prosperity. The "educational line" that filled the newspapers and flowed from the local chapter of the Home League promised that protection of industry would bring prosperity. Unemployment and insecurity, plus the promise that more industrialization would dispel the depression, were forcing a re-evaluation of the traditions that agricultural interests raised as goblins to frighten trespassers from their domain.

In Congress Fillmore could count for help on some of the country's most talented men. From his own state there was Francis Granger, still high and mighty in Washington circles. Sitting comfortably close to him was the grand old man of Whiggery, John Q. Adams. Gruff, bullish John Minor Botts, from Richmond, strained for another opportunity to castigate his fellow Virginian, John Tyler, and prove his own loyalty to the Whig party. Others were A. H. H. Stuart of Virginia, D. D. Barnard of New York, Indiana's Henry Smith Lane, Baltimore's John P. Kennedy, and Massachusetts' James S. Saltonstall,

[23] *Niles' Weekly Register*, 43:111; 66:188, 348-349; P. A. Stovall, *Robert Toombs: Statesman, Speaker, Soldier, Sage*, 46; see also, James E. Winston, "The Mississippi Whigs and the Tariff, 1843-44," *Mississippi Valley Historical Review*, 22:505-524.
[24] Julian P. Bretz, "The Economic Background of the Liberty Party," in *American Historical Review*, 34:250-264; see also speech of Alvin Stewart at the National Liberty Convention, May 12-13, 1841, in T. C. Smith, *The Liberty and Free Soil Parties in the Northwest*, 51; John R. Commons, "Greeley and the Workingman's Origin of the Republican Party" in *Political Science Quarterly*, 24:473-474.

Edward Everett, and Nate Appleton. Missing from the ranks of Congressional protectionists was Henry Clay. The old war-horse had left the Senatorial chamber in a peeve following the veto of the fiscal corporation bill and was stalking the country for the nomination in 1844. On Fillmore's shoulders rested the tariff leadership for both houses.

*   *   *   *   *

More than one barrier obstructed the protective tariff program. For years the government's income from the sale of public land effectively blocked higher duties. In these days, import duties were set by determining the difference between the government's income and its expenditures, and then setting rates that would return this difference. As long as the government had an income outside of import duties, those duties would not only stay down, but would fluctuate. In 1842 expenditures of twenty-seven million dollars were forecast. Of this five millions were to be obtained from public land sales. The remainder had to be made up by a tax on imports.[25] If, in the following year, land sales brought in twenty millions, then antitariff men would logically urge rate reductions. As long as the federal government could depend on land revenues, industrialists felt insecure, timid investors avoided new enterprise, and vested interests dreaded future fluctuations of tariff rates.[26] Nor did the "distribution" measure passed in the special session of 1841 give succor to protectionists. It halted "distribution" if tariff rates ever rose above 20 per cent. Since Fillmore planned rates as high as 85 per cent, all the evils of the land revenue would again be let loose on industry. For Fillmore one main objective was to preserve "distribution."

During the special session, the gathering protective tariff forces had marked time. But that session had created an obstacle:

[25]In that day there seemed to be universal agreement that excise and direct taxes should never be levied.
[26]See A. H. H. Stuart's speech against Tyler's first veto of the tariff, June 30, 1842 in *Niles' Weekly Register*, July 9, 1842 or *Congressional Globe*, 27 cong., 2 sess., 690-693. Distribution had as a scheme appeared again in Jackson's administration when it was used to try to eliminate the pet bank system by eliminating the government's surplus.

the rupture between Tyler and the Whigs raised the specter of a veto. Before the purge, Tyler had given assurances that he would approve higher rates, but now Whigs were uncertain. Tyler was coquetting for southern Democratic support. By January, so successful were his moves that Whig strategists grew alarmed. Something, they decided, must be done to break up the growing friendship between the President and the Democrats. The strategists fell upon the tariff as a method of driving a wedge between them. Unfortunately for industry, the plan would assure a veto of the tariff. But the tariff was no longer a simple economic measure: it was thoroughly enmeshed with Presidential politics.[27]

Fillmore knew that Tyler — never a protectionist — had earlier approved higher rates only to relieve the government's financial crisis. Further, the New Yorker understood that southern Democrats expected Tyler to oppose any protective measure as a sign of good faith. Yet Tyler's will to survive went beyond an alliance with Democrats, and the President hoped to keep some Whig support by proving that he was not wholly disloyal to the Whig program. If offered the proper measure, the President could accept it without endorsing the protective principle. He could claim that the bill was designed primarily for revenue and only incidentally offered protection. Fillmore, however, did not intend to give Tyler that opportunity.

*   *   *   *   *

To achieve all ends, protectionist and partisan, Fillmore resorted to a strategy of urgency. Until June, 1842, by one means or another, he had postponed action and blamed the delay upon the Treasury Department, which failed to supply his committee with adequate information to cast a tariff measure.[28] In each passing month after December pressure for action had mounted. Federal revenues had continued to decline and now in June the atmosphere was tense. In anticipation of the

[27]Chitwood, *Tyler*, 294, 302; see also Tyler's first message in James D. Richardson, comp., *A Compilation of the Messages and Papers of the Presidents*, 4:42-43.
[28]*Fillmore Papers*, 1:196-202.

loss of protection, many industrial firms had closed their doors.[29] The number of unemployed had grown. Finally at the peak of urgency, Fillmore pressed two tariff bills upon Congress. They were designed to achieve all that politicians and manufacturers could want — abandonment of the compromise, preservation of distribution, further embarrassment of Tyler, and relief to the manufacturing community. Fillmore's perspective was both short and long.

On June 9, pleading insufficient time to consider a permanent measure, Fillmore brought forth a stop-gap bill. It postponed for a month the compromise act's command to reduce rates on July 1. For the same length of time it postponed "distribution." Congress accepted the postponements, sent the bill to Tyler, giving him a choice of two methods of committing political suicide. Approval meant a sympathy with the manufacturing interests and unfaithfulness to the compromise: southern Democrats would cry traitor. If Tyler vetoed the measure, the Whigs would add another indictment to the true bill of arraignment. They would bandy him about as the man who refused to give the country a small measure of relief and as the President who placed his political ambitions above filling the Treasury while federal employees went unpaid. Although cognizant of the measure's implications for himself, Tyler made his choice. On grounds that the temporary tariff implied a retention of distribution, he vetoed the measure.[30]

While the first measure moved through the Senate toward Tyler's desk, Fillmore introduced the permanent tariff bill. It embodied "distribution" and raised rates high above the compromise level. Though conscious that Tyler's first veto meant death to the permanent measure, Fillmore pressed for early passage. At any stage of its passage, Fillmore could have made it acceptable to Tyler by simply eliminating "distribution." But politics and economics dictated another course. Fillmore prodded

[29]*Niles' Weekly Register*, 62:92, 101, 158, 173, 300.
[30]Chitwood, *Tyler*, 297; *Congressional Globe* 27, cong., 2 sess., 615, 688; Richardson, *Messages*, 4:180-183.

the House to keep his bill intact. And so, within three weeks, it went to the White House. As was expected, Tyler sent it back unsigned.[31]

Fillmore and the other Whig leaders now delivered the final blow to Tyler. They referred the veto message to a special committee of thirteen. John Q. Adams headed the committee, and Tyler's archenemy, John Minor Botts, was the committee's chief member.[32] Their report assailed the whole official conduct of the President and charged him with offenses of the gravest character. In order to prevent future "executive usurpation," the committee appealed for a constitutional amendment which would enable a majority in Congress to overrule a veto. The committee believed that the President deserved impeachment, but caution restrained them from recommending it.

While Whigs in Congress reaped political profits from Tyler's vetoes, Fillmore submitted still another tariff bill. This, the third in two months, abandoned the objectionable "distribution" scheme, and the President, who had vetoed the previous two on grounds of "distribution," approved the new measure. Tyler had a fetish for consistency, and since this bill met the qualifications he had laid down in his vetoes, he had no alternative.[33] But by signing the protective tariff bill, Tyler alienated his chary Democratic allies. They turned from him in scorn. Not only had Fillmore put the capstone on the Whig's legislative structure, but he had completely ruined Tyler's opportunity to break up the Whig party.

*   *   *   *   *

Tyler had won his struggle on "distribution," and his friends hailed the measure as a victory for him. But for nine years nullifiers had awaited the promised freer trade provisions of the 1833 compromise. A scant six weeks of low rates had

31*Congressional Globe,* 27 cong., 2 sess., 762, 852; veto message August 9; Richardson, *Messages,* 4:183-189. See also Chitwood, *Tyler,* 299-30.

32Fillmore was not on this committee; *Niles' Weekly Register,* 63:395-397; *Congressional Globe,* 27 cong., 2 sess., 894-896.

33For text of tariff see *House Documents,* 61 cong., 2 sess., No. 671, 120-139; for passage of measures see *Congressional Globe,* 27 cong., 2 sess., 912, 923-926, 960, 973.

rewarded their vigil. Fillmore and his friends had smashed the compromise, and though the full objective had failed, Fillmore's tariff of 1842 was a thumping protectionist triumph.

The Whigs not only stopped the downward trend, they actually imposed rates at the general 30 per cent level — 33-1/3 percent above the compromise level. Individual gains were enormous. Fillmore had used a common ruse to obtain 40 and even 50 per cent for some favored products. He had expanded the free list on noncompetitive imports, so that the general 30 per cent level was obtained by imposing higher rates on other articles.[34]

Two of the most active interests, woolen textile manufacturers and pig-iron producers, raised their protection at least 100 per cent by lifting the rates from 20 to 40 per cent. Manufacturers of hammered and rolled bar iron shot their schedule skyward to 85 per cent from a lowly 20. Though cotton textiles appeared to partake of the 30 per cent level, minimums of twenty cents and thirty cents on the cheaper grades belied the nominal 30 per cent rate.[35]

Fillmore had incorporated into the tariff of 1842 other provisions that enhanced protection. In that period of economic development, tariff writers had customarily fixed rates as a percentage of the value of the product — the so-called *ad valorem* duties. Manufacturers universally disliked the *ad valorem* system. It meant that real duties fluctuated with the value of the product. Worse in their eyes was that the amount of protection declined more rapidly than the decline of prices. When items sold cheaply, and protection was needed most, the amount of protection fell and profits tumbled. As a result, protectionists demanded specific duties of fixed amounts. Because the protectionist policy was obviously inherent in a specific duty system, Fillmore did not

[34]For products added to free list and revenues lost in that manner see *Niles' Weekly Register*, 63:38-40.
[35]For the effect of these higher rates on the iron and allied industries see M. R. Eiselen, *The Rise of Pennsylvania Protectionism*, 172-174; for effect on textiles, see Samuel Batchelder, *Introduction and Early Progress of Cotton Manufacturing in the United States*, 41-43.

introduce it into his tariff bill. He had neither the time nor the information at hand to rationalize a specific duty scheme with the pretended need for more revenue. But, he reasoned, if the evaluation of imports could be in the hands of friends of American industry, possibly they could modify the *ad valorem* system for the manufacturers' benefit.[36]

In the past a foreign exporter had declared the value of his shipments. If he were honest, the exporter based his evaluation upon the price structure of the exporting country, not on that of the United States. If dishonest, he might go to any limit to falsify invoices, which he and his American importing partner filed, in order to undermine American tariff rates. Many an American importer had lodged complaints with customs officials against dishonest foreigners. But, argued Fillmore, if American customs officials, appointed by friends of protection, instead of foreigners seeking to get into the American market by any means, set the value on imports, these values would be commensurate with the desires of the manufacturing community. The freight, dockage, insurance, and warehouse charges would also enter into the value of the product and would raise the real tax, even if the percentage rate remained the same. Thus Fillmore incorporated into his tariff bill the principle of determining the value of a product on the American side of the Atlantic.[37]

Then, if higher rates and American evaluation were not enough, Fillmore devised still another method of discouraging imports. Former Democratic tariffs permitted importers a year's grace to pay their import duties. Speculative importers, who could wait to unload their goods in a market enhanced by shortages, reaped the advantage. Great stores could be at the command of importers without their having tied up working capital in tariff duties. No one exerted pressure on them to sell until the market was favorable. The system encouraged them to import far beyond their means — which meant to the manufacturers a great abundance of competitive goods. To eliminate

[36]*Fillmore Papers*, 1:226.
[37]*House Documents*, No. 671, 61 cong., 2 sess., 121.

these speculative importers, Fillmore provided in his tariff for immediate cash payment of duties. Under the circumstances, he forced importers to limit their operations or risk the same competitive conditions that vexed American manufacturers.[38]

By reducing imports, Fillmore's tariff threatened to dip deeply into the pockets of the New York-New England shipping interests. To assuage this injury to their pocketbooks, he produced a refinement of England's old colonial system. As compensation to American shipowners for the loss of import trade, he gave them a chance to monopolize America's foreign trade by placing a 10 per cent surtax on the value of goods imported into the United States in other than American vessels.[39] If that did not take up the slack in shipping space, then the tariff measure of 1842 encouraged Yankee skippers to seek treasure in the Orient. Fillmore's tariff promised them a monopoly of the American market for Oriental products by taxing foreign competitors an additional 10 per cent.[40]

Though Fillmore had failed to achieve the full measure of protection that theorists and protectionists had desired, he had set the nation's economy a long way down the hallowed road. Few among his party supporters had cause to complain. But unlike these favored producers, Southerners could cry out in anguish along with the Charleston *Mercury*, that the Whigs "carry their reason, patriotism, conscience and religion in their purses . . . and . . . know no other voice but that of Mammon. . . . They have proceeded from one measure to another in sacrificing the people to capitalists, and giving the public chest into the hands of stock gamblers."[41]

* * * * *

[38] *Fillmore Papers*, 1:227, 228.

[39] *House Documents*, No. 671, 61 cong., 2 sess., 130.

[40] Under the Whigs, the promotion of the China trade took several forms. In 1842 the Whig Congress enlarged and began to modernize the Navy. It created an Asiatic squadron to offer armed protection to the Pacific traders. Webster meantime had induced Tyler and Congress to send a commission to China in quest of commercial privileges. Before the Whig administration had expired, Caleb Cushing and son Fletcher Webster obtained from the Chinese emperor, whom the Opium War had left in a chastened mood, a most favored nation agreement.

[41] Charleston, S. C., *Mercury*, June 30, 1842, quoted in *Niles' Weekly Register*, 62:312.

The joy of the manufacturing and merchant community at the passage of the tariff was unbounded. Almost as if to prove the Whig contention that protection would bring prosperity, the depression began to lift. Pennsylvania's iron-makers entered upon auspicious times, and New Yorkers experienced a rising tempo of industrial life. By mid-1846, a partisan observer announced that the tariff was "working wonders" in Connecticut and Massachusetts. "Every stream seems to turn a hundred wheels." Whether or not the tariff was responsible for the return of prosperity, Whigs were quick to claim the credit.[42]

In every quarter, grateful recipients of these favors lauded Fillmore for the masterful manner in which he had directed the Ways and Means Committee and the vigor with which he had espoused the cause of protection. Not only did his activities recommend him far and wide, but in the role of chairman, he revealed to the political world that behind his phlegmatic demeanor was a reservoir of untapped strength. Frequently during the session, he had risen in the midst of an uproar that would have borne down many a bold man, and in a commanding manner stilled the tempest to a whisper. Occasionally he gave evidence of powers of a higher order than many believed he possessed. He was always dignified, cool, self-possessed, conciliatory, clear, concise, and indefatigable; now and then he exhibited eloquence. "Fillmore," one of his audience remarked, "is a great man; but it takes strong pressure to make him show his highest powers."[43]

Few of his admirers would have believed, had he told them, that at this peak, when he was still a young man and the way appeared open to a still greater career, he had decided to retire from Congress.

[42]Eiselen, *Pennsylvania Protectionism*, 170-174; Barnes, *Memoir of Weed*, 131.
[43]Albany *Evening Journal*, April 16, July 19, 23, August 30, 1842; Greeley to Weed, August 13, 1842, Weed Papers; quotation that of Washington correspondent of New York *American* cited in Albany *Evening Journal*, January 26, 1843.

Chapter 8

Nativism and Defeat

N THE evening of October 29, 1841, the primate of American Catholicism, Bishop Hughes, harangued a gathering of his flock in New York City's Carroll Hall. A religious overtone, indeed, could be heard coming from the stage, but no evangelizing meeting was this. The theme was politics. The florid face of the bishop tightened with determination as his fist descended to the table. He called upon the gathering, not to repent their sins and return to the way of God, but to repudiate both political parties and come out "on their own hook."[1]

Under the ban of the bishop fell New York's candidates for the state legislature. They, charged the bishop, were unfavorable to his views, and before the evening ended, he persuaded the Catholic mass meeting to select a list of candidates — a "Carroll Hall Ticket" — dedicated to labor at Albany for Catholic privileges. The bishop smiled over the results as if to say, "This is our answer," and he looked northward toward the Society of St. Tammany, whose chieftains had abandoned the interests of 70,000 New York City Catholics.[2]

[1]Tuckerman, *Hone*, 2:96-97; John Hughes, *The Complete Works of the Most Rev. John Hughes, D.D., Archbishop of New York*, 1:666.
[2]Tuckerman, *Hone*, 2:97; New York *Tribune*, October 30, 1841.

Instantaneously, from out of the recesses of brooding minds, there arose the specter of a traditional fear. Men who imperiously regarded Catholicism as "un-American" again saw a Catholic "plot" developing in their midst. Once before that fear had led to action. In 1835 while visiting Vienna, Samuel F. B. Morse had learned of the Leopold Society and had warned his fellow Protestants back home that the Pope and the Holy Alliance had organized the society to convert America into a Catholic power. He had envisioned American Catholics, directed by a priestly hierarchy, seizing control of American politics and subverting cherished American liberties.[3]

Prodded by Morse's warning, vague antiforeign and anti-Catholic notions, long present in America, had welled to the surface and congealed into an organization called the New York Protestant Association. The Association had spoken out against popery, and after Catholics broke up one of its meetings, it had turned from rhetoric to politics. Tammany leaders, who counted most of the foreign and Catholic population of the city among their own, instantly had denounced the movement as a political device of the Whigs. Tammany had not misjudged the nativist outcry. In July of 1835 Natives and Whigs had formed an alliance which in two years had grown so strong that it won the local election.[4]

During the next few years, however, fears had subsided and Nativism had remained quiescent. But in 1840 the stimulus for a new outbreak had appeared. Governor Seward, cognizant of the great number of immigrant-American voters, had courted

[3]Carleton Mabee, *The American Leonardo, A Life of Samuel F. B Morse,* 162-168; Ray A. Billington, *The Protestant Crusade, 1800-1860, A Study of the Origins of American Nativism,* 101-102; Samuel F. B. Morse, *Foreign Conspiracy,* and, *Imminent Dangers.*

[4]Broadway Hall Riot on March 13, 1835 described in New York *Courier and Enquirer,* March 19, 1835. See also *ibid.,* April 3, 1835; New York *Post,* March 30, 1835. When nativism entered the national political arena in 1854-1855 as the American party, Whig editor Webb admitted, or even bragged, about his complicity in this early movement. His historical article in the New York *Courier and Enquirer,* June 7, 1855, is a valuable, if biased, review of nativism in America to that time. Basically Louis D. Scisco, in his early chapters of *Political Nativism in New York,* retains the story Webb tells.

their favor. Sympathetically he had noted that racial or religious prejudices often denied children of foreigners the advantages of public education. He, therefore, had asked the legislature to establish schools in which youngsters of immigrant Catholics might be instructed by teachers "speaking the same language with themselves and professing the same faith."[5]

In New York City, at the time, Catholics supported their own parochial schools, while the public school system was under Protestant, Democratic management. Prompted by Seward's expression, Catholics had demanded part of the public school fund for their institutions. But the anti-Catholic, anti-foreign sentiment had rallied behind the Public School Society to reject the request. Blocked locally, Catholics had carried their cause to Albany, where in May, 1841, the legislature, surprisingly aided and abetted by Tammany, had put the Catholic plea aside.[6]

It was under these conditions that Hughes had gathered his flock about him in Carroll Hall to urge the creation of a Catholic political party to discipline Tammany for its desertion of the Catholic cause. Instantly the old nativistic sentiment revived and gave enough support to the New York City Whigs so that, in spite of Bishop Hughes' vigorous call, the predominantly anti-Catholic Whig party had carried the election.[7]

Eventually the public school fund was adequately protected against Catholic incursions,[8] but this time, political nativism, instead of dying out, outlived its cause. After 1842, nativist sentiment was marshaled into the American Republican party, and in spite of Seward's and Weed's opposition, the city Whigs formed a permanent alliance with the group.[9]

[5]Seward, *Autobiography*, 460, 462.
[6]Hughes, *Works*, 2:459, 685; New York *Courier and Enquirer*, April 12, May 5, 1841.
[7]*Ibid.*, April 12, 1841; Mabee, *Morse*, 176-179; Scisco, *Political Nativism in New York*, 35; New York *Tribune*, October 25, 30, November 12, 1841.
[8]A compromise school bill took the New York schools legally out of the hands of the Protestants and placed them under secular state control, but the Catholics did not get any part of the school fund.
[9]New York *Courier and Enquirer*, June 7, 1855.

Encouraged by election results, the Native Americans raised their sights to broader horizons. In early 1844 they spread into New Jersey and into Pennsylvania. In Philadelphia the Natives and the Irish came to blows. Several Native Americans were murdered, and the Irish were hunted down by the light of burning homes and churches. The movement, meanwhile, spread elsewhere into rural counties near New York City and into Albany. In Brooklyn it polled 26 per cent of the vote, and Ulster produced a Native paper. A movement was afoot for a state-wide organization as the Presidential contest of 1844 loomed on the horizon.[10]

*   *   *   *   *

While Bishop Hughes pounded the table at Carroll Hall, three hundred miles northwest of New York City, in a cottage facing the village of Peterboro, New York, a middle-aged man mused over recent events. To the tremors of religious prejudice centering in the nation's metropolis he was insensible. He sat looking toward the village where he once lived in the "Mansion House." His neighbors knew this man — Gerrit Smith[11] — as a hemorrhoid-bedeviled eccentric, landlord of fifteen hundred tenants and mortgagees, and owner of the Oswego Canal Company and a million acres of New York land. The depression had forced him to abandon the "Mansion House" which he loved and to move his family to these modest quarters. His ledger said he had accounts receivable of almost $600,000 but only recently he had faced bankruptcy and had been forced to borrow money at 30 per cent to quiet the baying of his creditors.

Yet he was not brooding about business. Rather his thoughts were on abolitionism. He would much prefer to give his time to a "cause" than to business. Once in the past he had

[10]*Ibid.*; New York *Tribune*, February 2, April 4, 19, May 4, 7, 1844; Henry R. Mueller, *Whig Party in Pennsylvania*, 131-133.

[11]This sketch of Gerrit Smith and his role in turning the abolition movement into political channels is drawn largely from Ralph V. Harlow, *Gerrit Smith, Philanthropist and Reformer*, 22-171.

thought of giving up all other interests and going into the ministry. At other times he had found release in the activities of the Bible and Tract Societies, the Sunday School Union, and the Temperance Society. At present, the abolitionist movement filled his imagination. For eight years he had stood out as a leader among antislavery men, but in recent years factional quarrels among them had blighted their progress, and this bothered Gerrit Smith.

As early as 1836 friction had marred the harmony of the antislavery movement. Its national association — the American Anti-Slavery Society — and the local state organizations had quarreled incessantly over funds and the mode of accomplishing their aims. Bitter personal differences between William Lloyd Garrison, the intransigent leader of the Massachusetts group, and Lewis Tappan, merchant-president of the national society, had intensified the struggle. A schism had resulted, and within a few years abolitionism was speaking with many voices — a hodgepodge of local and state societies without unity or accepted objectives.

Smith had felt "sick, heart-sick," because of the "quarrels of abolitionists." It wounded him to see them waste ammunition on each other which they should be using against the enemy. He had thought long on a method of re-establishing harmony and revitalizing the movement. Before 1838 antislavery men had concentrated their efforts on "abolitionizing the mind" rather than society. Their propaganda had been pitched in a strong emotional key to persuade individuals to see the evil of slavery. By this moral suasion, they had hoped to see emancipation miraculously achieved. But moral suasion had not brought the desired results.

To invigorate their campaign, some abolitionists had begun to think about resorting to politics. Several had persuaded Smith to their view, and then slowly he had guided the New York antislavery men into politics. At first he had made no effort to form an independent party. In 1840, however, he took that step, and had suggested naming the new organization the "Liberty Party." When its delegates had met at Albany, they had nominated James G. Birney as their Presidential candidate. His vote in 1840 was farcical, causing wonder as to whether independent politics was worth the effort.

Now as Smith sadly ruminated over the chaos within antislavery ranks and reflected on its incursion into politics, he answered in the affirmative. Within the area of independent political action, he saw the solution to the abolitionist problems. Correspondents from afar confirmed his belief. Many men who had despaired took courage from Smith and assured him that the key to harmony and success lay with the Liberty party.

Early in 1842 Smith plunged into the task of blowing life into the feeble Liberty party. As his private business improved, he had more time to devote to the plan. In February he brought the New York Liberty party's nominating convention to Peterboro. A few months later he tried his hand at restoring harmony at an Albany meeting. Meanwhile, he corresponded east and west with leaders in Ohio, Pennsylvania, and Massachusetts who were organizing the cells for political action. As the seriousness of vote-getting impressed itself upon him, he gave his attention to the popularity and appeal of candidates. At one point he approached retiring Governor Seward on the Presidency. But the glow of Seward's antislavery principles was dimmed by the fire of his ambitions, and he rebuffed the abolitionist. Smith continued to labor incessantly for the Liberty party, scheduled to hold its national nominating convention in August at Buffalo.

*   *   *   *   *

From his seat in Congress in 1842, Fillmore fixed an anxious stare on New York. What he saw was enough to pain his stout Whig heart. At one end of the state, nativism's infiltration into the Whig party was disquieting. Already the party councils were divided on how to treat it.[12] At the other end of the state Fillmore could almost feel the drawing power of abolitionist

[12]Scisco, *Political Nativism in N. Y.*, 19-20; Albany *Evening Journal*, May 20, 1841.

activity. Upsetting reports had already filtered down to Washington. His former Antimasonic colleague, Myron Holley, was successfully herding western New Yorkers into the Liberty party. Dangerously they pressed in on Buffalo. Well might Fillmore have cried out with Weed: "For God's sake, don't incense such an element!" For a year Fillmore had been laboring with the strength of love to prevent Tyler from harming the party, and now he moaned: "We are in a bad way. The party must break up from its very foundations."[13]

Fillmore's solicitude had other grounds. In the election of 1841, New York Whigs had suffered a decisive defeat.[14] Publicly he assigned the humiliation to the "mental malady" of Tyler which drove him "on from folly to madness" and at last to "insane hostility to his former friends."[15] But Fillmore was capable of making nice calculations and could weigh the factors of decline in a more prudent manner. In the final reckoning he placed a great share of the responsibility on Seward and Weed. Their joint rule had done little to improve their party's position. On the contrary, they had driven many New Yorkers away.

Seward's proposal for giving public funds to Roman Catholic schools had aroused bitterness deep in the breasts of Protestant New Yorkers. Fillmore could appreciate that feeling, since he shared it. From early manhood he had defended the separation of church and state and had insisted that sectarians should pay for their schools. His teaching experience buttressed his belief that schools supervised by men who made a living by teaching dogma, did not necessarily promote lofty morals or good citizenship.[16]

Also, Weed's patronage policy, whose sharp sting Fillmore had experienced, was hardly above reproach. John C. Spencer,

[13]F. G. D. McKay to G. Smith, November 18, 1839, Josiah Andrews to G. Smith, November 26, 1839; M. Holley to G. Smith, March 9, 20, 1840, Gerrit Smith Papers. Weed to Granger, February 22, 1841, Barnes, *Memoir of Weed*, 89, Fillmore to Weed, February 22, 1842, *Fillmore Papers*, 2:242-243.
[14]Albany *Evening Journal*, November 11, 14, 19, 1841.
[15]*Fillmore Papers*, 2:242-243.
[16]Griffis, *Fillmore*, 31-32; *Fillmore Papers*, 1:276-281.

stalwart of the lean years but maligned by Weed in better times, showed his displeasure at the first good opportunity. A more dangerous opponent than Spencer could not be found. When Tyler's cabinet resigned, Spencer readily accepted Tyler's offer of the War Department. Subsequently, a nucleus of Tylerites appeared in New York to harm Whig fortunes.[17]

Seward's association with the McLeod affair, Fillmore noted, had also harmed the party. Three years after the Canadian rebellion, Alexander McLeod, an Englishman, visited New York. While imbibing at a tavern, he boasted that he had participated in the attack on the *Caroline* and that he had killed the only man shot in the encounter. The local sheriff immediately arrested him for murder and arson. Lord Ashburton, British minister, sprang to McLeod's defense and demanded his release. At the time Ashburton was deep in the throes of negotiating a treaty with Webster. One point they had under discussion was the *Caroline* affair. To have McLeod on trial in the midst of negotiations was most unpropitious. Webster tried to eliminate the embarrassment by repeatedly asking Governor Seward to dismiss the case. Each time Seward refused. Fortunately the jury found McLeod guilty of boasting and not murder. Yet the case had put Seward and Webster at odds. And New York friends of the "God-like Daniel" condemned Seward for his lack of cooperation.[18]

Seward also got into a heated joust with southern hotheads and hurt New York's coastwise traders. Virginia's governor had tried to extradite three colored men living in New York who had aided a slave to escape. A New York court would not permit extradition. Here the matter might have rested, but Seward's "overweening faith in his own sagacity"[19] led him astray. In advising Virginia's governor of the court's action, Seward volunteered, with questionable propriety, his own interpretation of the constitutional provision for the surrender of

[17]Tuckerman, *Hone*, 2:165.
[18]Seward, *Autobiography*, 518-520, 526-528, 538-541, 551-553, 566.
[19]Greeley, *Recollections*, 312.

fugitives from justice. His explanation was in poor taste, and though it was undoubtedly good law, it was poor politics. It needlessly aroused the indignation of Virginians, whose legislature retaliated by imposing special burdens upon vessels trading between Virginia and New York. City merchants in the southern trade consequently condemned Seward.[20]

Seward's most serious political blunder involved the construction of canals. Previously Democrats had kept annual canal expenditures limited to the state's surplus income. Theoretically, Democrats favored canal enlargements, but refused to go into debt for the projects. On the other hand, Whigs advocated speedy completion of public works, no matter what the cost. After 1838 the canal expansionists found in Seward a compassionate soul. His "natural tendencies," said a contemporary, "were toward a government not merely paternal, but prodigal — one which . . . [endeavored] to make every one prosperous, if not rich. . . . Few governors favored, few senators voted for more unwisely lavish expenditures than he."[21]

In 1839 he began improvements, the estimated costs of which his engineers woefully miscalculated. By 1841 the canal debt had risen from six to eighteen million dollars, and still the work was scarcely half finished. To add to the difficulties, state bonds depreciated over 20 per cent, which embarrassed the administration in its efforts to raise money. Democrats pounced on such a record. If this was what Whigs meant when they favored internal improvements, the Democrats wanted no part of it. The din of denunciation over Whig prodigality found ready response among voters. They thought it time to call a halt to such spending and in the election of 1841 they called it.[22]

In 1841 New York's repudiation of the Whigs was unique only in its decisiveness; elsewhere they also suffered defeats. By 1842 their buoyancy of a few short years ago had given place

[20]Seward, *Autobiography*, 428-429, 437-439, 463-464, 528-530.
[21]Greeley, *Recollections*, 312.
[22]Alexander, *Political History of N. Y.*, 2:49-50.

to fear and forebodings. Eighteen months of rule had left little save melancholy recollections.

By midsummer Fillmore, too, succumbed to the general gloom. The course of events in Washington and New York, and the prospects of another Congress under Tyler overwhelmed him. But Fillmore was seldom prompted by his emotions. In temperament he was always self-composed, and prudence usually guided his hand.

He surveyed his own position. At every hand he was being lauded for his success in steering through Congress the Whigs' most significant accomplishment: the tariff of 1842. Only Webster's treaty with Ashburton rivaled it in national importance. In the next few years, little more could be achieved in Congress. And he had no heart for two fruitless years in Washington. He might have enjoyed those years had a rumor that Senator Tallmadge of New York would resign from the Senate been true. Justifiably Fillmore believed he had some claim to the post.[23] He had asked Weed for his support and Weed had promised to give him "friendly consideration."[24] But Tallmadge had had no intentions of resigning, and the vacancy never occurred. Under the circumstances, Fillmore's enthusiasm for life in Washington waned. He reasoned that he could do more good during the next two years back in New York, where political fences were in need of much repair, than to continue serving in Congress. Thus, in July, 1842, after thorough reflection, he declined renomination and retired to the "quiet enjoyment of . . . [his] own family and fireside."[25]

*   *   *   *   *

In his retirement, a large and lucrative practice in the higher courts gave Fillmore constant and, to a person of his laborious habits, pleasant occupation. In this manner he passed the next few years, enjoying the esteem of his fellow citizens and laying

[23]Fillmore to Weed, February 6, 1841, *Fillmore Papers*, 2:219.
[24]Fillmore to Weed, February 16, 1841, Fillmore to Timothy Childs, April 29, 1941, *ibid.*, 2:220, 221.
[25]*Ibid.*, 2:241-245.

the foundation of an income that eventually enabled him to live in comfort and dignity.[26] But his hand still rested on the controls of the local Whig machine, and he eagerly read the political news from Washington and Albany.

Occasionally Buffalonians were reminded that their outstanding citizen had not abandoned all thoughts of returning to public life. In the summer of 1843 John Q. Adams visited the city, and upon Fillmore devolved the privilege of extending the official welcome. After Fillmore's speech — a eulogy that could not have failed to please Adams[27] — the "grand old man of Whiggery" prophetically addressed the audience. " . . . I cannot forbear to express here my regret at [Fillmore's] retirement in the present emergency from the councils of his nation. There, or elsewhere, I hope and trust he will soon return for whether to the nation or to the state, no service can be or ever will be rendered by a more able or a more faithful public servant."[28]

Neither Adams nor Buffalo had long to wait. For even before Adams uttered his oblique announcement of Fillmore's availability, Fillmore was planning a return to Washington. A week before his decision to quit Congress, a clue to his future course had been dropped. The Poughkeepsie *Eagle* had called for his nomination for Vice-President. Flattered, but not unwilling to consider it, he sent the notice to Weed.[29] At first Fillmore did nothing else to promote this candidacy, but by spring of 1843 he was inextricably entangled in behind-the-scene moves to win the post.

*   *   *   *   *

Except for politicians, few in the nation concerned themselves with Vice-Presidential maneuvers. Rather the country and its newspapers centered their attention on the Presidential contest. Long before the national convention, Clay's efforts to

[26]Chamberlain, *Fillmore*, 77-78.
[27]*Fillmore Papers*, 2:39-40.
[28]Chamberlain, *Fillmore*, 77-78; Buffalo *Commercial Advertiser*, July 27, 1843.
[29]Fillmore to Weed, June 28, 1842, *Fillmore Papers*, 2:241.

capture the nomination for himself had proved successful. And until the spring of 1844, it seemed certain, also, that Van Buren would lead the Democratic host.

Though party journals seldom reported Vice-Presidential politics, Fillmore's candidacy was progressing. He aimed his effort at winning the pledge of New York's delegates to the national nominating convention in Baltimore. There, with the state's large block of votes to maintain him, and his record on the tariff to recommend him, he hoped for success. Securing New York's delegation, however, was no slight task.

In 1842 a black cloud of dissatisfaction had ushered Seward out of the governor's office. His failures had brought forth a strong opposition faction whose vociferous leaders were largely from New York City. These city politicos, aided and abetted by other anti-Weed men, sharpened their knives for both Weed and Seward by offering John A. Collier as their candidate for governor.[30] Their second choice was Luther Bradish, and if both these men failed, the anti-Weed faction was willing to compromise on Fillmore.[31] Weed spurned all three. The friendship between him and Seward was as warm as ever, and if Weed could have dictated the state's choice of governor, it would have been his old friend. But he knew that Seward was impossible.[32] As a result he turned to Willis Hall.[33] For Seward, Weed had other plans — make him the Vice-Presidential candidate of the Whig party.

Learning of Weed's designs, Fillmore retaliated by arranging an understanding with John A. Collier, thus moving closer to the city crowd. For Collier's support in the Baltimore convention, Fillmore would throw his weight behind Collier for the governor's job.[34]

[30]New York *Tribune,* August 12, 1843; New York *Courier and Enquirer,* March 14, 19, August 16, 18, 1843; New York *Express,* August 16, September 23, 1843.
[31]Minturn to Weed, December 22, 1843, Weed Papers.
[32]Seward to Frederick Seward, January 14, Seward Papers.
[33]*Ibid.*
[34]*Albany Argus,* December 1, 1843; New York *Post* cited in New York *Tribune,* November 29, 1843.

Party chiefs foresaw a major struggle between Fillmore and Seward. But Seward, painfully aware of the hostility he and Weed had caused, refused to be considered for the Vice-Presidency. Half in humor and half in seriousness he informed Weed that he "had signed off everything" and put his "political estate into liquidation for the satisfaction of [his] creditors. . . ."[35]

Unable to change Seward's mind, Weed changed his own plans. He had "lived long enough to know that it is easier to swim with than against the tide."[36] Meanwhile, with each passing month, Weed's enemies were growing fonder of Fillmore. There was some talk that if Fillmore failed at the national convention the New York City group would drop Collier and take him up for governor.[37] As yet few knew that Fillmore had pledged himself to Collier.

That Weed's candidate, Hall, could be stopped if Fillmore's name went before the state convention no one doubted. But between Fillmore and Hall, Weed continued to prefer Hall. No open hostility existed between Fillmore and Weed, but in recent years their friendship had grown more formal, and Weed's favoritism for Seward had done little to change the trend. Now, however, Weed saw an opportunity to safeguard Hall and regain the confidence of Fillmore.

Asserting that he wanted to see Fillmore prosper, Weed arranged a meeting with Fillmore, Seward, and Hall. In this conference they agreed that Seward would not run for any office, that Seward and Weed would support Fillmore for Vice-President, and that Fillmore, should he fail at Baltimore, would not become a candidate against Hall. Then, to seal the bargain, Horace Greeley, editor of the New York *Tribune* and Weed's irascible and sometimes rebellious mouthpiece in New York City, raised Fillmore's name to the masthead as the *Tribune's*

[35]Seward to Weed, May 7, March 17, 1844, Weed Papers.
[36]Albany *Evening Journal*, May 4, 1844.
[37]J. C. Fuller to Weed, September 18, 1843, Weed Papers.

choice for Vice-President. Later Seward endorsed Fillmore and the Albany *Evening Journal* recognized his candidacy.[38]

All might have gone well except for one thing. In the midst of these arrangements, Willis Hall was struck down with an illness that rendered him useless as a candidate. Weed's predicament was patent. Instantly the chances for either Collier or Bradish becoming the party's nominee soared. Weed sought to save himself. He resurveyed all possible candidates. Briefly he reconsidered Seward's chances, but again dismissed him. Finally he concluded that Fillmore was the least of all evils. Approached, Fillmore rejected the suggestion.[39]

More concerned with his own salvation than Fillmore's destiny, Weed began a campaign to defeat Fillmore's Vice-Presidential candidacy and leave him no alternative but to run for governor. Weed boomed Fillmore as the only man capable of saving the state for Whigs and appealed to the party to reject him for Vice-President and nominate him for governor. It was a campaign couched in the most flattering terms for Fillmore, and it was calculated to allay fears of trickery on all sides. But Weed made a fatal mistake. The name of Seward was again heard as New York's candidate for the Vice-Presidential nomination.[40] Fillmore, instead of seeing Weed's predicament, saw this as another illustration of Weed's characteristic skulduggery.

"I receive letters," he confided to Francis Granger, "from my friends in various parts of the state stating that Governor Seward's most intimate friends are *killing me with kindness*. It is said they have discovered that it is indispensable that my name should be used for the office of governor, and that it would be unjust to me and ruinous policy to the Whig party in the state, if I am nominated for the office of Vice-President.

"I need not say to you that I have no desire to run for governor. . . . I am not willing to be treacherously killed by this

[38]Seward to [Frederick Seward], January 14, 1844, Seward Papers; New York *Tribune*, October 12, 1843.
[39]Seward to Weed, November 29, Hunt to Weed, December 15, 1843, Weed Papers.
[40]Seward to Weed, March 11, 1844, Weed Papers.

pretended kindness. . . . Do not suppose for a moment that I think they desire my nomination for governor."[41]

Under the circumstances, when Whigs met in national convention, Fillmore feared that the knife of Weedian politics would be stuck in his back. His fears were well founded. Though the New York delegation went to Baltimore pledged to Clay, they carried no instructions on the Vice-Presidency.[42] Weed himself journeyed to Baltimore and greeted the arriving members from other states with the gospel he had been spreading in New York. Everywhere he dropped the hint that the New York Whig party would be glad to see Fillmore passed by, since it wanted him to run for governor.[43]

In his ubiquity Weed failed to impress the delegates not to offer Seward's name. Then, after the unanimous nomination of Clay, and the cheers of thousands of voices subsided, the Vice-Presidential nominations began. Weed's mistake appeared almost immediately when Seward's name was offered along with Fillmore and three other candidates. Yet Weed had carried out the rest of his plan well, and there was little chance for Fillmore's nomination. On the third ballot, the convention gave Theodore Frelinghuysen of New Jersey a majority, and Fillmore's work of two years collapsed.[44]

*   *   *   *   *

Fillmore tried to bury his disappointment in good partisanship. On his way home from Baltimore, he met Frelinghuysen and Collier in New York City. There at a rally of Whigs all three appeared on the platform and showed public faces that smiled in unison. But Fillmore could not utterly conceal his feelings. Even the offer of the New York City leaders to cast

[41]Fillmore to Granger, April 7, 1844, Granger Papers.
[42]Seward, *Autobiography*, 688.
[43]This fact not generally known in 1844; there is even doubt that Fillmore knew about Weed's activities at the convention, though he suspected them, until 1850 when one of the delegates at that convention informed Fillmore. F. L. Gaines to Fillmore, July 12, 1850, *Fillmore Papers*.
[44]See proceedings of Baltimore convention in New York *Courier and Enquirer*, May 5, 7, 9, 12, 1844.

out Collier and join with Weed to make him the unanimous
nominee for governor could not dispel his chagrin. Peremp-
torily he dismissed the offer. His previous commitment to Collier
and his mistrust of the motives of Weed kept him from temptation.[45]

The growing antislavery movement in New York, however, began to pressure Fillmore toward a change of mind. Four
days before the Whig national convention, Clay had gone on
record against the annexation of Texas. Simultaneously Van
Buren had declared the same sentiment. Both thought they had
removed the vexing question from the campaign. But at their
nominating convention the Democrats rejected Van Buren and
made the issues of Texas annexation and occupation of Oregon
the leading ones of the campaign. Almost immediately the Democratic demand for all of Texas struck a responsive chord in the
South and West. Clay found himself in a difficult position.
Whigs in the South, though they had earlier indicated a willingness to support the no-annexation policy, began to change their
minds. Feeling the tide of popularity ebbing, Clay qualified his
position. In July he voiced the wish to see Texas added to the
Union "upon just and fair terms" and opined that "the subject
of slavery ought not to affect the question one way or the other."

Instantly Clay's new stand had repercussions in New York.
Those abolitionist voters who had remained with the Whigs,
and would have been willing to vote for Clay on a no-annexation platform, now veered to James G. Birney, nominee of the
Liberty party. Washington Hunt, a rising young politician from
Lockport, lamented: "We had the abolitionists in a fair way
until Clay seemed to be determined not to let them vote for
him."[46]

Inadvertently Fillmore now stood in a position where he
might aid the national ticket. During the past decade he had
acquired a sound reputation among abolitionists. Though he

[45]Albany *Evening Journal*, May 9, 1844.
[46]Hunt to Weed, Barnes, *Memoir of Weed*, 123.

did not have their zeal, he did oppose slavery, and accidents rather than design had placed him high on the abolitionists' list of acceptable public men. While in Congress in 1837-1838, he had acted with Adams in defending the right of petition.[47] In 1838, moreover, he had answered correctly all abolitionist questions. It mattered little that he had refused to pledge action on his own personal feelings.[48] Since by good fortune he was not a candidate for office in 1841, 1842, and 1843, he had escaped other inquiries. Yet at Baltimore the tinge of abolitionism had helped to make him unacceptable.[49] Frelinghuysen was a known slaveholder. When President Tyler had first begun to promote Texas annexation, antislavery inquiries had sought out Fillmore at his fireside. Salmon P. Chase had queried Fillmore on Texas annexation, and to Ohio's snooping antislavery leader, Fillmore had announced: "I am decidedly, unqualifiedly and uncompromisingly opposed to the annexation of Texas to the United States." He did not say it was because of slavery, but the impression was there.[50]

While antislavery sentiment began to rise ominously against the Whigs, Weed kept up the pressure on Fillmore to run for governor. His reluctance could not deflect Weed from his course, and others joined Weed. From the capital, Washington Hunt wrote: ". . . so far as I can judge at this distance you are right, and Fillmore is the man. I believe he is the strongest." Another political observer confirmed Weed's strategy. ". . . After Mr. Frelinghuysen was named for Vice-President, it struck me that Fillmore above all others was the man. You may rest assured he will help Mr. Clay to a large number of good men's votes." Determined to have Fillmore, Weed spoke out in the Albany *Evening Journal.* Weed's satellite press echoed the party line.[51]

47Weed, *Autobiography*, 588.
48Fillmore to W. Mills, October 17, 1838, *Fillmore Papers*, 2:174-175.
49Chamberlain, *Fillmore*, 82.
50Fillmore to Chase, April 8, 1844, *Fillmore Papers*, 2:255-256.
51Barnes, *Memoir of Weed*, 121; George W. Patterson to Weed, *ibid.*; Albany *Evening Journal*, May 9, 1844; Geneva *Courier, Washington County Journal*, Delaware *Express*, Attica *Democrat, Chenango Telegraph, Washington County Post*, Auburn *Journal* all quoted in *ibid.*, May 15, 17, 1844.

But Fillmore hung back. Publicly he went on record to scotch the mounting clamor for conscription. "When I saw from the public journals that many of my friends were committing themselves on this subject . . . I felt that the candor and frankness due to my political friends would not suffer me longer to permit them to remain in doubt as to my wishes on this subject. . . . I do not desire to be considered as a candidate for that office."

It would be "indelicate," he said, to reveal his private reasons. Yet if these were overcome, another reason restrained him. The candidate for governor "must be taken from among my political associates, and I feel that I owe too much to them," Fillmore confessed, "to suffer my name to come in competition with theirs. . . . To permit it would wear the semblance of ingratitude, or an overweening ambition for political preferment. . . . I can perceive no reason why I should subject myself to the imputation."[52] Weed published Fillmore's views and answered by listing fifteen newspapers which shouted from their mastheads: "We want Fillmore."[53]

Weed now understood the crux of his difficulty. Fillmore's reticence arose from his pledge to Collier. Consequently Weed redirected his appeal.[54]

If the pressure on Fillmore was great, that which now pressed on Collier became unbearable. Finally he could endure it no longer and withdrew in favor of Fillmore. But to the end Fillmore insisted that he did not seek the office. Yet as Collier bowed out of the race the stage was set for drafting Fillmore. Taking his own opinion, which he had often voiced, that the people had the right to draft any man for public duty, the convention nominated him by acclamation. For his running mate as

[52]*Fillmore Papers*, 2:257-259.
[53]Albany *Evening Journal*, May 25, 1844.
[54]*Ibid.*, May 9, 1844; *Broome Republican, Western New Yorker*, Elmira *Republican, Orleans American*, in Albany *Evening Journal*, June 1, 10, 1844. Washington Hunt remarked to Weed: "I perceive that our friend Collier is inclined to hold Fillmore to a rigid construction of his letter." Barnes, *Memoir of Weed*, 121.

lieutenant-governor, it chose Samuel J. Wilkins, an able, clear-headed lawyer, who, as far back as Morgan's abduction, had been identified as an Adams man.[55]

A few days later, Democrats selected Silas Wright as their candidate to oppose Fillmore. At the time Wright was a Senator from New York and would have preferred to stay in Washington, but he was a strict party man — a strong arm in Van Buren's army — and answered the call to duty. Forty-nine years old, he had been born in Massachusetts, grew up in Vermont and, when not in public service, practiced law in Canton, St. Lawrence County, New York. He was stout, square-built, and muscular. His open face, flushed with intemperate living, often lit up with a pleasing smile, and his manner was winning and honest. In the Senate his plain, spare words had carried great weight. If he slipped into rhetoric, he would apologize later for the "Bunkum." Horace Greeley conceded him to be the "keenest logician in the Senate." His heavy drinking frequently aroused the worry of his friends and the gibes of his enemies, but it had no effect on his general strength and character.[56]

*   *   *   *   *

Fillmore received the notice of his nomination with the laconic remark, "So I am in for it and there is no escape."[57]

Ever since his Congressional days, when he had first seen abolitionists and nativists turning to politics, he had known that these two groups would influence future campaigns. Now he, himself, had to contend with them — not in the fine terms carefully stated in public platforms, but as insidious ground swells. Though he personally felt that the abolitionists would not attack him, he knew, with Clay at the head of the ticket, that Whig voters with antislavery feeling would require careful handling.[58]

---

[55] Albany *Evening Journal*, July 12, August 18, September 12, 1844.
[56] The sketch of Silas Wright is drawn from J. S. Jenkins, *Life of Silas Wright*, and Arthur M. Schlesinger, Jr., *The Age of Jackson*, 105 ff.
[57] Fillmore to Weed, September 16, 1844, *Fillmore Papers*, 2:264.
[58] *Ibid.*, 2:265.

Earlier, his anxiety over nativism had led him to protect his standing with Buffalo's foreign population. This, however, was more German than Irish. German immigrants had settled along the great thoroughfare from New York to Cincinnati. They had acquired suffrage rights, and their numbers were so great that in many towns they exercised a controlling influence. Until Fillmore acted, Whigs had done little proselytizing among them.

Realizing that a few votes might change the election outcome in either Ohio, New York, or Pennsylvania, Fillmore thought it wise to establish a German-Whig paper at Buffalo, midway between New York and Cincinnati.[59] Acting with two other Buffalonians, he secured a German editor and set him up in business in 1843.[60] He solicited funds from outstanding Whigs on the plea that the Germans were "generally industrious and intelligent, capable of reading and writing in their own language and eager in the pursuit of political knowledge . . . it is of great importance both to them and us that the first impressions which they receive of our institutions be from a proper source."[61]

His effort to secure the German vote, however, was of little avail before other events that threatened to drive every foreign voter in New York into Democratic ranks. In New York City's spring election, the Native party had supplemented its hatred of foreigners and Catholics with a demand for economy and nominated James Harper, a businessman, for mayor. The program had given prospects of lighter taxes, which city Whigs had liked. Consequently Whigs had scuttled their own candidate in favor of Harper, and the election had ended in a thumping Nativist victory. Overjoyed at the Native success, city Whigs thought they had discovered the formula for keeping New York City out of the Democratic column in this Presidential

[59]Fillmore to Weed, December 29, 1843, *ibid.*, 2:253.
[60]W. A. Meyer had published the *Volksfreund,* and the new Whig organ was the *Freimuthig und West New Yorker Anzeiger.*
[61]Fillmore to Weed, December 29, 1843, *Fillmore Papers,* 2:254.

year.[62] Between May and November, Whigs and Natives in the city perfected their cooperative plans.[63]

Democratic newspapers seized upon the bargain and turned it into political capital. Democrats deserting to the Nativists were told that they were dupes of the Whigs. In interior counties the Democrats informed the foreigners that all Whigs were anti-foreign. In areas of large Catholic population, these editors branded all Whigs as anti-Catholic. Outside of the city, Whigs chafed under charges that were hard to deny. Bishop Hughes, himself, took to the platform and shook an angry finger at the Whigs.[64]

The cross-fire of the Democrats, Liberty men, and Catholic hierarchy forced New York Whigs to the defensive. Democrats, however, would not relax on the charges of nativism, and the abolitionists kept up a running attack on Clay's Texas and slavery position. To counteract their enemies' campaign, the Whig central committee imported Clay-supporting antislavery men for stumping tours. Seward, who had won the esteem of Irish-Catholics while governor, abandoned a reluctance to campaign and made a grand swing around the state. Fillmore was ubiquitous. He delivered anti-Texas speeches everywhere and endeavored to shift the issue to the tariff. The effort was tremendous, but as election day approached, a general gloom settled over the Whigs. They felt the tide of battle running against them.

[62]In round figures the vote was Native, 24,000; Democrats, 20,000; Whigs, 5,000. Of the Native votes, 14,000 were estimated to be Whigs. *Journal of Commerce,* April 12, 1844.

[63]Non-Whig elements among the Natives, heartened by the success, thought of creating a state-wide party. Whigs generally saw such a move as a threat rather than an aid to their own designs. A call went out on June 21 for a Native state convention. On September 10, one day before the Whigs met at Syracuse, the Natives met at Utica. A great debate ensued over the desirability of selecting an entire state ticket. The convention decided to postpone a decision, and with that postponement the threat to the Whigs subsided. A new general committee took control of the Native organization, and the Whigs and Natives drew closer together. *Journal of Commerce,* June 26, September 11, 12, 23, 1844. See also New York *Tribune,* August 27, 1846.

[64]*Albany Argus,* September 13, 19, 23, 30, October 7, 9, 10, 16, 18, 19, 1844. Hughes to Weed, August 29, 1846, Weed Papers; New York *Tribune,* October 10, November 11, 1844.

The returns justified their gloom; the entire Whig ticket went down in defeat.[65]

*   *   *   *   *

In election post-mortems, Whigs wrangled with each other over who had defeated them—the abolitionists or the foreigners.[66] Most Whigs eventually said both and sulked in the obscurity of retirement. If some doubt existed that the immigrant voters had defeated Clay, no doubt should have existed that Whig identification with nativism had defeated Fillmore.

Whig fear of the abolition vote had been real. When the last ballot was counted, however, the Liberty party candidates had polled only a few hundred votes more than in 1843.[67] In the Presidential year, therefore, no large number of Whigs had abandoned the party because of the Whig, or Clay's, position on Texas. Even where defection did occur, in the western New York stronghold of antislavery, Fillmore had run ahead of Clay by a little over 3,000 votes. The antislavery vote had remained with Fillmore even where it had deserted Clay.[68]

Yet in the entire state Fillmore had trailed Clay by 1,300 votes. In New York City and other urban areas, where foreigners and Irish-Catholics centered, Fillmore had lost out and Clay had fared better. In New York City, Fillmore ran 3,500 votes behind Clay. That probably meant that 3,500 foreign-born or Catholic Whigs had voted for Wright over Fillmore but remained with Clay. In Albany, Utica, Syracuse, and Rochester, though the numbers were smaller, the trend was the same.[69]

Even in Erie County the foreign vote reduced a customary 3,000 to 3,400 Whig majority to a meager 2,000. In the city of

[65]Albany *Evening Journal,* September 20, October 8, 9, 15, 22, 1844; Seward, *Auto-biography,* 725-728; Seward to Weed, June 20, 1844, Weed Papers.
[66]The final tally for governor in New York was Wright (Democrat) 241,090; Fillmore (Whig), 231,057; Stewart (Liberty), 15,136; for President, Polk (Democrat), 237,538; Clay (Whig), 232,408; Birney (Liberty), 15,216. *Civil List, State of New York* (1887) 166.
[67]*Albany Argus,* December 2, 1843.
[68]*Ibid.,* November 22, 1844.
[69]New York *Tribune,* November 15, 1844.

Buffalo, where in the previous four years over 1,400 naturalized citizens had acquired the franchise, the Whig majority narrowed dangerously. In his own Buffalo ward, which was rapidly filling with immigrants, Fillmore's old majority of 300 fell to a picayune 4.[70] Well might Fillmore in this year of bitter disappointments turn a skeptical eye on the recently naturalized citizens.

[70]Buffalo *Commercial Advertiser,* November 6, 7, 8, 11, 26, 1844; *Albany Argus,* November 15, 1844.

Chapter 9

The Comptrollership: Marking Time

LL IS gone—but honor!" soliloquized Fillmore when defeat was certain. Relieved from the strain of the campaign, he still brooded over the results. Deep in his heart he felt that his defeat — his only one — had been caused by the "foreign catholics," and that Weed and Seward, with possible malice, had led him into a trap.[1]

Yet Fillmore could do nothing to avoid retirement, and he gracefully resigned himself to a quiet, domestic life. He enjoyed living in Buffalo, and he stole many an hour away from business to be with his wife and two children. Powers had reached sixteen, and Fillmore took him into the law office as a student. Mary Abigail was entering the gangling stage of her early teens, and her music lessons were going well. Relations within the family were idyllic. Even around the hearthstone, the retired politician kept up the habit of gentle breeding in which he set so much store. After seventeen years of married life, Fillmore still treated Abigail with tender respect. She was the envy of the wives in their circle of friends as her husband continued to bestow on her the attentions and courtesies other men reserved for guests.[2]

[1]Fillmore to Weed, November 6, 1844, *Fillmore Papers*, 2:267; Fillmore to Clay, November 11, 1844, *ibid*.
[2]"Mrs. Haven's Recollections of Fillmore," *ibid*., 2:489.

In these surroundings of a busy professional and satisfying home life, Fillmore buried himself. Before long, however, the peacefulness, regularity, and uneventfulness of his days began to pall. Behind his smiling face and courteous bearing there slumbered a world of latent passion and power, "like the fires in the furnace of a great ship at rest, banked, and watched, but ready to call."[3] In spite of his protestations of devotion to the fireside, he could not sit idly by it. He had tasted the sweets of public acclaim and had sat at the table of the nation's honored few. The chancellorship of the University of Buffalo, which he helped to found, hardly satisfied his urge to be in the thick of public affairs. Politicians and statesmen on their way to a visit at the Falls stopped by frequently to remind him of the day when he had led Congress.

To make his retirement even less savory, each time he raised his sights beyond the confines of Buffalo, he saw events transpiring that filled him with agony. When James K. Polk won the Presidential election, Fillmore prophetically saw "a cloud of gloom" hanging over America's future, and prayed: "May God save the country; for it is evident the people will not. . . ."[4]

Before many months had passed he was forced to watch the Polk administration feed the expansionist appetite of the agricultural and planting interests with a diet of Texas, California, other vast areas of Mexico, and Oregon. While Polk catered to the lust for land, and all the interests lands served, his Administration ground down into dust the structure that Fillmore and the Whigs had labored so long to erect for the prosperity of merchants and manufacturers. The credit-killing sub-treasury scheme, which he despised, reappeared. His protective tariff measure of 1842 fell before the onslaught of the freetraders. A great program for river and harbor improvement in the Great Lakes area that promised better ways to market and more profitable markets died of a Presidential veto. Sarcastically

---

[3]Day, "Reminiscences," *ibid.*, 2:508.
[4]Fillmore to Clay, November 11, 1844, *ibid.*, 2:268.

Fillmore noted that "these ponds! Lake Erie, and Lake Ontario, and Lake Huron, and even Lake Superior, cannot be taken under the care of the constitution. . . ." Then, in protest, "I believe the constitution is not a salt water animal. . . . It can live as well in fresh as in salt water."[5]

The Mexican War, which broke out when Polk sent troops to support the boundary claims of Texas, moved, meanwhile, to its inevitable conclusion. The abolitionists greeted the war as a slaveholders' conspiracy. Those on whose toes Polk had trampled reinforced the abolitionists with charges of an unjust war — a war of conquest waged solely for the extension of slavery. These agitators prodded a growing body of Northerners to set themselves apart from the South. More and more, Easterners and those living along the shores of the Great Lakes thought of themselves as the great protagonists of a commercial and manufacturing economy. They believed this vastly superior to the planting economy of the South.

Fillmore stated the case quite bluntly. "The interests of the North" are being "sacrificed . . . while the" Administration incurs a debt of a "100 million dollars for the wild and wicked scheme of foreign conquest" to add "another slave territory to the United States." Though the "North has a majority of the votes, the South has managed to have the Speaker of the House about two-thirds of the time, and the Presidency about two-thirds of the time. Through the President, they control the patronage and foreign missions and are able to veto [northern] legislation. Through the speaker they control the committees and smother questions and hearings. . . . I cast no imputations upon the South for this, but ask: Shall we submit to our servile condition?"[6]

Fundamental to the interests of merchants was the need for expanding markets. In other years their markets had enlarged through foreign trade and coastal commerce, or by the construction of turnpikes and the use of flatboats on the Ohio and

[5]*Buffalo Express*, October 2, 1846.   [6]*Ibid.*

Mississippi rivers. Later canal construction had helped. Already some were beginning to see the potentialities of railroads. But in the mid-forties only 5,000 miles of rail existed in the nation.

At this point the greatest potential market was the Northwest — the lands that bordered the Great Lakes. For a generation the area had received countless immigrants and was now rich with people. Yearly the use of its natural waterway had mounted. By 1846 the traffic on the Great Lakes was almost equal to the United States export trade, and it promised in a few years to become greater than the whole foreign trade.[7] With use came pressure to improve its facilities. But the federal government did not open its generous purse to promote this new field of commerce.

As the Great Lakes area came into its own, Buffalo prospered beyond comparison. In one year, between 1845 and 1846, its population grew by 4,000 as it rose to 30,000. In another year 10,000 more active citizens crowded its limits.[8] The port's function had changed. Earlier it had acted as the great funnel through which hundreds of thousands of people moved to their new homes in the Northwest. Now it was collecting the products of the Great Lakes basin and moving them eastward to the coast.

Often a forest of masts sprouted from Buffalo's harbor, filling the basin with shipping from shore to shore. Captains of vessels, shipping agents, and merchants who awaited the unloading of cargoes, looked at these crammed conditions, lauded their significance in profits, but peering into the future saw the day when traffic would turn to other channels if the delays continued.[9] Already the city fathers thought of protecting themselves by building railroads out from the city like spokes of a wheel,[10] though they realized the present need for greater harbor accommodations and more basin slips to discharge cargoes. Hopefully they turned to Washington for funds to carry out expansion.

[7]*Ibid.*, March 27, 1847.   [8]*Ibid.*, February 9, 1848.
[9]*Ibid.*, November 30, 1846.   [10]*Ibid.*, December 1, 1846.

Buffalo was not alone in her hour of need. Merchants and lake captains at Erie, Cleveland, Sandusky, Toledo, Detroit, and Chicago complained of poor harbors and of the Buffalo bottleneck. They, too, turned to the federal government for aid. But in midsummer of 1846, Polk's veto of the river and harbor bill dashed their hopes.[11]

Immediately, citizens of the aggrieved area held protest meetings. At Buffalo, Fillmore and his partner, Hall, headed a group of dissenters and set up a committee of correspondence to gather strength for their cause.[12] As far east as Boston, merchants and manufacturers felt the impact of the veto. There Nathan Appleton and Abbott Lawrence led a gathering that paid respect to western commercial resources they were eager to exploit.[13] At Chicago a newspaper editor cried out: ". . . this harbor question is not a political one, but a sectional one. It is one between the North and the South."[14] The North "must be respected, and her commerce must be protected as well as that of other portions of the Union. . . ." The "iron rod wielded over" the North by "Southern despots must be broken. . . ."[15] Rapidly the committees of correspondence funneled the protests into a movement for a mass convention at Chicago.

In July, 1847, 4,000 delegates from nineteen states converged on Chicago to voice their plea and vent their spleen. Every politician of the Northwest who could make the journey attended the meeting. It was a splendidly organized affair with parades and decorations. Fillmore attended with the New York delegation, and one of his fellow Buffalonians, James L. Barton, was chosen temporary chairman. Before the convention adjourned, the delegates had set up a permanent committee to proselytize among Congressmen and knit the opinion of the convention into an unchallengeable demand for aid.[16]

Within a month, Fillmore attended a Buffalo meeting that

---

[11]*Ibid.*, June 7, 1847.   [12]*Ibid.*, March 22, 1847.   [13]*Ibid.*, June 7, 1847.
[14]Chicago *Democrat*, November 10, 1846.
[15]*Ibid.*, July 6, 1847.
[16]*Ibid.*, July 6, 7, 8, 15, 1847; *Buffalo Express*, July 12, 13, 1847.

echoed the demands of the Chicago convention and even went beyond its scope.[17] The position of Buffalo was peculiar. Here federal and state authority over internal improvements converged. Unless the state enlarged the canal to handle a greater volume of boats and increased the facilities for transferring from lake to canal shipping, nationally built harbor accommodations would be useless. Buffalo's attitude reflected commercial opinion throughout the state, for the canal was the major link between the Atlantic and the Great Lakes market. Harbor improvement and canal enlargement stood inseparably united. But the Democratic administration at Albany stood impassive on the canal,[18] and Democrats at Washington had already shown their hostility toward the harbor.

So as Fillmore watched and participated in action to preserve and nurture a way of life that was dear to him, he appreciated the need of winning the state back to the Whig party. Already New Hampshire, Maine, and Indiana had repudiated Polk's administration, and Fillmore hoped that New York would soon do the same.[19]

The Whigs of New York were scarcely a happy family, and in spite of Fillmore's hopes, their prospects for victory were not bright. After defeat in 1844, discord had mounted. Even Horace Greeley, consumed with a desire for public preferment, began to chafe under Weed's domineering behavior. Other New York City politicians went farther. Convinced that Weed and the wild notions of his protégé, Seward, were responsible for the recent failures, the city's leaders resolutely set themselves to dethrone the "Dictator," as they called Weed.

Fillmore was less drastic in attitude, and his thoughts were not on revenge but a Whig victory. He did not share New York City's bitter feeling toward Weed. To be sure, in the past few years Fillmore's relations with Weed had cooled, but this grew, not from hate or pettiness, but from Fillmore's growing ability to judge Weed's value to the party. Fillmore readily admitted

[17]*Ibid.*, August 21, 1847.   [18]*Ibid.*, May 19, 1847.   [19]*Ibid.*, October 2, 1846.

that no one had Weed's talents and that the Whig party needed him. But the Albany editor's compulsion to personal power needed restraint.

For his part Weed was less magnanimous. Already a vicious note was creeping into his cool treatment of Fillmore, forecasting what would one day become a malignant attack.

As the campaign of 1846 approached, Fillmore took it upon himself to try to promote Whig unity. He saw his own attitude as a possible compromise between Weed's ambitions and those of his enemies. Though he had no pretentions of being a "boss" like Weed, Fillmore could see that his own position in western New York might be used to balance, possibly to eliminate, the factional fights. In preparation he set about putting his own house in order. To control the local machine he induced his law partner, Solomon G. Haven, to run for mayor.[20] Haven won, and with that point achieved, Fillmore prepared the Erie central committee to back his former partner, Nathan K. Hall, for Congress. When the time came for nominations, Hall's easy victory showed how well Fillmore had smoothed the way.[21]

As the time approached for nominating a governor, Fillmore's movement toward unity without Weed's dictatorship gathered momentum. Weed sponsored Ira Harris, of Albany County, who had made his appearance in politics two years earlier as the friend of the Anti-Renters. He had championed the cause of the small, but volatile, Anti-Rent party that had arisen because aristocratic landlords had pushed exasperated tenants to the wall with hard bargains and foreclosures. Harris, though not a member of the Anti-Rent party, had received its endorsement and, once in the assembly, his sincerity and social outlook had continued to inspire the confidence of bedeviled tenants. Meanwhile, his marked ability had attracted Weed.

The second candidate, John Young, was a popular man of the hour. A nonentity a few years before, he had suddenly

20*Ibid.*, February 17, 19, 1846.   21*Ibid.*, September 19, 1846.

displayed powers of parliamentary strategy that won the calling of a state constitutional convention and passage of a large canal appropriation, both in spite of a hostile Democratic majority. Governor Wright vetoed the canal bill, but Young's action and prowess had quickened the heart of many Whigs. Weed eyed him charily.

New York City Whigs took kindly to neither Harris nor Young. Harris was Weed's candidate, and too radical, and they feared that Young was a demagogue because he had also bid for Anti-Rent support. As a result they looked about for a more trustworthy candidate of gubernatorial stature. The repeal of Fillmore's tariff only a few months before made them feel that a strong rally could be made around his name. And Fillmore did not, at first, scotch this hope. From both ends of the canal stemmed a movement for Fillmore's nomination.[22]

But his own nomination was not a part of Fillmore's plans, and he soon began to discourage the banner-waving.[23] He did "not feel at liberty" to enter the race, he asserted, because he had settled upon Young as his candidate. Not knowing, however, what might happen to his hopes to contain Weed, Fillmore did not summarily withdraw his name. After consultation with his friends, he left the way open.[24] The strategy was to nominate Young, and Fillmore pledged the Erie delegation.[25] If, however, Young could not win, Fillmore empowered his manager to accept for him the nomination, if it were unanimous. He was taking no chances of Weed's pulling out.

When the convention met at Utica on September 23, the New York City Whigs were still unconvinced of Young's trustworthiness. As balloting began, they concentrated on Fillmore. On the first ballot, he failed by one vote of a majority. Had his manager voted for Fillmore, he would have been the Whig

[22]Fillmore to Childs, October 8, 1846, *Fillmore Papers*, 2:269; Buffalo *Commercial Advertiser*, September 15, 1846.
[23]Fillmore to Horace Greeley, August 27, 1846, Fillmore Mss.
[24]Fillmore to Childs, October 8, 1846, *Fillmore Papers*, 2:269.
[25]George R. Babcock to Fillmore, March 4, 1850, Fillmore Collection.

candidate.[26] But instead he finally pursuaded the city delegation that they would find Young "as safe . . . a governor as Millard Fillmore would be."[27] Babcock withdrew Fillmore's name, and on the third ballot Young won.

Young carried the state that year, and the Whigs returned to power — something they had not been able to do under Weed's dominion. Thus the plan to reduce Weed to his appropriate size accomplished its purpose.

In the future all might have gone well for the Whigs if Weed had been content to play the role he was now assigned — wheelhorse for the party — or Fillmore had been more vigilant. But Fillmore was guilty of misjudgment. He was too prone to believe that others, like himself, were willing to subordinate themselves to the general good. Weed was constituted differently. He was very gloomy and informed Seward, who was anxious for office, that his prospects were extremely dubious. Yet he did not give up; he lived for the day when he would no longer have to share the leadership of the Whig machine.

In spite of their victory in the election of 1846, New York Whigs still lacked control of their state. The newly written Constitution of 1846 had opened to election all the major state offices that had formerly been filled by appointment. Yet the calendar placed their elections in the nongubernatorial years. Among the officers who would in 1847 be selected directly by the voters for the first time were the comptroller, secretary of state, state treasurer, state engineer, and the three canal commissioners. Not only were these the state's key administrative officers, but, as a group, they made up the canal board — probably the state's most powerful and significant agency. Therefore, after placing Young in the governor's mansion, Whigs trained their sights on absolute mastery of the state and aimed at 1847 as the banner year of victory.

The most significant office at stake was the comptrollership. In many ways it was the most important post in the state. It

[26]*Ibid.*   [27]New York *Express,* September 22, 1846.

lacked the pomp of the governorship but its possessor wielded powers far beyond those of the governor in shaping the economy of the state. The comptroller was not merely an officer, but a bundle of officers. He was a one-man government. Hardly a branch of the administration escaped his supervision. He was the chief of finances, the superintendent of the banks, and the virtual quorum of the commissioners of the canal fund, which made him the leading member of the canal board.

To salvage this post from their defeat in 1846, Democrats forgot their own differences and united on incumbent Azariah C. Flagg, the emerging strong man of his party. Knowing Flagg's ability, Whigs quickly realized that they needed their strongest man at the head of their ticket.

By this time politicos around the state were beginning to recognize what Fillmore, in his quiet and unpretentious manner, had done the previous year. Given this and his previous record all admitted that he was "the only man who would stand the first sight against A. C. Flagg."[28] Not only were his politics proper — midway between Weed and the city — but his talents were particularly fitted to the duties of the comptroller. He possessed what a later generation would call "administrative ability." A natural cast of mind that preferred business to show, a love of labor, a fondness for methodical work, and a compulsive natural grasp united to great capacity for details, energy, inventiveness — these were the qualities that recommended him for the post.[29]

When his friends approached him for permission to use his name at the convention, Fillmore did not hesitate. The blandishments were unnecessary.[30] He had decided to forsake "retirement" and re-enter political life as an officeholder. Though he would have preferred the post of United States Senator to that of comptroller, there were no Senate seats available, and

[28]*Buffalo Express,* October 9, September 28, 1847; New York *Express,* August 27, September 3, 14, 21, 22, 1847.
[29] [Chamberlain], *Fillmore,* 98.   [30]*Ibid.,* 106.

he was eager to lend himself to a cause he had fostered — Whig victory.

Fears of the "wild caprice of the everchanging multitude," which had once kept him out of the comptrollership, no longer haunted him. In the past twenty years, he had accumulated upwards of thirty thousand dollars in bonds and mortgages. He owned the homestead on Franklin Street, two houses on Seneca Street, and a vacant lot on the northwest corner of Main and Tupper, where some day he expected to build a luxurious dwelling for himself. With an independent income approaching three thousand dollars annually, in a day when six hundred maintained a family man in modest circumstances, he felt secure. Readily he acceded to his nomination. Anticipation of living in the thick of Albany's political life once again lured him on.[31]

The election returns justified the confidence which the party had placed in him. Leading his ticket, he obtained the largest plurality over a Democratic opponent — 38,000 — that any Whig had ever received.[32] This feat pleased his vanity almost as much as the sweeping Whig victory satisfied his political loyalty.

Shortly after his election, Fillmore visited Albany to secure apartments for himself and his family and to survey the comptroller's office. A warm reception at every hand encouraged him to extend the visit to three weeks. Basking in that welcome, he plainly saw that henceforth his life was not to be passed in the quiet practice of law, but in the full blaze of public life, where he was to be a prominent actor.[33]

Upon his return to Buffalo, filled with elation over the future, he closed out all his law matters. The cavalier manner in which he disposed of his law library to Haven revealed his high spirits.[34] A student-clerk made out a list of his books, and the two partners examined it and negotiated for the sale. After

---

[31]Day, "Reminiscences," *Fillmore Papers*, 2:503, 505.
[32]Albany *Evening Journal*, November 11, 1847.
[33]Day, "Reminiscences," *Fillmore Papers*, 2:503.
[34]*Ibid.*, 2:503-504.

considerable time, a difference of twenty-five cents a volume still separated them. Fillmore then bargained: "Mr. Haven, to settle this matter let us flip a cent. If it comes up head, you will pay me my price, if tail, you can have them at your price."

"Agreed," said Haven.

Fillmore started walking the floor, groped in his pocket as if in search of a certain penny. At last he produced a large, old fashioned coin and said challengingly, "Haven, here's a go."

"No! No!" shouted Haven, as he hurriedly made his way in front of Fillmore with both arms extended. "Mr. Fillmore," he remarked suspiciously, "you have been spending the last three weeks down at Albany with a political gang of cunning politicians, just long enough to learn their ways and tricks, and I want to examine that cent, to see if you have not got a double header." Haven took the cent and after a careful examination, handed it back. Fillmore smiled, Haven's countenance was unchanged, but the gathered office staff laughed heartily. The penny came up heads, and the bargain was closed.

In a less carefree manner, during the closing months of the year, Fillmore placed his Buffalo affairs in order for a long absence. To one of his students, who was soon to become a lawyer, he entrusted the management of his personal and private property. The Franklin Street house he rented furnished. With the law partnership dissolved and Haven unwilling to continue all the obligations of the firm, Fillmore stopped Powers' informal education and sent him to Harvard for the college education that his father had never acquired. Mary Abigail attended a Massachusetts finishing school. In the last week of the year, the Fillmores moved to Albany where every landmark revived memories of a political career begun twenty years before.[35]

Once settled amid the old haunts and installed in office, Fillmore conducted the comptroller's office in precisely the

[35]Fillmore to Weed, February 11, 1847, *Fillmore Papers*, 2:273; Day, "*Reminiscences*," *ibid.*, 2:505; Albany *Evening Journal*, December 20, 1847.

manner his supporters had expected. With his assenting voice joining those of others, the Whigs reversed the "Stop and Tax" policy. Soon canal enlargements began with fresh enthusiasm. Fillmore intervened personally in these affairs for the benefit of Buffalo and obtained an enlargement of the canal basin.[36] As bank supervisor, he framed the outline of a revised banking code.[37] In this outline, adopted by the assembly, he designed a currency system that Republicans in Congress sixteen years later adopted in the National Banking Act. It created a currency as light as paper, but backed almost exclusively by New York state and federal bonds instead of commercial paper as formerly. At the same time the act provided for the rapid elimination of the safety fund system that Whigs had condemned to a lingering death in 1839.

But while the routine of the office occupied most of Fillmore's time, his attention was steadfastly concentrated on the national scene where his destiny lay.

[36]Fillmore to O. Allen, November 28, 1848, *Fillmore Papers*, 2:265-266.
[37]See *Annual Report of the Comptroller of New York*, 1848.

Chapter 10

The Road Back to Washington

 STARGAZER, charting the future of Whiggery in 1846, might have forecast that in eight more years the party would wither away. But with all their wisdom, the party chiefs had no inkling of such a catastrophe. Instead, they allowed the insistent pressures of the moment, the need to win the local elections that were the key to national success, to draw them into actions that foredoomed their party. Their anxiety was understandable, for their successes in local elections, considering the whole county, were only 15 per cent as against their formidable opponents' 85. In a day when national issues were still far less significant than local, as the national government wielded less (and a more distant) authority, this was matter for despair.

It was true that since the creation of the Whig party the functions of the federal government had steadily increased. The parties, likewise, were turning more toward national issues, and the time was approaching when their leaders would dominate local elections with national issues. Northern Whig leaders, meanwhile, unconscious of the wider implications of their acts, and prodded by the need for success, fumblingly experimented with the national issue of slavery. It was this experimentation that proved fatal to both their own and the nation's unity.

The same professionals who had shunned the antislavery sentiment as a disease now thought to use it as a Whig issue. The Mexican War providentially threw the question to the front, creating a forum they could not suppress. They had earnestly sought tariffs, internal improvements, and uniform currency; they had tried antimasonry, nativism, and even ribald populism, to no avail. That they now willingly turned against their southern confreres revealed their desperation.

In New Hampshire the Whigs, fresh from castigating John P. Hale for associating with the abolitionists' Liberty party, elected him to the United States Senate. In Massachusetts John Quincy Adams and Charles Sumner, the latter rapidly rising as a Brahmin leader, created something new: the "Conscience" Whig, boldly antislavery and popular among country voters. Those who refused this lead, by default defenders of slavery, were derisively called "Cotton" Whigs. Since Nathan Appleton, Abbott Lawrence, and Robert Winthrop, their leaders, were associated with textile manufacturing, the term quickly took on a nasty second meaning. The two factions battled for organizational control in 1846, and the Cotton Whigs won because Daniel Webster gave them his support. He feared a change in the composition of his party. ". . . Others rely in other foundations . . . for the welfare of the country," he declared, "but for my part, in the dark and troubled night that is upon us, I see no star above the horizon promising light to guide us but the intelligent, patriotic united Whig Party of the United States."[1]

Southward in Pennsylvania, there was no Webster to stem the tide. There the Whigs, embittered by the repeal of the protective tariff, carelessly denounced the South and were quite prepared to cast aside their allies for the beckoning opportunities of the antislavery movement.[2]

Ohio Whigs, meanwhile, shamelessly flirted with the antislavery elements in their state. Although stopping short of

[1] Webster, *Writings and Speeches*, 16:322, Adams, *C. F. Adams*, 78.
[2] Philadelphia *North American*, August 5, 1846.

merger, their 1846 candidate for governor played the demagogue, talking against slavery in the Western Reserve but playing the heavy, impartial patriot along the Ohio River. The gross deceit brought him victory by a few votes.[3]

These maneuvers, not all, of course, so discreditable, were performed while the drama of the Wilmot Proviso was being played on the Congressional stage. Everyone understood that the Mexican War would add the territory west of Texas, including California, to the United States. The question was immediately posed whether this new territory should be free or slave. David Wilmot, a Democratic representative from northwestern Pennsylvania, tried to persuade Congress to pledge itself, in advance, to prohibiting the extension of slavery into any land that might be acquired. The House passed the measure in 1846, but the Senate withheld action. Antislavery leaders, meanwhile, made the Proviso their guiding principle and the movement's test of orthodoxy. Time and again, all through the war, they attached it as a "rider" to bills but each time it went down in defeat.

None of this was lost on the southern Whigs, who could hardly regard the new northern Whig experiments with composure. Since 1842 Dixie's Whigs had steadily lost ground, and these new developments left them in an anomalous position. They represented the large slaveholders while their northern colleagues harbored a growing antislavery element. Some escape must be found from the dilemma.

John J. Crittenden, Kentucky's governor, took the lead. He conceived a stratagem and gathered about him other leaders of the desperate southern wing of the party. One was a Senator from Delaware — six-foot-six, bibulous John N. Clayton. Another was North Carolina's pragmatic, forceful Willie P. Mangum. Soon the wizened introvert, Alexander H. Stephens, and his inseparable foil, the bulbous extrovert, Robert Toombs, joined the cabal. Nearly all of the southern states ultimately

[3]Edgar Allan Holt, *Party Politics in Ohio, 1840-50*, 214-292.

were represented. The stratagem they agreed to was simple: win the election of 1848 with a southern candidate untainted by antisouthern heresy. Victory would encourage the North's return to orthodoxy, and local victories would follow.

The blunders of several candidates simplified the problem of choosing a nominee. General Winfield Scott bowed himself out by arousing a national gust of laughter at his malapropisms. Next, John McLean's own Ohio party deserted him for Senator Tom Corwin. Then fate intervened.

Below the border an obscure general and sugar planter of Louisiana, Zachary Taylor, was leading an army from victory to victory against the Mexicans. · Both parties, thinking of Generals Washington, Jackson, and Harrison, sounded him out, finding him without party preference. During the winter of 1846-1847 General Taylor paid little heed to the overtures, except one, that of his relative and friend, John J. Crittenden. The War Department conveniently ordered Crittenden's brother, Thomas, to Mexico to join Taylor's staff. Soon the General's political fortunes were in the hands of a group, predominantly southern Whigs, known as the "Young Indians."

They had a very special problem in the renewed Presidential ambitions of Henry Clay, now restored to health by sane living after ostensible final retirement in 1844. The "Young Indians" unanimously agreed that Clay's candidacy was impossible but dared not boldly declare themselves. Fortunately Clay had said in 1845 he would emerge from retirement only upon unanimous demand of the country; his lukewarm colleagues now seized the statement and declared their disappointment with the lack of unanimity, suggesting Taylor to be the next best choice.

Taylor's campaign was pushed skillfully and vigorously. It was Whig where Whigs controlled; elsewhere, nonpartisan. The General's brilliant victory at Buena Vista clinched the matter, and even Clay began to wonder whether he would be drafted. As Taylor's popularity rose Clay finally was forced to take to the field, crisscrossing the country in a tour upon which he frequently responded to his friends' demands for a speech. Though political etiquette forbade open and insistent candidacies, he managed through this technique to announce his intention to run in November.[4]

While the dream of President-making unfolded in the South, Fillmore took stock of his own position. He had abandoned his profession in his forty-seventh year to obtain New York's comptrollership. Yet his ability transcended even the exacting requirements of the post. "He had the peculiar faculty of adapting himself to every position in which he served," remarked a contemporary. "When he was Chairman of the committee of Ways, members of Congress expressed their sense of his fitness for the position, by declaring that he seemed to be born to fill it."[5] This was always the case. Whatever job he held the same judgment prevailed.

If his administrative ability had always been unlimited, such was not the case of his ambitions. He had at first been timid about holding public office. Then for years he had subconsciously submitted to Weed and to Weed's judgment. In the past five years, however, a subtle change had occurred. He had a new confidence in his own destiny. He now recognized Weed as extraordinarily talented, but neither unerring nor universally just. Fillmore's own absence from office for five years — years that were enriched by a successful legal practice — had altered his perspective on politics. His own skillful manipulation of the party nomination in 1846, even if it were not generally acknowledged, had emboldened him. After his own election to the comptrollership, he probably could not have told an inquirer exactly where he wanted to go in public life — and the surviving record would offer no clue — but it made little difference, for opportunities for other offices were at hand. From the moment he arrived in Albany, he acted as if the future held something

[4]The story of the Southern activity behind Taylor's candidacy is best revealed in George Poage, *Henry Clay and the Whig Party*, 152-196; Arthur Cole, *Whig Party in the South*, 104-134; Holman Hamilton, *Zachary Taylor*, 2:38-86.
[5]A. H. H. Stuart to J. G. Wilson, April 29, 1878, Fillmore Mss.

for him beyond the comptrollership, and with this fate he was willing to cooperate.

He found the state capital in January of 1848 alive with speculation and intrigue over the Presidential nomination. Not unnaturally he looked to Weed as weathercock to the political winds. Politicking behind closed doors showed Weed's talents to the best advantage, and that the editor needed to be especially astute in this election Fillmore readily understood. Since 1846 Weed had been visibly chafing under the bonds that Fillmore and the party had placed upon him. Yet if Weed used the Presidential election correctly, he could break those bonds and recover his old power.

Fillmore found Weed suffering the tortures of the damned — twisting and turning to find the correct position in the Presidential race. Monthly the editor shifted from one candidate to another, first favoring one and then another as if seeking the role of President-maker. But he could not insinuate himself into a commanding position. What was worse, the party's most promising candidate appeared to be under the thumb of the southern wing. And Weed had been one of the northern Whig leaders who had begun to experiment with the antislavery vituperation as a way out of his troubles. "What plagues me," blurted out the still naive Washington Hunt, unconsciously stating one of Weed's perplexing problems, "is to think how I, after all I have said against slavery and its extension, am to look the Wilmot Proviso people in the face and ask them to vote for a southern Slaveholder."[6]

Possibly Fillmore should have shared Weed's disquietude. In 1846 he, too, had attacked the South. But his reasons were different. He had been hurt by the repeal of the tariff of 1842 and Polk's veto of the rivers and harbors bill. To Fillmore, southern Democrats were responsible for both these actions, and he had neither castigated nor rejected the southern wing of his own party. Rather, he knew southern Whigs to be fairly

[6]Barnes, *Memoir of Weed*, 165.

reliable in their support of northern Whig goals. Instead of causing him concern, the rise of a strong southern contender for the Whig nomination left Fillmore complacent and sanguine of victory.

Weed's antagonism on the other hand was not feigned. He was intent on recovering and wielding personal power and was a devotee of the new formula which would, eventually, require the elimination of the southern wing from the Whig party. Like some others who had directed the hate campaign against the South, Weed was deeply disturbed by Taylor's growing pre-convention strength. To offset it, Weed at first tried to promote Clay's candidacy. Later the editor talked of Webster, Scott, or McLean as possible compromise candidates between Clay and Taylor. Weed had no real enthusiasm for any of them, but someone or something had to stop Taylor.

Eventually Weed set his course and drew Seward and Horace Greeley to him for help. In the months before the nomination, when one of this triumvirate supported Taylor, the second supported Clay, and the third called for a compromise or maintained a benevolent neutrality toward all candidates. Each switched his position in turn. At length even McLean's manager in New York City became convinced that every move of the three men tended to check the progress of the candidate leading at the moment. He saw them as trying to secure an impasse by balancing the candidates' strength. Once this was achieved, the nomination of a dark horse — possibly Seward — might follow.[7]

Even if the effort failed there was profit in the strategy. The winning candidate's need for the triumverate's good will — in order to assure a maximum campaign effort in New York — would give Weed a strong bargaining position. He could demand either the Vice-Presidency, or a cabinet post, or a Senatorship for Seward, and certainly he could expect a large share of the

---

[7] *Niles' Weekly Register*, 73:19, 20; Poage, *Clay*, 163; see also letter of Seward to Weed, February 2, 1848, Weed Papers, in which he sighs for an "opportunity."

patronage in New York. A New York party that wavered in the choice of a Presidential candidate, therefore, would prepare the way for Weed's return to power.

He left no stone unturned. Early in 1848 he called on Fillmore to talk about Presidential politics. The Albany editor was not completely frank. He explained away his own somersaulting as a way of placing New York Whigs in a position where no matter who was nominated at the national convention, New York would be on the winning side. He urged Fillmore to accept this strategy which, at the outset, required an uncommitted delegation to the nominating convention.

"I will go along with Weed in this," Fillmore informed his former partner, Haven, "as long as it is not harmful to the best interest of the party. But we must win the national election."[8] Weed, of course, did not tell Fillmore of his hopes for Seward. The comptroller, however, knew Weed well enough to realize that he was bargaining for more than position, and that the rumor of Seward becoming a dark horse selection or a Vice-Presidential candidate had some substance behind it. Fillmore, maybe foolishly, did not turn Weed's proposal aside because he, too, saw some advantages in it. Looking ahead to the election, Fillmore was willing to risk the dangers of Weed's maneuverings if, by so doing, he could tie Weed to the Whig cause as it would be defined at the nominating convention. Fillmore had set himself up as a watchdog to guarantee Weed's conformity.[9]

Taylor's managers, meanwhile, had concluded that they must seek support among hesitant Northerners by linking a New England man to Taylor's name in the Vice-Presidency. Fearful of putting an antislavery man there, they settled on Abbott Lawrence. In money-making, if not in politics, few men were more eminent than Abbott Lawrence. He and his brothers, Amos and William, had devoted their lives to amassing a fortune from

[8]Fillmore to Haven, March 15, 1848, Fillmore Mss.
[9]Haven to Fillmore, January 22, February 16, 1848; Hall to Fillmore, February 16, April 3, 1848, Fillmore Collection.

trading and manufacturing textiles. "The sole object of trade is profit," said their eulogizing friend and biographer, Nathan Appleton. "It is true that some modification of the selfish principle may be said to lie at the root of all human action, but nowhere is it so naked and undisguised as in the profession of the merchant, whose direct and avowed object is the getting of gain."[10] So well had the Lawrence brothers succeeded in realizing the philosophy of their profession that by 1847 they had accumulated four and one-half million dollars, which placed them among the ten richest families in the nation.[11]

It was Abbott, the oldest and wealthiest of the brothers, whom Taylor's friends chose as his running mate. The choice was well calculated to serve their ends, but not to allay the anti-slavery Whigs. Instantly the charge arose, even from the Boston circle, that the Taylor-Lawrence team would mean cotton at both ends of the ticket. The Conscience Whigs could find no words strong enough in condemnation.

Fillmore and Weed also gave thought to the Vice-Presidential problem. Instead of being repelled by Lawrence's association with slaveholders, Weed saw an opportunity. By endorsing Lawrence, Weed could obtain an entry into Taylor's camp which might be useful in the future. Fillmore viewed the Vice-Presidential post differently. Even though some of his friends, who had supported him in 1844 for the Vice-Presidency, had begun, once again, to bruit about his name, Fillmore had his eyes on the party's success rather than on personal promotion. This had always been his attitude, and promotions had taken care of themselves. He made no move, consequently, to urge his own candidacy.[12] Rather he continued to watch Weed to see that the editor's talents and following remained staunchly behind Whig fortunes. Had Fillmore had designs on the Vice-Presidency, at this point, he would never have joined with Weed in

[10]Nathan Appleton, "Memoir of Abbott Lawrence," *Collections,* Mass. Historical Society, Sr. 4, 4:495-507.

[11]*Buffalo Express,* September 24, 1847.

[12]The author has been unable to find a single piece of reliable evidence which would indicate that Fillmore was trying to obtain the nomination for himself.

writing to Lawrence and urging the Bostonian to allow his name
to be presented to the national convention.[13] Nor would he
have journeyed later to New York with Weed to consult with
Lawrence at the Astor House.[14]

Fillmore believed that the Whig party needed Weed and
acted accordingly. If no fast friendship existed between the
editor and the comptroller, at least Fillmore bore his colleague
no ill-will. The rest of the group that had worked together in
1846 to reduce Weed's voice in the party were not as magnanimous toward the Albany editor as Fillmore. They were
more inclined to dislike, as well as distrust, him. Among these
were Bokee, Maxwell, Webb, and Brooks — all from New
York City and staunch Taylor supporters. Once the Executive
Mansion was in Whig hands, they had hopes of getting control
of the office of the Collector of the Port of New York. The
patronage power of that office was unequalled in the nation,
and if used properly could easily become the hard core of a
successful political machine. These men believed that they had
manacled Weed in 1846, and at first, as they watched Weed's
gyrations in the Presidential canvass, they had been amused.
Suddenly, possibly on warning from Fillmore, they realized
the implications of Weed's maneuvers. Seward might be imposed
upon them as either President, Vice-President, or Senator. Any
of these offices might give Weed, not themselves, control of
the collector's job. They quickly lost their complacency and
bestirred themselves to ward off Weed's thrust.[15]

Recruits to their cause were easily won. John A. Collier,
an ambitious Binghamton lawyer with a large following in the
southern tier of counties, a self-selected potential governor or
Senator, and often a victim of Weed's scheming, quickly joined
the group. Governor John Young, never Weed's friend, and

---

[13]Weed, *Autobiography*, 578.   [14]*Ibid.*, 585-586.
[15]Webb to Fillmore, March 3, 1848 Brooks to Fillmore, March 16, 1848; Fillmore
Collection; New York *Express*, February 16, 18, March 3, 9, 18, 1848; *Albany
Argus*, January 17, February 4, 7, 13, 26, March 7, April 14, 1848.

indebted to Fillmore for his election, also combined his future with theirs.[16]

Wariness of Weed tied these men together. In their hatred and fear of him, they strained to cut him down before he recovered his old dominion. Fillmore, however, imposed his more moderate attitude on these men, and instead of rashly attacking Weed for his tergiversations, they contented themselves with deep resolves to watch every action of the Albany editor. Time and circumstances appeared stacked against Weed, and unless events went awry at the convention, there existed little need to invite open rupture in this hour of national triumph for the Whig party.

In the spring of 1848, Whigs throughout the nation fought an exciting and bitter campaign among themselves. On one side stood southern partisans arrayed behind Taylor. They were determined to save themselves from their local rivals who were striving to create a sectional consciousness. Joining Dixie's Whigs in support of Taylor were a scattering of Northerners with a nest in New York City, and some Westerners who wanted to realize the benefits of the recent territorial growth.

On the other side was a large gathering of northern Whigs who had either given up hope of political success with the old alliance or who despaired of ever achieving the Whig economic program with an agricultural South and West, under any party label, in control of the national government. They had begun a campaign to unify the North. The voters who listened most attentively to their lashing of the South, however, were less dedicated to the Whig economic program than to the moralists' tenets of antislavery. Confusion over their Presidential candidate reigned among these antisouthern Whigs. Some of their leaders favored Webster, others Scott, and most accepted Clay, but without uniform enthusiasm or sincerity. Their confusion was compounded when a new political organization — the Free

[16]*Ibid.*, March 7, 26, April 14, 18, 1848; New York *Courier and Enquirer*, May and June, 1848, *passim*; Albany *Evening Journal*, May, 1848, *passim*.

Soil party — threatened to steal from northern Whigs both their antislavery and northern agricultural supporters by thumping for free homesteads and nonextension of slavery into the territories. Here was an attempt to create another northern party and some antisouthern Whig leaders advocated union with it.

These rumblings, however, could not divert the Taylorites from their purpose. In the preconvention caucuses, they captured delegation after delegation in the South. Still they knew no rest. As the doubtful delegates from the upper South and the West made their way to Philadelphia, Taylorites met them at the train and tried to convince them that only Taylor could be elected. By the time the convention assembled, Taylor's nomination was almost assured. Yet in spite of the attraction of the Taylor bandwagon, the fear of what Taylor's slaves would do to the vote in the North kept tension high, tempers brittle, and resistance strong. Throughout the proceedings, three-quarters of New York's delegates stubbornly opposed the party's will, and the hope that Clay might stop Taylor still prevailed among them and the rest of the opposition.

The stampede to Taylor developed on the fourth ballot. As member after member arose to promise his support of Taylor, a long period of tumult followed. Taylorites filled the hall with cheers of joy. Glum expressions revealed the undisguised disappointment of Clay's followers. Some men, with horror of having nominated a slaveholder stamped on their faces, frantically made for the platform. Among those who received recognition was slave-hating Charles Allen of Massachusetts. Choking with rage, he jumped to a table and shouted his opposition to Taylor. "The free states will not submit," he proclaimed to the assembled Whigs. The party, by this nomination, "is dissolved." Cheers and hisses arose in a deafening shout from the thoroughly excited convention, and only a quarter-hour of steady gavel rapping and the motion to proceed to the nomination of a candidate for the Vice-Presidency brought the house to order.[17]

[17]New York *Courier and Enquirer*, June 10, 1848.

At this moment, John A. Collier, the most prominent member of the New York delegation, who had been temporary chairman of the convention, seized the floor. He was an experienced and dextrous parliamentarian, with a quick, comprehensive mind, full of resourcefulness and ingenuity. Adroitly and felicitously, he identified himself with the antisouthern faction. He was chosen, he said, as a delegate for Clay for whom he had labored earnestly. He had voted for Clay on every ballot and was deeply disappointed at the result. But, he concluded, he was determined to support the convention's nomination, and magnanimously pledged New York State to the candidate. The convention was rapturous, and Collier had his audience's sympathy.[18]

With an eloquent picture of the sorrow and bitterness of Clay's friends before the assembly, Collier announced that he had a peace offering to suggest, which, if accepted, would reconcile the supporters of all the defeated candidates and prevent a fatal breach in the party. The delegates waited with bated breath. To the astonishment of his audience, he named Millard Fillmore for Vice-President.[19]

The speech, pitched in a subtle key, was perfectly timed to produce the desired effect. The nomination of Fillmore was assured the moment Collier mentioned his name. For a moment friends of Lawrence rallied to prevent a unanimous nomination, but not enough to stop Fillmore's nomination on the second ballot. Collier had achieved a *coup d'état*.

Fillmore had usurped the position of Lawrence on the Taylor ticket by an appeal that identified him with Henry Clay. Nothing could have been further from the truth. Not then nor ever was he a Clay man. To uninformed delegates, who were anxious to appease a hotheaded antisouthern faction for the sake of unity, Fillmore appeared to represent the peace offering pictured by Collier. Delegates remembered Fillmore for his tariff of 1842 and his intimate connection with the Whig program of 1842

[18]*Ibid.*, June 11, 1848.   [19]*Ibid.*

which Clay had directed. They remembered him for his gallant fight in 1844 to keep the antislavery vote of New York in the Whig column. They saw him now as a candidate from the North not identified with Taylor and, therefore, by specious reasoning, a Clay man. Most of New York had been in the Clay column on the Presidential balloting, and Fillmore was a New Yorker — and Collier implied he was a Clay man.

Collier had seized his opportunity to nominate Fillmore for reasons he had not stated. He wanted to prevent Seward from gaining the post, for Seward's name was before the convention, too. By so doing Collier would block one road for Weed's return to power. Collier also had a personal goal. He had seen a chance of becoming New York's junior Senator if the most available Whig in New York — Fillmore — were away in the Vice-Presidency. Rumor later charged Fillmore and Collier with scheming toward this end.[20] Rumor was partially justified, but never substantiated, when Fillmore's friends supported Collier for the Senatorship in January, 1849.[21]

No sooner had the campaign begun than Fillmore proceeded to demonstrate that he was no Clay man, nor an antislavery man in the sense that he had an intention of doing anything about slavery.

The Whig convention had met and adjourned without writing a platform of any kind. It would have been impossible to frame one. So it was up to the candidates to write it as the canvass progressed. Constantly the Democrats tried to embarrass the Whigs by pointing out that the Whigs were proslavery in the South and antislavery in the North.

In the South, Democrats attacked Fillmore by distorting the record. They made every effort to discredit him as an antislavery man. They even charged him with claiming that Congress had power to stop the interstate slave trade. Quickly he branded this charge as a lie.[22]

20*Albany Argus*, July 10, 1848; *Buffalo Express*, August 8, 1848, January 7, 1849.
21*Albany Argus*, January 2-14, 1849; Albany *Evening Journal*, January 2-15, 1849.
22Fillmore to Brooks, September 13, 1848, *Fillmore Papers*, 2:282.

On another occasion Fillmore informed Southerners that he had always "regarded slavery as an evil, but one with which the National Government had nothing to do. That by the Constitution of the United States the whole power over that question was vested in the several states where the institution was tolerated. If they regarded it as a blessing, they had a constitutional right to enjoy it; and if they regarded it as an evil, they had the power and knew best how to apply the remedy. I did not conceive," Fillmore continued, as he explained his record to the South, "that Congress had any power over it, or was in any way responsible for its continuance over the several states where it existed."[23]

Yet his southern friends were hard put to convince the South that he was not an abolitionist. A Rough and Ready club came to his rescue with a resolution "that the charge of Abolitionism recklessly advanced against Millard Fillmore, by unscrupulous partisan opponents, for the purpose of exciting sectional prejudice against him, has no foundation whatever in truth; but on the contrary is triumphantly disproved by the solemn declaration of our candidate for the Vice-Presidency, uttered long since in the councils of the Nation, that Congress has no power, under the constitution, to interfere with the institution of domestic slavery as it exists in the states of this union. . . ."[24] Whigs gave the resolution wide circulation, and Fillmore openly admitted that the resolutions "truly define my position and express my views on the subject."[25]

Yet in all his public utterances on slavery Fillmore never once mentioned slavery in the territory or the federal government's responsibility for it there. Likewise, to keep his appeal to the widest extent, he gracefully turned aside the advances of the Native Americans to commit himself on their program.[26] At the same time he bid for the Irish vote by extending his sympathy for Ireland's plight in famine and subjugation to England.[27]

23Fillmore to Gayle, July 31, 1848, *ibid.*, 2:280-81.
24Editor's note, Fillmore to Peyton, *ibid.*
25*Ibid.*
26Fillmore to Gowan, June 17, 1848, *ibid.*, 2:277-78.
27Fillmore to Titus and others, May 30, 1848, *ibid.*, 2:275-76.

As serious as the charges of abolitionism were to Fillmore in the South, his greatest trial came in the North. Smoldering resentment over Taylor's nomination was carried northward from the convention hall. Here and there an unregenerate called loudly upon northern Whigs to repudiate their slaveholding and slave-sponsored candidate. The clarion calls resounded in a wilderness until late in August when Taylor accepted the nomination of a small meeting of Charleston Democrats. Suddenly wild speculation swirled through the party structure and fanned the resentment into flames of destruction. Whigs immediately recalled that previous to his nomination, Taylor and his managers had played the nonpartisan game. It had been a shrewd game — and well calculated to cut deep into Democratic votes. But in the preconvention campaign it had set ill with staunch Whigs who disliked Taylor's agrarian support. They had brandished his nonpartisanship as tantamount to treason. They had remembered that the last man they had taken to their bosom for expediency — Tyler — had left them pinioned on expectancy.

At one point in the preconvention maneuvers, Taylor's managers had sought to frighten Whigs into abandoning Clay by having the General inform the world he intended to run regardless of the action of either Democrats or Whigs.[28] Northern Whig supporters who were more interested in measures than men had seen this as a threat to their well-being, and it had bolstered their determination to stop Taylor. A few days later, more judicious managers had hastily tried to withdraw this threat by having their candidate testify that he was a Whig who, if elected, would follow the nation's will as expressed in Congress.[29] But the second statement had only partially dispelled the distrust. Now suddenly Taylor came forth to accept the nomination of some Democrats. The news was received with indignation and incredulity, and among Whigs distrust resurged.[30]

In New York resentment flourished. Because Democrats

[28]The Richmond *Whig,* letter of April 20, 1848.
[29]First Allison Letter of April 22, 1848.
[30]Albany *Evening Journal,* August 21, 22, 1848; New York *Tribune,* August 21, 22, 1848; New York *Express,* August 22, 1848.

there had lost large numbers of both their workers and voters when Van Buren became the candidate of the Free Soil party, Whigs felt certain of a state victory no matter what happened nationally. Seward and Weed, moreover, had no enthusiasm for the election of either Taylor or Fillmore. Rather the national ticket appeared to be a hindrance to their ambitions.

Meantime Weed's prospect for recovering authority in the state improved when his candidate for the gubernatorial nomination, Hamilton Fish, began to get the support of the other faction. So cleverly had Fish's candidacy been managed that few appreciated that he was Weed's minion.[31] Sniffing local victory in the air, and uncertain of what a national Whig victory might do to his hopes, Weed felt that he could safely tamper with the national ticket at the coming Whig state convention. Taylor's acceptance of a Democratic nomination, and the fears it caused, pointed toward a strategy. Weed's focus was made sharper when Horace Greeley openly advocated scuttling Taylor in favor of Clay.[32] If New York's state convention were to select a panel of unpledged Presidential electors, other states might follow suit and change the whole national complexion of the Whig party. Win or lose, Weed and his alter-ego, Seward, would avoid the future onus of having traveled with Taylor and proslavery. Thus to create the necessary pressure on the state convention to desert Taylor, Weed put out a hurried call for a mass meeting of Whigs.[33]

On hearing of Weed's rumored design to bolt Taylor, Fillmore blanched. Whatever he thought of Taylor, Fillmore's whole future, and that of the Whig party, were tied to the Presidential candidate. With more heat than dignity, Fillmore sought out Weed in his editorial office to demand that the mass meeting be called off. Instead of being disdainful of Fillmore's request, the editor was all charm and suave concern for the wel-

[31]New York *Courier and Enquirer*, May and June, 1848, *passim*; Albany *Evening Journal*, May, 1848, *passim*.
[32]New York *Tribune*, June 20, July 7, 19, 30, August 1, 3, 8, 1848.
[33]Albany *Evening Journal*, August 22, 1848; Fuller to Fillmore April 15, 1848, Fillmore Collection.

fare of the party and Fillmore's election. Quietly and persuasively, but without revealing his ultimate purpose, Weed set about, in his most winning manner, to draw Fillmore into the scheme. But the Vice-Presidential candidate would not be trapped. The latent power that could raise him above himself in a crisis slowly began to have its effect on Weed as the two men spent the afternoon in consultation. Late that afternoon they abandoned the office and walked together to the steamboat landing to meet Mrs. Fillmore arriving from New York. On the way an agreement was reached. The mass meeting Weed had called would be held; but Weed succumbed to Fillmore's demand that "resolutions calculated to subdue the excitement should be adopted." With the bargain sealed the two men parted temporarily as Fillmore accompanied Mrs. Fillmore to the hotel, and Weed went back to his office to write the resolution.[34]

That evening, just at dusk, Fillmore re-entered the printing office and found Weed hunched over his desk, drawing up the resolutions. After a moment, Weed read them. Again alarm seized Fillmore. Weed had changed his mind and had phrased the resolutions in a way which would not allay excitement, but "defeat General Taylor."[35] All evening the two men stayed at the office and wrangled over the proposed mass meeting. Finally Fillmore again prevailed. They agreed on two points: first the mass meeting would convene the next day in the rotunda of the Capitol and be postponed for two days without any action being taken; and second, the two men would address a letter to Taylor and point the way out of the embarrassment to which he was subjecting the Whigs throughout the North.[36]

As agreed, the meeting was postponed through the diligent work of John A. Collier, and two nights later, the deliberations of the meeting were conducted and concluded precisely as Fillmore desired. The whole purpose of the mass meeting was turned on end. Instead of becoming a sounding board for dis-

[34]Barnes, *Weed*, 169-71.
[35]Fillmore to Brooks, February 10, 1855, *Fillmore Papers*, 2:350-51.
[36]Barnes, *Weed*, 169-70.

content with Taylor, it became the forum for discrediting Taylor's detractors. The resolutions it adopted asserted that New York Whigs found nothing in Taylor's action inconsistent with the welfare of the party. With that the meeting adjourned with cheers for Taylor and Fillmore.[37]

The letter that Fillmore and Weed had composed now went out under Fillmore's name to Taylor. The Presidential candidate, replying immediately, thanked Fillmore for his advice and promised to write again to his kinsman, Captain J. S. Allison, in a public letter and clarify his position. On September 4, Taylor's advisers wrote the letter in essentially the form Fillmore had suggested. Taylor, as a result, clearly defined himself as a Whig who would give Congress its head.[38]

This Allison letter salved wounded Whig spirits and quieted northern Whig carpers. Fillmore's successful joust with Weed saved the unity of the Whig party in New York. When the election returns were counted two months later, party statisticians who knew what had transpired in the office of the Albany *Evening Journal* paused momentarily in their celebration and shuddered at what might have happened. The election returns were close, and the Taylor-Fillmore victory had pivoted on New York's vote. Later even Weed admitted that had a fourth Presidential candidate been introduced into the New York election, Lewis Cass, the Democratic contender, would have carried the state and the election.[39]

For his role, Fillmore should have earned the gratitude of Taylor and the Whig party. But instead of bragging about his assistance and obtaining that gratitude, he was content to bask in the bright prospects of the future. As yet he did not anticipate Weed's next move.

[37]Albany *Evening Journal,* August 25, 1848.
[38]Weed, *Autobiography,* 579-83.   [39]Barnes, *Weed,* 171.

Chapter 11

"We could put up a cow . . . . "

HE FOUR months between election and inauguration were joyous for Fillmore. Wherever he went he exuded geniality and gracious charm. The week after the election, he went down the river from Albany to New York City to take part in a gala Whig celebration. "The versatile people were full of demonstrations of affection to the Vice-President," reported Seward, with a tinge of bitterness.[1] But in this, as in other public appearances, Fillmore's pink, rotund face glowed with good humor.

He had attained a position of real prestige, and the word was about that it would be one of influence, too. General Taylor, conscious of the great burdens that lay ahead of him, had sighed: "I wish Mr. Fillmore would take all of the business into his own hands. . . ."[2] With his naiveté concerning civil affairs, Taylor believed that the Vice-President was a member of the cabinet.

So certain was Fillmore of his position that he remained in Albany until the eve of inauguration to place the affairs of the comptroller's office in order. Blinded by the sudden shift in his career, he permitted magnanimity to dim his political vision.

[1]Seward to Weed, November 13, 1848, Weed Papers.
[2]Reported in Charles to Weed, January 14, 1849, Weed Papers.

The glow of success even corroded the hard principle of caution with which he regarded his New York rivals. Little did Fillmore appreciate that soon his exalted flight, like that of Icarus, would end in a plunge to the sea.

During these months the main issue of the day came no closer to a solution. Almost a year had passed since the treaty of Guadalupe Hidalgo had wrested California and New Mexico from America's southern neighbor. Meanwhile, the discovery of gold, like a lodestone, had attracted thousands of immigrants to the area. Bold adventurers crowded into the Eldorado, found their gold, and in doing so, forsook law and order. Only a military officer with a handful of soldiers stood by to protect the rights and privileges of inhabitants. Any observer of the national scene could perceive that Congress had no choice but to establish a strong civil government in the far western province.

Months were to pass, however, before Congressmen took up their obligation to the people of the Southwest — months devoted to pursuing patronage and maneuvering for position in the councils of the nation. In true political fashion, instead of dispatching their duties with vision, the nation's representatives approached the territorial problem only as a stage for other battles. No responsible officer seemed to care what happened to the people of California; rather, all were concerned with using the California and territorial issue to promote their own ambitions.

The plotters of one camp came from among the President's staunchest friends. They originally had urged Taylor's election as a way of stopping the corrosive effect of the free-soil movement in the northern wing of their party. This antislavery movement, because it threatened to drive the Whig voters of the South into Democratic ranks, had embarrassed these southern Whigs. Consequently, when Taylor was nominated they had sighed with relief. A Louisiana slaveholder at the head of the party, they reasoned, certainly would quiet the carpers at slavery in their own party and make the Whig label respectable in the South.

No sooner was Taylor elected than new circumstances, apparently, called for new objectives. Rather than purging the party of its free-soilers, self-perpetuation in office and re-election four years hence became the goal among many, with people such as William M. Meredith, William B. Preston, and John M. Clayton leading the way.

These three men, gathered together in the cabinet (Treasury, Navy, and State), guided many aspects of the politics of Taylor's administration. They induced Taylor to limit the influence of the extreme southern voice in Administration councils because victory in 1852 would require the support of the northern wing of the party. To win that support would necessitate an alliance with men like Weed and Seward. This then became the grand political strategy of Taylor's advisers, and it was a complete about-face from the original goal of the Taylorites.

*   *   *   *   *

During the months between election and inauguration, Weed and Seward did not suspect that Taylor's advisers were open to an alliance. Had the New York boss and his alter-ego perceived the aims of Clayton, Meredith, and Preston, the future would have looked less somber. Since only the election of Fillmore gave them a clue as to the future, they despaired. Weed thought long and hard about his predicament. For four years New Yorkers had strained to keep him from securing dictatorial power. Repeatedly, Fillmore had joined Weed's enemies, and now Weed saw Fillmore becoming the "New York leader in the general council of the Whigs of the Union."[3] For the next four, or even eight years, Weed and Seward faced the unpleasant prospect of opposing him.[4] Nor were they alone in this expectation. From New York City, Seward reported that the "politicians . . . are engaged in plans to take possession of General Taylor . . . . Weed is to be supplanted . . . ."[5]

Weed could see only one exit from his predicament. He

[3]Seward to Weed, June 10, 1848, Weed Papers.
[4]*Ibid.*
[5]Frederick W. Seward, *Seward at Washington*, 2:87.

had to curtail Fillmore's looming power. He must have a counterpoise to Fillmore at Washington. John A. Dix, New York's Senator, was about to retire, and Weed saw in this vacancy his means of salvation. He began to prepare for Seward's election to the post.

The former governor's old enemies, however, were ubiquitous. They had neither forgotten his distribution of patronage nor forgiven his sycophancy to Weed. Assuming that Seward as Senator would be harmful to their interests, they concentrated on his defeat by supporting John A. Collier.[6] It added to their strength, moreover, that Fillmore and Collier were friends. Collier's speech at Philadelphia had made Fillmore Vice-President, and his following naturally favored Collier. It was a noisy company, and for a time, gave Seward formidable opposition.

Between November and January, when the state legislature was to select the new Senator, intrigue became bolder. Some thought of compromising by switching to Hamilton Fish or Washington Hunt.[7] Though Seward modestly absented himself from the state, the harried Weed kept closely in touch with the political situation. At the crucial point, when Collier's chances soared, Weed made an audacious move. He appealed to his intended victim — Fillmore — for help.

Weed's cleverness was unbounded when his political objectives were at stake. He approached Fillmore when the Vice-President-elect's guard was down. In twenty years of association, Fillmore had had ample opportunity to become acquainted with Weed's habits, but the blandishments of the editor convinced Fillmore that Weed for once would rise above his habits. Weed asked Fillmore's support for Seward in the coming legislative caucus. For this support, Weed pledged himself and Seward to cooperate with Fillmore in every way for joint control of the state. To Fillmore and Weed, this meant consultation and

---

[6]New York *Express*, August 27, 30, September 6, 7, 9, 14, October 23, November 6, 9, 15, December 2, 14, 18, 30, 1848.
[7]*Ibid.*, December 5, 18, 20, 1848; New York *Herald*, December 15, 18, 28, 1848.

agreement on the distribution of federal and state patronage. It was wise politics for Fillmore to secure such a promise on the eve of a national career. It was also for the best interest of the party. In good faith, but with bad judgment, he accepted Weed's offered partnership. Instead of continuing in the anti-Seward movement, Fillmore encouraged all his political friends in the legislative caucus to accept Seward. As a result Seward won.[8]

Just before leaving for Washington in late February, 1849, Fillmore dined with Seward and Weed at Albany. It was a love feast. Pledges of cooperation and openhanded relations were renewed. Everything was pleasantly arranged. "The Vice-President and Senator were to consult from time to time, as should become necessary, and agree upon the important appointments to be made in our state," recorded Weed.[9]

Seward's private instructions were different. As Weed's emissary, Seward had a two-fold task: to destroy Fillmore's possible control over the federal patronage for New York and secure that control for Weed's machine; and to ween Taylor away from southern influence.[10]

*   *   *   *   *

Inauguration day, Monday March 5, dawned chilled and cloudy. A hint of snow freshened the air, but the snow itself would not arrive until after the ceremonies. As usual, Fillmore arose early that morning even though the official carriage that would carry him and the retiring Vice-President, George Dallas, to the capitol would not arrive until 11 o'clock. He was staying at the Willard, his old haunt when he had been a Congressman.

A week before, when he had first arrived in Washington, Fillmore had found Zachary Taylor at the Willard, too. Immediately he had paid his respects to the President-elect. Nothing but pleasantries had passed between them. They had been thrown

[8]Hall to Fillmore, December 22, 1849, Fillmore Collection, cf. with Barnes, *Memoir of Weed*, 174; New York *Herald*, December 15, 18, 28, 1848.
[9]Weed, *Autobiography*, 586-587.
[10]Seward to Weed, February 21, 1849, Weed Papers.

together again on March 1 at a White House dinner that President Polk gave for the incoming administration. About forty leading statesmen of the day — both Democrats and Whigs — had been present, but "not the slightest allusion was made to any political subject."[11] And so it had gone all week long. A steady line of visitors had pressed to see the President-elect, but Fillmore had been too considerate to press his own attention upon Taylor in the last days before inauguration. For his part, Taylor was still putting together his own cabinet, yet never once did he call upon his running mate, whose knowledge of the party's leaders went back twenty years, for advice. At this point the oversight had caused Fillmore no concern.

Throngs of visitors, meanwhile, had been arriving for several days at the capital by rail, steamboat, carriage, horseback, and even on foot. Washington's overnight accommodations were filled beyond capacity, and though the uncomfortable patrons paid record high prices, they still kept coming. Eventually the sightseers, office seekers, and well-wishers formed the largest inaugural crowd in the city's memory, and an infectious din of merriment seeped into every corner of the city. By inauguration day nasty weather could not dampen the holiday mood that had seized the visitors as they gathered for the parade down Pennsylvania Avenue to the capitol, and pressed in around the temporary platform before the capitol steps.[12]

It was, of course, more Zachary Taylor's day than Fillmore's, but as the Vice-President-elect drove along the Avenue, thousands of Americans, of all parties, cheered. Fillmore's broad, flushed face beamed with the spirit of the day, and as he removed his hat from time to time — his long white hair flowing in the breeze, his kindly blue eyes surveying the crowd — he looked the picture of dignity and propriety.

His own inauguration ceremonies, unlike the President's, took place in the Senate chamber, the right wing of the stately

[11]Milo M. Quaife, ed., *Diary of J. K. Polk*, 4:352-353.
[12]*National Intelligencer*, March 1, 4, 5, 1849.

white building of the lawmakers and Supreme Court justices. Visitors had never failed to be delighted with this classic little Senate hall, redolent of the genius of Latrobe.[13] Solemnly, and flanked by a Senatorial honor committee, Fillmore entered shortly before noon with the thought that he would spend his next four years in the intimate quarters of this semicircle presiding over the debates of statesmen. But now the room was packed with all sorts of celebrities. Even while Congress was in session, visitors had always found it easy to crowd into the room and rub elbows with the Senators themselves. On this festive occasion, it was, therefore, no surprise to see celebrities and their ladies, dressed in the height of fashion, mingling with the legislators. The tiny visitors' gallery, too, was so crammed that before the ceremonies started three women fainted.[14]

As Fillmore stepped forward to take his oath, the buzz of voices subsided, but the rustling silk and endless flutter of fans continued to punctuate the silence. His own expression was serious, but as he repeated the oath after the Chief Justice, his voice was loud and deep. Then he turned to the Senators — for the Upper House was in official session to seat their presiding officer — and briefly addressed the legislators. He expressed his faith in America's "capacity for self-government," and looking into the future, he hoped that this capacity, even in times of extreme crisis, might carry on so that "the glorious Union may endure forever." It was a short panegyric on the processes of American government, and a vague call for patriotism in the impending crisis.[15] Politely the assemblage heard him out, and then adjourned. Noisily and cheerfully, all moved outside, as if by signal, to the steps of the capitol where in a few more minutes, Zachary Taylor performed the main show of the day.

That evening Fillmore drove from the White House with President Taylor through a snow storm and over Washington's rutted streets to three inaugural balls. Their first stop was Carusi's

[13]Harriet Martineau, *Society in America*, 1:180.
[14]*National Intelligencer*, March 6, 1849.
[15]*Fillmore Papers*, 1:287-288.

Saloon, on the northeast corner of Eleventh and C Streets, where visiting soldiers were being entertained. They then made their way to Jackson Hall, on Pennsylvania Avenue, where the Democrats danced away the disappointments of defeat. Finally, an hour before midnight, Fillmore and Taylor reached the City Hall. Here between four and five thousand persons were present to greet the President's party and to dance the new Administration into power. As the evening grew older the veneer of grace wore thin, and bejeweled guests, in all their finery, pushed to the tables for refreshments and struggled for room on the dance floor. Long before the dawn, when the festivities ended, Fillmore had returned to the Willard tired and a little nettled. Though he had been in the company of the President all evening, he was no closer to him now that he had been a week before. Either Taylor's warmth for his Vice-President — so evident after the election — had been mere civility or, in the intervening months, his advisers had made him extremely circumspect.[16]

* * * * *

If Fillmore's stock had neither risen nor fallen as a result of his brief encounter with the President, happenstance was aiding Seward in his plan to deal the Vice-President a mortal blow. As soon as Seward arrived in Washington he began to work furtively for the grand objective.[17] He cultivated Taylor's brother as a way of finding a back door to the President's favor, and he made a point of becoming intimate with all potential and indicated cabinet officers. On March 1, he reported to Weed: "General Taylor, Mr. Clayton and Mr. Ewing are frank, open and confiding towards me."[18]

Seward's careful buttonholing of high ranking men of Taylor's administration might have won him nothing had not the triumvirate of Clayton, Meredith, and Preston been ready with their own ideas. It was obvious to them that their plans for the future could not succeed without the support of northern

[16]*National Intelligencer*, March 6, 1849; H. Hamilton, *Taylor*, 2:149-161.
[17]Seward to Weed, February 23, 1849, Weed Papers; New York *Express*, February 21, 23, 28, 1849.
[18]Seward to Weed, March 1, 1849, Weed Papers.

Whigs. In the past two years on the main issue of the day —
slavery in the territories — these northern Whigs had identified
themselves as friends of the Wilmot Proviso. To obtain their
support, Taylor's administration must give them the substance
of the Proviso, but at the same time Taylor's advisers knew that
they must avoid alienating southern Whigs.

The task of placing the Administration on both sides of
the territorial issue looked like a juggling act that must fail. Yet
the President's advisers had faith in their own ability to succeed.
Already they had experimented with a promising technique.
Both Clayton and Preston, serving out Senatorial terms before
taking on their cabinet posts, had just come away from the lame-
duck session of the Upper House where they had urged dividing
the Mexican cession into states and admitting them to the Union.
Territorial status would thus be avoided and the new states,
rather than Washington, would decide the question of slavery
for themselves. By accepting this course of action Taylor's
administration could escape the vexing problem of going on
record in favor of free or slave territory and could parry the
charge of free-soilism that might come from the South. Moreover, since the preponderance of the population in the Far West
was antislavery, the plotters could expect that their policy would
result in creating free states. By the *fait accompli* of statehood,
Preston and Clayton — later Meredith — hoped to achieve the
objective of the Proviso without endorsing it. It was cunning
politics.

In the coming months they were to do their work well. A
few weeks after the inauguration President Taylor would send
Thomas Butler King, a prominent Whig representative from
Georgia, and several army officers to California. With the
cooperation of the military commander already there, Taylor's
agents would prod Californians into a seemingly spontaneous
movement for statehood. A convention would meet and draft
a constitution, and the military would turn over the reins of
government to this illegally conceived state. By the time Congress
reassembled in December, 1849, "free" California's two Senators

would be on their way east prepared to request their seats in Congress.

Because of this high-level scheming, Seward had an opportunity to work his way into the confidence of the Administration. While King and the army were moving west, Taylor's advisers sought to find friends in Congress against the day when Taylor revealed his hand. Seward's happiest stroke of fortune came when Preston consulted him. By this meeting an alliance between Taylor's administration and the Weed machine began to form. At first, and possibly never, Taylor was not fully apprised of the purpose of his advisers. As a result the alliance started out as an attestation of friendship. Eventually, however, the metes and bounds of the agreement were set. For Seward's support, Weed would have control, with rare exceptions, of the patronage controlled by Preston, Clayton, and Meredith in New York — irrespective of the agreement between Fillmore and Weed. Caution would be exercised, however, to give the impression that the Albany agreement between Weed and Fillmore was recognized by the Administration.[19]

Through all these preliminaries Fillmore remained ignorant of Seward's moves. Instead, the Vice-President was painfully conscious of the pressure of office seekers for decisions; and still innocently expecting to be guided by the Albany agreement, he approached Seward. The Senator, at the crux of establishing himself with Taylor's advisers, begged Fillmore for time in deciding on appointments. "I have stipulated," Seward wrote to Weed, "for time and inaction concerning marshals, postmasters, district-attorneys, and there I leave these matters."[20]

On one appointment action could not be avoided. For important services rendered before the nomination, Taylor gave his New York City friends the privilege of naming the revenue collector for the Port of New York, which, except for several

[19]Poage, *Clay*, 219-220; Seward to Weed, March 3, 1849, Weed Papers.
[20]Seward to Weed, February 21, 1849, *ibid.*

cabinet posts, was the most important appointing office in the nation. On receiving the news New Yorkers gloated with satisfaction and quickly settled on John Young, former governor and hated enemy of Weed and Seward. By this time, however, Seward was sufficiently close to the Secretary of the Treasury to persuade Meredith to block the appointment. As a result the Administration asked the New Yorkers to name another. This time they chose Hugh Maxwell. The choice still did not meet the approval of Weed, but as yet Weed and Seward dared not reveal their hand too openly and had to acquiesce. Possibly the Senate might fail to confirm Maxwell.[21]

Had the collector's job in New York's port been kept open a while longer, Weed might have had more success. A short time later Clayton was ready to dispose of one of New York's more influential offices, that of marshal of the northern district. By arrangements with the Secretary of State, Fillmore and Seward agreed to meet on a fixed date in Clayton's office and offer him a candidate satisfactory to both men. When the scheduled day arrived Clayton postponed the meeting and set another day. Taking advantage of the interval, Seward and Weed arranged a hoax. A messenger appeared at Clayton's office and pretended to be sent from both Seward and Fillmore with the name of their selection — P. V. Kellogg. Actually Kellogg was Weed's selection, and the messenger's story was a blatant lie. Before Fillmore knew what had taken place, Clayton accepted the decision and recommended Kellogg to Taylor, who readily acceded.[22]

Now, at last, Fillmore discovered how he was being duped. He realized again that the pledge of Weed and Seward was black with insincerity. Quickly he appealed to Taylor, but the President refused to act without consulting Clayton.[23] How Taylor would finally act would determine the future of New York's party. A crisis in the plans of Weed and Seward was at hand.

[21]Seward to Weed, February 23, 1849, *ibid.*, New York *Express,* February 21, 23, 28, 1848.
[22]*Buffalo Express,* May 9, 1849; Fillmore to Taylor, March 22, 1849, Fillmore Mss.
[23]*Ibid.*

At this point, Weed, unwilling to trust such fine manipulation to Seward's less dextrous hands, hurried to Washington. He made haste to see the President's brother and indirectly caused himself to be sent for by the President. Publicly Taylor wanted to stand with neither faction, but privately the influence of the triumvirate began to show. By the time Weed left the White House, he had convinced the "old man" that he, too, desired peace; that the struggle between Seward and Fillmore was purely personal, and that all New York Whigs were in favor of harmony. With deft logic, but tongue in cheek, Weed persuaded Taylor that the surest way to solve the problem was to take patronage out of the hands of Fillmore and Seward and put it in the hands of Governor Fish, who all agreed was unbiased. The President was delighted with the solution and might even have suspected that Fish was Weed's tool. With the point established, Weed left town. To Seward he left the task of polishing his gem of deceit.[24]

By March 24, 1849, Seward could write to Weed: "Well! The beginning has been successful beyond anticipation. Things have ripened until suspicion has given place to confidence, and weakness to strength. . . . The cabinet are sound, the Senators wise. . . . Let Governor Fish now write to me when you have advice to give the Cabinet. Some of the members take *that* point with great respect. It is the state administration at Albany that is to be strengthened, and the Governor is its acknowledged head. This saves the necessity of deciding between the V. P. and the Senator."[25]

Leaving matters to the governor meant supremacy in the state for Seward and Weed. Fillmore's candle was not entirely snuffed out, but it soon ceased to be counted as one of the lights of the Administration. Both Seward's aim to secure control of

[24]Haven to Fillmore, April 2, 24, May 2, 1849, Fillmore Collection; Stetson to Weed, January 14, 1849, Seward to Weed, March 16, 19, 21, 23, 25, 1849, Weed Papers; Albany *Evening Journal*, March 29, 1849; Seward, *Seward at Washington*, 2:87, 106; Frederic Bancroft, *The Life of William H. Seward*, 1:215-216.
[25]Seward, *Seward at Washington*, 2:107.

New York patronage and the cabal's desire to win Seward's support were accomplished.

With the mask torn from his pretense, Weed now opened his attack on the Vice-President. Soon Fillmore was to learn how merciless Weed could be. Fillmore's recommendation of John A. Collier as New York naval officer was ignored in favor of Philip Hone, whom Weed had designated. The postoffice job in New York City eluded Fillmore's man because of the prodding at Washington of Bishop Hughes, who had in turn been prodded by Seward.[26] Simultaneously, Weed turned loose an undercover campaign in New York State to undermine Fillmore. Agents appeared in every county to prepare delegates for the coming state nominating convention and to proselytize among state officers for pledges to oppose Fillmore and his friends.[27]

In May, 1849, Weed delivered the *coup de grace*. He invaded western New York and Buffalo itself. In Fillmore's political fortress, Weed found a partially illiterate political hack, Levi Allen, whom Meredith appointed collector of the Port of Buffalo over Fillmore's candidate, William Ketchum.[28] Weed chortled over his triumph and unleashed a belittling press campaign. A Vice-President, ran the cant, could never wield any authority, so any man with ambition for appointment should abandon him. "We could put up a cow against a Fillmore nominee and defeat him," gibed the Weed press and pointed to Buffalo as proof.[29] The unpledged members of the party flocked to Weed and deserted Fillmore as too feeble to aid even his closest friends. His popularity plummetted, and lukewarm friends, failing to win offices, took up the germ of Weed's besmirching and complained loudly that Fillmore should have protected their interests.[30]

[26]Haven to Fillmore, April 2, June 7, December 26, 1849, Fillmore Collection.
[27]Hall to Fillmore, December 22, 1849, *ibid*.
[28]Hall to Fillmore, December 19, 1849, *ibid*.
[29]Buffalo *Express*, May 31, 1849; Fillmore to Hall, December 18, 1849, Fillmore Mss.
[30]Buffalo *Express*, May 24, 1849.

By mid-1849, Fillmore's situation had become desperate. A half year had wrought a political revolution. Weed had recovered a great deal of the power he had lost in the previous four years and was using it to destroy the Vice-President. The battle of patronage on which the revolution turned, Fillmore had lost by being generous of heart and magnanimous of spirit.

* * * * *

Fillmore was not alone in his hour of distress. By summer, events in California and the assignment of places in New York aroused suspicions in at least two camps. New York City politicos looked askance at the federal appointments in their state and soon began to complain as their suspicion of Taylor's administration became aroused.[31]

Southward in Dixie a group of keen-nosed Taylor supporters scented trouble. Almost as soon as the understanding between Seward and Preston was reached, the highly perceptive Alexander H. Stephens suspected it. He drew Secretary of War Crawford and Georgia's Robert Toombs into his confidence. During the summer of 1849 they confirmed their suspicions. The Administration's encouragement of free-soilism augured ill for southern Whigs. To reidentify the Whig party with the Wilmot Proviso would cast the fortunes of southern Whigs back to the nadir of 1846-1848.[32]

Among the victims of the grand strategy, none fully knew how thoroughly the Administration had adopted the goal of the Wilmot Proviso. All suspected that Seward had cast a spell over the President. All professed to think that the spell could

---

[31] *Journal of Commerce*, January 8, 10, 1850; Charleston *Mercury*, reported in New York *Post*, September 15, 1849; Richmond *Enquirer* in New York *Express*, February 5, 1850; New Orleans *Commercial Bulletin* in *Journal of Commerce*, January 8, 1850; see also "A Traveller" in *ibid.*, January 24, 1850; Barnard to Fillmore, January 31, 1850, Fillmore Collection.

[32] Clayton to Crittenden, December 13, 1848, April 18, 1849, Crittenden Papers; Crittenden to Clayton, December 19, 1848, April 11, 1849, Clayton Papers; G. Duncan to Crittenden, January 15, 1849, Crittenden Papers; Morehead to Crittenden, December 25, 1849, Crittenden Papers; Washington *Republic*, December 19, 24, 1849, January 6, 1850.

be broken by appealing directly to Taylor. All — Fillmore and his friends, the New York City politicos, and Stephens, Toombs and their segment of southern Whigs — marked time. They awaited the reopening of Congress before making a final judgment. As yet none cared to brand as traitorous his own party's Administration.[33]

Chapter 12

Toward the Compromise of 1850

Y THE time Congress assembled in early December, 1849, intense distaste for Taylor's program in California had seized wide segments of the South. During the summer and fall, rabid prosoutherners had learned enough to arouse them to extreme acts. In October a Mississippi state convention had called upon all slaveholding states to send delegates to a "Southern Convention." It would meet on the first Monday in June, 1850, probably after Congress had adjourned, and pass judgment on the Administration's activities. South Carolinians, meanwhile, expecting the worst, had formed committees of safety and correspondence in imitation of the American Revolutionists and were prepared for rebellion. Mississippi, Florida, and North Carolina legislatures had passed resolutions in defense of slavery's interests in the territories; other meetings in Alabama, Georgia, and Tennessee also indicated a strong leaning toward united southern resistance to Taylor's plan. As if he were speaking for all the discontented of the South, J. H. Hammond shouted out that there was a growing conviction that the Union had always "been and always . . . [would] be a disadvantage" to the South. Observers everywhere could readily see that the

"President's Plan" for California was causing a southern reaction that might erupt at any moment into strident nationalism.[1]

The display would have been less alarming had it been confined to Democrats. But some southern Whigs were lending their weight to the movement, and what might have otherwise been simple partisanship now became a dangerous affair.

These southern Whigs had no real desire either to carry slaves into the territories or to make the West into slave states. Under different circumstances, they could easily have settled for a "free" California. Yet they dared not act on their feelings. In the mind of many southern voters a generation of propagandists had planted the idea that the South was a national entity deserving of patriotic loyalty. To this concept all southern public men must either pay homage or leave public service. Southern Whigs could readily recall that earlier their party had been legitimately charged with being antisouthern, and as a result, its numbers in the South had declined rapidly. For survival's sake, they had tried to cleanse their national party of this charge by supporting Taylor, a slaveholder, for the Presidency. Much to their chagrin, once Taylor was elected, they discovered that they had misjudged him, for on the territorial issue he could readily be identified as antisouthern. As a result some southern Whigs dared not support their President's program for the territories. Further, if political oblivion were not to be their lot, they must either change the Administration's plan or stand openly against it. Southern Whigs were less concerned about a "free" California than they were about the effect a Whig-created "free" California would have on their own fortunes.

The leadership of Dixie's distraught Whigs fell to Georgia's two militant Congressmen, Alexander H. Stephens and Robert

[1]*Congressional Globe,* 30 cong., 2 sess., 440; C. S. Boucher, "The Secession and Cooperative Movements in South Carolina, 1848-1852," *Washington University Studies,* 5:no. 2; C. P. Denman, *The Secession Movement in Alabama,* 1-13; J. C. Siterson, *The Secession Movement in North Carolina,* 38-53; Dorothy Dodd, "The Secession Movement in Florida," *Florida History Society Quarterly,* 12:3-19; Richard H. Shryock, *Georgia and the Union in 1850,* 178-216; Cleo Hearon, *Mississippi and the Compromise of 1850,* 16-90; J. H. Hammond to Calhoun, January 4, 1850, *Annual Report of the American Historical Association* (1899), 2:1193.

Toombs. After a summer in the South brooding over Taylor's hobnobbing with free-soilers, Stephens and Toombs returned to Washington determined to break the "nefarious" relation. They visited Taylor at the Executive Mansion and demanded that he abandon his free-soil plan for the West or suffer the consequences. Neither words nor threats would change the President's mind.

Failing at the White House, the Georgians carried their attack into the party's council. With a band of southern Representatives loyally following their lead, they tried to put the Congressional caucus on record against the President's plan. Once again they failed, but they would not give up their crusade. They carried their battle to the floor of the House.[2]

Here, near equality in numbers existed between Democrats and Whigs. Neither possessed a majority, and the balance was held by a handful of uncontrollable dissidents and free-soilers. The Whig caucus, meanwhile, with the blessing of the Administration, selected Robert Winthrop of Massachusetts as its candidate for the Speakership. The greater part of the Democrats united around Howell Cobb of Georgia. The outcome of this election would determine the control of the House committees and the nature of all legislation for the next two years.

Seeing their opportunity either to eliminate or pigeonhole Taylor's program for the West, Stephens, Toombs, and their following bolted the caucus selection. Though it could not be predicted with certainty, this action probably meant that no Whig Speaker would be elected until the President saw the light of reason and bargained with the southern wing of his party. Should he remain adamant, in all likelihood one of two things would happen. The House would either remain unorganized and no legislation would pass, or a Democrat would win and all the committees would be stacked against the Administration.

[2]Clayton to Crittenden, December 13, 1848, April 18, 1849; Morehead to Crittenden, December 25, 1849; G. Duncan to Crittenden, January 15, 1849, Crittenden Papers; Crittenden to Clayton, December 19, 1848, April 11, 1849, Clayton Papers; Washington *Republic*, December 19, 24, 1849, January 6, 1850.

Either result, to southern Whigs fighting for their lives in their own section, was better than the consequences of Taylor's program.

Their calculation was hazardous but it worked. Day after day during the month of December, almost down to Christmas day, balloting proceeded, and though the candidates changed, no one could win a majority. Not until the weary House changed its rules to permit election by plurality did Howell Cobb, the original candidate of the Democrats, emerge the winner. Even then Stephens, Toombs, and company held the balance of power, for in the final tally the vote stood 102 to 99 with Georgia's Whigs supporting Georgia's Democratic candidate. With the opposition in control of the House — and Senate, too — the future looked black, indeed, for Taylor's far western policy.[3]

*   *   *   *   *

During the summer and fall of 1849, Fillmore's mind and spirit were far away from the developing crisis in Washington. Rather his own plight in New York occupied his attention. Though the enormity of Weed's perfidy had staggered him, Fillmore had no intention of submitting docilely to its result. Once again his latent strength — that quiet and undramatic perseverance that kept him constantly on the edge of greatness — began to show. Weed would never really subdue him. For all his power and cunning, Weed would never obtain his most cherished goals largely because Fillmore stood in his way. As a result Weed's bitterness toward his former friend would know no bounds. Even after Fillmore passed away, Weed would continue his besmirching and belittling.[4] Yet the alchemy of time and ink could not reverse the course of events, which had begun in the early 1840's, and which were once again set in motion as Fillmore fought for his political life.

---

[3] *National Intelligencer*, December 1849, *passim; Congressional Globe*, 31 cong., 1 sess., 1-27; Benjamin Perley Poore, *Perley's Reminiscences of Sixty Years in the National Metropolis*, 1:360.

[4] Weed's *Autobiography*, on which most former evaluations of Fillmore have been based, was published in 1883-1884.

That summer he began to gather about him an active group of men who took his goals as their own. He drew to himself several top leaders, but more significantly he organized, town by town, a group of "young, zealous, active Whigs" who were "intelligent and industrious. . . ." And all dedicated themselves to restoring the balance in the New York party that Weed had upset.[5]

To aid in the process of recovery Fillmore encouraged his friends to create a newspaper at Albany. Even though friendly newspapers existed elsewhere in the state, he knew that he could never expect a fair hearing through Weed's Albany *Evening Journal.* And because the capital city press was universally regarded as the party's official organ, he knew that he needed one there, too. Such a paper, the Vice-President predicted, would "restrict, and tame Weed and his dependencies — harmonize and strengthen the party — protect our friends from proscription and slander, and weaken, if it does not destroy this arbitrary, and over-shadowing central influence" in Albany.[6]

Serious negotiations for establishing the paper did not begin until Fillmore had arrived in Washington in November of 1849. Soon thereafter John T. Bush was assigned both the jobs of raising enough money to start a paper and finding a suitable editor. He tried to engage Henry J. Raymond but discovered Webb had hired him to run the *Courier and Enquirer* instead. Bush then turned to other prospects.

Fillmore, meanwhile, had another inspiration. He advised Bush to set aside the idea of a new press and do double service for the Whig cause by purchasing the Albany *Evening Journal* — even "at a sacrifice of $10,000." Convert it into an "inde-

[5]Duer to Fillmore, December 18, 1829; Bush to Fillmore, December 3, 1849; Collier to Fillmore, December 2, 1849; Young to Fillmore, December 9, 1849; Kellogg to Fillmore, December 12, 1849; Henshaw to Fillmore, December 24, 1849; Wood to Fillmore, December 22, 1849; Colgrave to Fillmore, December 20, 1849, Fillmore Collection; see also lithograph letter in *ibid.* dated July 24, 1849; also Fillmore to Weed, October 29, 1849, *Fillmore Papers*, 2:290.
[6]Hall to Fillmore, December 2, 1849, Fillmore Collection; Fillmore to Babcock, March 7, 1850, *Fillmore Papers*, 2:293.

pendent Whig paper, devoted to the Whig Party and the Whig cause, and to nothing else — not *selecting* its favorites and *neglecting* the rest, but leaving the selection of candidates to the appropriate conventions, and giving support to those who are fairly and regularly nominated." The idea was tempting, and Bush made the effort, but Weed could not be had for a price.[7]

Instead, in March of 1850, the New York State *Register*, well-endowed for a long fight, began publication at Albany. Bush had collected $10,000 to launch it in a day when $2,000 put a local paper on its feet. Most of the backers were high-ranking New York Whigs and New York City merchants. Fillmore himself pledged $500. Bush, moreover, had found two competent men to act as editors. One, Jerome Fuller, was a former state senator and acquaintance of Fillmore's. Soon Fuller would become Fillmore's chief contact with New York City's men of means. The *Register's* other editor was Alexander Seward — no relative of his namesake in the Senate — who, as former owner-editor of the Utica *Gazette*, had been a tireless opponent of Weed.[8]

The news of Fillmore's activities was no secret to Weed. On the way to Washington in November, months before Fillmore's newspaper went to press, the two rivals met by accident in New York City. It was their first meeting in many months, and it put a personal climax into their long-range battle. They exchanged cold accusations, and thereafter the last shred of pretense disappeared.[9]

This encounter helped steel Fillmore to the need of facing the up-hill battle he must have with President Taylor and his executive family. At the bottom of Weed's recovery of power

[7]Fillmore to Babcock, March 7, 1850, *Fillmore Papers*, 2:293.

[8]Fuller to Fillmore, January 1, 4, 18, 25, March 22, 1850; Bush to Fillmore, January 5, February 23, 1850; Campbell to Fillmore, January 8, 1850; Ketchum to Fillmore, January 25, 1850; Bokee to Fillmore, January 26, 1850; Bemus to Fillmore, April 5, 1850; Haven to Fillmore, April 27, 1850; White to Fillmore, July 3, 1850; Babcock to Fillmore, April 8, 1850, Fillmore Collection.

[9]Fillmore to Weed, December 22, 1849, *Fillmore Papers*, 2:290-91; Fillmore to Hall, December 16, 1849; Hall to Fillmore, December 19, 1848, Fillmore Collection.

lay the Administration's favoritism, and unless this were nullified, Fillmore would never be able to survive the onslaught of Weed's attack. Yet Fillmore dared not declare open war on the Administration. Not only was his party loyalty too deeply engrained for such an act, but it would gain nothing except entrenching Weed even deeper in the favor of the executive family. Nathan K. Hall, who was engaged with his former law partner in this struggle for survival, sounded the theme of what Fillmore had to accomplish: "We must either be put 'victors in curia' by your individual efforts at Washington . . . unless indeed we conclude to lie down quietly and submit like whipped spaniels to Weed's dictatorship."[10]

No sooner did Fillmore arrive in Washington than he called upon the President. To him Fillmore demonstrated that the Administration's appointments were undermining his whole position. He did not press to have Taylor withdraw the most irritating of all appointments, Levi Allen, since the Vice-President undertsood that Taylor could not retreat. But he informed the President that he felt grievously mistreated and wanted to know if in the future he "was to be treated as friend or foe." Then, leaving Taylor, the Vice-President visited Secretary of Treasury Meredith and repeated his case. Both President and Secretary assured him that he would be treated more justly than in the past. Temporarily this satisfied Fillmore that more of New York's patronage would go to his friends and that Weed's position with the Administration would not be as secure as it had appeared. A fair beginning had been made even though he was still locked out of the Administration's council.

*   *   *   *   *

As they exchanged words, neither Fillmore nor Taylor fully appreciated that within ten months their individual actions — not unrelated to their conversation — would drastically alter the course of history. Though discontent in the South already promised trouble, it did not forecast how serious the crisis would be.

[10]Hall to Fillmore, December 2, 1849, *ibid*.

Soon the nation would become so torn with strife that only heroic action in Congress — frankly called a compromise — could restore peace.

Yet President Taylor was unaware that this crisis would be brought on by his plans to make California a free state. Even the Stephens-Toombs bolt from party regularity, and the battle over the Speakership, did not upset him. Little wonder, then, that at first Fillmore had small cause to concern himself with the President's program. Except when the Senate was deadlocked, he had no vote to cast; nor did he have other powers to wield, for Senate rules made him only a presiding officer. What power he possessed came not from his office but from his political influence. And against that the Administration's advisers had erected a barrier by denying him their confidence.

For the next seven months, immobilized by his office and by the President's advisers, Fillmore sat on the sideline of the greatest political battle of the era. Unfortunately, by forcing this idleness upon him, the Administration wasted much needed talent. Few of Taylor's legislative leaders had Fillmore's skill for guiding measures through the Congressional mill. Memory of his success in obtaining the tariff law of 1842, when another struggle between the President and Congressional leaders had troubled the party, were still fresh. But Taylor's friends preferred Seward's vote and voice in the Senate to their Vice-President's skill at management. It was a blunder. Seward brought them no additional support, while Fillmore's active participation in the Administration might have saved the day for them.

What Taylor's administration lost, posterity gained. Forced into inaction, Fillmore could only become a student and observer of the battle that raged about him. Inadvertently he was placed in a position where he could gauge the simple truths that lay behind that war of words and cunning. And when in seven months the call finally came for him to act, he was able to go to the heart of the matter with quick, deft strokes and restore peace to the harassed political world.

The national crisis started with an uncomplicated cause: Congress had to give some kind of government to the vast region the nation had acquired from Mexico. Finding an acceptable one, however, was difficult. It would have been easy to satisfy Californians and people of the Southwest, but these were not the ones who caused the trouble. Rather the character of the new government had to be acceptable to Congress, and here no majority could agree on a single solution.

Party discipline was useless. Democrats and Whigs alike forgot party lines and divided into three different camps. One group wanted a solution that favored southern ideals and interests. The second group called for a solution that fit the dreams of northern antislavery men. In between was a third group whose members placed other considerations above the North-South issue. Within this third group there was no agreement on goals, but because their attitudes were not pronouncedly sectional, they were frequently referred to as the "Nationals." The power of solution rested with them, and if they could be induced to act with one or the other group, they could shape the future.

Blithely ignoring the fact that his party neither controlled Congress nor was in agreement with him, Taylor laid his solution to the problem of governing the Far West before this divided Congress in his annual message. He implied that Congress need not concern itself — in a creative sense — with the nature of the government for California and the Southwest. A way existed for all the territorial problems to solve themselves. During the summer and fall, Californians had formed themselves into a state and would shortly ask for admission to the Union. Further, New Mexico, the southern half of the Southwest, would soon repeat California's action. He recommended that Congress accept both requests for statehood when they arrived.

If it were not immediately clear how this proposal would solve all problems for Congress, Taylor later spelled it out. The nub on which Congress would stumble into an impossible political morass was the question of allowing slavery to exist in these territories. By accepting Taylor's plan — skipping the territorial form of government in favor of statehood — Congress could leave that decision to the new state. A second cause for sectional controversy was a boundary dispute between Texas and New Mexico. If Congress settled this by creating the Territory of New Mexico, warned Taylor, the resulting definition of boundaries would produce another North-South outburst. Congress could avoid this issue, too, by admitting New Mexico to statehood. Then the boundary dispute, constitutionally, would become a matter for the Supreme Court to decide.[12]

Even as the clerk read the messages to Congress, Taylor knew — and so did most of the nation — that Californians had decided to keep slavery out of their state. In all likelihood New Mexicans would do the same. Taylor's proposal, therefore, set the stage for the admission of two new "free" states into the Union from a region which Southerners were most responsible for acquiring.

Northern partisans whooped with joy, and herein lay the key to Taylor's strategy for persuading Congress to accept his plan. From among the three divisions in Congress he expected the antislavery group — Whigs, Democrats, and Free-Soilers alike — to give him their solid support. In this he would not be disappointed. To pad their numbers into a legislative majority, however, would require help from a great number of those in the middle or "National" group. To them, Taylor's proposal held out the hope of side-stepping political embarrassment by avoiding action; he was wagering that a great share of the "Nationals" desired and dared to shed their responsibility for the course of events in the Far West.

"National" Whigs, who were prone to follow the party's course most loyally, would be able to say that no matter what Congress did, the people of the Far West had spoken, and the fate of the area could not be changed. Democrats of the

[12]*Congressional Globe*, 31 cong., 1 sess., 69, 87, 90, 103, 150, 195-196, 200-209; Richardson, *Messages*, 5:26-30.

"National" group might easily justify supporting Taylor's program, for, when analyzed, it was the fulfillment of the doctrine of popular sovereignty, already a well-worn plank in the Democratic platform.

On the surface Taylor's strategy of merging "Nationals" and northern extremists into a legislative majority held promise. But it failed to take into account two things: the tremendous effort some hotheaded Southerners would make to defeat the plan; and in turn, the effect this southern movement would have on the members of the middle group in both parties.

A number of southern Congressmen were prepared to fight the President's Plan with nearly every weapon in their arsenal. Hot words, uttered in anger and desperation, flowed from them.[13] Some were willing to go the limit: secession. Robert Toombs blasted at the "discreditable trick" that the Administration was practicing on the South. Pointing a finger at an Administration man, he warned: "Sir . . . . if by your legislation you seek to drive us from the territory of California and New Mexico . . . I am for disunion; and . . . I will devote all I am and all I have to its consummation."[14] For a man who had always fought the professional "fire-eaters" these were strong words. Others were just as threatening. So cool an observer as John C. Calhoun, whose many years of trying to unify southern action had tempered his hopes, suddenly warmed to the task. "The Southern members are more determined and bold than I ever saw them," reported Calhoun. "Many avow themselves to be disunionists, and a still greater number admit, that there is little hope of any remedy short of it."[15]

How serious the movement was no one could accurately gauge. But the rebellion-like activity, begun during the summer in South Carolina, continued. Texas was rumbling with threats to use its militia to enforce its boundary claim. And scheduled

[13]*Congressional Globe,* 31 cong., 1 sess., 51-59, 119-123.
[14]*Ibid.,* 27-28.
[15]Calhoun to Andrew Pickens, January 12, 1850, *Annual Report of the American Historical Association,* 1899, 2:780.

less than a half-year away was a convention of southern states
that might easily become the guiding body for creating an independent South.

Southern reaction gave Congressmen of the middle group
reason to pause and reflect upon the wisdom of supporting
Taylor. Those among them who were genuinely concerned
about the nation now wondered if Taylor's plan — admittedly
feasible, even clever — was safe. Why invite disunion when some
other plan, equally feasible, might prevent it? Other Congressmen of this middle group who were less worried about disunion,
because they felt that the threats to secede were mere bombast,
were troubled, nonetheless, by the South's violent reaction. Here,
again, extremists were making an undisguised and potent appeal
to southern "patriotism." No southern Whig or Democrat, who
numbered himself among the moderates, dared face a constitu-
ency aroused by such means unless he, too, could appear the
defender of southern interests. Before Taylor's plan could receive
his approval, it needed modifications that would take the sting
out of its antisouthern provisions.

Neither these southern moderates, who needed a face-saving
device, nor the alarmed patriots, were the only "Nationals" who
distrusted Taylor's program. Others foresaw that the southern
reaction would irreparably harm the parties. Since both parties
revolved on a North-South axis, their southern wings might
have to take the course of Stephens and Toombs if discontent
was as earnest as it appeared. With the break would go all the
dreams of those whose political life was tied to the old alliance.
This concerned northern Democrats of a moderate persuasion
more than Whigs because Democrats drew upon the South for
a greater share of their strength. But Whigs of the same view,
even though smaller in number, were equally moved. Politics
of the North-South axis would not permit these men to accept
Taylor's policy for the Far West.

No one would ever know how Taylor's plan would have
fared had it been put to a vote, but the line-up of "Nationals"

against it seemed to spell its doom. For various reasons these "Nationals" dared not accept Taylor's program without modification, and until this were certain, they would not permit it to come to a vote. This month of heated vituperation further served to convince politicians of the middle group that Taylor's program was dangerous to them. Their major purpose came to be the devising of modifications that would remove the danger of a southern explosion harmful to their nation, party, or person; this was complicated by the need to retain the votes of Taylor's supporters.

In mid-January, 1850, Henry S. Foote, short, bald, hot-headed, and eloquent Democratic Senator from Mississippi — who before the session ended would brandish a pistol and threaten fellow-Democrat Thomas Hart Benton with his life — was the first of the "Nationals" to step forward with a plan. It was less comprehensive than the scheme Henry Clay would soon devise, but it represented an effort to overcome the difficulties of the President's Plan. Instead of statehood for California and the Southwest, Foote called upon Congress to create three separate territories: California, New Mexico, and Deseret. Anticipating, however, that California would soon become a "free" state, he proposed dividing Texas and admitting another "slave" state, thus maintaining the historical balance between the sections. Foote's proposal was too poorly thought out to solve the dilemma that all "Nationals" faced, but it at least indicated what a southern Democrat who belonged to the middle group would be willing to accept.[16]

Two weeks later, after much preparation and anticipation, Henry Clay obtained the attention of the Senate. The old man of seventy-three, wracked by a cruel cough, rose in the Senate chamber on January 29 and began his last great legislative effort. "I hold in my hand," he announced, "a series of resolutions which I desire to submit to the consideration of this body." If accepted, he continued, they will produce "an amiable arrange-

[16]*Congressional Globe,* 31 cong., 1 sess., 101-5.

ment of all questions in controversy between the free and slave states, growing out of the subject of slavery."[17] On this note of promise he then laid out a program of legislation which showed that border-state Whigs also believed Taylor's proposal would need extensive revision before it could become acceptable to a Congressional majority.

Only on one point did Clay agree with Taylor: California should be admitted to the Union as a "free" state. Thereafter Clay proposed to alter the rest of the President's Plan. Instead of erecting the New Mexican region into a state, as Taylor desired, Clay suggested that the area be given two separate territorial governments. On the question of slavery in these territories he urged Congress to refrain from doing anything, but rather to let nature take its course. Here Clay was trying to give extreme Southerners hope without discouraging antislavery men. Southern "Nationals," moreover, might better be able to face their constituents if they supported such a measure rather than Taylor's.

The third part of Taylor's plan gave the Supreme Court the responsibility for settling the boundary dispute between Texas and New Mexico. Contrarily, Clay called upon Congress to draw the boundary and suggested a line that would favor New Mexico. Since this would be a bitter draught for Texans to swallow, he offered them something to sweeten it. For five years Texans had been trying to persuade the federal government to assume the state debt they had contracted in their war for independence. Now, Clay proposed this be done. Thus Texans would trade away their claim to a vast piece of real estate for a large sum of money.

To this point Clay had dealt with the same problems as Taylor. Hereafter, however, the Senator moved further afield to find the combination of concessions and gains that would satisfy enough northern extremists and "Nationals" to obtain a settlement. To make the whole proposition more acceptable to antislavery men he proposed that the slave trade in the District

[17]*Ibid.*, 244.

of Columbia be abolished. And to tempt Southerners to support these measures he called for a new and more effective fugitive slave law. In both cases Clay was harkening to twenty years of agitation.

Thus, by proposing a compromise, Clay tried to point the way toward political peace.

By introducing his resolutions Clay set in motion important legislative machinery, but the authorship of the compromise was not to be his. Without Stephen A. Douglas, Illinois' Democratic junior Senator, compromise would have been impossible. Chubby, full and manly in both torso and head, Douglas' legs were so dwarflike that they made him the shortest Senator in history. But his stature was measured in other ways, too. Everyone called him the "little Giant." Elected to Congress when he was thirty, he was now only thirty-six and already marked as a man of destiny. His vibrant energy, which led one admirer to describe him as a "steam engine in britches," gave him his leadership in the national legislature. Though a distinguished speaker he left his mark on the coming compromise less by oratory than by skillful negotiations in cloak rooms and by manipulating legislative procedures.[18]

On the territorial issue he was less concerned about what happened to slavery than in preserving the Democratic party as one that should revolve on a North-South axis. While his own House listened to the forensics inspired by Clay's resolutions, a crisis developed in the lower chamber that threatened to put Democrats at odds with each other. James Doty, Democratic Representative from Wisconsin, introduced a resolution that demanded immediate and unconditional admission of California. If voted on it would have forced the Democrats to divide into northern and southern factions. Better, thought Douglas, that the Democratic party should go down on record with a vote that could be defended in both halves of the nation. Like his

[18]George F. Milton, *Eve of Conflict*, has the best description of Douglas's role in the compromise.

counterpart among Whig "Nationals" he did not want to see the two wings of his party separate. He needed a plan which the great majority of Democrats could support. And since passage would require help from Whigs, he sought out their "Nationals" in private conference.

His chief aide in the project was Representative John A. McClernand of Illinois, the chairman of the House Territorial Committee. A handful of Congressmen met with McClernand at Speaker Cobb's house to arrange an understanding. Of those assembled the two Georgian Whigs, Stephens and Toombs, held the key to success. They had already identified themselves as implacable foes of Taylor's plan, but in spite of this, they were anxious for some settlement which would permit their party to stay alive in the South. Douglas saw that if Stephens and Toombs would define their requirements in line with the need for northern support, it would go a long way toward swinging "Nationals" of both parties behind a specific compromise.[19]

At the conference the Georgians stated their position with great frankness. They would willingly accept a "free" California in the Union *after* the South got concessions elsewhere. Congress, they insisted, must organize all the rest of the Southwest into two territories — New Mexico and Utah — and permit the local inhabitants to decide the question of slavery within their territorial bounds now, and again when admitted to the Union. This was "popular sovereignty," long advocated by some Democrats, and it was completely acceptable to Douglas and McClernand. Shortly thereafter, McClernand reported out of his committee bills to carry this agreement into effect, and these bills rather than Doty's resolution became the focus of discussion in the House. Later Douglas would report similar bills from his committee in the Senate. Eventually these measures would be at the core of the compromise.[20]

[19]*Ibid.*, 58-59; Robert P. Brooks, "Howell Cobb and the Crisis of 1850," *Mississippi Valley Historical Review*, 4:285.

[20]A. H. Stephens, *A Constitutional View* . . . ., 2:202-214; New York *Express*, February 20, 21, 1850; *Congressional Globe*, 31 cong., 1 sess., 375-376, 592, 628-629.

The McClernand-Stephens, or Douglas, plan differed from Clay's proposal by leaving untouched the issues of fugitive slaves, slave trade, and both Texas' boundary and her debt. Further, it gave the people of the territory the chance to decide about slavery while a territory, whereas Clay's proposal left this problem hanging in mid-air until the area became a state. Irrespective of their differences, however, Clay, Douglas, Stephens, and Toombs were all moving around the same pivot. They were looking for a way to make it possible for "Nationals" to support a program for governing the Southwest that could be made to appear advantageous to both pro- and antislavery voters. President Taylor had provided no such face-saving feature in his own plan.

In terms of the tripartite division of Congress, Clay, Douglas, Stephens, Toombs, and company were using the "Nationals" as the main source of support and hoped to draw help from the less extreme sectionalists, North and South. Taylor, contrarily, rested his cause with the northern extremists and hoped to obtain the remainder of the votes needed for a legislative majority from northern and border-state "Nationals."

On the last day of February, John Bell, Whig Senator from Tennessee, presented another compromise scheme. Like Douglas, he ignored the slave trade and fugitive slave issues and limited his proposal to the territory acquired from Mexico. But, unlike Douglas, Bell concerned himself with Texas' boundary and debt. For very minor concessions of land Texas would receive enough money to handle her debt. Then California would be admitted as a free state. In the area between Texas and California, Bell provided for three territorial governments that would eventually become three states. While this region was under territorial governments, however, nothing would be done about slavery. In essence Bell was trying to provide a plan that would be more acceptable to Southerners, and he had mixed together features from both Clay's and Douglas' proposals.[21]

* * * * *

21 *Ibid.*, 436-439.

From his raised dais in the Senate chamber, Fillmore watched the drama of the compromise unfold. He appreciated its significance, yet because of his faith in American political processes, and his profound understanding of politicians, he had little apprehension that the territorial question could not be solved. Since he had been nudged out of the Administration's confidence, he had almost no direct opportunity to influence the settlement. Nor did he desire to shape it. Rather he saw himself in the role of observer and umpire, and in the Senate he presided over the great debate without prejudice. Slavery in the territories was the Administration's problem more than the Vice-President's.

For the curious, however, Fillmore's past record could have revealed his ultimate position. He was not an extremist. No passionate, fanatical impulse gripped his soul or limited his frame of action. Usually he would cooperate with the party's collective judgment. If, however, fate challenged him to decide between solutions, he would make the choice most acceptable to the nation at large. If asked to describe his position, he would probably call it "National."

In spite of his calmness, his own destiny would soon be inextricably entangled with the oratory that sounded about him. But at first the more pressing problems of his own future, rather than the merits of the compromise plans, troubled him. Nathan K. Hall's charge that "We must either be put 'victors in curia,'" or "submit like whipped spaniels to Weed's dictation" still rang in the Vice-President's ears. He could only see that the entente between Taylor's administration and Weed must be broken, and that the means for doing so were not readily at hand. In January, however, the territorial issue and Fillmore's fate began to move closer together.

Back in Albany, Weed was bludgeoning the New York legislature into an endorsement of the Wilmot Proviso. Fillmore, perceiving a small opportunity, pounced upon this action, for in it he saw, correctly, a slight variation from Taylor's plans. To point up the disparity, Fillmore had a counterresolution introduced into the state legislature. It was more in keeping with Taylor's message on California. Weed, however, pushed through the original resolutions, and Fillmore, immediately, reported the affair to Taylor. Had the relations between Weed and the Administration rested on creed, instead of convenience, Fillmore's tale-bearing might have produced results. But Taylor quickly forgave his ally.[22]

Fillmore's interference in Albany tended to identify him with the President's Plan. The illusion only lasted briefly for in New York City a new force, which would help move him toward a more compatible position, had begun to gather. There in the nation's first city, powerful merchant princes had suddenly and unexpectedly become active foes of Taylor's program even though they had supported him in the election and had been, for some time, hostile to the expansion of slavery. To this point bombast from southern extremists had left this community of traders unmoved.[23] Most merchandise going into the South cleared through New York City, and unusually heavy orders from southern customers had encouraged New York merchants to discount the seriousness of the southern movement. Cyrus W. Field wrote gleefully to a southern customer: "Our Spring trade has already commenced, and promises to be very large, and we hope therefore to do much more with you this year than we have ever yet done."[24]

Soon he and his colleagues were jolted out of their dream. By the beginning of February, southern customers were sending scores of letters to New York merchants. All indicated that purchases for the spring trade would be delayed, and possibly entirely curtailed, because of the "agitation of the great national questions in Washington."[25]

[22]Fuller to Fillmore, January 4, 25, February 18, 1850; Dox to Fillmore, January 5, 30, February 2, 18, 1850; Bush to Fillmore, January 5, 1850; Bokee to Fillmore, January 26, 1850; Barnard, January 31, 1850, Fillmore Collection.

[23]Simeon Draper to Weed, September 23, 1849, Weed Papers.

[24]Quoted in Philip S. Foner, *Business and Slavery*, 15.

[25]*Journal of Commerce*, January 8, 10, March 6, June 27, 1850; Fowle to Weed, January 28, 1850; Abell to Weed, February 6, 19, 20, 1850; Spaulding to Weed, February 18, 1850, Weed Papers; Dix to Fillmore, January 5, 1850, Fillmore Collection.

In the city two publications which suddenly appeared amplified the alarm now beginning to arise among the merchants. Muscoe R. H. Garnett's *The Union, Past and Future, How it Works and How to Save It* first pointed to the value of the Union to northern merchants. Then, in terrifying language, it described how secession would eliminate business prosperity. An article by Thomas Prentice Kettel, *Stability of the Union,* repeated the theme and urged businessmen to exert themselves to preserve the structure of government upon which so much of their prosperity depended. Both authors argued that English businessmen were encouraging Southerners to secede. If New Yorkers did not beware, warned Garnett and Kettel, foreigners would seize the valuable southern trade. Southern correspondents, meanwhile, kept merchants informed on the rising tide of secessionist sentiment.[26] By the second week of February, they learned that six states had already appointed delegates to the coming Southern Convention to be held in Nashville.[27]

Almost in unison, New York merchants forgot their hostility to slavery extension. For them no choice existed between prosperity and depression. At this very moment Henry Clay came forward with his compromise plan. Like desperate men, they embraced it and urged it upon Congress. The southern threat of economic retaliation had revolutionized their thinking.

At the time Jerome Fuller was in New York City scouting for funds for Fillmore's newspaper. To Fillmore he reported that every businessman he met had "undergone a change" in attitude. "There is evidently a reaction beginning to take place on the question of slavery," and "the tendency is to be less ultra."[28] Taking advantage of their changed sentiment, Fuller assembled a group of them at the home of Morris Ketchum. Among them were some "of the strongest and some of the wealthiest men of the city." There he urged them to help start

[26]Foner, *Business and Slavery*, 23.
[27]A. C. Cole, "The South and the Right of Secession in the Early Fifties," *Mississippi Valley Historical Review,* 1:375-399.
[28]Fuller to Fillmore, February 18, 1850, Fillmore Collection.

a newspaper to fight Weed. If they contributed to it, Fuller promised, it would voice the desire of New Yorkers for a rapid settlement of the territorial issues. They accepted the offer and made heavy subscriptions.[29]

These merchants had more in mind than helping Fillmore. Two days later almost the same group[30] formed themselves into a merchants' committee and called a mass meeting.[31] Twenty-five hundred of their colleagues answered the call. So enthusiastic was the response that the local Whig General Committee voted to cooperate in sponsoring the committee. And from this point forward New York City Whigs and the merchants' committee worked hand in glove.[32]

Thus were conjoined three New York groups: Fillmore's upstate machine, New York City's local Whig Party which the anti-Weed faction dominated, and a well-endowed and organized pressure group composed of the city's merchants. Though each sought something different, each felt that a change in Taylor's plans for the territories would be helpful to its objective. Once before these groups had worked together and had given direction to New York's politics, but this time, unknown to them, they would shape the course of the nation's history.

The alliance eventually gave Fillmore great strength. For the moment, however, it placed him in an awkward position, though he would not have rejected the help from New York City to avoid his embarrassment. In a day when ward-heeling politicians constituted the major voice in party conventions, Fillmore knew that it took more than propaganda to influence nominations and win elections. To secure himself against the machinations of Weed, Fillmore had to find favor with the petty party lieutenants who attended local caucuses and who sent

[29]*Ibid.*; Simeon Draper to Weed, July 22, 1850, Weed Papers.
[30]Hiram Ketchum, Henry Grinnell, Stephen Whitney, George and Nathaniel Griswold, Frederick R. Lee, William B. Astor, Snydam, Sage & Co., Kent, Page and Co., Daniel Lord, N. T. Hubbard and Sons, William H. Livingston and Co., Marshall O. Roberts, Ralph Mead and Co., and Olyphant and Sons.
[31]New York *Express*, February 19, 1850.
[32]E. G. Spaulding to Weed, February 18, 1850, Weed Papers.

delegates to county, district, and state conventions. Only one appeal influenced them. They followed the man who got them jobs. Under the circumstances, the whisper campaign that Weed could put up a cow against a Fillmore selectee and have it confirmed had delivered telling blows. Already men who had long labored for Fillmore in less belligerent days had deserted his cause.[33]

Only through the President could Fillmore hope to recover some appointing power and stop the ebbing tide. As a result he tried to win his way back into the President's favor, not by sycophancy, but by making the President conscious that he had done his Vice-President an injustice. All through the first year of Taylor's Presidency, Fillmore and his press had assiduously refrained from blaming the President for these appointments. Rather Fillmore's press agents concentrated their attack on the President's cabinet as a pack of ungrateful, conspiring advisers. Fillmore, himself, had said absolutely nothing on the issue of compromise, and that had helped establish the impression that he stood behind the Administration since almost everybody else in the Senate was attacking it.[34]

Now, in late February, to have his upstate machine in alliance with vocal anti-Taylorites placed Fillmore in a delicate position. He saw no tangible advantage in abandoning his personal tact with Taylor, nor was he willing to sacrifice his allies even though they, by calling for compromise, were causing him embarrassment. Publicly he chose to remain between the two camps.[35]

[33]Fillmore to Brooks, May 24, 1852, *Fillmore Papers*, 2:323-324; Ketchum to Fillmore, January 29, 1850; Haven to Fillmore, January 27, 1850, February 5, 1850; Henshaw to Fillmore, February 5, 1850; Macy to Fillmore, February 10, 1850; Bowen to Fillmore, March 11, 1850; Ketchum to Fillmore, March 23, 1850; Charles to Fillmore, March 11, 1850, Fillmore Collection.

[34]Fillmore to Brooks, May 24, 1852, *Fillmore Papers*, 2:323-324; Hard to Fillmore, January 4, 1850; Dox to Fillmore, January 30, 1850; Hard to Fillmore, February 9, 1850; Resolutions of the Whig Young Men in General Committee, copy dated February 15, 1850; Dox to Fillmore, February 2, 1850, Fillmore Collection; New York State *Register*, March, April, May, 1850, *passim*.

[35]Fillmore to Brooks, May 24, 1852, *Fillmore Papers*, 2:321-324.

Fillmore's tactics were not hopeless. A change in the cabinet might alter the entire picture. Recently Weed's ally, Secretary of the Treasury Meredith, had become involved in a multi-million-dollar scandal that rocked the Treasury, and his dismissal might come at any time. Should that happen, a cabinet reorganization might follow. In any event Weed's influence in the cabinet would be weakened.

A fortnight later, Daniel Webster helped Fillmore maintain his footing. On March 7, following the lead of other Senators who one by one were making set speeches on the territorial issue, Webster rose to his peroration. He understood, as few others did, that the struggle over slavery in the territory was in many ways a sham battle. As he saw it, behind it all, other than the fears and ambitions of politicians, was the industrial revolution. To him the future belonged with the city, the financier, and the industrialist. Agriculture was declining to inferiority and dependency, and in the slavery battle one branch of agriculture was making a desperate effort to stave off the end. Webster, therefore, spoke with moderation as he made a great national appeal. The Union, he declared, could no more be dissolved than could the "heavenly bodies rush from their spheres." Secession without civil war was an utter impossibility. Yet by concessions both could and must be avoided. The question was: who should make the concessions, North or South? His answer: the North because she would lose nothing by generosity. She was superior in size and strength, and since she had married herself to the industrial revolution, the future inevitably by the "operations of time" belonged to her. She could, therefore, afford to be patient. The abolitionists, moreover, need not fear that concessions at this time would strengthen or extend slavery. There was not left "within . . . any territory of the United States, a single foot of land" where "some irrepealable law" of nature did not forbid slavery, he assured them. Nature need not be re-enacted by legislation. Slavery was doomed. Webster was willing, therefore, in spite of his belief that slavery was a moral and political evil, to give it full constitutional rights. He would agree to support all that Henry Clay had proposed. The Union was worth temporary concessions.[36]

Even as Webster was speaking, Fillmore wrote privately to a friend that the speech was "truly statesman-like."[37] The Fillmore press took up the cue, and this coincided with the reaction of the New York City merchants who were overjoyed with Webster. For weeks nothing could be heard on Wall Street but excerpts from the seventh of March speech. Philip Hone reported that the famous exordium was in "every man's mouth,"[38] and Lewis Tappan, antislavery leader, heard with disgust "merchants," "Brokers," "monied men," and "owners of Bank, Railroad and manufacturing stocks" quoting excerpts from the address.[39] Such reaction gave Fillmore means for continuing to be both for and against Taylor's plan: have his friends praise Webster's stand, say nothing specifically in favor of Clay's program, and continue to profess loyalty to the President.

Fuller expressed the strategy in this manner: "We have a good many sides to please. New York City generally prefers a compromise to the President's Plan. Clay has a host of friends there and elsewhere upon whom we must retain our hold. Webster men are in favor of territorial government. Clay's friends are calling upon us to say something in his favor. If the adjustment passes, then we shall be on the strong side; if it fails, then we shall go in with all our might for the President's recommendation, and urge its adoption among others for the reason that the compromise has failed. In that way we shall save our credit with Clay's friends and hope to keep in position with the President."[40]

*   *   *   *   *

Through April and May, sentiment for compromise gained momentum. The progress of debate revealed little interest in

36Webster, *Writings and Speeches*, 16:327-45.
37Fillmore to Babcock, March 7, 1850, *Fillmore Papers*, 2:293.
38Hone, *Diary*, March 14, 1850.
39Tappen to Scoble, April 24, 1850, *Tappan Correspondence* in *Journal of Negro History*, 12:429.
40Fuller to Fillmore, June 6, 1850, Fillmore Collection.

abstractions and focussed attention upon practical measures. Thus Congress must deal with admission of California, the organization of the territories, the settlement of the Texas-New Mexico boundary, and a new fugitive slave law. On this both Northerners and Southerners agreed. But opinions were far apart on how they should be treated.

A majority favored some sort of compromise that would give each side a feeling of success. Yet, the order in which victories should be doled out kept the compromisers apart. Administration men, northern free-soilers, and even some northern moderates insisted that California be admitted to the Union before considering any other proposal. Yet southern "Nationals" who were willing to see California "free," regarded this procedure with knitted brows. They feared that once California were in the Union, Congress might not pass any other measure. Their anxiety had foundation in the realities of politics. Because free-soilers would pour unbearable scorn on their heads, generous northern "Nationals" might not dare to vote for concessions to the South, and without their help no legislation was possible. Should this fear prove groundless, another existed. President Taylor might veto all measures except those that carried out his own desires. This fear arose from a growing awareness of Taylor's stubbornness. He would accept no changes in his proposal and could not be convinced that any were needed. To him the source of all the trouble was Clay, who the President believed had suggested compromise as a way of stealing the stage. Open hostilities between Taylor and Clay were delayed only because the Senator carefully avoided an overt utterance. Then, at the end of April, Clay blundered into criticism. Taylor's suspicions instantly caused an open breach, and it appeared that if any compromise measures now reached Taylor's desk, they would be vetoed.[41]

Compromisers, worried that their colleagues' backs were not stiff enough, and mistrusting Taylor, sought to avoid the

[41]Brown to Crittenden, January 11, 1850, April 19, 1850, Crittenden Papers; New York *Express*, April 29, 1850.

snare of pressure and trickery. In February, Senator Foote had pointed the way around the real or imagined pitfalls when he had proposed that all the various measures be brought together into one bill — an idea that earned the name "Omnibus." When first broached, the Omnibus proposition had found little support. Even Clay had sniffed at it suspiciously. But Stephens and Toombs and their extreme element of the southern "National" Whigs made the Omnibus the *sine qua non* of their support. As the debate dragged on, and others began to appreciate the character of Taylor, and the breach between Taylor and Clay widened, others saw the practicality of an "Omnibus Bill." Taylor and Congressmen alike, in order to get what they wanted, would have to accept what they disliked.

Supporters of the Omnibus idea complicated its acceptance as a form for presenting the compromise by arguing over how the measure would be put together and who should do it. Southern compromisers wished to have the bill constructed by a special committee; the northern supporters, like Webster and Douglas, wished to have it put together by the Senate itself through a series of amendments to a particular measure. A committee-made Omnibus would give no one the opportunity of killing any part of the measure, and every Senator, after voting, would needlessly share the responsibility for those parts of the measure repugnant to his section. Contrarily, in a bill put together on the Senate floor, each could disclaim responsibility for the repugnant parts by voting against offensive amendments, though permitting the Omnibus to pass. The committee-made Omnibus was in the spirit of true compromise; the other, a politically expedient compromise.[42]

Finally, after Clay accepted the Omnibus principle, the Senate created a special committee of thirteen, and the Bell resolutions were referred to it. By disregarding the rules of the Senate, and through the special indulgence of Vice-President Fillmore, Clay's resolutions were also referred to the committee.

[42]See Holman Hamilton, "Democratic Leadership and the Compromise of 1850," *Mississippi Valley Historical Review*, 41:406-7.

Later Clay became chairman of the group. On May 8 he reported back three measures; one dealt with the fugitive slaves; the second with the slave trade in the District; and the third was the Omnibus Bill. In the Omnibus Bill was embodied a slight modification of the solutions that Stephens and Douglas had worked out, back in February, for the problems of California's statehood, of the Southwest's government, and of Texas' debt and boundary.

With the measures before the Senate, once again the vocalizing was taken up in earnest. Vociferous as it was, it could not obscure the conclusion that at last a strife-weary Congress would find its way through the maze of opinion and principles that had hindered an adjustment for over a year. The revolt that had started in the South against Taylor's plan might soon produce results.

*   *   *   *   *

As June approached compromisers sensed that victory might be theirs. Unofficial counting of noses indicated a narrowly achieved success for the Omnibus Bill. Summer heat made Congressmen anxious to desert Washington, and the Senators sat back to wait for the last of their orators to have his say. Then suddenly Taylor brought on a crisis that "knocked in the head all previous calculations."[43]

A half-year earlier, Taylor had informed Congress that he had urged New Mexico to pursue the same course as California. After the treatment California received, few had regarded Taylor's suggestion as more than a wish — few except the Texans. Fearing loss of an imperial domain to New Mexico, should she become a state, Texas had established her authority at El Paso and, while the Senate debated the Omnibus Bill, had sent commissioners on to Santa Fe to bring her into the fold. But here in the heart of New Mexican territory, Texans had encountered Colonel Monroe, the federal commander.

[43]New York *Express*, June 25, 1850.

Following his instructions from Washington, Colonel Monroe turned back the Texans, denied their claim, and then proceeded to create the area he occupied into a state. He called together a constitutional convention that, by May 25, framed a state constitution. Quickly this news reached Texas. There the prospect of losing 100,000 square miles of land produced intense excitement. By the middle of June, Governor Bell informed the Texan Congressmen of the crisis and vowed he would resort to force to uphold Texan claims. He also wrote the President, demanding disavowal of Colonel Monroe's action. To give his militancy wider support, the governor called a special session of the Texas legislature for August 12.[44]

Taylor, meanwhile, carried to Congress the tale of Texas' drive to take Santa Fe. The news of a possible clash between federal and Texan troops disrupted the course of the compromise. A week later, the telegraph brought from St. Louis the news that New Mexico had adopted a constitution. This, together with Taylor's message, created an entirely new state of affairs at Washington. Northern slavery haters, worn down by time, suddenly revived and saw in New Mexico's action a chance to win the region unmistakably for freedom. Texas debt-holders throughout the nation shuddered as they saw the boundary dispute, which they were using to bargain for federal assumption of the Texas debt, being snatched from their hands to go into the Supreme Court where bargaining stopped. Southern states, especially Mississippi, hastened to encourage Texas by offers of assistance, while it was reported that Texas' Sam Houston was about to resign his Senatorship in order to assume command of the Texan force. The long-awaited Southern Convention now began its meeting in Nashville, and southern members of Congress began to hold caucuses. The cause of Texas was at once made the cause of the whole South. Rapidly the

[44]*Ibid.*, June 26, 27, July 6, 10, 1850; W. C. Binkley, "The Question of Texan Jurisdiction in New Mexico under the United States, 1848-1850," *Southwestern Historical Quarterly*, 24:1-38. Bell to Taylor, July 3, 1850, Fillmore Collection. (This letter reached Washington after Taylor was stricken and was opened after his death by Fillmore.)

compromisers lost ground as the attitudes of extremists on both sides stiffened. The old forces which "Nationals" had tried to dispel by putting the compromise in the Omnibus form returned with renewed vigor. In the heat of the heightening crisis, "Nationals" themselves might not dare to accept concessions that ran counter to sectional prejudices. Further, Taylor might even veto the Omnibus in order to have a chance — now possible — of getting both a "free" California and a "free" New Mexico. The chances of passing the Omnibus, which a few weeks before had appeared so good, withered.[45]

In spite of fading hopes, Clay moved to push the compromise bills to a vote — whatever the outcome. Again the gallery statisticians began to count votes. Suddenly in mid-June they turned the national spotlight upon Fillmore. It became more and more possible, as the heat of argument increased, that Fillmore would be called upon to break a tie in the Senate. The prospect did not please him. His heart was with the compromisers — but politics dictated placation of Taylor. On June 18, writing confidentially to a friend, he said: "I think the Compromise Bill will pass the Senate, but it may come to my casting vote — as to that — *Quaere?* I shall wait till I see what shape it assumes before I determine to say yea or nay."[46]

Fear that the Omnibus would fail or fall victim to Taylor's veto prodded southern compromising Congressmen to renewed efforts to change the President's mind. On the night of July 1, a southern caucus appointed C. M. Conrad of Louisiana, Humphrey Marshall of Kentucky, and Robert Toombs of Georgia to remonstrate with the President about his New Mexican policy. They were all "original Taylor men." They warned Taylor that if he insisted on the admission of California and New Mexico as states and persisted in his hostile attitude towards Texas, all his southern friends would be driven into opposition. Taylor was adamant. He insisted on California's right to come

[45]Binkley, "Texan Jurisdiction in New Mexico," 1-38; New York *Express*, June 23, 26, July 2, 6, 1850; Washington *National Intelligencer*, July 4, 1850.
[46]*Fillmore Papers*, 2:321.

in at once and declared he would recommend the admission of New Mexico as soon as her constitution arrived. He scouted the claims of Texas to the Santa Fe country. Since he must in any case offend one wing of his party, he said that he could hardly be expected to sacrifice eighty-four northern men for twenty-nine from the South. In view of the President's well-known obstinacy, it was evident that further remonstrance was useless.[47]

But on July 3, Stephens again attempted to alter the President's policy. Again he failed, and he and Toombs sought the aid of Preston. Their heated discussion ended in a threat by Stephens to impeach the President if he ordered troops to Santa Fe. The next day, on July 4, Stephens published a card in the *National Intelligencer* warning that a military collision in New Mexico would send the whole South rushing to the aid of Texas with arms.[48]

The President's answer to the threat of impeachment and war was to order the drafting of a powerful and comprehensive message on the general state of the country. This would have forced the resignation of two cabinet members, Crawford and Johnson, who were both swinging toward compromise. The President had also decided to free his administration of the Treasury scandal by sacrificing Meredith. Accordingly he began to consider cabinet appointments and on July 3 he conferred with Thurlow Weed. Stanley of North Carolina was slated to succeed Crawford, and Bell, or possibly Crittenden, to replace Johnson. By Weed's advice, the President assigned the Treasury to Governor Hamilton Fish of New York. Official announcement of cabinet reorganization was delayed by the Independence Day holiday.[49]

The character of rumored cabinet changes demonstrated to Fillmore the futility of his cautious silence on the compromise.

[47] J. P. H. Claiborne, *Life and Correspondence of John A. Quitman*, 2:32-33.
[48] *National Intelligencer*, July 4, 1850; New York *Express*, July 6, 9, 18, 1850; Avary, *Stephens*, 26-27.
[49] New York *Express*, July 13, 18, 1850; Weed, *Autobiography*, 590, 591.

Reluctantly he dropped his guard before a private correspondent. "I perceive the papers are discussing the probability of my casting vote on the Compromise. *'Of that Knoweth no man.'* I think it never will be given, but if it is, it will be for which I think right upon the whole, regardless of all personal consequences. I have nothing to gain or lose, but in the independent and faithful discharge of my duty, regardless of demagogues, North or South."[50]

Only a few days before, Fillmore had heard that Weed had gone to the White House; he knew that a cabinet reorganization was about to occur; and with Weed at Taylor's elbow, Fillmore realized that the new cabinet, like the old, would be stacked against him. But to avoid ruffling the old General's feathers more than necessary, Fillmore again visited Taylor. He informed the President that he might be called upon to give the casting vote in the Senate on the compromise, "and if I should feel it my duty to vote for it, as I might, I wished him to understand, that it was not out of any hostility to him or his Administration, but the vote would be given, because I deemed it for the interests of the country."[51] Thus in the gentlest terms possible he firmly notified the President he was prepared to end the compromise issue in the nation.

Congress recessed for Independence Day, and the quiet in Washington was like the lull before a storm. For seven months Congress had labored in passionate heat to solve the slavery issue. It had progressed from an Administration-sponsored plan that was free-soil to a realization of the need for a compromise on the basis of establishing an equality of dissatisfaction in all camps. As Congress reached the end of its labors, the extremists, led by the President, had made a last-minute sally that might lead to civil war. The situation was desperate. Although no one knew it, within a week Fillmore was to end the crisis.

[50] *Fillmore Papers*, 2:322. [51] *Ibid.*, 2:323.

Chapter 13

President Fillmore Wrecks the Omnibus

ATE Tuesday evening, July 9, while Fillmore fumbled uninterestedly over his correspondence, an impatient knock at the door interrupted him. Since Mrs. Fillmore and Mary had left Washington a month before to escape the capital's summer heat, he bestirred himself to answer. There stood a breathless messenger from the Executive Mansion, pale with the news he bore; only minutes earlier, President Taylor had passed away.[1]

Throughout the evening, the Vice-President had been waiting for this message. During the day he had spent hours in the sickroom of the dying President and had come away at the dinner hour to obtain some relief from the chatter and oppressiveness of the anteroom.

Taylor's illness had developed suddenly. On Thursday, Independence Day, the President had attended a celebration at the Washington Monument. The oration was long, and the President had listened to it with his head uncovered and exposed to a merciless sun. Later that day he had had a fair quantity of iced drinks and fresh fruit. By the next morning he was sick with what the doctors called "cholera morbus." No one at first had thought his condition too serious, but over the weekend he

[1] *Fillmore Papers,* 1:430-431.

had grown weaker, and on Monday his condition had become grave.[2]

Fillmore's first realization that he might become the President of the United States had come the very noon of that fateful day. In the Senate chamber, while South Carolina's Senator Butler was declaiming against the President's Plan, a messenger had called Fillmore from his chair and told him he was wanted at the Executive Mansion immediately, because the President was slipping fast. Fillmore, pale and dazed, hurried unceremoniously out of the room. The messenger then "tripped about" and whispered the news to Webster, Clay, and Cass. The chamber hummed with the realization of what was happening. The orating Butler, on hearing the news, "dropped at once in his seat" and the Senate immediately adjourned.[3]

At the White House Fillmore had found the cabinet members and other dignitaries already assembled in the anteroom. They had all settled down to wait, and as the hours passed, the doctors periodically had reported that the President was failing to respond.[4] What Fillmore had thought about during those long hours was unknown. In all likelihood he had been numb with disbelief.

Now as he stood in the doorway of his room at the Willard, he read the message from the cabinet: "Sir: The . . . painful duty devolves on us to announce to you that Zachary Taylor . . . is no more. . . ."

Reality now burst upon Fillmore with terrible force. For a moment his strength dissolved, and he realized how unprepared he was for the great responsibilities that faced him. He sat down, deliberately closed the channels of his panicked imagination, and awkwardly informed the cabinet: "I have no language to express the emotions of my heart. The shock is so sudden and unexpected that I am overwhelmed. . . . I . . . shall appoint a time and place for taking the oath of office. . . ." at the "earliest moment."[5]

[2]*National Intelligencer*, July 6, 9, 10, 11, 1850.
[3]*Ibid.*, July 11, 12, 13, 1850.   [4]*Ibid.*, July 13, 1850.
[5]July 9, 1850, *Fillmore Papers*, 1:329.

He then locked his door to all, but, visitors or no, that night was a sleepless one.[6] Most Presidents have four months before taking office to form their policies. He had one night. He was fully aware of the taut condition of the bonds of union. No President had ever taken office in the face of such impending disaster.

Only a few days earlier a Washington journalist had reported that in "less than six weeks" Texas would send "2,500 men" to New Mexico. Colonel Monroe's federal troops numbered "about five or six hundred" and 600 more would join them. Texans would in all likelihood overwhelm Monroe and "arrest" him and his officers for "obstructing" the laws of Texas. Rumor had it — and Fillmore was in no position to know anything to the contrary — that Taylor had instructed Monroe to resist Texas to the last man. On hearing this, Alexander H. Stephens had screamed in the House: "The first federal gun" fired "against Texas . . . will signal . . . freemen from the Delaware to the Rio Grande to rally to the rescue."[7]

So impassioned had the question of Texas, the Southwest, and slavery become, that on Saturday, July 6, ninety-one Congressmen, using the Treasury scandal as an excuse, had passed a motion to "censure the President."[8] Only two weeks earlier, 180 leaders of the South had assembled at McKendree Methodist Church in Nashville. Amid fiery speeches they served notice that their beloved Dixie would never brook interference with its rights and demanded as a minimum condition for peace the right to carry their slaves into the Southwest. Later generations of analysts would discount the seriousness of the Nashville Convention because it failed to bring on secession. But to the statesmen of the day who understood its potential, it was a frightening spectacle. Its adjournment without dissolution, moreover, did not end the fright, for the delegates had provided for another session, six weeks after Congress adjourned, to review the work of Washington in the light of their ultimatum.

[6]Louisville *Journal*, March 16, 1854.   [7]Hamilton, *Taylor*, 2:377, 378.
[8]*Congressional Globe*, 31 cong., 1 sess., 1346-47, 1351, 1360, 1362-63.

Little wonder that Fillmore spent a sleepless night. Later he reported[9] that he "reviewed during those hours . . . his own opinions and life." From his youth up, he had "cherished . . . a feeling, even a prejudice, against slavery." Yet reason told him that there was no immediate or simple solution to the slavery problem. Instead, he saw in the gathering clouds in the North and the South, a storm which was likely to overwhelm him, "and . . . his country, also. . . . ." He could only conclude that it was high time that so pernicious a topic should be withdrawn from national politics. At this point almost anything would be better than the unceasing agitation that threatened disunion and civil war. How to accomplish this he did not know, but he resolved "to look upon this whole country, from the farthest coast of Maine to the utmost limit of Texas, as but one country, the country of his birth" and not as a group of regions each demanding exclusive loyalty. Deep within him, where his reason could not reach, his muffled conscience told him that what he was about to do might cost him his political future. "I well knew, that by so doing, I must lost the friendship of many men . . . especially in my own state, and encounter their reproaches." But, he said, "to me, this is nothing. The man who can look upon a crisis without being willing to offer himself upon the altar of his country is not fit for public trust."

The next morning Fillmore informed Congress of the President's death. At noon before a joint session of both houses, with the cabinet present, Judge Branch of the district court administered the Presidential oath of office. As Fillmore repeated the words, faces in the audience were distorted. Some tried to keep the mask of grief over their fears, and other struggled to conceal their joy for they were beginning to suspect that a revolution was in the offing.[10]

*   *   *   *   *

The seven members of Taylor's cabinet were painfully aware

[9]*Fillmore Papers*, 1:431; Louisville *Journal*, March 16, 1854.
[10]*National Intelligencer*, July 11, 1850; Buffalo *Express*, July 13, 1850; Babcock to Fillmore, July 10, 1850, Fillmore Collection.

of the revolution the night had wrought. For sixteen months they had remorselessly proscribed Fillmore's friends, and only recently, as his vote became important, had they relaxed and treated him civilly.[11] In turn, Fillmore's press had relentlessly attacked the cabinet. With unrivaled vigor, his editors had persecuted the cabinet officials who were implicated in a money-grab that scandalized the nation. Between Taylor's official family and Fillmore, there was no love lost.[12]

They did not know Fillmore's intentions, but to forestall expected dismissal, each member of Taylor's cabinet offered his resignation on the evening of Fillmore's inauguration. He accepted them without hesitation, but he asked the retiring officials to stay in office for a month while he reorganized the Administration. They gave him only a week, and the harassed President had to work feverishly to gather about him a cabinet of acceptable advisers.[13]

During his first sleepless night as President, Fillmore had settled on Webster for his cabinet's premier. On the day of inauguration the two went into conference. The aged statesman from Massachusetts, Fillmore learned, was still willing to abide by the principles of his March 7 speech and was willing to take the post of Secretary of State. Doubt about who would replace Webster in the Senate and whether Webster's financial friends would continue to pay for his services in the new position hindered an immediate appointment. Both wanted Robert W. Winthrop to succeed Webster. A typical Brahmin representative, Winthrop was alive to the same interests Webster had served. Trained in Webster's law office, Winthrop was the hand-picked heir apparent to Webster's leadership in New England. For several sessions prior to December, 1849, Winthrop had been Speaker of the House, but in this Congress he had been retired to the House floor. During the debates he had taken a moderate,

[11]New York State *Register*, July 12, 1850.
[12]New York *Express*, April 17, May 14, June 28, July 1, July 28, 1850.
[13]Letters of Clayton, Johnson, Ewing, Meredith, Preston, Collamer to Fillmore all July 10, 1850, Fillmore Collection. New York *Express*, July 12, 13, 16, 17, 18, 20, 24, 1850.

almost "National," position on the slavery crisis. The fate of
Webster's seat in the Senate rested, however, with the Massachusetts governor, Briggs, who coveted the position for himself.
Only extreme pressure from Fillmore and Webster forced Briggs
to forego his own ambitions and appoint Winthrop. Webster's
friends, meanwhile, raised a fund for him, and by July 17 all
was arranged for Webster to enter the cabinet.[14]

Even before Briggs relented, Fillmore turned to other cabinet
appointments. Time pressed upon him with almost unbearable
force. Every decision reflected the need to act quickly. Admirers
of Webster were prone to give him credit for selecting the cabinet
since he and the President frequently conferred. This was not
true. The two men saw the state of the nation through the same
spectacles, and Fillmore was happy to have the help of the lion
of Boston, whom he had always admired. But almost all of the
Whigs approached, or thought of, as possible cabinet members
were Fillmore's nominees. Webster's main contribution in putting together the cabinet was that of a go-between: he sounded
out candidates before a position was offered by Fillmore.

In search of men who would reflect his desire for sectional
peace, Fillmore dug deep into his memory, particularly into those
Whig years 1841-1843 when he had led a Whig House through
its most fruitful accomplishments. It was to become characteristic
of him whenever a vacancy occurred in high places "to run over
in his mind, the names of his acquaintances, who would probably
be best qualified to fill the position, and after weighing the
qualities of each, to make the appointment."[15] It made no difference if the man were still active in politics. He tested each with
the same question: was he a Whig whose outlook was national
rather than sectional — a man who could rise above his con-

---

[14]For Webster and funds see Claude M. Fuess, *Daniel Webster*, 2:249; also Lawrence
to Cooks, September 11, 1850, forwarded by latter to Fillmore, September 13, 1850;
Granger to Fillmore, July 16, 1850; Charles to Fillmore, July 30, 1850; Barnard
to Fillmore, July 10, 1850, Fillmore Collection; Daniel Goodwin, *In Memory of
Robert C. Winthrop*, 19. There was some indication that had this maneuver failed,
Webster would have remained in the Senate and Winthrop gone into the cabinet
as Secretary of State. Davies to Fillmore, July 16, 1850, Fillmore Collection.
[15]Stuart to Wilson, April 29, 1878, Fillmore Mss.

stituents on slavery? Twenty-four hours after he took the oath of office, he had canvassed the nation for moderate leaders and discovered a host of acceptable men.

Fillmore felt that if John J. Crittenden and William Alexander Graham could be brought into the cabinet, both would strengthen the cause of peace. Webster agreed that both were excellent choices.[16] Between them, Crittenden and Graham represented a sizable portion of the "National" southern element. Although originally a Taylor man, Crittenden in recent months had deserted the fold and had tried to persuade the Administration to forsake its hardheaded insistence on the President's Plan.[17] Graham's asset lay not in his work toward compromise, for he was in political retirement in Hillsborough, North Carolina, but in past performances where he had displayed orthodox Whig traits. During the thirties he was North Carolina's staunchest Whig; in the early forties, as United States Senator, he had stood solidly behind internal improvements and Fillmore's tariff measures; and as governor of North Carolina from 1844 to 1849, he had built and financed a state railroad.[18] Both men readily accepted their appointments, Crittenden as Attorney-General, and Graham as Secretary of the Navy.[19]

The remaining cabinet positions required more deliberation. For the Treasury post, Fillmore originally had slated Samuel Finely Vinton of Ohio, a Whig who had voted moderately on the questions still resounding in the halls of Congress. When, however, the retiring Ohio representative in Taylor's cabinet, Thomas Ewing, pressed too hard for Vinton's appointment, Fillmore grew cold.[20] He transfered his favor to Thomas Corwin, who was Ohio's most revered Whig. Reluctant at first to join the Administration as Postmaster-General, Corwin finally consented to come in as Secretary of the Treasury.[21]

16Memorandum of Webster to Fillmore, July [11], 1850, Fillmore Collection.
17Washington *Republic*, April 3, 4, 6, 12, 16, 20, 23, 24, 25, 1850.
18Graham to Fillmore, July 25, 1850, Fillmore Collection; see also Montford McGehee, *Life and Character of the Hon. William A. Graham*, 18-60.
19Crittenden to Fillmore, July 31, 1850, Fillmore Collection.
20Ewing to Fillmore, August 18, 1850, *ibid.*
21Webster to Fillmore, July 19, 1850, *ibid.*

For his Postmaster-General, Fillmore considered several well-known political figures,[22] and finally decided to give the post to a very close associate, his former law partner, Nathan K. Hall. Fillmore felt he could prevent that important patronage-dispensing office from being abused with the trusted and unambitious Hall acting as its guardian.

Two men whom the President sought for his cabinet he failed to obtain. Both were of the "National" type with whom he was packing his council. Senator James Alfred Pearce of Maryland, an unprofessional politician, was a quiet, scholarly man, who devoted himself to improving the Library of Congress and cultivating a circle of friends among the literati.[23] For a decade, ever since Pearce had helped Fillmore fight the pretensions of Clay in 1841, the two had been close friends. Fillmore offered Pearce the Interior Department. As much as the Senator would have liked to become a part of the official family, he felt obliged to remain in the Senate.[24]

Turned aside by Pearce, Fillmore now asked Edward Bates of Missouri to choose between the War and Interior departments. The Chief Executive wanted Bates in as a representative of the Northwest. Though from Missouri, he was well respected in Iowa, Illinois, and Wisconsin. At first Bates accepted, but on August 1, fearful of being exposed to the danger and casualties of political life, he declined.[25] Fillmore now experimented with the opinions of several other Northwest representatives,[26] and finding them little to his liking, turned southward to Louisiana for his final choice of a Secretary of War, Charles Magill Conrad.[27] Fillmore knew Conrad as a sound Whig who, as a Senator in 1842, had supported the tariff measures with exceptional skill, and who now, as a Congressman, was cooperating

---

[22]One was William L. Dayton, the other L. B. Ruggles. Webster to Fillmore, July 7, 19, 1850, *ibid.*
[23]B. C. Steiner, "James Alfred Pearce," *Maryland Historical Magazine*, 16:319.
[24]James A. Pearce to Fillmore, July 19, 21, 1850, Fillmore Collection.
[25]Bates to Fillmore, August 1, 1850, *ibid.*
[26]Henry L. Geyer, a Missouri Whig, and Charles Jenkins, a Georgia Whig. Buffalo *Express*, September 9, 1850; Geyer to Bates, August 6, 1850, Fillmore Collection.
[27]Conrad to Graham [August 9, 1850], *ibid.*

with the Stephens-Toombs-Douglas combination to break Taylor's policy.[28]

The importunate Pennsylvania delegates, who saw their favor with the Administration dissolve with Meredith's demise, forced Fillmore to promise a cabinet post to a Pennsylvanian. He wavered between Andrew Stewart, a Uniontown iron-monger who as Congressman was known as "Tariff Andy," and Thomas M. T. McKennon, a close friend of Pearce. Fillmore offered the Interior post to McKennon, only to have him resign a month later.[29] Thereupon he turned aside Webster's suggestion and bestowed the post on an old acquaintance from Virginia, the Union-loving Alexander H. H. Stuart who had been in political retirement for seven years.[30]

*   *   *   *   *

Few in the nation knew, as they read the newspaper reports of Fillmore's first week in the Presidency, to which side — compromise or Taylor's plan — Fillmore would direct the force of the Executive. Since the debate in Congress abruptly halted, and official Washington marked time out of respect for the departed President, who lay in state at the Executive Mansion, nothing happened to indicate a trend. The cabinet selections, kept secret, offered no clue.

Washington correspondents began to speculate. Some suspected that the feud with Seward would force the new President into the arms of the compromisers. Others delved into Fillmore's past, learned of his reputation as an antislavery man, and concluded he would take up Taylor's policy. But throughout the commercial community of the East, where Fillmore's character was best understood, a deep sigh relaxed the tension that had each merchant peering anxiously at his ledgers. "Men of discernment" in Boston "met together, and without saying a word,

---

[28]Binkley, "Texas Jurisdiction in New Mexico," 24:1-38.
[29]Kennedy to Fillmore, August 9, McKennon to Fillmore, August 26, 1850, Fillmore Collection.
[30]Stuart to Wilson, April 29, 1878, Fillmore Mss.; Webster to Fillmore, August 26, 1850, Fillmore Collection.

sufficiently manifested to one another that in their judgment, a highly important . . . change had taken place."[31]

Speculation was short, for as soon as decorum would permit, Washington officialdom settled down to business, and Fillmore's plan for the compromise materialized rapidly. Whether a settlement of the territorial crisis came as an Omnibus Bill or a series of separate measures had no bearing on his approach. To him the ritual was insignificant — he wanted the substance of a compromise — a cessation of all the agitation that had the nation pitting its armed force against a state and that turned men's minds away from the real needs of the nation. As a public official he refused to let a "higher law" than the Constitution govern his action. As a party leader, however, Fillmore was no disciplinarian. He would tolerate wide latitude of opinions among Whigs on slavery,[32] if for the time being they would cease prodding the nation to fits of suicide. Peace over slavery was his objective and to obtain it he adopted a flexible approach.

The great debate had revealed a weakness in the Omnibus strategy. "Nationals" had devised it to discourage Taylor from vetoing measures he disowned and to encourage the less extreme sectionalists to vote for measures that were unpopular in their states in order to get measures that were popular. The strategy had not worked as well as its sponsors had hoped. Instead of being willing to take the bad with the good, some sectional "Conscience" Senators preferred to be identified with only the interests of their area. Thus the Omnibus's chances for success had hung on a narrow margin.

With Fillmore in the Executive Mansion, however, and Taylor's threat of a veto gone, the Omnibus was no longer the only way toward success. Should it be broken into its several parts, the sectionalists would vote for those measures which they approved. Then if enough "Nationals" joined them, each meas-

[31]New York *Express*, July 1, 13, 1850; Ketchum to Fillmore, July 27, 1850; Allibone to Fillmore, July 19, 1850; Webster to Fillmore, October 14, 1850, Fillmore Collection; Philadelphia *Sun*, July 11, 1850.
[32]P. Greeley to Fillmore, December 16, 1850, Fillmore Collection.

ure might receive a legislative majority. From the point of view of political wisdom, for both party and officeholders, this was sound. Stephen A. Douglas, leader of the Democratic block of "Nationals," had persistently advocated it.

With these possibilities in sight, Fillmore turned his full attention to Congress, which on July 15 once again took up its burden. Two days later, Webster, still a Senator, laid the basis for the Administration's action. He obtained from Douglas a promise to support the provisions of the compromise as separate measures if the Omnibus Bill failed.[33]

With that promise ringing in his ears, and filled with patriotism, Webster delivered his Senatorial peroration — his last appealing address to the Senate for the Union. He called for the enactment of the Omnibus, and if that failed, then the immediate acceptance of its detail in separate bills.[34] Simultaneously Fillmore let it be known that he would sign any constitutional measure passed by Congress.[35] With these two unofficial announcements Fillmore's peace offensive began to unfold. The new Administration now waited for Congress, encouraged to act and freed of fears of a veto, to take one or the other road toward peace.

Before a week had passed, the Senators were ready to press the Omnibus to a vote "and let the agony be over."[36] For seven months they had maintained their battle lines, and as the whips of the Omnibus counted noses, it again looked as if one or two votes would decide between defeat and victory. At a caucus on July 29, Clay and his associates made one last move to win a few more votes. They modified the Texas boundary settlement of the Omnibus Bill. Instead of drawing the boundary line by legislative enactment, they proposed to appoint a commission to investigate the boundary. While that commission conducted

[33]*Congressional Globe,* 31 cong., 1 sess., app. 2:1266; New York *Express,* July 20, 1850.
[34]*Congressional Globe,* 31 cong., 1 sess., app. 2:1260-1270.
[35]New York State *Register,* July 15, 18, 20, 22, 27, 1850; New York *Express,* July 15, 17, 20, 1850.
[36]*Ibid.,* quoting from Washington correspondent of Baltimore *Sun,* July 18, 1850.

its survey, the operation of the territorial government for the disputed territory would rest in abeyance. The provision — known as the Dawson Proviso — encouraged southern ultras to believe that all of New Mexico east of the Rio Grande would eventually become Texas' westernmost counties, and therefore additional slave territory. The next day the Senate accepted the caucus-drawn Dawson Proviso, and friends of the Omnibus were jubilant.[37]

But Clay had committed a blunder. In altering the Omnibus, he miscalculated the true spirit of Fillmore's goal. Since the Dawson Proviso failed to settle the Texas boundary and merely postponed its solution to another day, it left the way open for Texas to assert her claim to Santa Fe with armed force. Already Governor Bell had called a special legislative session to determine Texas' course. Should the nation be fortunate enough to avoid an armed clash during the proposed survey, in only a matter of months, when the commission submitted its work to Congress for approval, the whole volatile question would again be exposed to the inflamed debates of Congress.[38]

Fillmore perceived the dangers in the revised Omnibus, and he moved quickly to restore its original decisive quality. He called his friend, Senator James Alfred Pearce, to the Presidential Mansion, and together they laid out the strategy: either eliminate the Dawson Proviso or clear the way for a complete settlement by breaking the Omnibus.[39] Into the sweltering Senate chamber, Pearce carried his plan, unknown to the great crowd of notables who jammed the galleries until the hall "actually steamed with perspiration." They had come to view the passage of the Omnibus Bill, which the Dawson Proviso had seemingly assured. The complicated parliamentary situation compelled Pearce to resort to heroic means to accomplish Fillmore's purpose — nothing less than a motion to strike out the entire New Mexico section and

[37]New York *Express*, July 25, 27, 29, 30, August 1, 1850; *Congressional Globe*, 31 cong., 1 sess., app. 2:1443, 1466, 1481-1482.
[38]Binkley, "Texas in New Mexico," 24:29.
[39]Steiner, "Pearce," 16:332. See Pearce's letter of August 5. 1850. New York *Express*, August 1, 2, 1850; *Congressional Globe*, 31 cong., 1 sess., app. 2:1470-1488.

then to reinsert all but the Dawson Proviso. Consternation seized the friends of the Omnibus, and in the confusion dozens rushed to Pearce's side with words of caution and entreaties for reconsideration. But Fillmore's spokesman stood his ground.

Divining the impossibility of restoring the original Omnibus, Pearce permitted himself to be led into a Machiavellian trap. He granted an extreme Southerner's request[40] to divide his motion. In the ensuing vote, the motion to "strike out" carried,[41] but the motion to "reinsert" failed,[42] and the Omnibus was shorn of one of its provisions. Panicked friends of the Omnibus sued for time by urging an adjournment, but its foes pressed home their advantage. They struck out the California section,[43] and the emasculated bill, now reduced to a simple organization of Utah, passed.[44] In a fleeting moment, when success was in sight, the Omnibus expired — a victim of Fillmore's desire for peace.[45]

Upon the death of the Omnibus, as he had promised, Douglas assumed leadership to effect a compromise with separate measures. He called up a California bill and pushed it toward enactment. But again executive pressure altered the course of the compromise. The same factors that had prompted Fillmore to set Pearce on his course pressed with ever-increasing force upon the President. Texas Congressmen were importuning him to repudiate Colonel Monroe's action. They claimed they had inside information that Texas' militia would march against Santa Fe and seize the disputed region. Succumbing to Texan threats was not Fillmore's way, and he addressed a stinging message to Governor Bell, which went out under Webster's name, that upheld the federal government's title to the area. Neither was stubbornness Fillmore's way; for while he scolded Texas, he, Webster, and Douglas shaped the provisions of a new Texas boundary bill which made more concessions to Texas than the original provisions of the Omnibus. The new bill drew a boundary that conceded Texas 33,000 square miles, but denied

---

[40]Yulee of Florida.   [41]Vote: 32-22.   [42]Vote: 25-28.   [43]Vote: 34-25.
[44]Engrossed 32-18 and passed the following day without record.
[45]*Congressional Globe,* 31 cong., 1 sess., app. 2:1470-1488.

her 70,000 other square miles which she claimed. Under considerable pressure, the Texas Senators agreed to support this measure, and Pearce was again called upon to act as the instrument of the Administration.[46]

On August 5, Pearce introduced the bill into the Senate, and the next day he tried to secure precedence for it over the California bill which held first place on the calendar. Momentarily he failed. Again Fillmore rushed to the rescue. That same day he hurriedly sent to Congress an alarming description of the Santa Fe situation, and after reviewing the history of the controversy, pointed out that the boundary question could never be settled by a review of the documents. No one really knew where it was. Because of this, he appealed to Congress to make its own decision quickly. It "is . . . my deep and earnest conviction" he said, that Congress must make

> an immediate settlement of the question. . . . Domestic tranquility calls for this. It seems to be in its character . . . the first . . . of the questions . . . now requiring decision. . . . If judicial proceedings were resorted to . . . years would pass . . . before the controversy could be ended. . . . Such delay . . . might be the occasion for disturbances and collisions. For the same reason I . . . doubt . . . the expediency of the appointment of commissioners [to examine the boundary]. . . . Congress is as capable of deciding . . . now as it would be after a report of the commissioners. . . .
>
> I repeat my conviction that every consideration of public interest manifests the necessity for settlement of the boundry dispute before the present session is brought to a close."[47]

The message, hailed everywhere as a master stroke of timing and persuasive moderation, prepared the way for peace.

[46]New York *Express*, August 7, 8, 1850; J. W. Sheahan. *Life of Stephen A. Douglas*, 132-34; George D. Armond, "Douglas and the Compromise of 1850," *Journal of the Illinois State Historical Society*, 21:451-99; Webster, *Writings and Speeches*, 12:153ff., Webster to Haven, August 10, 1850, *ibid.*, 16:558-9; Webster to Fillmore, July 30, 1850; Texas delegation to Fillmore, July [22], 1850; Rogsdon to Fillmore, July 22, 1850; Howard to Fillmore, July 13, August 1, 1850; Webster to Fillmore, [August 6, 1850], Fillmore Collection.
[47]Richardson, *Messages*, 5:72-73.

The next day the President's wish for precedence was granted,[48] and almost overnight the hiatus between thought and action dissolved. With a haste that its previous procrastination made to appear unbecoming, the Senate passed the Texas boundary bill. Still possessed by a spirit of accomplishment, the Senate readily placed its stamp of approval on the California, New Mexico, and fugitive slave measures. It threatened to regress to its former ways on the bill to abolish slave trade in the District of Columbia, but by September 13 that too received Senatorial sanction. Down the corridor, the Representatives were doing their part. The obstacles to compromise and concession having been removed by the Administration's policy, the Representatives by mid-September had enacted all the measures into law.[49]

Except for the Fugitive Slave Act, Fillmore affixed his signature as rapidly as the bills came to him. On the Fugitive Slave Act he hesitated. Personally it was repugnant, and he knew it would "draw down upon his head vials of wrath" from abolitionists. Yet Fillmore knew all along he would sign it. He regretted its necessity, but the Constitution required the giving up of fugitive slaves, and it was not for him to decide whether this was a wise provision of the Constitution — it was a compact, he had sworn to maintain it, and he would do so to his last hour. In the North the papers had raised grave doubts about the constitutionality of the act, since it denied fugitive slaves the right to a jury trial. Fillmore had no doubts of the act's constitutionality, "but from deference to public opinion of the northern people, and to avoid the imputation of hasty and unconsidered action" he referred the matter to his Attorney-General. Crittenden sustained Fillmore's constitutional view, and thereupon, without reference to the cabinet, Fillmore signed the bill.[50]

[48]*Ibid.*, 5:68-72; *Senate Journal*, 31 cong., 1 sess., 543.
[49]Buffalo *Express*, August 21, 1850; Graham to Fillmore, September 9, 1850; Webster to Fillmore [August 6, 1850]; Clay to Fillmore, August 10, 1850; Fish to Fillmore, October 12, 1850; Barnard to Fillmore, August 12, 1850, Fillmore Collection; *Congressional Globe*, 31 cong., 1 sess., app. 2:1520-21, 1531-33, 1543-1678 *passim*, 1690, 1743-44, 1750, 1784, 1794-95, 1805, 1809-10, 1817, 1829-30 1837, 1630-74.
[50]Stuart to Wilson, April 23, 1878, Fillmore Mss.; Marshall to Wilson, January 27, 1882, *ibid.*; *Fillmore Papers*, 1:432-33.

As if by magic, the clouds of disunion, which hovered threateningly over the nation, disappeared. In ten short weeks, Fillmore's administration had solved the problem of territorial government that had plagued Congress ever since American and Mexican troops first clashed four years ago — a problem that had sacrificed all else to its devouring demand for attention.

Chapter 14

Warfare: The Bolt of the "Silver Greys"

LMOST immediately after hearing of Taylor's death, Fillmore's family had set out from Buffalo for Washington. They arrived too late for the simple inauguration ceremony but their presence helped the new and harassed President over the personal hardships of the first weeks. Amid the fearful responsibilities that had been thrust upon him, it was comforting to have close at hand those whom he loved and who loved him. Mrs. Fillmore, unfortunately, was ailing and could not take on the duties of the First Lady without help. But her comely, talented daughter, not yet out of her teens, turned to the task with an inborn felicity and graciousness that did credit to her parents. Young Millard, already a lawyer in his own right, became his father's private secretary and did yeoman service in the post.

His family, however, was the President's only comfort. Elsewhere, even though he had won the battle in Congress, there was no respite from anxiety. If he had expected the Compromise measures to establish peace automatically, he was mistaken. Though reduced in intensity, the problems were still with him. Free-soilers and fire-eaters alike redeployed their forces to widely scattered sectors on the home front and now, in guerilla fashion, sniped at the settlement. The Chief Executive's work was cut out for him. If he were to be true to the high resolve that the crisis of July 9 had forged in his soul, the fight for sectional peace must now be carried to the home front. He must persuade the guerillas to accept the Compromise as a permanent part of the American scene. He had little time to prepare for battle on this front, for even as he was signing the last measure, his old enemies in New York threw down the gauntlet of challenge.

*   *   *   *   *

For over a year, Weed and Seward had waged open, merciless warfare against Fillmore. They had persecuted his friends and had maligned him as an ingrate. All this they had done because, mistakenly, they had regarded the Vice-President as Seward's chief rival for the Presidency and Weed's chief rival for mastery of the state party. During those fifteen months Fillmore had fought back with persistent stubborness and had rallied to his cause both upstate and New York City interests. But Weed had been confident that Seward's intimacy with the Administration ultimately would wreck whatever influence Fillmore might still retain.[1]

Then the fatal news of July 9 flashed across the nation, and the high spirits of the editor of the Albany *Evening Journal* tumbled into depression. The man Weed and Seward had tried to crucify commanded the entire force of the federal government. In their imagination they saw the axe of revenge fall. They expected to see heads roll and their appointees, whose confirmations they had not had the courage to push in the face of Fillmore's position in the Senate, dismissed in wholesale lots. The future looked somber and uninviting, and in their fright, they impulsively struck out against the Administration.[2]

But again Weed and Seward misjudged Fillmore. By their own standards he had ample justification for reprisals. Yet vengefulness was not a part of his character. He had no desire to carry on a vendetta against them. A double transformation had taken place. No longer need he be concerned with his own political

[1]Hammond to Fillmore, July 12, 1850, Fillmore Collection.
[2]*Buffalo Express*, July 12, 1850, August 15, 1850; Albany *Evening Journal*, July 10, 16, August 15, 30, 1850; Barnard to Fillmore, July 10, 1850; Sign to Fillmore, July 10, 1850, Fillmore Collection.

health. Further, the responsibilities of his office had raised his vision to encompass the entire American scene. What he saw from the height of the Presidency determined him to seek the role of a statesman rather than that of the politician.

After the crowded days of his first weeks in the office had passed, he felt that his political life had run its course and that he owed the nation a great obligation. He had obtained the highest honor of the land, and beyond that there was little more except an extra four years of being President. Only the lust for power, the kind of hankering that kept Weed going in the face of all discouragement, would make additional years in the Presidency attractive or desirable. Yet lust for power never had motivated Fillmore. He had sought respect, position, wealth, and comfort, but never power. And now he was committed, with an honesty of feeling that could not be doubted, to a policy of restoring peace to the land. The haunting realization that the nation must be freed from sectional discord, whether expressed by words or by guns, tempered his approach to New York politics.[3]

Weed, as he struck out for his own interests, was the first to challenge the Compromise settlement. But, determined to serve the cause of peace, Fillmore met this mailed fist with an olive branch. Instead of wielding the federal patronage axe against Weed, Fillmore tried to draw the Albany editor to the support of the Compromise. The President understood that Weed was capable of changing his line if he saw an opportunity to advance toward his own goals. Even though Fillmore's friends were hot for the blood of "the dictator and his minion," the President ignored these calls for revenge. He hoped to avoid confusing the Compromise with Weed's and Seward's personal hatred for himself and he, therefore, shielded the New York boss from the wrath of his old victims. At this crisis, cautioned Fillmore, if Weed were not provoked into rash, defensive acts, he

[3]Ullman to Fillmore, September 24, 1850; Young to Fillmore, August 1, 1850; Fuller to Fillmore, July 10, 1850, Fillmore Collection.

might be brought around to accepting the Compromise by silence, if no other way.[4]

In the first three months of his administration, Fillmore withdrew only a single Weed appointment. The one removal was a balm to the President's dignity: he fired Levi Allen, Weed's appointee to the Buffalo collectorship and the symbol of Fillmore's former undoing.[5] It was his sole victory indulgence. He hoped that such restraint might induce Weed and Seward to give up the sectional issue as a vault to power, since their own strength would plainly not be threatened by Fillmore's rise to the Presidency.[6]

Time would soon show that Fillmore's attitude toward Weed and Seward arose from misplaced hope. Through each stage of the Compromise Seward had opposed its provisions. He had thoroughly aligned himself with antislavery sentiment, and even had he wanted to, he could not have readily reversed his stand without real embarrassment. Both he and Weed, moreover, had long doubted the value of the Whig party, as then constituted. If Seward ever were to be President, it would be only as the candidate of a section, and they had been thinking of reshaping their party rather than adjusting themselves to it. Taylor's death confirmed their feelings, and instantly they adopted the strategy of trying to retain the control of the New York Whig party as a nucleus for building anew. Once before in his long career, Weed had behaved in the same fashion. That was when he gave up hope for the Antimasonic party. Now, again, the first step in the campaign was to keep New York Whiggery committed to a free-soil ideology and await the future.[7]

[4]Young to Fillmore, September 5, 1850; Ketchum to Fillmore, September 30, 1850; Hall to Fillmore, September 2, 1850; Fuller to Fillmore, September 10, 15, 1850; Spencer to Fillmore, August 7, 1850; Thompson to Fillmore, July 29, 1850; Corning to Fillmore, August 15, 1850; Barnard to Fillmore, July 12. 1850; Haven to Fillmore, July 19, 31, 1850; Kellogg to Fillmore, August 5, 1850, *ibid.; Rochester American,* July 26, 1850; Syracuse *Daily Star,* July 13, 1850.
[5]He replaced Allen with William Ketchum, his old friend and original recommendation.
[6]*Buffalo Express,* August 8, 1850; Buffalo *Commercial Advertiser,* August 5, 1850.
[7]Haven to Fillmore, September 14, 1850; Fuller to Fillmore, September 15, 1850; Mower to Fillmore, August 18, 1850; Charles to Fillmore, July 30, 1850; Barnard to Fillmore, July 10, 1850, Fillmore Collection. *Buffalo Express,* August 16, 1850.

With their sectional objective in mind, Seward and Weed tried to turn Fillmore's desire to maintain peace to their own advantage. They instructed their friends to encourage the Administration in its misplaced hope. Meanwhile, they made every effort to prepare the ground for a coup that would carry them toward their goal — a general announcement that the New York Whigs would neither accept the Compromise nor abandon their antislavery feelings.[8]

*   *   *   *   *

The President's policy of restraint was soon tested. Less than a week after the passage of the final Compromise measure, New York Whigs were scheduled to hold a state nominating convention at Syracuse. The eyes of the nation turned to it. Here would be answered the question: would free-soil Whigs accept the work which Congress and Fillmore had just completed?[9]

From every direction, delegates descended upon Syracuse, and some bore instructions or advice from the President. A hand-picked Buffalo delegation came prepared to put down what Fillmore called that "two cent system of politics which builds up individual and personal interests upon abstract and non-essential points, affecting prejudices and not actualities."[10] Fuller and Barnard arrived from Albany with the attitude of the President in mind; Maxwell and Young came up from New York City determined to convince the party that abolitionism must be abandoned. The head of the city delegation, Daniel Ullman, carried Fillmore's direct instructions on the attitude his friends should adopt. Avoid all untoward incidents, Fillmore cautioned Ullman, and make every effort to get along with

[8]"The time will come son, I think, when we must make open war on this administration . . . . " Seth Hawley to Seward, September 21, 1850, Seward Papers. Hunt to Fillmore, July 25, 1850; Hewitt to Fillmore, August 10, 1850; Diesendorf to Fillmore, July 11, 1850; Calhoun to Fillmore, July 12, 1850, Fillmore Collection. *Buffalo Express,* August 16, 1850.

[9]Hull to Fillmore, July 29, 1850; Ullman to Fillmore, September 24, 1850; King to Fillmore, August 22, 1850; Curtis to Fillmore, September 18, 1850; Hoxie to Fillmore, August 26, 1850, Fillmore Collection.

[10]Fillmore quoted by Haven to Fillmore, September 9, 1850, Fillmore Collection.

Weed and Seward. The convention should say and do nothing offensive to either faction; the ticket should represent both groups. For the time being, postpone all hostilities toward Seward and Weed, and concentrate on the greater objective of displaying to the nation that New York was willing to forsake its slavery agitation for the general welfare of the nation. William Duer, Congressman from Oswego, arrived from Washington with a platform. He had been huddled with the President and was told that in the event that Weed refused to cooperate, the convention should assure the nation that New York's Whigs were not in accord with the "higher law" doctrine.[11]

Hopes of success ran high among Fillmore's friends. On the first show of strength, Francis Granger, grown silver-grey in the service of the party, and now tied to Fillmore's cause, won the chairmanship of the convention. Here was a good beginning. Washington Hunt then easily won the nomination for governor. Though some delegates were afraid that Hunt was Weed's tool, they had accepted him at Fillmore's behest. The rest of the ticket was entirely satisfactory to both sides. Then Duer, as chairman of the committee on resolutions, brought in a moderate plank on the Compromise from a committee previously picked by Granger. The Whigs of New York, ran Duer's statement, "acquiesce in the creation of territorial governments for New Mexico and Utah in the confident belief that these acts will result in the exclusion of slavery from the territory ceded by Mexico to the United States." Here was a left-handed acceptance of the Compromise that placated the free-soilers by assuring them they had won their battle on the territories.[12]

Up to this point all had gone well. Though Weed and Seward had a majority of the delegates, they had restrained themselves. Fillmore's failure to remove Weed's friends from federal offices

---

[11]Duer to Fillmore, October 2, 1850; Ullman to Fillmore, September 2, 1850, September 24, 1850; Fuller to Fillmore, September 20, 1850, Fillmore Collection.
[12]*Buffalo Express*, October 1, 1850. Young to Fillmore, August 21, 1850; Fuller to Fillmore, July 9, 1850; Hunt to Fillmore, September 18, 1850; Graham to Fillmore, September 9, 1850; Stuart to Fillmore, September 7, 1850, Fillmore Collection.

had apparently worked to the good of the Compromise. Then
suddenly the "two-cent" spirit flared out. A delegate from
Seward's home district arose and offered a substitute set of
resolutions. In only two respects were they different. "As
territorial governments are established for New Mexico and
Utah without any prohibitory clause, upon the assumption that
slavery is prohibited" by nature, declared one statement, it is
the solemn duty of Congress to prohibit slavery in these territories "on the first indication" that nature was not doing her
duty. The second blatantly extended the "thanks of the Whig
Party" to Seward for representing the views of New York so
cogently in the Senate.[13]

Instantly Fillmore's friends were on their feet in protest.
This was exactly what they had tried to avoid. All day long, in
the spirit of conciliation, they tried to defeat the substitute
resolutions. But they had arrayed themselves against a well-
disciplined majority directed from Weed's hotel room. When
the substitute resolutions passed 70 to 40, Francis Granger gave
the cue to Fillmore's men. He threw down his gavel and stalked
out of the convention. His long, silver-grey hair seemed to
stand out like a mane as he strode up the aisle. Behind him
followed the other forty delegates.[14]

One observer instantly wired Fillmore: "Affairs at a crisis.
Convention split open. Granger and your friends gone to
another house." Another reported: "We have nailed the colors
to the mast and we'll fight to the last for you and your administration. . . . The line is drawn." The line was, indeed, drawn —
right down the middle of the party. Fillmore's conciliatory
policy had failed.[15]

                    *   *   *   *   *

[13]*Buffalo Express,* October 1, 1850. Faxton to Fillmore, October 3, 1850; Conkling
to Fillmore, October 1, 1850; Duer to Fillmore, October 2, 1850; Ketchum to
Fillmore, September 30, 1850, Fillmore Collection.
[14]Young to Fillmore, September 29, 1850, *ibid.;* Syracuse *Daily Star,* September 28,
29, 30, 1850.
[15]Maxwell to Fillmore, September 28, 1850; B. F. Hall to Fillmore, September 25,
1850, Fillmore Collection.

Fillmore's bland and controlled face did not reveal the emotions that seized him as he read the telegrams from Maxwell and Fuller. Weed had rejected the formula for harmony and had thrown down a challenge. Between them there was to be no peace. Smoldering resentment tempted him to pick up the gauntlet and do personal battle with his former ally. Quickly, however, the real purpose of his offer of cooperation repossessed him. The fate of the Compromise might well be in the balance. The thought quenched his impulse and covered him with anxiety.[16]

Among the bolters, whom Weed instantly dubbed the "Silver Greys" because of Granger's flowing grey locks,[17] was a strong contingent from New York City. What this group might do, cut loose from the party organization, crowded thoughts of impulsive action from Fillmore's mind. They were his supporters but their background was a history of rash acts. In this hour of crisis, audacity might be disastrous for the cause of Compromise.[18] Yet Fillmore could not deny that extreme

[16]The following letters written by Haven, next to Hall, Fillmore's closest friend, to Fillmore, bear this out.
    October 3, 1850: "Yours of the 29th ult. rec'd. . . . The situation is delicate, as you suggest. If Hunt is passed by at Utica we will have cause for anxiety. I know how you feel about Weed and I have not always been in agreement with you but I think we should have cut off all the Sewardites from office that if we are not extremely carefully now Weed will do us in like last year. Why don't you make some demonstration in Washington that will assure our friends that they can depend on the administration . . . ?"
    October 5, 1850: "Yours of the 2nd ist. rec'd. . . . I agree that the action of our friends at Syracuse was 'indiscreet.' They should have published the address placing them on a national platform and then endorsed the Whig Ticket. The call of a convention was sheer folly. If this was your policy, then we've been misled because every act till now points toward a profound consideration of the enemy. Had you wanted the move, I've been telling our friends here, you would have told us definitely that the knife was sharpened. . . . "
    October 14, 1850: "I dare not trust the convention at Utica and so I had our meeting adopt the precise resolutions reported by the committee of 8 at Syracuse. And then ratify the Syracuse nominations heartily, and then adjourn.
    "I think this will do the most good at Utica. They will find that if they wish to make a new nomination that they cannot force it upon us. I now think we shall elect Hunt & I have thought so from the beginning in case it was not kicked over in Utica."
    All letters in Fillmore Collection.
[17]Albany *Evening Journal*, September 29, 30, October 5, 1850.
[18]See Fillmore's actions below.

pressure from New York City merchants was impelling the city's Whigs to incautious acts.

Early in 1850 Gotham's merchants had endorsed the Compromise as a means of breaking the southern boycott of northern products and services. Much to their dismay, however, the passage of the Compromise did not quiet the slavery agitation. Southern extremists still threatened secession, and southern buyers continued to boycott the New York market. The merchants appealed to their southern customers to call off the dogs of reprisal and cried out that others, not they, were responsible for the antislavery movement in New York. They laid the blame at the feet of Weed and Seward, and as a token of good faith, they resolved to silence the Albany editor and his cohort.[19]

On the method of achieving their object, however, the merchants divided. One group, led by professional politicians, sought to win the confidence of southern customers by supporting Fillmore's administration. The other group, led largely by merchants who occasionally dabbled in politics, scoffed at this solution. This was the impulsive element in the party, and it called for drastic action. Its members felt that both major parties were fatally afflicted with the " 'potato rot' of negroism."[20] Only the creation of a new party around the pro-Compromise elements of the old parties would achieve the economic peace they sought.[21]

Now as Fillmore laid down the telegrams bearing the dramatic news from Syracuse, he saw how hard it would be to restrain the impetuous merchants. They had been presented an opportunity to organize a new party around the bolting "Silver

[19]Davis to Fillmore, October 7, 1850; Ketchum to Fillmore, September 30, 1850; Young to Fillmore, September 29, 1850; Barnard to Fillmore, September 30, 1850, Fillmore Collection. Draper to Weed, October 2, 1850, Weed Papers. *Journal of Commerce,* October 1-6, 1850.

[20]Davis to Webster, August 9, September 12, 1850, Webster Papers.

[21]Draper to Weed, August 5, 1850; Lyman to Weed, September 23, 1850, Weed Papers. Ketchum to Fillmore, August 22, 1850; Barnard to Fillmore, September 17, 1850, Fillmore Collection.

Greys." This was what troubled Fillmore's thoughts. A division of Whigs into two independent organizations, one led by himself and the other by Weed, would not bring peace. Rather such a dissolution would leave Seward and Weed in the field with no alternative but to beat the drums of sectional discord. Agitation would heighten rather than decline. Against this Fillmore had set his face.

Only hours later, another group of telegrams confirmed Fillmore's fears. Following the walk-out, the "Silver Greys" reassembled in another hall. Almost all were shaken by a tempestuous will to strike back.[22] Had they simply wanted to protest the pro-Seward resolutions, they would have endorsed Washington Hunt for governor, and passed Fillmore's resolutions on the Compromise. Instead the seceders, not having Fillmore's insight, called another state convention for October 17 at Utica. It portended the formation of an independent party with its own platform and candidates. To Fillmore the news boded ill.

Rather than independent tactics — or as some were suggesting, union with the pro-Compromise segment of the Democracy — Fillmore preferred to keep the Whig party intact and smother the sectional issue in a great public display of magnanimity, forbearance, and nationalism. Knowing Weed's lust for power, Fillmore still believed that if he dangled the right bait before Weed, he would voluntarily cease agitating the slavery question. The bait before Weed was still the prospect that some day soon, if for the time being he quit agitating the slavery issue, he might again control an undivided Whig party.[23] Fillmore appreciated that to carry out this program against a wily and astute opponent like Weed and a skitterish wing of his own followers would be a difficult task. But New York's importance in the struggle for acceptance of the Compromise was manifest, and Fillmore threw himself unsparingly into the work. Hardly had the Syracuse convention divided before he put into effect

[22]Syracuse *Daily Star*, September 31, 1850.
[23]Haven to Fillmore, September 29, 1850, December 18, 1850, Fillmore Collection.

his complicated scheme to repair the damage which his friends had unintentionally done.

First he let the patronage axe fall once, and the head of Lewis Benedict, postmaster at Albany, rolled.[24] Benedict had helped pack the Syracuse convention with Seward boosters. His dismissal reminded the lowly in the ranks of Weed's henchmen that too close an identity with Weed might earn for them the same treatment. Cautiously, however, Fillmore refrained from wholesale proscriptions which would have driven the small politicians into wild hysteria.[25]

Next the President turned his attention to make sure that the "Silver Greys" would nominate Washington Hunt at the Utica convention, as well as endorsing the platform he had sent to Syracuse. This would spike the new party movement without harming the Compromise. For years Fillmore had known Hunt, and in recent months the two had corresponded freely. He believed Hunt was safe and not the blind tool of Weed and Seward. But to convince the doubtful and to take some of the force out of the new party movement, Fillmore entrusted Francis Granger with drawing out Hunt. Fillmore, meanwhile, instructed trusted delegates how to behave at the coming Utica convention, and he charged James O. Putnam, his special emissary to the meeting, with preventing independent party action.[26]

In the meantime, Fillmore's friends urged New York City businessmen to cooperate. On October 11, at the behest of Hugh Maxwell, a group of sixty "heavy merchants" were brought together at the palatial Fifth Avenue home of Morris Ketchum.

[24]Barnard to Fillmore, September 30, 1850; Benedict to Fillmore, October 9, 1850, *ibid*.

[25]Ullman to Fillmore: "Your kind favor of the 3d is before me. Your line of policy is certainly judicious. It appears to me, however, that Kellogg . . . and Clawes [postmaster at Troy] should be exceptions. Those men are so foul mouthed, and active in their opposition that our friends feel that they should be decapitated in order that they may be a terror to others." October 5, 1850, *ibid*.

[26]Haven to Fillmore, October 6, 1850; Kellogg to Fillmore, October 8, 1850; Granger to Fillmore, October 19, 1850; Hunt to Fillmore, October 25, 1850, *ibid*. *Buffalo Express*, October 24, 1850.

Maxwell reported to Fillmore that these merchants were "alive to the vast interests New York City has in stopping agitation."[27] By playing upon this feeling, he persuaded them to give large sums of money to carry out a state-wide campaign to sell the Compromise to the average voter. A committee, packed with Administration friends, was empowered to spend the money. The meeting also revealed how strongly they were opposed to Weed. They called for the nomination of someone besides Hunt whom they considered Weed's tool. This was what Maxwell, at the prompting of Fillmore, was trying to avoid. Quickly Maxwell assured the group that Hunt was reliable, and after much persuasion they finally agreed to support Hunt if he came out unequivocally in favor of the Compromise and the national Administration. In response to this understanding, that evening the New York City delegation left for the Utica convention. It was instructed to cooperate with the Buffalo delegation.[28] The next day at Utica, Fillmore's friends obtained the endorsement of Hunt on a Compromise platform.[29]

All appeared to be going according to plan. The action at Utica saved the party from dissolution, and Fillmore still had his bait dangling before Weed. A few days later, Granger drew out Hunt. He placed himself behind the Compromise — but with one equivocation. He urged some "modifications" in the Fugitive Slave Act. What he asked was barely a half step out of line with the "Silver Grey" position. As a politician, Fillmore understood that since Hunt was the candidate of two factions, it was necessary to take a position between them, and he was satisfied with Hunt's reliability.[30]

The merchants, however, were quick to find fault with Hunt's hedging. They charged him with kowtowing to the

[27]Stuart to Fillmore, October 12, 1850 for quotation; see also October 3, 1850, Fillmore Collection.
[28]Maxwell to Fillmore, October 12, 1850, *ibid.*
[29]New York State *Register*, October 15, 1850; *Buffalo Express*, October 23, 1850.
[30]*Journal of Commerce*, October 18, 1850; Ketchum in *ibid.*, October 26, 1850. Granger to Fillmore, October 19, 22, 1850; Stuart to Fillmore, October 21, 1850; Davis to Fillmore, October 18, 1850, Fillmore Collection. *Washington Hunt to Francis Granger* . . . Morgan to Weed, October 31, 1850, E. D. Morgan Letterbook.

spirit of Sewardism. Talk of a new party reappeared, and once again the merchants threatened to get out of hand. They called for a giant "Union Meeting" of their community at Castle Garden. Ten thousand merchants signed the call "without distinction to party" to assemble together to voice their approval of the "peace measures" and to take any action "best calculated to avert the further progress of political agitation in the north." The state election was only a few days away. Rumors spread that a new "Conservative Union Party" would emerge from this meeting. But Fillmore's friends moved in on the mass meeting and confined its action to a broad pledge to vote only for safe and sure men.[31]

The threat of independent politics, however, did not pass so easily. The Castle Garden meeting appointed a huge committee — called the Union Committee — staffed it solely with merchants, and charged it with achieving its object. At any moment it might launch a third party. Then, on the eve of the election, a faction of the committeemen, calling themselves the "Union Association," recommended in newspaper broadsides that voters divide their ticket between Whigs and Democrats. They printed a "Union Ticket" and urged the selection of the Democratic nominee for governor over Hunt.[32]

Here was defection, but not an independent party that Fillmore had feared ever since the Syracuse convention. He watched the birth of this Union Ticket unruffled. This kind of coalition was common among the city merchants. As long as they confined their Union Ticket to the city and made it a mixture of other parties' candidates, Fillmore was satisfied. It would not break the unity of the Whig organization and create a sectional party.[33]

[31]Lathrop and Carleton to Webster, October 23, 1850, Webster Papers. David to Fillmore, October 24, Fillmore Collection. *Journal of Commerce*, October 23-25, 1850.

[32]*Ibid.*, October 24, 26, 30, November 4, 5, 1850; Hunt to Fillmore, October 5, 1850, Fillmore Collection.

[33]Ketchum to Fillmore, November 7, 30, 1850; Brooks to Fillmore, November 16, 1850; Bush to Fillmore, November 20, 1850, *ibid.*

Although Fillmore had no part in designing it, the Union Ticket proved a boon to his objective. It won the support of "men of wealth and character." Before the election, the *Tribune* had predicted that the ticket would gain the votes of a majority of the merchants, and it had warned the rural Whigs to intensify their efforts to nullify "mercantile defection." The results amply justified these fears. Hunt was elected by barely 300 votes, and in New York City received 962 fewer votes than his rival, Horatio Seymour. On the other hand, Cornell, the Whig and Union candidate for lieutenant-governor, received a majority of 4,437 votes in the city. Unquestionably, the mercantile Whigs had cast their votes for Seymour, fearing that Hunt was a Seward man. In business circles, the election results aroused considerable joy because reports revealed that Southerners interpreted New York's election as a decisive blow to Seward, and as a victory for Union and Compromise.[34]

Fillmore nodded his approval. He had what he wanted even if it had not come by his plan of tempting Weed to support the Compromise. By shrewd political work, amid ever-changing conditions, he had made it possible for his native state to sustain the Compromise. Although not as decisive an endorsement as he would have liked, it left the impression that his party was willing to accept the measures as the best possible solution of a knotty problem. He had out-maneuvered Weed in a political game in which Weed was a past master. And Fillmore had done it in so subtle a manner that the promise of permanent silence of the Sewardites on the slavery issue came within sight.

[34]Hone, *Diary*, November 4, 1850. Davis to Fillmore, October 7, 24, 1850, Fillmore Collection. *Journal of Commerce*, November 7-14, 1850. Stetson to Weed, November 7, 1850, Weed Papers. Hunt to Fillmore, November 10, 1850; Phoenix to Fillmore, November 6, 1850; Davis to Fillmore, November 7, 1850, Fillmore Collection. Grinnell to Crittenden, November 18, 1850, Crittenden Papers.

Chapter 15

The Great Silence

ILLMORE'S campaign for sectional peace required constant vigilance. During the previous six years, antislavery agitators, by fighting against the extension of slavery, had won a sympathetic hearing. With that issue they had reached more hearts than the abolitionists had ever done with their moral suasion. But now in 1850, the Compromise, by eliminating the issue, had completely cut the ground out from under them. For the time being they were forced to turn to other propaganda. They seized upon the Fugitive Slave Act.

It, unlike the other parts of the Compromise, did not settle an issue with one stroke. Because it required constant enforcement, the Fugitive Slave Law offered continuing material for attack. In unison antislavery leaders turned upon it. They denounced Fillmore for signing the measure; and anonymous fanatics threatened him with physical violence and affixed skulls and crossbones to their threats. In later years, when sectional emotions clouded men's reason, these charges would shroud Fillmore's name with iniquity.

Ostensibly the agitators directed their fire against the law of 1850. Neither that law, nor the law of 1793, nor indeed any enactment for the rendition of fugitive slaves would have escaped their attack. Previous to 1850, they had attacked the law of 1793 that Washington had signed. Its enforcement had depended upon the full cooperation of state and local officials.[1] In the 1830's and 1840's, however, the agitators obtained regulations designed to deny that cooperation. In consequence, execution of the law devolved on the officers of the United States alone. Already overburdened with other work, they could give it little attention, and by the mid-forties, the act had become inoperative.

Aggrieved slave owners had long demanded the more effective law[2] that they had obtained in the act of 1850.[3] In essence the new law reduced the need for local help. Instead, the rendition of fugitive slaves was entrusted entirely to federal officials whose powers and numbers were greatly increased.

It was against this new act, that undid the work of several decades, that the agitators clamored. Legally the act grew out of the constitutional injunction prohibiting any state from freeing a fugitive slave. Actually, by their own admission, antislavery men were trying to annul this constitutional obligation. When all was said, no matter what their motives, when the complications of argument and appeal were stripped to their basic precepts, the antislavery leaders based their attack against the law on the plea that the constitutional injunction was not binding. Men of conscience, men with compassionate hearts,

[1] It had authorized the master to seize and arrest his slave wherever he found him and take him before a judge of the United States courts, or any magistrate of a county, city, or town in the state in which the arrest was made. If such a judge, or magistrate, was satisfied that the owner's claim was valid, it was the officer's duty to give a certificate to the owner to remove the slave to the state from which he had fled.

[2] The defects they had sought to eliminate were the law's failure to provide: sufficient number of United States officers for its execution, for the arrest of fugitives in any other manner than by the claimant himself, for adequate force to prevent reckless fanatics from rescuing captured fugitives, and a definition of the proof necessary to justify a certificate for fugitive's surrender.

[3] This new law appointed a suitable number of commissioners who had concurrent jurisdiction with the judges of the United States Courts in hearing and determining these cases. The United States marshal of the district was entrusted with the arrest of the fugitive and his retention pending decision. He had the power to call out the posse to aid him in pursuing a slave or hold his charge against a mob. To establish the fact that the fugitive was a slave, a court could take proofs in the state from which the fugitive had fled. In case the owner anticipated trouble in carrying his slave back to the South, the commissioner had the authority to direct the marshal to give him a safe conduct. These were the leading provisions of the act of 1850 which distinguished it from that of 1793.

must obey the "divine law" of humanity, which they called "a higher law," rather than the Constitution. Where divine law and Constitution collided, it was man's duty to repudiate the Constitution.

By this definition Fillmore was hardly a compassionate man. Scarcely had the act of 1850 received his signature, when antislavery men defied him to enforce it. From Pennsylvania came the first challenge. There a marshal, in order to hold a captured fugitive against a mob, called upon the local citizenry to act as a posse — his right under the new law. They ignored his charge and, instead, stormed the temporary jail, and whisked the Negro away to freedom.[4] Two Pennsylvania judges, seeing the weakness of the marshal when he was forced to rely upon the posse, addressed themselves to the President. They asked for a general order authorizing the employment of United States troops in such an emergency.[5]

Fillmore looked upon this request as "a grave and delicate question." Immediately he promised to "exert whatever power I possess under the constitution and laws" to enforce the observance of the act.[6] But the act was silent on the use of troops. Yet without them the law might possibly become as dead a letter as the act of 1793. Not concerned about the plight of the slave owners who had lost slaves, but worried over the effect forcible rescues of slaves would have on southern secessionists, he determined to follow a policy of denying fire-eaters the opportunity for agitation.[7] " . . . I mean at all hazards to do my part towards executing this law. I admit no right of *nullification* North or South."[8] Such a policy would require absolute faithfulness in enforcing the act.

At this crisis, two of Fillmore's cabinet members, Webster and Crittenden, were absent from Washington. To test the

[4]Philadelphia *Daily Sun*, October 11-14, 1850.
[5]Judges Grier and Keane to Fillmore, Fillmore Collection; Fillmore to Webster, October 23, 1850, Claude H. Van Tyne, *The Letters of Daniel Webster*, 436.
[6]*Ibid.*
[7]Philo Fuller to Fillmore, November 12, 1850, Fillmore Collection.
[8]Fillmore to Webster, October 23, 1850, Van Tyne, *Webster's Letters*, 436.

opinions of his official family, Fillmore called in the remainder. After two meetings, they unanimously agreed that the President had the authority, and the duty, to use military force to aid civil officers in executing the law. In this particular case the commanding officer of the marines at Philadelphia was instructed to answer the plea of the marshal, or the deputy, if the latter were sustained by a United States judge. Shortly afterwards, a public announcement of the decision to use force went out to all marshals and commissioners.[9]

Fillmore's policy was not a doughface endorsement of slavery, nor one aimed at breaking the back of the fanatics with military persecution. "God knows that I detest slavery, but it is an existing evil, for which we are not responsible, and we must endure it, and give it such protection as is guaranteed by the constitution, till we can get rid of it without destroying the last hope of free government in the world,"[10] he wrote to Webster. "My object, however, has been to avoid the use of military force as far as possible, not doubting that there is yet patriotism enough left in every State north of Mason's and Dixon's line to maintain the supremacy of the laws; and being particularly anxious that no state should be disgraced, by being compelled to resort to the army to support the laws of the Union, if it could be avoided, I have therefore commenced mildly — authorizing this force only in the last resort, but if necessary, I shall not hesitate to give greater power, and finally to bring the whole force of the government to sustain the law."[11]

*   *   *   *   *

Though Fillmore hoped that the antislavery agitation would cease without federal intervention, the agitators would give him no rest. Even while he was meeting the cabinet and deciding on the army policy, Boston became the scene of another challenge to the spirit of compromise. Two years earlier the "under-

[9]Fillmore to Webster, October 28, 1850, *ibid.*, 438-439.
[10]Fillmore to Webster, October 23, 1850, *ibid.*, 437.
[11]Fillmore to Webster, October 28, 1950, *ibid.*, 439.

ground railroad" had brought William and Ellen Crofts to
Boston. Since no fugitive had been returned to slavery from
the Bay State for a generation, Boston was thought to be a safe
haven from pursuing captors. With impunity the abolitionists
had openly heralded the arrival of the Crofts. Gleefully the
abolitionist press had broadcast the escape to the nation and
twitted the owner to do anything about it. Knowing how fruitless action would be, the owner, Robert Collins of Macon,
Georgia, had suffered his loss in silence. But the act of 1850
gave Collins courage, and he sent two slave-catchers to Boston
to recover his servants.[12]

Indiscreetly the agents let it be known that they were after
the lionized Crofts. The news quickly found its way to Boston's
antislavery headquarters, where instead of starting the fugitives
on their way out of the country, the agitators decided on a
demonstration. They concealed the Crofts in the homes of two
elite Boston families and publicly prepared to foil the slave-
catchers. In the last week of October and in early November,
placards appeared on the streets calling for a public meeting of
protest against the Fugitive Slave Act. There resolutions were
adopted and a committee for the Crofts' defense designated. Because Boston's officialdom was honeycombed with abolitionists,
the plan was feasible. Though not one of them, United States
Marshal Devins, by delaying and fumbling with the warrant
for the arrest, played into the abolitionists' hands. Meanwhile
a bevy of lawyers turned upon Collins' agents all of their legal
talents of obstruction. Three successive times the agents were
arrested on trumped-up charges.[13]

In the midst of these tactics, Webster and Fillmore interfered. The ailing Webster bandaged his rheumatic legs and
journeyed from his Marshfield retreat to Boston. There he
poured starch into the marshal's backbone. Simultaneously,
Fillmore announced his determination to enforce the Fugitive

[12]William Still, *The Underground Railroad*, 368-374.
[13]Webster to Fillmore, November 15, 1850, Fillmore Collection.

Slave Act at all hazards and with troops if necessary. Almost overnight the abolitionists' position became untenable. Instead of risking the arrival of troops and the freedom of the Crofts, the abolitionists now secreted the two runaways on a vessel bound for London. By the time the legal restrictions on the agents had relaxed, the Crofts were away, and the agents of Collins returned to Georgia empty-handed.[14]

Fillmore's and Webster's action had not saved the slaves for their master, but the firmness of their tone threw the abolitionists into paroxysms of denunciation. Fillmore endured the slurs with no intention of striking back. Rather he wanted to see the excitement lose its force. When Collins petitioned Fillmore to fire Marshal Devins for dereliction of duty, the President stilled that complaint, too. Action on Collins' plea might be the cause of a new outbreak, so he dismissed Collins with a respectful acknowledgment that he was willing to discharge any officer who failed to perform his duty, but Collins' charge rested solely on newspaper commentary.[15]

*　　*　　*　　*　　*

Fillmore's attitude toward the Fugitive Slave Act was dictated by more than the action of northern fanatics. Concern over the southern ultras contributed to his problem. The fear of insurrection and secession that from the first had helped him settle on a policy of conciliation was still present in his mind. In recent years firebrands had greatly intensified Southerners' consciousness. For years these agitators had been pointing with alarm at the threatening northern aggression and exploitation. If the South, they had warned, did not unite and stop the North, all that was cherished would be destroyed.

Now that the Compromise had succeeded, they claimed that their predictions had come to pass. Except for the Fugitive Slave

[14]Henry Wilson, *Rise and Fall of the Slave Power*, 2:325.
[15]Fillmore to Collins, *Fillmore Papers*, 2:301-304.

Law, they felt, the Compromise was a complete rout. The South had lost California, would probably lose New Mexico and Utah, had suffered on the slave trade, had failed to get what it wanted for Texas, and with violent resistance to the Fugitive Slave Act beginning in the North, would see that, too, go by the board. The Compromise, they asserted, had reduced the South to inferiority.

The governors of Georgia, Mississippi, and South Carolina doubted whether the South could honorably continue in the Union after it had been thus insulted, despoiled, and defrauded by the adjustment. Whatever the objective — secession or defense — the drum-beating continued; and they scorned the sectional peace Fillmore sought. It would never improve their cause to let the spirit of compromise offset the psychological gains they had made thus far. A second Nashville Convention had been called for November 12, 1850, and the firebrands now planned to use it to concentrate all southern discontent into challenging solidarity.

These Dixie agitators did not confine their activity to words alone. One faction planned bold deeds. In late October of 1850, with the Nashville Convention about to assemble, a revolutionary spirit stalked the land. The public was almost unaware of the danger, but the President and cabinet were informed of all that was going on. Alexander H. H. Stuart, the Secretary of the Interior, was in continual correspondence with James L. Petigru of Charleston, South Carolina, who was the Administration's chief informant of the moves of South Carolina fire-eaters. From him Fillmore learned of plans to seize the federal forts at Charleston as the first step toward secession. By way of preparation, in order to obstruct federal retaliation, the United States attorney and other important federal officers in the state resigned. Fillmore had difficulty finding suitable men to fiill the vacancies. It appeared that a concerted plan was afoot to keep the posts vacant. He offered Petigru the job of attorney, but he declined on the ground that it would interfere too much with his general practice. Fillmore then appointed another, who turned out to be a secessionist and soon resigned. The job went begging. On the eve of the Nashville Convention, the most important law-enforcing office in South Carolina was empty. Then suddenly Petigru, impressed with the gravity of the situation, changed his mind and took the office.[16]

So alarmed had Fillmore become that he brought General Scott into the cabinet meetings to prepare for the insurrection. On Scott's advice, the fortifications at Charleston were strengthened. Troops were sent into South Carolina, and stationed at points in North Carolina and elsewhere so that they could, in case of an outbreak, be concentrated at the point of attack. The governor of South Carolina called upon Fillmore to explain this hostile act of stationing so many troops in the vicinity of Charleston. Fillmore replied curtly, but with dignity, that as Commander-in-Chief of the army of the United States, it was his duty to station the troops at such points as he deemed most advantageous to the public interests, and that he recognized no responsibility for his official action to the governor of South Carolina. Thus prepared, Fillmore awaited the action of the fire-eaters, who in turn watched the November elections in Georgia for the signal.[17]

South Carolinians would have been willing to lead secession, but they realized it might better start from a state which had not so long borne the odium of radicalism. Earlier, Georgia's legislature had declared that the admission of a "free" California would be an act of aggression requiring drastic counteraction. The California bill had passed. "What will Georgia do?" became the inevitable question, and fire-eaters now placed their hopes in Georgia. They had not long to wait. Almost immediately Governor Towns issued a spirited proclamation for a

[16]This story is related quite fully in Stuart to Wilson, May 8, 1878, Fillmore Mss; see also B. E. Perry, *Reminiscences of Public Men*, 257, 286-88; *Letter to Governor W. B. Seabrook on the Dissolution of the Union.*
[17]Stuart to Wilson, May 8, 1878, Fillmore Mss.; Perry to Fillmore, April 22, 1851, Petigru to Fillmore, May 30, 1851, Fillmore Collection.

state convention to meet on December 10 to determine Georgia's course.[18]

Against this kind of agitation, Fillmore personally could do little. But his southern Whig supporters, cutting short their rejoicing over the Compromise, did battle where Fillmore could not. Their strategy called for the election of convention delegates who were pledged to the Compromise. Stephens and Toombs led the campaign. Both took to the stump. Soon others joined them. They defended the admission of California and asserted that secession was no proper remedy for existing grievances. Georgia, the empire state of the South, they said, owed much of her prosperity to the Union and would enjoy inestimable advantages from her continuance in it. They called themselves Union men, members of the "Union and Southern Rights Party," for they relaxed the regular party line to welcome the cooperation of those Democrats like Howell Cobb who shared their sentiments. Their spirited campaign carried the election and sent a great majority of Union delegates to the Convention.[19]

The Union victory in Georgia dampened the ardor of the secessionists. A few days later the Nashville Convention met. This was supposed to have been the crux of secessionist endeavors — the place where Georgia's election should have sparked the South to action. But the signs that had once encouraged had brought only discouragement. Trying to bolster their spirits, the Nashville delegates spent six days delivering fire-eating speeches to each other and passing resolutions condemning the Compromise. Yet their meeting was hardly noticed. Attention was still centered on Georgia. There within a month under the guidance of Charles J. Jenkins, whom Fillmore had once considered for Secretary of the Interior, the Union men proclaimed Georgia's acquiescence in the Compromise. Only if it were modified, they asserted, would Georgia consider resistance. Coming from the state that secessionists had hoped would take

[18]*National Intelligencer*, September 28, 1850.
[19]Washington *Republic*, October 15, 1850; Stovall, *Toombs*, 83-85; Avary, *Stephens*, 27.

the initiative, this message acted like a balm on all the souls that fire-eaters had seared. South Carolina's preparations to seize federal authority in the state ceased. In Washington the Administration breathed more quietly.[20]

*   *   *   *   *

Following the elections of 1850, Fillmore faced an insidious challenge to peace. It was unlike the abolitionists' attack against the Fugitive Slave Act or the secessionists' condemnation of the Compromise. This challenge was subtle and treacherous. The Fugitive Law had made it possible for freed, as distinguished from fugitive, slaves to be condemned back into slavery by unscrupulous slave traders. And even before any actual case of spiriting away a freeborn Negro occurred, demands were heard to eliminate this hazard. Because what was asked was reasonable, it appealed to moderate men.

At first even Fillmore thought it reasonable. To Webster he wrote: "It seems to me . . . that the . . . true ground for our friends to take is this: that the law hav'g passed, must be executed. That so far as it provides for the surrender of fugitives from labor it is according to the requirements of the constitution and should be sustained against all attempts at repeal, but if there be any provision in it endangering the liberty of those who are free, it should be so modified as to secure the free blacks from such an abuse of the object of the law, and that done we at the North have no just cause of complaint."[21] Later Webster voiced the same opinion.[22]

Because the proposal was reasonable, it lent itself to political ends, if indeed, politics had not been its chief purpose. Official party endorsement of the Compromise was forcing antislavery Whigs into fellowship with slavery. Understandably sensitive, and wishing to hold the antislavery vote, they now seized upon the modification proposal. It could be used as evidence that

[20]R. M. Johnson and W. H. Brown, *Life of Alexander H. Stephens*, 259-260.
[21]Fillmore to Webster, October 23, 1850, *Fillmore Papers*, 1:334-335.
[22]Webster to B. B. Ayer, November 16, 1850, Van Tyne, *Webster Letters*, 443.

their loyalties were still with the abolitionists without repudiating the Compromise. Among them were Weed and Seward, who were convinced that their future lay in catering to the antislavery spirit; they and their entire following adopted "immediate modification" as the symbol of their unity and of their resistance to the Administration.

Seeing the twist that Weed and company were giving to modification, Fillmore changed his view. He had no desire to see it become the sounding board for Weed's sectionalism — got up for political effect. And when the President gave his first summary of policy to the nation on December 2, he buried approval of modification in the stipulation that no change should be made "until time and experience shall demonstrate the necessity of further legislation to guard against evasion or abuse."[23] Between "immediate" and "until time and experience shall demonstrate" was a gap into which New York politics was to drop. Here was a chasm between Weed and Fillmore that was to cause the President more trouble than all the other resistance to his policy.

The election of 1850 had jolted, but not unseated, Weed. The shock had weakened his grip on the New York party enough to prevent him from playing the role of President-maker for Seward. But he had no intentions of resigning himself to this fate. Accustomed to thinking of patronage as the source of all factional strength, he made arrangements with Democratic Barnburners, who controlled the state's canal board, to replace all "Silver Greys" among the canal's officeholders with his faithful followers. In return he promised that the Whig governor would treat the Barnburners generously in other posts.[24] Then he set his sights on capturing the major source of real Whig opposition to himself in the state — New York City's important patronage-dispensing offices. It was only through Fillmore that he could acquire control of Young's and Maxwell's offices. Suddenly, then, after the election — as if contrite over the

[23]Richardson, *Messages*, 5:93.   [24]VanDeusen, *Weed*, 183.

captiousness of his followers — Weed pretended to be reconciled with Fillmore.

In late November and December of 1850, letters from Governor-elect Hunt and retiring Governor Fish bombarded Fillmore with appeals for peace between himself and Weed.[25] Hunt, on a plea that he would be embarrassed by Whig feuds, called for peace and harmony within the party; Fish, as a Whig candidate for the United States Senate, called for harmony, too. Then a seemingly impartial New York legislator from Albany — Samuel P. Lyman — showed up in Washington to plead the cause of mutual forgiveness. Each evening, while masquerading as a neutral torn and wounded by party strife, he wrote long reports of his progress back to Weed.[26]

Lyman visited Fillmore, Corwin, Webster, Hall and the other cabinet members and assured them that all that kept Weed hostile to the Administration was fear that his friends would be discharged from office — particularly in the New York City customhouse. Weed had no other objectives, Lyman asserted. If the Administration would get rid of Maxwell and Young, who were the guiding geniuses of the opposition to Weed in New York City, all would be well. If he could feel that he was not deserting his friends, Weed would even sell his paper and take a trip to Europe. To preface these importunings, the Albany *Evening Journal* suddenly reversed its attack on Fillmore and lauded him for his annual message to Congress. So noticeable was the change of tactics that Haven, Fillmore's former law partner, wrote from Buffalo: "What's the matter with Weed? Is he Sick?"[27] If Maxwell and Young could not be removed, Lyman suggested that at least they take orders from Grinnell and Minturn — two respected merchants of New York City. He did not mention that Grinnell and Minturn were Weed's closest partisans among city merchants.[28]

[25]Hunt to Fillmore, November 16, 30, 1850; Fish to Fillmore, November 18, December 23, 1850, Fillmore Collection.
[26]Lyman to Weed, December 1, 2, 5, 6, 8, 1850, Weed Papers.
[27]Haven to Fillmore, December 10, 1850, Fillmore Collection.
[28]Lyman to Weed, December 1, 2, 5, 6, 8, 1850, Weed Papers; Lyman to Fillmore, December 15, 1850, Fillmore Collection.

Fillmore recognized Weed's agent for what he was.[29] But for the benefit of silence from Weed and his absence from the country, Fillmore decided to toy with Weed's new attitude. For five months the President had stayed the axe of proscription, and this was no time to forsake a strategy that might yet work. So to Lyman, Fillmore voiced his desire for complete harmony. He regretted that for the sake of peace he could not remove Maxwell or Young, but he assured Weed through Lyman that he had no desire to make any removals from office, whether Weed's or his own friends.[30] As a measure of good faith, Fillmore hastened to reinstate one of Weed's friends whom Maxwell had removed. Lyman was gleeful.[31]

Hardly had Lyman left Washington, self-satisfied with his "peace-making," than Fillmore called in Maxwell. Instead of being upbraided and disarmed, the collector of the port returned to New York City unaffected by Weed's machinations. Rather, he was newly commissioned for another political task. By Christmas day he was trying to buy, if Weed were sincere, the Albany *Evening Journal*. He kept Fillmore posted on the progress of these negotiations.[32]

If Lyman was pleased with himself, Weed was not. He knew that Fillmore had spotted his trick, for the President had gone no further than he was always willing to go. Weed had not won control of the city's patronage and was awkwardly caught saying kind things about the Administration and professing a desire for reconciliation.

Taking advantage of Weed's pretense, Fillmore pressed to put New York Whigs officially on record as accepting the Compromise and endorsing his formula on the Fugitive Slave Act. Under his guidance, J. B. Varnum, an assemblyman for

[29]Fuller to Fillmore, December 15, 1850, *ibid*.
[30]Lyman to Weed, December 1, 1850, Weed Papers.
[31]Lyman to Weed, December 8, 1850, *ibid*.; Fuller to Fillmore, December 7, 1850, Fillmore Collection.
[32]Maxwell to Fillmore, December 18, 25, 29, 1850; Bush to Fillmore, January 1, 1851, *ibid*.

the city, mooted about that he would introduce an appropriate resolution into the legislature when it met in January. This was not what Weed wanted. Henry J. Raymond, speaker of the lower chamber, and Weed's henchman, acted quickly. In the appointment of committee chairmen all of Fillmore's friends were forgotten. Simultaneously, the myth of Weed's desire to sell the Albany *Evening Journal* exploded, and the honeymoon month of December gave way to three months of warfare.[33]

Varnum quickly altered his plans. He saw that a defeat of the resolutions would be worse than no action or no comment. And a defeat was certain.[34] He and the other Fillmore men turned to still another method of getting New York Whigs to endorse the same resolutions. New York was due to elect a United States Senator. If the legislature chose a man who accepted Fillmore's formula, it would amount to the same thing as passing the resolution.

Hamilton Fish was regarded as the logical Whig candidate against Democratic incumbent Daniel S. Dickinson. Fish was even acceptable to the New York City Whigs. He had remained silent on the Compromise, but secretly he had accepted Weed's yoke. As governor he had worked with Weed and had acquired his dislike, if not his hatred, for Fillmore. In his anxiety to become a Senator, Fish had nevertheless swallowed his pride and entered into correspondence with Fillmore to win the President's support. All of the letters he permitted Weed to censor, and the Albany editor ruled that under no circumstances was Fish to accept the exact wording of Fillmore's formula for peace. When Fillmore discovered that Fish believed the Fugitive Slave Act should be modified and failed to attach the mystical words "when time and experience demonstrate the need," he extended the correspondence with diplomatic but penetrating questions. So anxious was Fish not to earn Fillmore's hostility that he assured the President, in spite of Weed's interdiction, that he

[33]Bush to Fillmore, January 5, 1851; Varnum to Fillmore, January 13, 15, 1851; Hall to Fillmore, January 13, 1851; Maxwell to Fillmore, January 13, 1851, *ibid.*
[34]Varnum to Fillmore, January 13, 1851, *ibid.*

believed Fillmore's interpretation of the country's need was correct. Though the ritualistic words were absent, this satisfied
Fillmore.[35]

This exchange of views remained hid from all except Fish,
Fillmore, and Weed; and Fillmore had pledged himself not to
use the letters without Fish's approval. Ignorant of the correspondence between Washington and Albany, the Union Safety
Committee of New York interposed its strength. Greatly heartened by its success in the November election, it had set itself
up as a permanent committee to act as the watchdog of the
Compromise. Both Maxwell and Young joined, although they
could not control the group. The committee, meanwhile, seized
upon Fillmore's formula for modification — "When time and
experience demonstrate the need" — and made it the test of
orthodoxy. It threatened to crush anyone in the state who would
not conform.[36]

At the end of January, Varnum, hearing of the committee's
demand, innocently approached Fish, fully expecting him to be
cooperative. Much to his surprise, Fish refused to take a public
stand on the Compromise. Varnum assured Fish that all he
wanted was a written statement that he acquiesced in Fillmore's
formula. But Fish remained adamant, and his suspicious mind
whispered to him that Fillmore, while writing one thing to him,
had set the "Silver Greys" on his trail. Bitterly he informed
Weed that he had repulsed the enemy.[37]

When the Union Safety Committee heard of Fish's stand,

[35]Buffalo *Express*, November 27, December 4, 1850. Gilbert Davis to Fillmore,
November 7, 1850; Varnum to Fillmore, November 21, 1850, January 13, 15,
1851; Fuller to Fillmore, January 4, 1851; Bush to Fillmore, January 5, 1851;
Fillmore to Fuller, February 23, 1851, Fillmore Collection.

[36]Varnum to Fillmore, November 22, 1850; Davis to Fillmore, November 25, 1850;
Ketchum to Fillmore, January 10, February 17, 1851; Fish to Fillmore, November
27, 1850; Williams to Fillmore, December 5, 1850; Lyman to Fillmore, January
7, 22, February 3, 4, 1851, *ibid.* Charles Cooke to Weed, November 8, 1850,
Weed Papers.

[37]Fish to Weed, January 31, 1851, *ibid.* Bush to Fillmore, February 3, 1851, Fillmore Collection.

its members resolved either to force Fish to a "finality" position or see him defeated. Varnum, acting under different orders, approached Weed again. He asked for a reconsideration of the resolution, intimating "Silver Grey" resistance to Fish as the alternative. If Fillmore discharged Maxwell and Young, bargained Weed, the Administration could have its resolution — after Fish's election. At this, Fillmore balked.[38]

Even before the election day, the affair had reached an impasse. Feverishly the Union Safety Committee organized the "Silver Greys" of the city against Fish and told all that it was Fillmore's wish. Fillmore, though satisfied with Fish's private attitude, could not bring himself to repudiate the New York City group — his staunchest supporters. His silence implied that the Union Safety Committee really represented the Administration. Already Weed hinted that Fillmore was treacherously trying to defeat the party's candidate for the Senate. Varnum, meanwhile, desperately tried to reach some sort of compromise, while Fish, made more stubborn than ever by distrust and dislike for Fillmore, and acting under orders from Weed, remained resolute.

Reviewing the affair, Fillmore concluded that "Silver Greys" dared not have the responsibility for Fish's defeat on their hands. Weed would have a handle for claiming that the Administration had deserted the party, and "Silver Greys" would be on the defensive. At balloting time Fillmore wired George Babcock, his special emissary from Buffalo in the legislature, to have his friends vote for Fish even without a resolution. This threw consternation into the ranks of the "Silver Greys" who had fallen in behind the Union Safety Committee. Yet when balloting occurred, all "Silver Greys" followed Fillmore's directive — all except one, Senator James W. Beekman of New York City, who was intimately connected with the Union Safety Committee, and whose vote for Francis Granger cast the election into a tie between Dickinson, the Democratic candidate, and Fish. The Union Safety Committee rejoiced and ordered the

[38]*Ibid.*

firing of a cannon at the Battery in honor of the victory. A few days later, it succeeded in getting the city's Whig General Committee and Whig Young Men's General Committee to adopt resolutions in praise of Beekman.[39]

Instantly Weed assigned the cause for Fish's plight to Fillmore. It was a falsehood, and Weed knew it, but by half-truths, innuendo, and circumstantially weighted evidence, Weed "proved" that Fillmore was responsible for it. Fillmore did not like the unjust attack on himself, but did nothing publicly to refute it. Yet he saw that it could have telling effect. If a Democratic victory resulted, party workers might more readily believe Weed's charges. Again, at Fillmore's behest, the triumvirate of Varnum, Fuller, and Bush asked Fish to take a forthright stand on the Compromise. But Fish held out, bitter against the Administration whose hand he mistakenly saw behind the maneuver. Fillmore's friends offered Fish the opportunity of saving his face, by withholding any statement until after his election. He refused. They asked permission to make public parts of his letters to Fillmore. Still he refused. Fillmore, himself, then switched the tactic and asked Beekman to change his vote, but the New York City senator was as stubborn as Fish.[40]

It looked as if the election were permanently stalemated. During the remainder of February and well into March, 1851, strict factional discipline kept the affair in precarious balance. But in late March, a trick proved unexpectedly fruitful. While

[39]Ketchum to Fillmore, February 14, 17, 1851; Fuller to Fillmore, February 17, 1851; Beekman to Fillmore, March 4, 1851; Ketchum to Fillmore, February 15, 1851, *ibid.*

[40]Fish to Weed, February 4, 6, 20, 1851, Weed Papers. Bull to Seward, February 1, 1851; Benedict to Seward, February 5, 1851; Blatchford to Seward, February 5, 1851; Draper to Seward, February 7, 1851; Bronson to Seward, February 8, 1851, Seward Papers. Bush to Fillmore, February 23, 1851; Davis to Fillmore, February 19, 1851; Maxwell to Fillmore, February 18, 1851; Hunt to Fillmore, February 10, 27, March 23, 1851; Varnum to Fillmore, February 9, 1851; P. Fuller to Fillmore, February 2, 1851; Fuller to Fillmore, February 7, 1851; Ketchum to Fillmore, February 4, 1851; Lyman to Fillmore, February 3, 4, 5, 9, 26, 1851; Patterson to Fillmore, February 24, 1851; Hall to Fillmore, February 12, 1851; Foote to Fillmore, February 7, 1851, Fillmore Collection. Fillmore to Fuller, February 23, 1851; Fillmore to Babcock, February 23, 1851; Fillmore to Hunt, February 23, 1851, Fillmore Mss.

two Democrats were absent, the Sewardites sneaked through an election vote. It was designed to catch George Babcock, Fillmore's special and personal agent in the New York legislature, off guard. They hoped that Babcock would vote against Fish in an effort to overcome the loss of two Democratic votes. Should he do so, they would have completed the chain of evidence that they had been forging to prove Fillmore responsible for Fish's defeat. Babcock had always voted for Fish, did so this time, and by this single vote Fish was finally elected.[41]

Immediately Weed and Seward claimed Fish's election meant New York had rebuked both Fillmore and his Compromise. The Administration, however, could indulgently smile at this bravado. During March, while Fish's election was stalemated, Fillmore had circulated among key Weed supporters the private letters he had written to Babcock, Bush, and Fuller. These were intended to show that he was supporting Fish. They also showed that Weed was masking personal objectives behind a fight on principles. The truth had begun to dawn on some of the more neutral of New York's Whig politicians that Weed, not Fillmore, was the troublemaker in the Whig party. Weed, himself, could not believe he had scored a great success. He decided that a period of hibernation to await mistakes of his enemies was due. In haste — and weary, too, of winning skirmishes but losing the main campaign against a tireless enemy — Weed left for Europe. The Albany *Evening Journal's* raucous shouts began to diminish.[42]

Fillmore had failed in a second try to get a solid endorsement of his policy from his state's party, but he was not discouraged. He drew consolation from the fact that Weed also had failed to obtain a victory, and that elsewhere the Administration had been eminently successful. In the long view, time and

[41]Brooks to Fillmore, [March 1, 1851]; Bush to Fillmore, March 4, 1851; Babcock to Fillmore, March 18, 1851; Fuller to Fillmore, March 19, 1851, Fillmore Collection.
[42]Maxwell to Fillmore, February 26, 1851; Foote to Fillmore, March 2, 1851; Bush to Fillmore, March 4, 1851; Haven to Fillmore, March 5, 1851, *ibid.* Albany *Evening Journal*, March, *passim.*; Van Deusen, *Weed*, 184.

Fillmore's perseverance were accomplishing what his undramatic action seemingly had condemned to failure.

One thing was certain to the President as he stood aside to see where everything was leading — the policy of trying to buy Weed's silence by restraining proscription had failed. The President decided to give in to the pressure from New York City and use the weapon of proscription on their common foe. By February 23 he informed Governor Hunt that there would have to be some judicious removals of officeholders; and by mid-March he gave the signal to Maxwell to clear out the customhouse. Even before the election of Fish was achieved, Babcock was taking stock of the loyalty of federal officers around Albany. No sooner was the evidence in than two key Weed men lost their jobs. The fight between Weed and Fillmore was about to take another direction.[43]

* * * * *

By the summer of 1851 the Administration's nationwide repression of agitation became effective. Like a thick blanket of fog it crept slowly, silently, engulfing the flames of turmoil in its smothering embrace. Here and there an occasional tongue of fire licked through the cloud to give evidence that the embers still smoldered. Yet like men on guard to watch a dying fire, the President and his cabinet carefully removed as much inflammable material as possible from the reaching grasp of the flames.

For a short time after the spring of 1851, each of three slave rescues threatened to bring new eruptions. In each, without dramatics, without any beating of the breast, government officials

[43]Hancock to Fillmore, January 31, 1851; Granger to Fillmore, February 20, 27, 1851; Bush to Fillmore, February 23, March 4, 1851; Fuller to Fillmore, February 23, March 27, 1851; Kidd to Fillmore, February 24, 1851; Thompson to Fillmore, February 27, 1851; Haven to Fillmore, February 28, 1851; Hall to Fillmore, March 27, 1851; Maxwell to Fillmore, March 7, 28, 1851; P. Greeley to Fillmore, March 27, 1851; Mann to Fillmore, April 11, 1851; Duer to Fillmore, March 27, 1851; Willard to Fillmore, March 19, 1851; Babcock to Fillmore, March 17, 1851; Hunt to Fillmore, March 23, 1851, Fillmore Collection.

prosecuted some of the persons involved in the rescues. Two brought convictions. In the third, near Philadelphia, troops had rounded up a bevy of Negroes and three whites who had defended seven runaway slaves against captors. Negroes and whites alike went on trial charged with insurrection and treason. Though the charges collapsed before a jury,[44] never before had city, state, and federal officials worked so closely together in bringing the law-breakers to trial. Philadelphia flung wide her prison doors to admit the federal prisoners. Later Pennsylvania repealed her fifteen-year-old injunction against using her jails for holding runaway slaves. The abolitionists complained bitterly, for the cooperation between the three areas of jurisdiction gave evidence of faithfulness to the Fugitive Slave Act that went deeper than the Administration. Everywhere the shadow of a "higher law" grew less somber, and Compromisers brightened in the changing light.

The sweep of time worked in harmony with the Administration's "great silence." The nation appeared to be wearying of sectional suspense. For the most part, public opinion was ready to receive pronouncement of forty-four Congressmen of both parties and all sections that the Compromise was to be regarded as the final settlement of all it treated.

In the South the talk of secession had been more than gasconade. It had been a real danger. That the South did not act was due, in part, to Fillmore's policy. The appeal of the fire-eaters had fallen on the deaf ears of the large slaveholders. Until these people could be made to see the advantages of secession, no southern movement could be successful. For years the planting capitalists had aligned themselves with the Whig party of the North to protect themselves against the more rabid Democrats of their own area. Nationalism had become their forte. As yet they saw little reason for deserting the national alliance in favor of one with their enemies who led the southern unity movement. Only fear that the Whig party was a trap

[44]Philadelphia *Daily Sun*, April 1851, *passim*.

rather than a bulwark of their own defense could have made the southern Whigs move into the Democratic party. As long as Fillmore directed the force of government against the northern agitators, that fear did not exist. They continued to spurn the temptation of a sectional party. Sectionalization of parties slowed down, and temporarily froze, during Fillmore's administration. Everywhere intelligent Union men, who had testified to the genuine seriousness of the crisis, came out of it with praises for Fillmore on their lips.[45]

Deafness to the appeal for southern unity afflicted more than the large slaveholders. With the Fillmore administration, and partly because of it, the South entered into a period of prosperity. "Thirteen cents a pound for cotton . . . make[s] civil war and revolution exceedingly distasteful . . . ." wrote General James Hamilton after a trip across central Georgia. "Prosperity makes the masses indifferent to the crisis," was the comment of Governor Seabrook.[46] "The present apparent prosperity of the South is one of the causes of whatever there may be of reluctance among her people to advocate resistance; because there is plenty to live on, because we are out of debt, and cotton brings a good price, many are in so good a humor and so well satisfied with themselves and things around them as to shut their eyes to the future in the consoling reflection that the future cannot hurt them."[47]

The cities — strongholds of another sector of southern Whiggery — were especially prosperous, and therefore out of step with the radicals. Richmond, Charleston, Savannah, Mobile, New Orleans, Natchez, and Memphis were all Compromise centers. References to their Yankee flavor and their unsound and uncertain character were often on the lips of the states' rights enthusiasts. Furthermore, the masses "refused to throw up their caps and shout for the dissolution of the Union." A

[45]A. H. Stephens to J. Thomas, *Annual Report of the American Historical Association* (1911), 2:184.
[46]Richard H. Shryock, *Georgia and the Union in 1850*, 290.
[47]*Niles' Register*, November 18, 1850.

Georgian complained to a fellow fire-eater: "You cannot imagine how perfectly quiet the whole people are on the subject of all the stir and fuss at Washington. Nobody at home, Whig or Democrat, believes that any man there feels what he expresses of ultraism."[48]

Fillmore tried to direct the attention of the country into other channels. Beyond preserving the Union, the object of peace was to give the economic forces of transportation, commerce, and industry a chance to develop the nation's resources. When the opportunity arose to honor one of the largest undertakings of the day — the completion of the Erie Railroad — Fillmore turned the ceremonies into a gala peace demonstration. He and the entire cabinet, along with other notable politicians from both parties, accepted the invitation of the directors of the road to travel its length from New York to Dunkirk. En masse the group assembled in New York bedecked in ambassadorial finery. Wearing top hats, frock coats, ascot ties and their best public smiles, they climbed aboard the special train and like picnickers stiffened by their formal clothing they made their way to Dunkirk. The smoke from the billowing stack whipped back over the coaches, drifted through the open windows, and kept the celebrants busy avoiding the hot ashes.

Soot and discomfort did not stop them. At stations along the way, from the Atlantic shore to Lake Erie, Fillmore appeared on the rear platform. Behind him his cabinet assembled and listened as he addressed the local citizens who had gathered about the train. The speeches were short, but in each, after he had congratulated the promoters of the road, he tried to impress upon his audience the necessity of accepting the Compromise. It was a steam-powered stump tour through one of antislavery's heartlands. Bulking large in these talks was the inference that prosperity went hand in hand with sectional peace.[49]

[48] J. H. Lumpkin to Howell Cobb, October 5, 1850, *Annual Report of the American Historical Association* (1911), 2:214; James A. Meriwether to Cobb, August 24, 1850, *ibid.*, 211; M. Fulton to Cobb, November 6, 1850, *ibid.*, 217-218; H. V. Johnson to Calhoun, October 20, 1849, *ibid.* (1899), 2:1196.
[49] See speeches, *Fillmore Papers*, 1:409-416.

In September of 1851 he took advantage of more railroad celebrations to visit New England. The occasion was the opening of new railroad lines that connected Boston with Canada and the West. His theme was the same. If the nation wanted more prosperity, it must have sectional peace. Only two members of the cabinet accompanied him on this trip. They were Conrad and Stuart, who represented the deep South in the federal administration. Wherever Fillmore went, he displayed these men. It was like putting two Southerners on the stage for abolitionized New Englanders to stare at and learn, by seeing, that Southerners were not the monsters characterized in the abolitionist press.[50]

The nation, as if picking its inspiration from the Administration, ushered in a new era of prosperity. The period was one of industrial development. Railroads supplanted canals as freight carriers and opened the prairies to profitable settlement. In the North when the pursuit of money was not the topic of conversation, then it was Jenny Lind or the Rochester spirit-rappings. Slavery was not forgotten, but it slipped into the back of people's minds; and everyone except northern abolitionists and southern fire-eaters wished it to remain there.

Immigration reached a new high level as the victims of famine, rebellion, and tyranny sought succor in the New World. It portended a new nativistic movement in politics, but in the summer and fall of 1851, thought, not action, was applied to the immigrant deluge. Industrial expansion and westward migrations allowed wages to keep pace with rising prices. The nation had already entered the beginning of its industrialization, and the Fillmore administration stood in the van of the movement to offer government encouragement to the harbinger of industrialism — the railroads. Only days after the passage of the Compromise measures, the national policy of granting federal lands to subsidize railroad building was inaugurated. Agitation had already begun for the federal government to build or subsidize a transcontinental railroad, and Fillmore recommended its consideration to Congress.

[50]See speeches, *ibid.*, 420-425.

In the labor movement talk gave way to action. Unions began to appear. They concluded trade agreements with their employers, federated nationally on craft lines, and avoided politics. The American workingman ignored Utopia but demanded two dollars a day and roast beef. Neal Dow won a famous victory with the Maine prohibition law, and Arthur's *Ten Nights in a Bar Room* spread the gospel of temperance. Baseball became popular, yacht racing and intercollegiate rowing were introduced, together with vulgar luxury. In New York, Newport, and Saratoga, according to the season, could be found "a set of exquisites — daintily arrayed men who spend half their income on their persons, and shrink from the touch of a woolen glove . . . delicate and lovely women, who wear fine furs and roll in the most stylish equipage."[51]

Into the ostentatious living of his day the President easily gravitated. Helping him were grateful New York City money-makers who lionized him on every visit to the city. Seeking to give him a token of their esteem, but wanting to avoid any untoward suggestion, they gave the First Lady a "splendid coach" and a pair of horses.[52] One of the donors, enamored by the magnificence of his own gift, described it as a Clarence coach made expressly for the President. "It is made," he glowingly reported to Fillmore before the President had seen it, "of the richest materials, and finished in a style that reflects credit on the artizans employed to do the work. The body and running gear are painted dark invisible green, and the door panels are relieved by a very . . . artistical painting representing the coat of arms of New York, with motto 'Excelsior' nicely defined in a scroll. . . ." On each side of the driver's box is a silver lamp, very ornamental and chaste. A spread eagle of solid silver sur-

[51]Buffalo *Commercial Advertiser*, June 15, 1851.
[52]Donors of the carriage were: C. V. Newhall, Jos. R. Taylor, Jonathan W. Allen, Seth Geer, Moses Maynard, Jr., Robert H. McCarty, Robert T. Haws, James B. Taylor, Shepherd Knapp, Thomas Cornley, Silas C. Herring, George Briggs, Ambrose C. Kingsland, Henry E. Davies, Jos. V. Varnum, Jr., Charles H. Marshall, Marshall O. Roberts, D. D. Howard, Edmund Griffin, James S. Thayer, William V. Brady, William Tyson, Harvey Hart, Nicholas Dean, Lebedee Ring, Robert Smith. [Donors] to Fillmore, November 25, 1850, Fillmore Collection.

mounts each of the reflectors, and the plated glass, ground and polished, is fitted in diamond-shape, and thus presents a neat and rich appearance. . . . The whole . . . [interior] . . . will excite universal admiration. The seats, the sides, front and back, are covered with rich blue watered silk, through which a vine or sprigs of white run, that in a glare of light resembles burnished silver. They are stuffed with curled hair of the best quality, in rools and diamonds, that make the easiest and most comfortable lounge that has ever been invented. The lace of the carriage is of the same material with large blue and silver bullions attached to the holders. The top is covered with the same rich material which forms a pleasing contrast with the rich Turkey carpet on the bottom of the carriage. . . . To each of . . . [the ten windows] is attached a spring curtain of beautiful blue silk finished with rich festoons and tassels. The handles and rollers are made of pearl and silver . . . The cost is $1500."[53]

It was the most magnificent coach Washington society had ever seen. Prosperity and sectional peace had made it possible for the President and his lady to join the elite and "roll in the most stylish equipage."

[53]Henry E. Davies to Fillmore, November 23, 1850, *ibid.*

Chapter 16

The Lure of the East

ROM the veranda of society's hilltop Bellevue House, a starched gathering watched bengal lights and rockets flare across Newport's night-capped harbor. With each brilliant display in the September sky, modest exclamations escaped from the group. From the sparkling, filigreed decorations of the ballroom behind them came the strains of a British cotillion and the chatter of a happy throng around the punch bowl.

Amid the gazers, expansive with conviviality, stood Millard Fillmore. Most of Massachusetts' state officials and railroad promoters milled about him. They had touched off this celebration, and he was their guest of honor. The full meaning of these fireworks, coming from the anchored steamers and sailing vessels in the harbor, was not lost on him.

The festivities marked the completion of a long chain of railroads connecting the Canadas with Massachusetts, the Great Lakes with the ocean, and the commencement of a line of steamers between the capital of New England and Liverpool. Forging a modern network that tied Boston to the world was adequate reason for its promoters' rejoicing. For Fillmore, however, as he beamed benignly on the assembled, delight arose from a different source.

Long had the Erie Canal focused his attention on commerce. Unlike those about him on the veranda, he did not view trade as a participant, for he never owned any business, and the closest he ever came to actual promotion arrived much later in his life when he invested heavily in railroad stocks and bonds. Yet during the debates on the Compromise, while others were pre-occupied with slavery, he had cooperated with Stephen A. Douglas to arrange the first federal land grants for railroad con-struction. This action opened the era of federal aid to railroads and contributed greatly to their development. Unfortunately, federal subsidies would one day be fraught with favoritism and scandal, but when Fillmore smiled down from Presidential heights on trade and commerce he served no special group or venal interests. Rather his regard was visionary. Commerce to him was god-like — modern man's chief provider and benefactor — and he honored its leaders and advanced their cause wherever he could.

A half year earlier, at another railroad celebration, while he complimented the Erie, he had revealed his own economic philosophy. "As a general rule," he noted, "it [had] been sup-posed that nations and states alone could accomplish such works as these. . . ." But the builders of the Erie Railroad, "at a cost of $23,000,000" have "accomplished all of it by" their own "enterprise. . . ."[1]

Now to the men gathered around him watching the pyro-technics in the night sky, he again revealed his broader appre-ciation of commerce. "I am glad that" Massachusetts "has stretched forth her iron arms to the great West and to the Canadas," he told his audience. "I am entirely in favor of all means by which States and countries can be bound together by the ties of mutual business interests and relations. . . . I rejoice in all measures which extend and increase our means of inter-course with foreign countries, and strengthen and enlarge our foreign commerce."[2]

[1] *Fillmore Papers*, 1:415.
[2] Story to Fillmore, November 12, 1851, Fillmore Collection, contains the original clippings of Fillmore's speeches on this New England tour. They had been edited to a considerable degree before they appeared in Severance's volumes.

Here, whether he wished to reveal it or not, he was also exposing the bedrock foundation of his foreign policy.

*   *   *   *   *

In 1850 the overseas area that beckoned American traders to strengthen their ties and multiply their profits was the Orient.[3] China was no new place for American merchants. Her treasures had long tempted Yankee skippers. For almost half a century, whalers and sealers had carried on their profession in Chinese waters. In the sweep of this trade, Hawaii, too, had become the rendezvous for the Pacific Ocean traffic. There sprang up in Honolulu a brisk local trade followed by an invasion of foreign immigrants. New England merchants opened stores; capitalists organized bands of workmen to cut sandalwood; and often a sailor, weary of the lash and salt pork on shipboard, deserted his command, fled into the interior, and settled down with a native wife to a softer life under genial skies. Hawaii's sandalwood entered into the China trade as Yankee ship captains paused at this haven in mid-Pacific for food and water. To Far Eastern cargoes was added the abundant furs of the Oregon country.[4] Fillmore's tariff of 1842 had further encouraged skippers to ply the Pacific waters by taxing their competitors at higher rates.

Until 1842 the China trade, under any flag, was largely illegal. But in that year the British forced the emperor to open several ports to British ships. The following year, under Whig auspices, Caleb Cushing returned from the Orient with a most-favored-nation treaty that gave Americans all the privileges of the British in the Chinese treaty ports. By the late 1840's, if China was no new place for American traders, the double garland of tariff and treaty gave it new attractiveness. Long before the Mexican war ended, a veritable "Oriental fever" seized

[3] K. S. Latourette, *The History of Early Relations between the United States and China, 1784-1844*, 213.
[4] H. W. Bradley, "The Hawaiian Islands and the Pacific Fur Trade, 1785-1813," *Pacific Northwest Quarterly*, 30:275-299; R. S. Kuykendall, *The Hawaiian Kingdom, 1778-1854*, 304-313.

Americans as they dreamed of multimillion-dollar transactions in the Far East. They rushed scores of vessels into the trade and bade fair to overwhelm their British competitors who thought themselves sole heirs to the traffic by reason of their Opium War.[5]

The Chinese trip from Atlantic ports was a tremendous haul. Venturesome captains had the choice of rounding either the Cape or the Horn. Even before the United States had acquired a definite Pacific frontage, some Americans were calculating how best they could shorten these routes to the Orient. They became interested in three possible crossings of the Central American isthmus: Panama, Tehuantepec, Nicaragua. Any one of the three would cut thousands of miles and a hundred days from the journey. Soon an enterprising group procured transit rights across the Panama isthmus, and the State Department, in response to calls for help, threw a protective covering over this private undertaking in the treaty of New Granada. At the time hopes for a canal through Panama were dim, and the transit right was thought of as having value only for a highway or railroad.[6]

On the heels of this move, several events occurred to give added drive to the search for a shorter route to the Pacific. The Polk administration canceled joint occupation of the Oregon country with Britain; gold was discovered in California; and Mexico ceded California to the United States. Overnight America acquired a Pacific domain to which thousands began to migrate. A host of new interests, appreciating how long and arduous was the trip to the Pacific, and only dimly perceiving the possibility of a transcontinental railroad, joined hands with the China traders in their clamor for a speedy route to the Pacific. Even the government, in the negotiations for peace with Mexico, tried to buy the transit rights across the Tehuantepec isthmus. It failed, but at best this was only a railroad route, and already there were dreamers who were thinking of an all-water route through

[5]H. B. Morse and H. F. MacNair, *Far Eastern International Relations,* 114; Adams, *Memoirs of Adams,* 102; C. M. Fuess, *The Life of Caleb Cushing,* 1:422.
[6]J. B. Lockey, "A Neglected Aspect of Isthmian Diplomacy," *American Historical Review,* 41:305. See also Hunter Miller, ed., *Treaties and Other International Acts of the United States of America,* 5:115-160.

Central America. Their eyes were turned on Nicaragua where the engineers of the day thought the only possible isthmian canal route lay. Hastily a group of American promoters began to negotiate with the Nicaraguan government for the right to dig that canal.

These quick strokes staggered the British. Should Americans get control of the isthmian routes, they would have one of the most important nerve centers of the world trade. Worse, they appeared to be maneuvering themselves into a position to monopolize Pacific commerce.

The British were willing to sacrifice much before they permitted Yankees a clear title to Pacific trade. As Britons saw it, the gravest threat to their welfare lay in the proposed Nicaraguan canal. To forestall its construction, Lord Palmerston acted in a belligerently imperialistic spirit with hardly a nod to international decorum.

The eastern terminal of the proposed canal was the San Juan River, miles from which lived a savage tribe known as the Mosquito Indians. Over these aborigines, the British had long claimed a protectorate. Now in 1848, taking advantage of their relation with the Mosquitos, the British seized San Juan (renamed Greytown) at the entrance to the San Juan River, ostensibly to protect their ward, "His Mosquito Majesty," against the Nicaraguans.[7] Across the isthmus, on the Pacific side, the Gulf of Fonseca lay in a position to command the possible Pacific terminal, and in October, 1849, a British naval officer entered that body of water and seized Tigre Island. The London authorities eventually retired from the island, but they retained possession of San Juan and dared the world to dispute their right to stay.

The American group of canal entrepreneurs, meanwhile, had obtained from Nicaragua the right to dig that canal, but they knew their contract was useless as long as the British held San Juan. United States Secretary of State Clayton went to their

[7] R. W. Van Alstyne, "Central American Policy of Lord Palmerston, 1846-48," *Hispanic American Review*, 16:352-57; Miller, *Treaties*, 5:705-706.

aid. Anxious to see construction begin, he tried to dislodge the British. He was not bellicose. He recognized, rather, one of the root causes for Palmerston's action: Britons feared that if Americans owned the canal, they could close it to British use at any time. Such action would imperil millions of pounds of investments.

To allay this fear Clayton offered to guarantee the neutrality of the proposed canal if the British would accept the same obligation. Thus, with fear of closure eliminated, Clayton expected the British either to retire from San Juan or, at least, to ease the way for construction to begin.

The British accepted Clayton's offer, and three months before Fillmore became President, the two nations wrote their agreement into the Clayton-Bulwer treaty. For a time expectations for a canal were bright. Whatever her original intention, however, once the treaty was law, Britain dashed those hopes to the ground. She refused to budge from San Juan or to use her position to promote construction. It appeared that Clayton had inadvertently tied the nation's hands, for to obtain a canal, the United States must now forcibly eject Britain from San Juan. War, even if desirable, would be ludicrous. Should America defeat Britain, the two enemies would then become partners in the defense of the territory which Britain had lost. As Americans became aware of the trap they had helped forge for themselves, they grew bitter and came to despise the Clayton-Bulwer treaty as a cunning British triumph over America.[8]

From another quarter, meanwhile, aid came to American Pacific Ocean traders whose dreams of a canal seemed to have been blighted by the British. Shipwrights and Yankee salts were working a miracle in design and time. In one month of 1850, thirty-three sailing vessels from New York and Boston skirted the Horn and entered San Francisco Bay after an average passage of 159 days. Then there came booming through the Golden

[8]R. W. Van Alstyne, "British Diplomacy and the Clayton-Bulwer Treaty, 1850-1856," *Journal of Modern History*, 9:157, 161; M. W. Williams, *Anglo-American Isthmian Diplomacy, 1815-1915*, 80-105.

Gate the clipper ship, *Sea Witch*, of New York, ninety-seven days out. This fabulous ship had cut over sixty days from the journey — almost as much as the proposed isthmian canal had promised. At once the cry went up for clipper ships at any price. This new type of sailing vessel — the flowering of four millenniums — was characterized by great length in proportion to breadth of beam, enormous sail area and long concave bows ending in a gracefully curved cutwater. It had been devised for the New York-China tea trade, and the voyage of the *Sea Witch* showed its possibilities.[9]

Even while the British occupied San Juan, the cloud of sail that carried the clipper ships speedily captured the traffic in Far East products. England's East-Indiamen humbly waited while American clippers sailed off with cargoes of tea at double the ordinary freight. When the *Oriental* of New York appeared at London, ninety-seven days from Hong Kong, crowds thronged the West Indian docks to admire her. The London *Times* challenged British shipbuilders to set their "long practiced skill, steady industry and dogged determination" against the "youth, ingenuity and ardour" of the United States. What isthmian engrossment had failed to do for Americans, the clipper ship seemed to have accomplished. Maybe the British hold on San Juan would prove useless to her design and Americans would still obtain a monopoly of the Pacific trade.

Yet farsighted observers knew that the clipper was a fad, useful only for a limited purpose where speed, not cost, governed the shipper.[10] The depression seven years later would confirm their belief. But already at hand were portents of the future. Steam had captured river and coastwise commerce. The shallow draft and the side or stern wheel of the river trade, however, were unsatisfactory for ocean traffic. Not until the screw propeller was applied were steam vessels practical for ocean commerce.

[9]Carl C. Cutler, *Greyhounds of the Sea*, 175-190.
[10]H. I. Chapelle, *History of American Sailing Ships*, 225.

The idea of a screw propeller was a hundred years old before it was applied to ships. But apathy, the lack of a suitable engine, and the reluctance of naval architects to drill a hole below the water-line retarded its development. In 1836 John Ericsson demonstrated his screw on the Thames by towing four British Admiralty members on a barge at the unbelievable speed of ten knots. But hidebound British naval experts rejected it. Though Ericsson's screw failed to win over the British board, it did impress Captain Robert F. Stockton of the United States Navy and some shipbuilders. Stockton prevailed upon Ericsson to come to America. Under Whig guidance, in 1842-1843, the frigate *Princeton,* which became the first war vessel propelled by screw, was built. Merchantmen began to adopt the screw propeller to their purpose, and thereupon steam entered into stiff competition with sail for priority of the sea. That steam did not supplant sail immediately was due to the problems of sacrificing freight space for a coal supply.

Governments were now enrolled to solve the fuel problem by providing coaling stations along the trade routes and by reducing trade mileage. In response to this call, foreign offices and navy departments the world over began to contend for the shores of narrow seas that served as throats of commerce and for islands that might serve as way stations in the trackless ocean. The British, already possessed of a great number of these strategic points, had little difficulty maintaining their supremacy in all places except the Pacific. But there the stepping-stone islands became objects for seizure by others, and the proposed isthmian projects threatened to give Americans first place in the race for steam-carried produce.

So while the clipper appeared to obviate the need, the future of steam required the construction of either canal or railroad across the isthmus.

*   *   *   *   *

"I rejoice in all measures which extend and increase our means of intercourse with foreign countries . . . " Fillmore had said. And he inherited, as President, the problem of promoting American trade in the Pacific against British rivalry. The beneficent figure of the Bellevue House, who had offered the transportation world his compliments, now had his chance to perform deeds. In the realm of foreign affairs his word was more than a declaration of faith — it carried a special scepter of authority. He knew, moreover, that the United States must prepare for the day, not far distant, when steam, not sail, would propel ocean commerce.

A great share of the conduct of foreign affairs devolved on him. Chronic catarrh, rheumatism, and morbidness frequently drove his Secretary of State, Webster, into hiding at his Marshfield estate. Instead of resenting his absence, Fillmore encouraged Webster, always in the spirit of friendliness, to rest. Never once did Fillmore suggest that the lion of New England resign. The President had offered Webster the State post more to weight the Administration on the side of the Compromise than to draw upon his experience in foreign affairs. Rather than lose Webster's name from the roster of the official family, the President himself, when the occasion demanded, took an active role in the foreign office, even though he had never had any experience with foreign affairs.

His foreign policy was simplicity itself: promote, by honorable means only, every legitimate interest of Americans. This meant that bellicose action or unwonted greed on the part of either foreigners or Americans must be restrained. He cared neither to flaunt the power of America nor to test the strength of others. And when his term of office was over, his record would be remarkably clear of bluff, bombast, or aggression.

Each of the three isthmian routes — the beginnings of the Pacific highway — offered opportunities for action that could have either tempted or forced the President away from his policy of peaceful, but firm, promotion of America's interests abroad. The British, however, did not interfere with the New York combine that was building the Panama railroad and seemed to be satisfied with the guarantees of the treaty of New Granada. There the Washington government had bound itself to maintain the "perfect neutrality" of the route to the end that "free transit of traffic might not be interrupted."[11] The promoters, too, acted angelically, and the thankful President reported to Congress in December, 1851, with evident satisfaction, that a "considerable part of the railroad . . . [had] been completed," and he promised "mail and passengers" would "in the future be conveyed thereon."[12]

By contrast, the Nicaraguan route was fraught with turmoil. The canal promoters dared not proceed so long as the British stubbornly refused to budge from one of the terminals. It was "obvious" to Fillmore that the ship canal "would be indefinitely postponed" if the British continued to display or parade their military force.[13] Patience, however, marked his support of the canal group. Though he felt that the British were violating the Clayton-Bulwer treaty by continuing to occupy San Juan, he never turned to the warmonger's solution.[14] Twisting the lion's tail he scorned. No fanfare heralded him as the champion of American rights. His method, not unlike Clayton's a short time before, was to persuade Britons of America's good faith and thus induce them to withdraw from San Juan.

To Minister Abbott Lawrence, cotton and shoe manufacturer versed in the arts of selling,[15] fell the task of convincing the British that the United States had no objectives in Central America that were inimical to British interests. Against a vivid memory of "Fifty-four-forty or fight," and the annexation of Texas, New Mexico, and California, it was hard for the British to give credence to these protestations of good faith. Yet Fillmore earnestly threw his official weight behind the campaign.

[11]Lockey, "Isthmian Diplomacy," 305; Miller, *Treaties*, 5:115-160. The treaty with New Granada paved the way for the Panama railroad which was completed by Americans in 1855.
[12]Fillmore's second annual message in Richardson, *Messages*, 5:121.
[13]*Ibid.*, 5:81.
[14]Fillmore to Webster, December 7, 1851, *Fillmore Papers*, 1:359.
[15]Webster to Fillmore, July 10, 1851, Van Tyne, *Webster Letters*, 483.

"It is to be hoped," he announced, "that the guarantees which" the treaty offered would be "sufficient to secure the completion of the work. . . ."[16]

At one point, Palmerston, with tongue in cheek, hinted that he might withdraw, but further intimated that he would cede San Juan to Costa Rica. Instantly Fillmore, Webster, and Lawrence perceived the ruse. This suggestion would provide a way for Britain to back out of a tenuous claim on San Juan, and let Costa Rica prevent the building of the canal. For a canal it was necessary to have the entire route covered by a single jurisdiction — Nicaragua. Official Washington scoffed.[17]

Chance saved Palmerston the trouble of reaching a final decision. In the midst of these hints, a violent struggle broke out between Nicaragua and Costa Rica over their boundary. Then the personal avarice of a few Nicaraguan leaders, who played to the mob with a nationalistic theme, led to the overthrow of a government friendly to American canal promoters. For months, reported Fillmore to the nation, Nicaragua was "the theater of one of those civil convulsions from which the cause of free institutions and the general prosperity . . . [had] so often . . . suffered. Until quiet" could be "restored . . . no advance" could "prudently be made in disposing of" the canal question.[18] Try as they would, Americans could not restore order with peaceful means. The American chargé d'affaires to Nicaragua could not find a government to accept his credentials, and even the Nicaraguan minister in Washington, Mr. Marceletta, threw up his arms in disgust for lack of a government to represent.[19] Palmerston now justified San Juan occupation by pointing to the ferment in Nicaragua.

Matters might have rested at this point had not an untoward event occurred. In November, 1851, the captain of the American steamship, *Prometheus,* refused to pay a small sum in port dues

[16]Richardson, *Messages,* 5:81.
[17]Webster to Lawrence, January 16, 1852, Van Tyne, *Webster Letters,* 514.
[18]Richardson, *Messages,* 5:121.
[19]Webster to Lawrence, January 16, 1852, Van Tyne, *Webster Letters,* 514.

claimed by the city authorities at San Juan and started out of the harbor. Under orders from the British consul, who was Britain's special protector of His Mosquito Majesty, the English brig-of-war, *Express,* gave chase. She fired a round of shot at the American vessel, compelled the captain to heave to, douse his fires, and forced him to pay, under protest, the 123 dollars required.[20]

When the news reached Washington, the New York City canal interests were in arms.[21] Fillmore almost lost his composure and cried out, "It is a direct violation of the treaty."[22] Webster informed Lord Palmerston that no "protectorate over the Mosquito coast could justify . . . the collection of port charges . . . by British ships of war. . . ."[23] Fillmore promptly ordered an armed vessel to the scene.

At this point, Lord Granville succeeded to the foreign office, and seeing the danger of England's position, as soon as the facts were confirmed, disavowed the firing on the *Prometheus.* The crisis passed quickly. But it opened the British foreign office to common sense. Crampton replaced Bulwer at Washington, and negotiations began to settle the whole Mosquito question.[24] By the end of April, 1852, they had perfected a convention by which the four nations concerned — United States, Britain, Costa Rica, and Nicaragua — settled their problems.

The plan was excellent. Fillmore's policy of patient persistence had recovered what his predecessor had inadvertently lost in the Clayton-Bulwer treaty. Shipping interests trading west again looked forward to an isthmian canal. But the rejoicing was short-lived. Nicaraguan revolutionists now took up where Britain and Costa Rica had left off. They repudiated the work of their minister and would have nothing to do with the treaty.

[20]New York *Express,* December 3, 1851; New York *Herald,* December 3, 1851.
[21]*Ibid.,* December 6, 1851.
[22]Fillmore to Webster, December 7, 1851, *Fillmore Papers,* 1:359.
[23]Webster to Lawrence, December 3, 1851, Webster, *Writings and Speeches,* 14:405.
[24]Webster to Bulwer, February 10, 1852, *ibid.,* 16:640.

In the time left, Fillmore's administration could not persuade the Nicaraguans to change their attitude.

For the remainder of the decade, the affair dragged on. A change of parties at Washington, and the filibustering activities of an adventuresome Southerner, William Walker, a shy individual weighing scarcely a hundred pounds, who led three expeditions into Central America, dissolved the confidence between the United States and Britain that Fillmore had established. Not unnaturally, the British felt that this prince of filibusterers was but the advance guard of Manifest Destiny and that he was engaged in a covert attempt to secure territory for the United States in Central America. Before the decade was over, the labor of Fillmore's administration was lost. Had he approached the problem of promoting this American highway to the Orient with less than peaceful means, his Administration might have produced a canal a half century before history recorded it.

*   *   *   *   *

The third route between the Pacific and Atlantic oceans cut across the Tehuantepec isthmus in Mexico's extreme southern domain. The length and the nature of the surrounding terrain prohibited the digging of a canal. For a railroad, however, it was ideal, and if constructed, the road would reduce the journey between east and west by hundreds of miles even over the Nicaraguan and Panama routes.

When Fillmore took office, the American promoters of the Tehuantepec railroad were surveying the route.[25] Behind them lay eight years of troubled history, and ahead lay insecurity. In 1842 bellicose Santa Anna, president of Mexico, had granted to a fellow Mexican, Don José de Garay, the exclusive right of communication over the isthmus. The monopoly was for sixty years, and in place of financial aid to Garay, the profligate Mexican government contributed what they had in abundance — land. For ten leagues on either side of the proposed one hundred-

[25]Following summary from *Report of Committee on Foreign Relations in the Senate,* August 30, 1850.

mile railroad, Garay received a fee-simple title to the land. Only one string remained attached to this million-acre gift. Garay had to begin construction by July, 1844.

In the wake of the grant, there followed a period of revolutions, and in such turmoil, Garay was unable to begin his railroad. He sought an extension of his deadline. From his benefactor, Santa Anna, he obtained an extension of one year. Still turbulence raged on all sides, and as the day of forfeiture approached, with no railroad begun, Garay again sought relief. This time, with Santa Anna out of power, he appealed to the Mexican congress for a law extending his time until 1848. Before the deputies could act, General Mariano de Salas dispersed the congress, and momentarily the Garay grant lapsed. But Dictator de Salas in November promulgated a decree which was a duplicate of the proposed law. This third reprieve gave ample time actually to begin construction.[26]

Meanwhile, uncertain of his right to the grant because of the lapse and disheartened by popular agitation against officially supported tyranny of church and aristocratic clique, Garay peddled his charter to foreign investors and entrepreneurs. On February 5, 1848, by a devious route, the rights of Garay became the property of an American citizen, Peter A. Hargous. In order to secure capital to begin construction of the railroad, Hargous transferred two-thirds of his holding to a group of New Orleans capitalists headed by Judah P. Benjamin.[27]

Just as Fillmore was taking up the duties of President, the New Orleans directors of the Tehuantepec project were sending out a company of American engineers to complete the survey. As in Panama and Nicaragua, Fillmore tried to cast the cloak of governmental protection around these railroad builders. On the eve of their departure, he was doing all in his power to "impart a feeling of security to those who may embark their property

[26]On Garay grant see *Senate Executive Documents*, 32 cong., 1 sess., X(621), No. 97.
[27]*Ibid.*, 163-174, 175-177; Pierce Butler, *Judah P. Benjamin*, 124; *American Railroad Journal*, 23:689, 757; 24:90, 295, 372, 451; 25:236.

in the enterprise."[28] To Robert Letcher, American minister in Mexico City, Webster sent instructions to negotiate a convention for almost unlimited authority over the railroad. Mexico's foreign minister objected, and modifications were substituted that divided the guarantee of the right-of-way's tranquility jointly between the two governments. In January, 1851, Letcher and President Herrera signed the treaty, which the United States Senate ratified immediately. But fears prompted the Mexican Congress to another course.[29]

One of the articles of the treaty recognized that the Garay grant was still valid, and thus his successors, the Americans, possessed all his rights. With the memory of the consequences of the Texas grants to Americans still fresh in mind, Mexican deputies looked fearfully at the million-acre grant as another way for Manifest Destiny to subtract a large province in the south from Mexico. In May, 1851, instead of accepting the treaty, the deputies invalidated the Garay grant on grounds that he had lost his privileges in July, 1846, and that De Salas' decree was an act of a usurper. Instructions went out to governors in Tehuantepec, and the American engineers found themselves forcibly prevented from continuing their work.[30]

Instantly Benjamin was at the Executive Mansion. At first he urged Fillmore to treat Mexican authorities roughly in order to protect the railroad's interests. Fillmore gave him a flat refusal. Then Benjamin threatened that he would insist on his rights to the isthmus and that the railroad company would "send out 500 men to prosecute the work" who would "be prepared to resist any attempt to drive them off." If such a collision occurred, stormed Benjamin, it would force the two countries to war. In one way or the other the 100,000 dollars already invested must be protected.[31]

[28]Richardson, *Messages*, 5:81-82.
[29]Miller, *Treaties*, 5:765-775. *Senate Executive Documents*, 32, cong., 1 sess., X(621) No. 97, pp. 36-38, 41-43, 29-35, 47-50.
[30]*Ibid.*, 46, 50-52, 75-79, 80-85, 88. *American Railroad Journal*, 24:517.
[31]Fillmore to Webster, July 19, 1851, *Fillmore Papers*, 1:347.

Fillmore calmly and firmly replied that though he deemed the Tehuantepec railroad" a very important national enterprise," he was not willing to go as far as Benjamin to achieve it. He was "prepared to do anything [he could] honorably do to sustain" the company, but "I am not willing to see the nation involved in war with Mexico to gratify . . . the cupidity of any private company."[32] All Fillmore was willing to do was to urge upon Mexico the wisdom of accepting the treaty.[33] He refused to threaten war. Benjamin, faced by a determination he did not expect to find, quickly abandoned his blustering. His change of tactics and the President's forbearance, however, did not alter the Mexican attitude. That nation remained suspicious and would not accept the treaty.[34]

Dour over this failure, Fillmore drew consolation from his belief that "nothing was left undone that could have been done, to secure the rights of this company, and guarantee them by a treaty. . . ." To fend off the complaints of the stockholders, he pointed out that the "rights of the company, like the rights of every other contractor with a foreign nation . . . are rights growing out of a private contract, and if the Mexican government refuses to fulfill that contract, the proprietors doubtless have a claim for pecuniary indemnity, but that is to be settled, like every other claim of the kind. . . ." Fillmore had to agree with Mexicans that Garay's grant was too large and could "justly" make them "apprehensive . . . that it might turn out to be another Texan colony."[35]

Even if the New Orleans company had suffered, Fillmore did not give up hopes of finding a peaceful way to get a railroad across Mexico. After a new Mexican minister arrived in Washington, correspondence with President Arista was resumed, and Fillmore learned that Mexico would be willing to grant the right

---

[32]*Ibid.*
[33]He wrote to President Arista urging re-submission of the treaty and ratification. *Sen. Ex. Doc.*, 32 cong., 1 sess., X(621) No. 97, p. 157-90.
[34]*Ibid.*, 144.
[35]Fillmore to Webster, May 20, 1852, *Fillmore Papers*, 1:365-366.

of way to American citizens if it were made on less liberal terms than the Garay grant.[36] This suited his objective, and Webster, following the President's lead, suggested that Hargous and Benjamin try to obtain the new contract.[37] They did, but in the scramble among speculators, the Mexican government awarded it, on February 5, 1853, to Colonel A. G. Sloo, a New Orleans rival of Hargous and Benjamin.

Again Fillmore's administration showed that it was concerned with the fate of the railroad rather than the promoters. As soon as Americans had reacquired the right to build, the State Department placed its protective arm around the project. Roscoe Conkling, Letcher's replacement in Mexico City, negotiated a treaty with the Mexican government and obtained for the United States the right to "extend its protection as it shall judge wise to the company, in the construction and completion of the road and the enjoyment of their privileges. . . ."[38]

Success, however, was only short lived. The old Garay claimants would not quit the field, and for years their insistence that their grant was still valid haunted the project and discouraged investment in Sloo's company.[39] The Conkling treaty, moreover, arrived in Washington after Franklin Pierce became President, and he refused to submit it to the Senate for ratification. Apparently the hope, which Fillmore and his State Department had brought into being, that Pacific trade could be promoted by the construction of a railroad across the Tehuantepec isthmus, was foredoomed to be the victim of business and political rivalries.[40]

*   *   *   *   *

36*Ibid.*
37Webster to Fillmore, July 8, 1852, Fillmore Collection.
38*Senate Executive Journal*, 32 cong. 1 sess., 19:260.
39*De Bow's Review*, 14:407; Garber, *Gadsden Treaty*, 58, 59.
40Miller, *Treaties*, 5:839. Eventually after tortuous twisting through diplomatic and legislative tangle, it appeared that Fillmore's policy of peaceful persistence would succeed when his objectives were incorporated into the Gadsden Purchase by the work of his friend and crony, and Whig sympathizer, Senator Bell of Tennessee. But once again inept entrepeneurs fumbled their opportunities. *Sen. Ex. Jr.*, 9:299, 302, 306, 310; Garber, *Gadsden Treaty*, 135-40.

With the gathering of American interests for an assault on the China trade, it was natural that the State Department should endeavor to draw the Hawaiian Islands more tightly into the American sphere. Long before the mystic phrase "open door" had been invented, Americans were following its essential principle in their relations with Hawaii. Basically the "open door" was the only alternative open to a nation denied by tradition the advantages of colonial exploitation. The "open door" precluded other mercantile powers from encroaching upon a backward nation and encouraged it to sustain its independence. In this way a backward nation could maintain an equality of relationship among all foreigners within her land.

To give the "open door" reality in Hawaii, the United States government had been the first to acknowledge the kingdom's national existence. Soon several other governments followed this lead, and in the first fifty years of relations between the Sandwich Islands and the rest of the world, little of an untoward nature occurred. It was to America's advantage to support the islands' independence. "We were influenced in this measure," recounted Fillmore in a review of history, "by the existing and prospective importance of the islands as a place of refuge and refreshment for our vessels engaged in whale fishing, and by the consideration that they lie in the course of the great trade which must at no distant day be carried on between the western coast of North America and eastern Asia."[41]

More than once the State Department had served notice on foreign powers to keep Hawaiian independence inviolate. On one occasion in 1843, when an overzealous British naval officer seized the islands, the State Department announced that "we might even feel justified . . . in interfering by force to prevent" the islands from "falling into the hands of one of the great powers of Europe."[42] That same year, the British and French signed an agreement by which they bound themselves not to annex the

[41]Richardson, *Messages*, 5:120.
[42]Legare to Everett, July 13, 1843, *Senate Executive Documents*, 52 cong., 2 sess., No. 77, p. 109.

Hawaiian Islands. Though applauding this step, Washington refused to join the powers in such a statement of self-denial.[43]

Soon America's "open door" policy for Hawaii was again challenged. In 1849 Napoleon III seized Honolulu, and America's protest resounded in Paris. Though the French withdrew, rumors that they might return wafted through the Hawaiian capital and on to Washington. This time it was Fillmore who was forced to define his attitude toward the island kingdom.

In the United States, meanwhile, a genuine flurry for annexing Hawaii had developed. A San Francisco newspaper declared: "The native population are fast fading away, the foreign fast increasing. The inevitable destiny of the island is to pass into the possession of another power. That power is just as inevitably our own. . . . The pear is nearly ripe; we have scarcely to shake the tree in order to bring the luscious fruit readily into our lap."[44] A naval officer, knowing the importance of the islands to the commerce of the Pacific, reported from his Pacific squadron that "the Hawaiian Islands would prove the most important acquisition we could take in the whole Pacific Ocean — an acquisition intimately connected with our commercial and naval supremacy in those seas."[45]

As rumors of French overt action persisted, the Hawaiian king thought of means to defend his islands. Naively he gave Fillmore the opportunity for annexation. Encouraged by American citizens who filled his ears with advice, the native ruler proposed a secret annexation which would be valid only if French hostility proved true. Eagerly the American commissioner, Luther Severance, sought Washington's sanction for this proposal. Neither Fillmore nor Webster shared Severance's enthusiasm. Instead of using the proposal as a lever for annexation, Webster cautioned his commissoner to remain aloof from such shady affairs. If the king wanted to make a bona fide offer,

---

[43]R. W. Van Alstyne, "Great Britain and the United States and Hawaiian Independence, 1850-55," *Pacific Historical Review*, 4:15-16.
[44]Quoted from Kuykendall, *The Hawaiian Kingdom*, 408.
[45]*Ibid.*, 415.

Severance should transmit it to Washington. Fillmore and Webster deemed that the pear should not be shaken into the American lap under cover of darkness.

While this decision was being made, French designs materialized. In 1851, rather than risk occupation, Napoleon changed his tactics. His commissioner, M. Perrin, presented the native monarch with a list of demands that would reduce the islands to a French protectorate. Severance called on Webster for guidance, but Washington took matters into its own hands. Webster sharply informed Napoleon that Hawaii must remain independent in spirit as well as law. If it would lose its independence, it would be to America.[46] Like the British eight years earlier, the French retired.

The drama of the Sandwich Islands had not ended — but a threat to this essential steppingstone to the Orient had been parried by an Administration whose vision could see squadrons of American ships plying Far Eastern waters.

*   *   *   *   *

Since it provided a way station on the trip to the Far East, an independent Hawaii served Fillmore's purpose. Though the clipper ships had captured the imagination of the world, practical men of commercial affairs saw that future world trade belonged to the steamship. Honolulu served equally well for refreshing clippers or refueling steamers. Beyond this mid-Pacific refuge stretched numberless miles, sparsely dotted with island havens. None belonged to America, none was fitted out for coaling, but one possessd a coal supply.

Already steeped in the tradition of servitor to commerce, professionals in the American navy had conceived a philosophy of action in the Pacific that was to accomplish results in the years to come. That philosophy, as set forth with great care by Commodore Matthew C. Perry, was startling in its simplicity. "We cannot expect," he said, "to be free from the ambitious

[46]Webster to Severance, July 14, 1851, Van Tyne, *Webster Letters*, 484.

longings of increased power, which are the natural concomitants of national success." This seemed axiomatic. "When we look at the possessions in the East of our great maritime rival, England, and the constant and rapid increase of their fortified ports, we should be admonished of the necessity of prompt measures on our part. . . . Fortunately the Japanese and many other islands of the Pacific are still left untouched by this unconscionable government; and some of them lie in a route of great commerce which is destined to become of great importance to the United States. No time should be lost adopting active measures to secure a sufficient number of ports of refuge."[47]

Acting on such assumptions, the Commodore at one time had seized the Bonin Islands and raised the American flag at Port Lloyd. When less sympathetic Democrats returned to power, the flag was lowered in the Bonin Islands, and Japan reasserted her sovereignty. Perhaps it was not an accident that the first American naval officer to formulate imperial designs for opening commercial ports — Commodore Perry, a sailor from Providence, which was long one of the chief centers of the China trade — was the one eventually selected to bring Japan into business relations with the United States. Certainly it was no accident that this was achieved under a Whig administration headed by a man whose very soul and entire life was wrapped in the wonders of canal and lake commerce, and a Secretary of State who under another Whig administration had been responsible for sending a mission to open the gates of China to New England traders.

For over 200 years Japan had kept her ports closed to foreign trade — save for one harbor where the Dutch were allowed to carry on a small amount of business. And since the turn of the century, enterprising captains and nations had periodically knocked at Japan's door to inquire if she had changed her mind. In 1792 and 1804, two Russian captains, under the guise of returning Japanese seamen, had attempted to

[47]Dennett, *Americans in Eastern Asia,* 92.

carry away a boat-load of Japanese goods, but both failed. In 1807 an American ship carrying a Russian flag unsuccessfully sought trade at Nagasaki. The following year a British frigate put in at the same port and received the same rebuff. In Van Buren's administration an American ship, *Morrison*, returned some Japanese sailors to Yedo, but again the hoax failed.[48]

The trade with China, meanwhile, had grown with alacrity. Japan and her island chains lay athwart the direct route between San Francisco and Shanghai, and the requirements of steam navigation made imperative the establishment of coaling stations in the Land of the Rising Sun. Farsighted American businessmen were also looking hungrily upon Japan as a prospective market. As early as 1852, *De Bow's Review,* an influential southern journal, prophesied a 200,000,000-dollar annual trade with Japan. The Japanese, meanwhile, were treating shipwrecked mariners, chiefly from America's large whaling fleet, as felons. Some alleged that they had been required to trample and spit upon the Christian cross and that their companions had died as a result of having been shut up in small cages and exposed to the elements in stocks.[49]

The rising importance of the Far East trade continued to bring numerous sallies against Japan's exclusiveness. Two British surveying ships and two French warships visited Japan in the forties. In 1846 an American expedition under Commodore Biddle visited Yedo, to find the port closed; another American ship visited Nagasaki in 1849 to receive some shipwrecked sailors. All attempts to persuade Japan to emerge from her chrysalis failed to move the shogun who ruled in the name of the emperor.

Hitherto the efforts had been only halfhearted, but with Fillmore in the Executive Mansion, a virile determination seized Washington. Late in 1850 Fillmore transferred Commodore Aulick from the South Atlantic command to the East India

48*Ibid.,* 83-114.
49*De Bow's Review,* 13:562.

Squadron. His instructions, drawn up by Webster, were based on broad principles. "The moment is near when the last link in the chain of oceanic steam navigation is to be formed," predicted Webster. "It is the president's opinion, that steps should be taken at once," he continued, "to enable our enterprising merchants to supply the last link in that great chain which unites all nations of the world by the establishment of a line of steamers from California to China." To achieve this end, Webster forecast, "it is desirable that we obtain, from the Emperor of Japan, permission to purchase from his subjects the necessary supplies of coal. . . ."[50] A year later Fillmore wrote: "We understand there is a great abundance of coal and provisions in the Empire of Japan."[51]

Commodore Aulick became involved in a *faux pas* while a Brazilian minister was a passenger on board his vessel to Rio de Janeiro that made him unacceptable for diplomatic duty, and as a result he was taken off the projected Japanese mission. The determination of Fillmore and Webster to complete the chain meantime had grown greater. And they concluded to give the mission a more imposing aspect by sending out an independent fleet under the command of Commodore Perry, who was clothed with full powers of negotiation.

Meanwhile Fillmore and Webster labored under a mist of ignorance about the Japanese Empire. Little was really known of the land except as the Dutch learned it. To the files and personnel of the Dutch foreign office the American minister to the Netherlands repaired. There he searched out the reply of the shogun in 1844 to an address by William II asking that ports be opened to foreign trade.[52] Fillmore, in the meantime, had prepared an absurdly childish address to the emperor that reflected the Western World's complete inability to imagine the correct protocol to be employed in addressing a god-emperor.[53]

[50]Webster, *Writings and Speeches*, 16:322.
[51]*Fillmore Papers*, 1:395.
[52]Folsom to Fillmore, December 30, 1851, Fillmore Collection.
[53]See letter, *Fillmore Papers*, 1:344-345.

When a translation of the shogun's reply to the king of the
Netherlands arrived in Washington, Edward Everett, who on
November 6, 1852, became Secretary of State on Webster's
death, drew up another letter that incorporated much of the
childishness of the first one.[54]

The instructions to Perry, however, were untouched by
the mystery of the unknown. Prepared by Conrad, Secretary
of War and acting Secretary of State, they charged Perry with
obtaining protection for shipwrecked sailors, permission to
secure supplies, especially coal, and the opening of one or more
ports for commerce. These objects were to be obtained by
"argument and persuasion"; but if necessary he was to state
"in the most unequivocal terms" that American citizens wrecked
on the coasts of Japan must be treated with humanity "and that
if any acts of cruelty should hereafter be practiced upon citizens
of this country . . . they [sic] will be severely chastised." Since
the "president has no power to declare war, his mission [was]
necessarily of a pacific character," and he was not to "resort
to force unless in self defense in the protection of the vessels
and crews under his command, or to resent an act of personal
violence offered to himself, or one of his crew." He was,
further, to be "courteous and conciliatory, but at the same time,
firm and decided." He should, therefore, "submit with patience
and forebearance to acts of discourtesy to which he may be
subjected . . . but . . . " should be careful to do nothing that
would "compromise . . . his own dignity, or that of the
country." He would, on the contrary, "do everything to
impress them with a just sense of the power and greatness of
the country . . . . "[55]

Perry understood his instructions well. In July, 1853, six
months after leaving Norfolk with four warships, he entered
the Bay of Yedo. The Japanese had never before seen steamers
of this type; and as the American flagship, belching black smoke,
steadily moved up the bay in face of a strong headwind, the

[54]Everett to Fillmore, November 10, 1852, Fillmore Collection.
[55]Dennett, *Americans in Eastern Asia*, 158.

people were struck with consternation and made haste to defend themselves. With firm dignity Perry delivered the President's address into the hands of the shogun, and in ten days, with a promise to return later with an even larger force, he steamed out of the bay again.

Internal conditions in Japan were ideal for such a display of force and restraint. Whatever their desires, the Japanese knew that the British had broken through the barriers of China by arms and that both British and Russian battleships were at hand waiting to work their will on Japan. The country was ripe for change, since the feudal system of Japan was breaking down, and a new commercial and urban class, eager for power, was rapidly rising. Since the early seventeenth century, the shogunate, which represented the military, had exercised *de facto* sovereignty in Japan, though in theory subordinate to the emperor. Japan's more progressive leaders, who were reasonably well informed about the outside world, favored opening negotiations with Perry, and their counsel prevailed.

When Perry returned in February of 1854, this time with seven black ships, the country's leaders were ready to talk. The negotiations proceeded smoothly, and amidst sumptuous feasting and various kinds of liquors, which were fully appreciated, the treaty between Japan and the United States was signed.[56] By it Perry obtained all that was asked of him. Though meager, the concessions revolutionized the former Japanese policy. Fillmore's administration had prepared the ground for sweeping changes in the relations between the East and the West, and his highway to the Orient was taking shape.

[56]F. L. Hawks, *Narrative of the Expedition of an American Squadron to the China Seas and Japan,* 1:438.

Chapter 17

Fillmore Obstructs Manifest Destiny

THE DESIRE for China's trade had created the constructive side of Fillmore's foreign policy. It had made it necessary for him to open Japan, keep Hawaii out of foreign hands, and attempt to build railroads and canals across the Central American isthmus. Aggressive in these matters as he was, Fillmore was no worshiper of acquisitive Manifest Destiny. Willingly he repressed the bumptious spirit of Americans as they entered into a new era of prosperity, freed from the distress of sectional conflict. To him it was just and honorable to use the Presidential authority to promote commerce, but degrading, no matter what the object, to seize another's land.

*　　*　　*　　*　　*

Off the coast of Peru lay a group of islands, uninhabited, barren, and waterless. For tens of thousands of years, seafowl had used it as a resting place. During these millenniums their excrement — called guano — had accumulated in the islands' caves and crannies until in some places there were deposits thirty feet deep.

A generation before Fillmore's administration, the fertilizing value of guano was discovered. Because it brought a handsome price — five pounds a ton — some ships plying the Pacific waters brought it back to the northern world. At first there was no difficulty except transportation. In the thirties and forties, Peru laid claim to the archipelago, although it lay far enough off the coast to fall outside of littoral islands under international precedents. Until 1850 the Peruvian government did little to enforce its ownership. Then a revolution brought into existence an administration that threatened to turn back with fire any ship that came to Lobos seeking guano.

In New York City, meanwhile, speculative traders and shipowners had sampled the guano profits and, finding them high, prepared to make a killing. At the head of the New York combine was A. G. Benson, erstwhile pioneer in trade and colonizer in the Pacific Northwest against the competition of the Hudson's Bay Company. Joined with him were numerous Wall Street entrepreneurs, including the politically active Hiram Ketchum, one of the city's largest capitalists. They proposed sending a hundred ships to the Peruvian islands and returning with thousands of tons of guano. In the midst of their planning came the hostile rumblings from Peru. Convinced that Peru's protests could be ignored, and that the guano islands were a Pacific no man's land, the bold New Yorkers continued their preparations. To be sure of his position, however, Benson asked Webster to arrange protection by the United States navy, and Webster readily complied. Not trusting the word of Webster alone, Benson sent Captain Jewet to Washington to determine if Webster's order had gone through to the navy. Navy Secretary Graham upbraided him for even asking such a question. Webster's letter was the act of the government, and Graham "had issued the order to the Commodore for 'full and complete protection.' "[1] With such assurances, preparations went ahead.

Hearing of the enterprise, the Peruvian minister protested, and the affair came to Fillmore's attention. Webster, rapidly declining in health, was spending most of his time at his Marshfield retreat. Fillmore reviewed Peru's claims and concluded that

[1]Benson to Fillmore, September 8, 1852, Fillmore Collection.

the islands were hers.[2] He did not know of Webster's promise to Benson or Graham's order to the navy. A few days later, Fillmore was confirmed in his belief of Peru's ownership by the attitude of the British. Palmerston, who was always willing to shoulder a gun for British traders, had concluded also that Peru's claim to Lobos was good. If Britain conceded this, Fillmore had no doubts about it.[3] The United States, therefore, could not protect Americans if they sought to take guano without Peru's consent.

Before Fillmore's decision reached Benson, the fleet had sailed; and when the group heard that they had lost official protection, consternation seized them. From every quarter letters of protest arrived in Washington. Fillmore now learned of Webster's promise.[4] Sharply he questioned Webster, and the Secretary of State admitted he had blundered.[5] The adventurers bid fair to lose a fortune; but Fillmore remained stubborn in his refusal to use the navy. He shook his head as he imagined the project failing and the group petitioning the government for indemnification.

All appeared hopeless for Benson's expedition until he devised a plan to save the day. He proposed that Peru permit the flotilla to load without paying Peru's extraction price. Then if Fillmore insisted that the islands were Peru's, the government, which had encouraged the expedition, would pay the cost to Peru. The Peruvian minister was won to his side, and Benson aproached Fillmore. Either the government pays Peru, warned Benson, or it will face the wrath of the New York merchants and a welter of private compensation bills in Congress. To his aid Benson brought the New York City politicians, James Brooks of the *Express*, Fillmore's recently appointed New York naval officer, D. A. Bokee, and an astute politician who looked after

---

[2]Fillmore to Webster, July 8, 1852, *Fillmore Papers*, 1:369-71.
[3]Fillmore to Webster, July 16, 1852, *ibid.*, 1:371-72.
[4]Benson to Fillmore, September 9, 1852; Hoxie to Fillmore, September 10, October 29, 1852; Hunter to Fillmore September 29, 1852; Bokee to Fillmore, October 26, 1852; Brooks to Fillmore, October 29, 1852, Fillmore Collection.
[5]Webster to Fillmore, September 9, 1852, *ibid.*

the city's business community, Joe Hoxie. The pressure was too great, and Fillmore succumbed. For the future, however, the group of capitalists abandoned all thought of freely exploiting the deposits, and the President could draw consolation from the nation's untarnished honor.

* * * * *

From another group giving free play to expansionist tendencies Fillmore got less compliance. Since the opening of the century, Americans had looked across their southern border at the changing fortunes of Latin America. As each Spanish colony shook loose the mother country's hold, fears that a strong imperial power would grab the fledgling states haunted the American State Department. By 1830 all except Cuba had passed through revolution to independence.

Because of Cuba's commanding location off America's southeastern coast the old fear of foreign intervention was strong should Cuba join the free Latin American states. As long as a weak Spain controlled Cuba, the State Department was content. But it occasionally raised its voice to announce that it would not tolerate a formidable rival off American shores. Webster, himself, during his first term as Secretary of State, had guaranteed the islands to Spain.

The Mexican war developed an appetite for Cuba among Americans themselves, and President Polk attempted to purchase the Pearl of the Antilles from Spain for 100,000,000 dollars. Havana was a natural port of call for ships engaged in trade with newly acquired California and Oregon; if Havana were to fall to an unfriendly nation, American commerce could be hampered seriously by annoying regulations. Cuba's position also commanded the vital isthmian routes to the Pacific. But probably a more important factor in promoting a desire for Cuba was the need for slaves. With vast Texas, and possibly California, to populate with slaves, the demand was causing prices of field hands to rise. Already an illicit slave trade with the West Indies had grown to serious proportions. Some outspoken Southerners even argued publicly for the reopening of the slave trade. If the Spanish West Indies became American possessions, these islands might become the breeding grounds of slaves for Dixie's expanding cotton fields.

Those who saw the positive advantages of annexation perceived as well the danger of a continuation of weak Spanish rule in the island. Rumblings of Cuban racial unrest portended evil days; Spain might even be forced to free the slaves. Worse still was the chance that Haiti's grim slave revolt might be repeated on a larger scale. It would not do to have another Negro uprising at the South's doorstep.

When Polk's efforts to acquire Cuba through purchase failed, filibusterers took hold of the reins of Manifest Destiny. President Taylor suffered no small amount of annoyance from these men, whose object it was to start revolutions in Cuba. Most of the trouble revolved around Narciso Lopez, a picturesque Venezuelan adventurer who insisted on fitting out his expeditions in the United States. Lopez readily enrolled hundreds of restless Mexican War veterans eager to carry out the dictates of Manifest Destiny. Some of these adventurers doubtless looked upon themselves as bearers of the torch of liberty. Many more were attracted by promises of rewards, such as confiscated sugar plantations.

In other ways filibustering for Cuba had its origin in motives of cupidity. To American speculators Lopez sold, at large discounts, bonds of the revolutionary government he hoped to establish, pledging in their support the public lands, property, and fiscal resources of Cuba. The means of payment, Fillmore later noted, were "only to be obtained by . . . bloodshed, war, and revolution."[6]

On his first two attempts Lopez and his band of Americans fell afoul of fortune. Undaunted, he busied himself at New

[6]Richardson, *Messages*, 5:115.

Orleans with more preparations. For a third time a President was called upon to stop this "palpable violation of the laws of the United States," and this time Fillmore was in office.

On receiving word of Lopez' activities, Fillmore lost little time. He alerted the customs and naval officials and by public proclamation warned those whom Lopez had inveigled into the scheme of the penalty they would incur.[7] For some time Fillmore hoped these measures would forestall the expedition.[8] The hope proved delusive.

Before Lopez' band set out for Cuba, a slight insurrectionary movement had taken place at the eastern end of the island. American newspapers exaggerated the power of the revolt, and the young adventurers, believing that Cubans had set their revolution in motion, rushed to enlist under the banner of Lopez. Very early in the morning of August 3, the steamer *Pampero* stealthily cleared New Orleans harbor. On board were upwards of 400 armed men.[9]

Eight days later they landed at Playtas, within twenty leagues of Havana. The main body moved inland; others remained behind to unload and transport supplies. On the morning of August 13 the small rear-guard group undertook to join their companions. Spanish troops intercepted them, and a bloody conflict ensued. The invaders retreated to the place of landing. There about fifty of them obtained boats and sped toward the safety of the open sea. Among the keys near the shore, however, the filibusterers fell captive to the coast guard and were carried to Havana. Hailed before a military court, they all admitted the charge of being hostile invaders. Three days later all lay dead — the victims of public execution.[10]

At the time of this trial and execution, the main body of invaders was still in the field. Gradually the Spanish troops closed in, and on August 24 Lopez was captured and executed.

[7] See proclamations of April 25, October 22, 1851, *ibid.*, 5:111, 112.
[8] *Ibid.*, 5:113.   [9] *Ibid.*, 5:113, 114.   [10] *Ibid.*

Many of his remaining followers were killed or died of hunger and fatigue. The rest, about 160, were made prisoners and sent to Spain.[11]

All this had transpired rapidly. Hardly an opportunity presented itself to the American government to save the filibusterers. The invasion, battles, trials, and executions had come and gone at a pace that showed a certain indifference to forms of justice on the part of Spain. She had quelled the uprising, but her summary justice brought down about her ears a hornets' nest of public opinion. Many scions of pretentious southern families had fallen before Spanish fire.

Had Fillmore been an expansionist, the opportunity for retaliation was patent. But for the filibusterers he had no sympathy. He refused to use the occasion for an annexation movement. Quickly and effectively he disavowed the action of Lopez, admitted the right of Spain to treat the invaders as she did, and thus allayed Spanish suspicion. Further, he laid the blame for the catastrophe on foreigners, deluded youths, and greedy American speculators.[12]

*   *   *   *   *

Espying in Lopez' expedition American preliminaries for annexation, the English and French foreign offices jumped to protect their real and fancied interests. To the Caribbean waters they dispatched warships with instructions to watch for other filibusterers, an action portending search on the high seas. Though Fillmore had disavowed the filibusterers, he would not tolerate a revival of the old search and seizure that England had employed in the Napoleonic wars. Protests went out to London and Paris, and Conrad ordered several units of the navy to the Caribbean. The situation became tense.[13]

Before the strain relaxed, a blustering New Yorker readied himself for the role of war inciter. George Law, aggressive Latin American trader and owner of a line of steamships that sailed the

[11]*Ibid.*   [12]*Ibid.*, 5:115.   [13]*Ibid.*, 5:117.

West Atlantic, had run afoul of authorities at Havana. On his *Crescent City* he harbored a purser who had purveyed information to a Cuban revolutionary junto in New York that had published articles derogatory to Spain. In high dudgeon, the authorities at Havana demanded that Law fire his purser or no ships of his company would be permitted in Cuban waters.[14]

Unaccustomed to respecting the rights of others, and convinced that his own desire to see the American flag flying over Cuba was also the Administration's secret goal, Law protested Cuba's action to Webster. Much to Law's chagrin, the Secretary of State advised him to get rid of the offensive purser. But Law saw an opportunity to act the firebrand. He continued the purser on the payroll and had the effrontery to threaten that he would force the Administration to war. He proposed to defy the Spanish authorities, force them to fire on his ship, and compel Fillmore either to come to his aid with military force or face an outraged public made conscious of "national honor" by expansionist propaganda.[15]

Fillmore bristled. He thought Law to be either a knave trying to embarrass the Administration, or a fool fired with grandiose imperial designs. Quickly he ordered Bokee and Maxwell to prevent the departure of the *Crescent City*. Publicly he denounced all efforts of private citizens to declare war on a friendly nation. Taken aback by this decisiveness, Law acceded to Fillmore's wishes. He remained unconvinced, however, that his position was untenable. Fillmore, too, was unconvinced that he could control Law's actions by this method, and as a result, he promised to try to adjust the difficulty between Law and Havana through diplomatic channels.[16]

England, meanwhile, endeavored to turn Fillmore's opposition to filibustering to her own advantage. She sought to relieve her fears of an American Caribbean hegemony. To Paris and

---

[14]New York *Express*, September 3, 5, 15, October 12, 1852.
[15]Maxwell to Fillmore, November 11, 13, 16, 1852, Fillmore Collection; Fillmore to Maxwell, November 12, 1852, *Fillmore Papers*, 2:334-336.
[16]*Ibid.*; Richardson, *Messages*, 5:165.

Washington she sent notes suggesting a treaty between France, Britain, and the United States in which each would pledge herself never to take possession of Cuba.[17] But the British misjudged Fillmore's motives. He had no intention of permitting British traders to forge a trap for America. To Edward Everett, Webster's successor in the State Department, fell the task of parrying this British move.

The President, said Everett to England, considered the question of Cuba an American, not a European question, and objected to the proposed treaty because it assumed that the United States had no other or greater interest in the island than France or England. ". . . The compact, although equal in its terms, would be very unequal in substance. England and France by entering into it would disable themselves from obtaining possession of an island remote from their seats of government. . . . The United States, on the other hand, would . . . disable themselves from making an acquisition which might take place . . . in the natural order of things." Since Cuba, reasoned Everett, "commands the approach to the Gulf of Mexico, which washes the shores of five of our States . . . it bars the entrance to" the Mississippi river and "keeps watch at the doorway of our intercourse with California by the Isthmus route. If an island like Cuba," continued Everett with deft analogy, "guarded the entrance to the Thames or the Seine, and the United States should propose a convention like this to England and France, those powers would assuredly feel that the disability assumed by ourselves was far less serious than that which we asked them to assume."[18]

A few days later, in his annual message to Congress, Fillmore balanced Everett's assertion that the United States had a special interest in Cuba by assuring the world he had no plans for acquisition. "Were this island comparatively destitute of inhabitants, or occupied by a kindred race," Fillmore argued, "I

[17]Webster to Fillmore, October 1, 12, 1851, Fillmore Collection; Richardson, *Messages,* 5:165.
[18]*Senate Executive Documents,* 32 cong., 2 sess., no. 13, pp. 17-18.

should regard it, if voluntarily ceded by Spain, as a most desirable acquisition. But under existing circumstances, I should look upon its incorporation into our Union as a most hazardous measure." Its different "national stock, speaking a different language," cooled whatever ardor Fillmore had for Cuba. And if that were insufficient, the fear that acquisition "might revive those conflicts of opinion between the different sections of the country, which lately shook the Union to its center," chilled him further. Hopes of filibusterers and English merchants alike suffered at the hands of the President.[19]

*　　*　　*　　*　　*

Momentarily Fillmore's action in blunting the edge of Cuban filibustering restored a degree of repose to the State Department. Haunting echoes of former gasconades, however, just as quickly upset it.

In 1848 Louis Kossuth, the Hungarian landed aristocrat, had headed a revolt against Austrian domination. The natural sympathy of Americans with any insurrection against monarchs led to an idealization of Kossuth and his cause. In the summer of 1849, President Taylor had appointed A. Dudley Mann as a secret agent to investigate the situation. He had power to negotiate a commercial treaty, and even to recognize Hungarian independence. Before Mann could reach Hungary, Kossuth suffered defeat and fled to Turkey, where he was thrown into jail.

Meanwhile, the Austrian government, by skillful espionage, had secured a copy of Mann's instructions; and the Chevalier J. G. Hulsemann, Austrian chargé d'affaires in Washington, had complained informally of the attitude taken by Taylor. Nothing came of this diplomatic exchange until Taylor publicly condemned Austria, in late March, 1850, by transmitting to the Senate all the correspondence with Mann. Hulsemann at once took official offense, and his government was still bubbling with indignation when Fillmore took up the reins of government.

[19]Richardson, *Messages*, 5:165-166.

To the newly installed Secretary of State, Hulsemann dispatched a note which undiplomatically accused the United States of being "impatient for the downfall of the Austrian monarchy" and of using language "offensive to the Imperial Cabinet."[20] This note reached Webster's desk on October 2. The next morning he sent a copy to Fillmore, with the comment: "We shall have a quarrel with Austria. I have foreseen it for some time."[21]

Webster, William Hunter, his chief clerk, and Edward Everett put their heads together, and they concocted an answer that was to become a notable document in American diplomacy.[22] It quickly received Fillmore's approval. Their object was less to answer Hulsemann than to beat the drums of nationalism. Webster later admitted that he wished "to tell the people of Europe who and what we are, and awaken them to a just sense of the unparalleled growth of this country," and to "touch the national pride, and make a man feel sheepish and look *silly* who should speak of disunion."[23]

The letter was an extraordinary document.[24] It was couched in the conventional style of diplomacy but possessed a boastfulness and self-assertion seldom found in the correspondence between sovereign powers. With an indifference to consequences, which he probably would not have shown if he had been in controversy with a country like Great Britain, Webster declared that circumstances had made the American people "the representatives of purely popular principles of government"; that, although the United States was powerful and prosperous, it had abstained "from acts of interference with the political changes of Europe"; but that it could not help wishing success "to countries contending for popular constitutions and national independence." As to any retaliation on the part of Austria, the

[20]Full text of letter in Webster, *Writings and Speeches*, 12:162-164.
[21]*Ibid.*, 18:394.
[22]Paul R. Frothingham, *Edward Everett, Orator and Statesman*, 322, 323; Poore, *Reminiscences*, 1:403; Curtis, *Webster*, 2:535-536; Webster to Fillmore, November 13, 1850, Fillmore Collection.
[23]Webster to Ticknor, January 16, 1851, Webster, *Writings and Speeches*, 16:586.
[24]*Ibid.*, 10:165 ff.

people of the United States were "quite willing to take their chances and abide their destiny." The tone of the note was that of a young and ambitious country, asserting its rights by bluster and bombast.

During the exchange, Congress had caught the Administration's spirit of bravado, and in that mood it had instructed the President to obtain the release of Louis Kossuth from his Turkish prison. At the same time it had invited the Hungarian rebel to come to America. The American minister at Constantinople duly interceded, won freedom for the "Noble Magyar," and early in September, 1851, placed him on the warship *Mississippi* bound for New York.

Now Fillmore and Webster had to listen to the music they had helped compose but never wanted to hear. Already Hungary's revolt had aroused enthusiasm in the hearts of Americans, and when Kossuth's gaunt, round-shouldered figure descended the gangplank, New York's multitude greeted him with hysterical enthusiasm. Salutes were fired from forts and warships in the harbor. Hungarian and American flags flapped in the breeze. A spontaneous cheer arose from a hundred thousand throats.[25] Kossuth raised his bearded face to the tribute and momentarily the wrinkled brow lost its anxiety. He thought New Yorkers mad, but such madness suited him. He saw a chance to induce the American government to intervene between Hungary and Austria to secure Hungary's independence.[26] From that moment, every day and every hour, he pressed that message upon popular attention. New York's welcome was just the beginning of an ovation that had no parallel in the past.

Sitting at his desk, Fillmore read of the excitement and pondered his own conduct. He "knew Kossuth was not a statesman. . . ."[27] and he mistrusted the Hungarian patriot. There was never any question in his mind on what to do about Hungarian freedom. What troubled him was the enthusiasm Kossuth

[25]New York *Times*, December 6, 1851.
[26]New York *Express*, November 19, 23, December 12, 29, 31, 1851, January 3, 1852.
[27]*Fillmore Papers*, 2:316-317.

was arousing. The shade of Citizen Genet had returned with a beard. Also a distinct possibility existed that some designing politician would link Kossuth with the abolitionists by a semantic play on "freedom." Already Seward was preparing to join the Kossuth entourage.

Webster and Fillmore went into consultation. "It requires great caution," warned Webster, "so to conduct things here, when Mr. Kossuth shall arrive, as to keep clear both of Scylla and Charybdis. We shall treat him with respect, but shall give him no encouragement that the established policy of the country will be any degree departed from."[28]

On December 3, after brief visits in Philadelphia and Baltimore, Kossuth reached Washington. Senators Seward and Shields met him at the station, and instantly they repaired to the State Department.

"Kossuth has called at the Department," Webster reported to Fillmore later, "and he desires an introduction."

"If he desires simply an introduction," Fillmore replied, "I will see him, but if he wants to make a speech to me, I must most respectfully decline to see him."

"He has promised me not to make a speech," replied Webster.

"Very well, then, I will see him."[29]

That evening Kossuth and his suite were entertained in Brown's Hotel at the expense of Congress. They consumed enormous quantities of food and wine, and during the night's revelry did considerable damage to the furniture.[30] As one of the after-dinner speakers, Seward crowned the Magyar rebel with a rich garland of words. Kossuth's hopes ran high.

[28]Webster to Haven, December 23, 1851, Webster, *Writings and Speeches,* 18:497.
[29]From an interview with Fillmore appearing in the New York *Herald,* September 16, 1873.
[30]Poore, *Reminiscences,* 2:405.

The next day he appeared at the White House. Senators Seward and Shields were in tow. The previous evening's panegyrics still rang in Kossuth's ears. On being introduced to Fillmore, he confidently launched into a long speech and formally made known his wants. This unwelcome turn did not throw Fillmore off his poise. What had not been accomplished unofficially, now had to be done directly.[31] ". . . As an individual," he addressed Kossuth in a few cool and forcible words, "I sympathized deeply with you in your brave struggle," but as chief magistrate of this nation, "my own views . . . are" to adhere to the principles laid down by Washington, and there can be no departure from that policy.[32]

It was the first note of discouragement that Kossuth had received, and it came from the highest source in the land. The next night at another feasting, Webster appeared to lighten the blow. His objective was otherwise: not to let such an anti-administration man as Seward reap the reward of identity with the Kossuth craze. He therefore made a powerful argument for Hungarian independence. "We shall rejoice to see our American model upon the lower Danube and on the mountains of Hungary." As a toast he offered: "Hungarian Independence, Hungarian control of her own destinies; and Hungary as a distinct nationality among the nations of Europe."[33] But all through the dinner Webster did his utmost to make the patriot realize that the warmth of his reception did not mean that the United States would interfere in his behalf.

Mollifying as were the words of sympathy, the cold blast from the Chief Executive froze Kossuth's plans. From that hour, his mission was a failure. He left Washington for a tour of the West and South where he met little encouragement. A return visit to the national capital called forth no formal demonstrations. He was better treated in New England, where he raised a considerable sum of money. But the mob mania had died almost

---

[31]"Tribute of James O. Putnam to Fillmore" in *Fillmore Papers*, 2:467-468.
[32]Interview of Kossuth with Fillmore, *ibid.*, 1:426.
[33]Webster, *Writings and Speeches*, 13:452 ff.

as suddenly as it had arisen.   Sobered, Kossuth and his wife
departed for Europe.

*   *   *   *   *

Over the passing years of his administration, Fillmore's
attitude toward foreign nations clearly harmonized with his
personal precepts and prescriptions for the nation at home. His
concern for railroads, canals, rivers, harbors, and uniform
currency — the foundations of commerce in the domestic
markets — had shaped his public policy before becoming President and nurtured his attitude toward sectional peace. So, also,
his firm conviction that government owed the business world
its guidance caused him to use the President's responsibility in
foreign fields to expand the overseas trade. Isthmian canals and
railroads, Pacific and Caribbean islands, oceanic way stations,
fueling facilities for steamships, and the oriental trade — all these
he promoted to the best of his ability. For all his aggressive promotion of American interests abroad, however, he had never
fallen victim to the disease which led statesmen to find plausible
excuses for land-grabs. Obtaining colonies abroad fitted neither
into his scheme for expanding commerce nor his desire for
domestic peace.

Chapter 18

Self-Sacrifice: "The Hopes of Good Men"

N DECEMBER 7, 1851, lanky, learned Dr. Thomas Foote paused before the White House door. He was only half conscious that his wrinkled and linty traveling cloak was hardly appropriate for calling on the President. Rather his thoughts dwelled upon a letter he carried in his pocket. All night and all day, as rapidly as train, steamer, and stage could carry him, he had traveled from Albany to answer the summons of that letter. It was from the President, and though it had not hinted at what troubled Fillmore, the politician-editor-doctor had his suspicions.

Since his return a year before from the legation at Bogota, Dr. Foote had entered into the confidences of the President even more often than when he had stood behind him as editor of the Buffalo *Commercial Advertiser*. Only six months before, at Fillmore's request, Foote had bought into the *Albany Register* and replaced John Bush as a co-editor.[1] Since then, the *Register* had been interpreting the Fillmore administration to New York voters with becoming sympathy. Now the doctor suspected something big was afoot.

He was ushered quickly into the President's study and found Fillmore dabbling with some state papers, waiting for his old friend and crony to arrive. Soon he unloaded on the

---

[1]Haven to Fillmore, April 12, 1851; Bush to Fillmore, April 29, 1851; Maxwell to Fillmore, April 30, 1851, Fillmore Collection.

doctor's shoulders the burden of his summons. Foote's suspicions were confirmed: Fillmore had decided to withdraw from the Presidential race of 1852.

*   *   *   *   *

The decision had originated seventeen months earlier. From the fateful day of Taylor's death, Fillmore had felt no desire to succeed himself. "When I was . . . called" to the Presidency, he later recounted, "the country was agitated by political and sectional passions . . . patriots and statesmen looked with apprehension to the future. In that feeling I participated most profoundly. . . . I was oppressed by a sense of the great responsibilities that rested upon me, and sincerely distrusted my ability. . . . To prepare and strengthen myself . . . I endeavored to lay aside . . . every personal ambition."[2]

All through the harrassing months of struggle for sectional peace, he had kept his resolve. Yet he had guarded it as a secret. To talk of withdrawing from the Presidential race would only help the enemies of the Compromise. There was of course a certain temptation to disclose his renunciation so that he might indulge himself in a priggish satisfaction in his own virtue, but his vanity was better served by accomplishment. That egotism which sometimes led to fanaticism in other men became in him hard practicality. Alexander H. H. Stuart, his Secretary of the Interior, saw this trait in the President. Fillmore "was a man of decided opinion," recounted Stuart, "but he was always open to conviction." ". . . When he had carefully examined a question & had satisfied himself that he was right, no power on earth, could induce him to swerve from what he believed to be the line of duty. . . ." As early as his first month in office, Fillmore had considered standing for re-election, had found it undesirable, and had rejected it. For pragmatic reasons he had kept his own council, and his temperament helped him in his silence. Few

[2]Louisville *Journal*, February 16, 1854. In a letter to Ullman, Fillmore said, after the passage of the Compromise measures, that he believed he was "at the end of my political race." Quoted in Ullman to Fillmore, September 29, 1850, Fillmore Collection.

realized how chary he was of irresponsible speech. A mistake might lead to sectional discord. Members of his cabinet eventually came to appreciate that he never said a word for which he was sorry. "I remember on one occasion," remarked Stuart, "Mr. Corwin, Mr. Crittenden & I were walking together within the President's grounds . . . when Mr. Crittenden stopped me suddenly and remarked, 'Gentlemen, this President of ours is a very remarkable man. We have now been in daily intercourse with him for nearly three years, yet I doubt if either [sic] of us can say that we ever heard him utter a foolish or unmeaning word, in all that time!' "[3]

Although Fillmore did not make his decision known, a shrewd observer might have penetrated his silence. From the beginning his actions were not those of a candidate. Had he wanted to stand for office his power over federal patronage could have guaranteed him the chance, but he refrained from using it. Actually nothing short of a crisis ever induced him to swing the patronage axe. Placing Nathan K. Hall in the Postmaster-General's office was an effort to keep the post out of the hands of designing politicians rather than the selection of a trusted hatchet-man. Judge Hall had neither the experience nor the temperament to be an unscrupulous patronage dispenser. Eventually Weed's stubborn disregard for sectional peace did force the President to use his power over officeholders. Instead of dismissing his enemies in wholesale lots, he cut out only a few malignant offenders of "sectional peace."[4]

[3]Stuart to Wilson, April 29, 1878, Fillmore Mss.

[4]Fuller to Fillmore, March 26, 1851, remarked that both Maxwell and Young "are willing to comply with your suggestion." Both "think a half dozen well placed removals will do the trick of restoring confidence to friends . . . more would be unwise." Fillmore Collection.

See also Robert G. Campbell to Fillmore, March 31, 1852, "The Times, Tribune, and Journal are all harping on your removal of Seward's friends from office. We should silence their noise by listing all that have been removed and in each case the cause was delinquency." *Ibid.*

During Fillmore's administration, there was only one mass removal of New York officeholders. That was in the New York City customhouse. Maxwell acted the executioner of about 200 Sewardites, at the behest of pressure from the Committee of Safety rather than of Fillmore. Fillmore acquiesced in this by reason of the same philosophy whch would permit him to keep Sewardites in office. See Harvey to Fillmore, May 10, 1851, *ibid.*; cf. *Buffalo Express*, April 7, 1852.

In Boston, the focus of electioneering for all New England, a collector of the port, Phillip Greeley, Jr., labored cunningly against the President. While assuring him that the Administration was receiving Greeley's support, he worked for Seward. Warned against this man, Fillmore did nothing.[5] Yet, by one reckoning, had Greeley's office been used to promote Fillmore's cause, he would have obtained his party's nomination.[6]

In Philadelphia, another port collector, the confirmed braggart, William D. Lewis, played both sides of the Whig field. Here, too, warnings could not budge the President to act against Lewis. Nor did Fillmore do anything to hinder the candidacy of Winfield Scott, the chief candidate of the anti-Fillmorites.[7] Elsewhere the President showed the same apathy toward electioneering. Though Ohio's most powerful Whig was a member of his cabinet, the President did nothing to encourage the Ohio machine to accept him as its candidate. The President's friends in Illinois lamented the post office appointments because there, as elsewhere, he did not try to build an engine for re-election. Like a man whose vision was dimmed by other sights, Fillmore neglected opportunities that a Presidential candidate would have seized avidly.[8]

In December of 1850 Fillmore wanted to announce his withdrawal from the race. Charges from Weed's paper that

[5]Charles to Fillmore, February 19, May 8, 1852; P. Greeley to Fillmore, March 5, 6, 1851, March 9, 1852, Fillmore Collection. P. G[reeley] Jr. to Seward, April 14, May 22, 1852, Seward Papers.

[6]Had P. Greeley's influence really been turned to Fillmore's benefit, the Scott delegates from Massachusetts might have been Fillmore's and those from Maine, on which Greeley worked, would have been Fillmore's. The combination could have given Fillmore the nomination on the first ballot.

[7]Mueller, *Whig Party in Pennsylvania*, 181-192. Harvey to Fillmore, June 16, July 17, October 19, 1851; Mitchell to Fillmore, July 10, 1851; Smith to Fillmore, October 15, 1851; Randall to Fillmore, October 18, 1851; Lewis to Fillmore, October 19, 1851; [Anon.] to Fillmore, October 17, 1851; Hedges to Fillmore, May 17, 1852; Kelley to Fillmore, April 20, 1852; Lewis to Fillmore, April 21, 1851, Fillmore Collection.

[8]Chicago *Daily Democrat*, May 17, 1852. Thompson to Fillmore on Indiana politics remarked, November 6, 1852: The "eternal carpers about slavery . . . true complaint is that you have not consented to make the spoils system the basis of your government," Fillmore Collection.

he was using his Presidential power to get re-elected irritated and wounded him. He feared, however, that if he himself announced his withdrawal, it would turn his whole administration into a politicking circus. Wanting no part of a dissident administration, he still tried to refute the charges indirectly. He called upon his friend Dr. Foote to prod Dame Rumor into whispering that Fillmore did not seek election. Foote advised against the method. But Fillmore persisted, and in March, 1851, Foote complied.[9] The doctor was right. Planting rumors was no way to withdraw. No one believed them, especially when simultaneously an almost unanimous Whig voice from the South demanded Fillmore's nomination.

*   *   *   *   *

Sincere as he was in trying to remove himself from the election, circumstances were against him. Troubles in the South were contriving to make Fillmore the only candidate for whom southern Whigs could vote. They were in a desperate position. Their long campaign (the so-called "Union Movement") to check the fire-eaters had completely disrupted their state organizations. Only through joint action with "Union Democrats," to the neglect of their own party, had southern Whigs been able to stop the fire-eaters' revolt against the Compromise. As the need for joint action declined, however, some of these Whigs resisted returning to the fold. Either they had lost confidence in their party or they were convinced that the issues on which the Whig party had been founded were dead. The vague latitudinarianism that remained could not, they felt, again bring victory.[10]

Southern Whig wheelhorses, straining against this inertia, concluded that their party and their constituents' interest would be served only by a time-tested candidate who might be presented to the southern voters as their friend.[11] As they looked about

---

[9]Foote to Fillmore, February 7, March 2, 1851; Fuller to Fillmore, March 22, 1851, *ibid.*
[10]Cole, *Whig Party in the South*, 212-228.
[11]Governor Thomas Brown to W. G. M. Davis, September 4, 1851 in Washington *Republic*, October 22, 1851.

for such a candidate they, quite naturally, espied Fillmore. Here was their ideal man. By his firmness and fairness in the executive office, especially in the execution of the Fugitive Slave Act, he had ingratiated himself in southern hearts.[12]

The move to nominate Fillmore was not confined to the South. In spite of the violence he had done to antislavery sentiment, Northerners turned to him, too. His position on slavery would soon become the overwhelming faith of the North, and some were willing to reward him for establishing domestic peace by electing him to the Presidency.

From all quarters Fillmore received protestations of support. Early in October, 1850, J. B. Mower, the generation's greatest dabbler in Presidential politics, saw Fillmore as the only possible Whig candidate for 1852.[13] "If you run, Dauphin County is yours," wrote a Harrisburg correspondent.[14] "After a business trip through Penna., the Western States, and then to Georgia, I believe that either you or Mr. Webster will be the next candidate," wrote another.[15] By the fall of 1851, organized efforts were afoot to capture delegates still to be elected to the national convention. "I . . . can safely say our [Iowa] delegation to the National Convention will be [for] Fillmore. . . ."[16]

By that time Vermont had already selected its delegates, with three possible and one definitely a Fillmore man.[17] In other parts of New England Webster was the favorite, but Edward Everett revealed to Fillmore the character of the Webster movement. All of Webster's friends were Fillmore's, Everett assured him, and like others, Everett had taken Webster as first choice because of long years of political and social friendship. "But the issues of the coming election are far too momentous to be decided by personal preferences," he told Fillmore, "and I shall hold

[12]Cole, *Whig Party in the South,* 221.
[13]Mower to Fillmore, August 5, 1850, Fillmore Collection.
[14]Saunders to Fillmore, February 18, 1851, *ibid.*
[15]Smith, W., to Fillmore, June 18, 1851, *ibid.*
[16]Madeira to Fillmore, October 10, 1851, *ibid.*
[17]Nale to Fillmore, April 23, 1852, *ibid.*

myself in a position to give cordial support to your nomination. . . ."[18]

In Philadelphia the *Daily Sun* flung wide Fillmore's banner in March, 1851,[19] while G. W. Knight organized a Fillmore Union Club, which he claimed was one-third larger than the Rough and Ready Club that had carried Philadelphia for Taylor in 1848.[20] In October, 1851, a large enthusiastic Workingmen's meeting endorsed the President for re-election.[21]

So persistent was the movement to nominate Fillmore that Thurlow Weed threw up his hands in desperation. Harassed by his reflections upon political trends, Weed saw only a dark future. He again took refuge in a trip to Europe and advised his lieutenants to give the Compromise Whigs a *carte blanche* in the selection of the Presidential candidate for 1852.[22]

* * * * *

Had Seward accepted Weed's counsel, Fillmore might have become the unwilling candidate of his party despite his wishes. With Weed absent in Europe, however, Seward sparked a drive against his New York rival that ended in disaster for all concerned. Party circles mentioned seriously only two other men as possible candidates: General Winfield Scott and Daniel Webster. As a military hero whose drabness could be forgiven, a Southerner, and a man committed quietly and unaggressively to the Compromise, Scott was available. His name had appeared in each of the three previous campaigns, and now some Whigs in Indiana, Pennsylvania, Ohio, and the South declared for him. Then suddenly in the spring of 1851, the whole Seward camp moved behind Scott's candidacy. Seward's association was enough to frighten off southern support. As a President-maker,

18Everett to Fillmore, November 26, 1851, *ibid.*
19Philadelphia *Daily Sun*, March 31, 1851.
20Knight to Fillmore, March 12, 1851, Fillmore Collection.
21Bryant to Fillmore, October 25, 1851, *ibid.*
22Van Deusen, *Weed*, 191. See also David to Fillmore, April 9, 1851; Baker to Fillmore, May 5, 1851; Mumford to Fillmore, June 29, 1851; Throckmorton to Fillmore, n.d.[1851]; Chalmer to Fillmore, March 3, 1851, Everly to Fillmore, October 17, 1851, Fillmore Collection.

Seward's sincerity was questionable. He cared less about Scott's victory than Fillmore's defeat. The despondency of Seward and Weed at this point, when the pro-Compromise campaign had reached its peak, was leading them to operate on the philosophy that things must get worse before they got better. "Worse" meant breaking the Whig party if that was the only way to defeat Fillmore; "better" meant reorganizing the political parties along sectional lines. But whatever his motive, Seward breathed life into Scott's candidacy.

Webster, meanwhile, placed himself in the race. No man's ambitions ran higher than his. He had longed passionately for the Presidency. He wanted it not only because of glory, but because an election would vindicate his life. He felt that he had earned it by his services to his country. "But, sir, it is a great office," he told William Bates, when asked what the Presidency could do for him, "it is the greatest office in the world; and I am but a man, sir, I want it, I want it."[23] Seventy years of heavy work and intemperate living had weakened his body so that his enemies were not far wrong when they pictured him as "an ordinary looking, poor, decrepit old man, whose limbs could scarcely support him; whose sluggish legs were somewhat concealed by an overhanging abdomen; with head downcast and arms dangling almost helpless by his side, and incapable of being magnetized for the use of the orator."[24] His frame may have sagged, but Webster's will was indomitable.

From the time he took office under Fillmore, everything Webster did was calculated to achieve his nomination. Webster's capacity for friendship was something more than camaraderie, or buoyant good nature. Throughout his life, though he had made many enemies, he was surrounded by men who admired and loved him. Even when they doubted his public stand, they stood by him, and he by them. As early as June, 1851, a self-appointed committee of friends began an organized effort to

---

[23]Quoted in Fuess, *Webster,* 2:268; see also Foote to Fillmore, May 2, 1851, Fillmore Collection.
[24]W. P. and F. J. Garrison, *William Lloyd Garrison,* 3:330.

capture the nomination.[25] Webster closely watched the work of
the committee, and late in November, they formally threw his
hat into the ring.[26]

*   *   *   *   *

Without envy Fillmore watched Webster's campaign unfold.
Rather, he welcomed it. In the late fall of 1851, just before
Webster's campaign formally opened, George Ashmun, one
of Webster's sponsors, received Fillmore's secret approval of
Webster.[27] With Webster's name now prominently displayed,
Fillmore thought it safe to announce his withdrawal, and he
planned on making it in his annual address to Congress in
December, 1851. Yet in the opinion of a large segment of the
party, Fillmore's intention was premature.

The news of his decision quickly spread through the grape-
vine, and instantly from every quarter came cries of anguish
and pleas for reconsideration. Since the sectional crisis many
men had stopped and analyzed their party. It led at once to
doubts over the ability of the Whig party to reach its goals.
Since 1848 factionalism had torn the organization seemingly
beyond repair. Where desertions to the Democratic party had
not marred the symmetry, or headlong ambitions had not
broken its unity, then apathy or disgust had paralyzed its acts.
At every side evidence mounted that soon the party would dissolve. But the objectives for which the core and heart of Whiggery stood were still to be won.

Oran Follett, one Whig soothsayer and well-wisher, who
had an uncanny ability to see the forest as well as the trees,
expressed his view when he urged Fillmore not to withdraw
from the race. "If you . . . [withdraw]," he warned Fillmore,

[25]P. Greeley to Fillmore, June 19, 1851, reported that these men were Rufus
Choate, E. Everett, Geo. Ashmun, E. P. Tileston, Ansel Phelps, Jr., J. P. Bradlee,
Geo. T. Curtis, Peter Harvey, Fillmore Collection.
[26]Webster to Harvey, November 12, 1851, Webster, *Writings and Speeches*, 16:629.
[27]Webster wrote to Haven in a cryptic but decipherable letter: "Mr. Ashmun
leaves for home this afternoon. He has seen many persons, & he thinks the coast
will be clear, & known to be clear, in due time." *ibid*.

"it will cut the ground from under the 'Old Guard.' . . . You may not seek nomination, but you cannot turn it down. Important interests will be jeoparded by such a course." To Follett the accomplishment of the Whig economic program overshadowed all political loyalties. For him the Whig party existed only to enact measures to encourage business. He lamented that the "clap-trap of . . . politicians" had sacrificed the fundamental Whig cause. In his eyes only one glimmer of hope existed: a new party founded upon "Old Guard" principles must be created. And for that purpose, Fillmore held the key to success. "Upon all genuine 'Republicans' . . . a work has devolved, which they cannot perform successfully," Follett cautioned the President, "if you surrender our single prominent advantage [that] they possess through you and by you. . . . Remove your name and your enemies who are occupied with attacking you will turn to new plots. . . . I know well the men who are training their forces against you. Take the word of an old tactician for once, and await a sign from the Gods. Lying oracles only have as yet mouthed the 'vox populi.' "[28]

Follett did not lack for company among Whig leaders who were toying with creating a new party with a national outlook. New York City's Union Safety Committee made no bones about its desire to effect a union of "National" Democrats and Whigs.[29] This attitude had troubled Fillmore at the time of the "Silver Grey" bolt. Since then, the Union Safety Committee was winning a growing body of New York City Whigs to the idea. Already Maxwell, Young, Bokee, Brooks, and Webb, who made up the core of Whig politicos in the city, were touched by the heresy. After constantly rubbing elbows with the Committee, the city's politicians felt their future lay in a "new relation."

Webster, too, though seeking the Whig nomination, was convinced that it was vain to labor to reconstruct either major party. Both were resolved into their original elements, he asserted.

[28]Follett to Fillmore, November 19, 1851, Fillmore Collection.
[29]Foner, *Business and Slavery*, 66-67.

Neither had cohesive power. Henceforth all efforts should be directed to the building of a great Union party with a grand national man as its representative and leader. He pointed to Georgia as the center of the movement and to himself as the "great national man."[30] His nomination by the Whigs would coalesce the forces needing a "great union party," for he expected not only to retain the "National" Whig support, but he was interpreting "the . . . personal attentions of Democrats as proof that they will vote for him. 'Tis a delusion harmless to all but himself," commented a critic.[31] Yet Webster asked Fillmore to agree "that the time is fast approaching, for the formation of political parties upon new distinctions."[32]

While Oran Follett was calling for "new relations" in an abstract sort of way, and the city Whigs were becoming contaminated with the strategy of the Union Safety Committee, and Webster and his followers were looking for a new Union party stemming from the Union movement in the South, still a fourth possibility offered itself for consideration. In Philadelphia the dormant seed of nativism again began to germinate under the cultivation of Lewis Levin, Ingersoll, the *Daily Sun,* and the recently organized American and Foreign Christian Union.[33] Dropping the name of Native American party and restyling itself the American Democratic party, it put itself behind the Cooper-Fillmore-Webster faction in Philadelphia. Already the secret patriotic society, Order of the Star-Spangled Banner, a brain child of Charles B. Allen of New York, was growing beyond its feeble conception and crawling to the city of Brotherly Love. The fraternal organization of the order and the political program of the Americans were soon to be working as complements. So efficiently had its secrets been guarded, few outside the order knew of its existence. And fewer still suspected how important nativism would become. But for those who had eyes

---

[30]Foote to Fillmore, August 27, 1852, Fillmore Collection.
[31]Foote to Fillmore, May 2, 1851, *ibid.*
[32]Webster to Fillmore, August 6, 1851, *ibid.*
[33]Chalmer to Fillmore, March 3, 1851; Harvey to Fillmore, June 16, 1851; Everly to Fillmore, October 17, 1851, *ibid.;* Philadelphia *Daily Sun,* March 31, 1851.

to see, here was a "new relation" that could be used to avoid the dead hand of the past that would accompany a union of factions.

Was this call for a new party the oracle Fillmore should await? Fillmore did not think so. A new party might achieve sectional peace, but the tactic was foreign to the President's former course. Once begun, a new party would create so much confusion that no one could safely forecast the result. In the confusion of organizing a Union party out of the "Silver Greys," plans might go awry and produce a sectional party. Better to take the safer, more cautious approach, Fillmore reasoned, and smother fanaticism behind the curtains of the Whig councils.

Instead then of getting behind the new party movement, Fillmore, until at least the November elections, hoped to preserve the Whig party. During July, August, and September, so that the party would have a united front in the November elections, he directed an effort to obtain a unity conference with Seward's followers.[34] Against the centrifugal force of the Union Safety Committee he called upon Maxwell, Bokee, and Young to use obstructing tactics. Maxwell, feeling the force of Fillmore's hand more keenly than that of the Union Safety Committee, recanted his tendency toward heresy and reported that "we have made a manifestation which takes the wind out of the Union Committee's sail. . . . We do not intend to be accused by our Whig friends elsewhere that we have faltered in supporting the Whig State ticket. I know the danger of such a belief in reference to future action."[35] Two days earlier Maxwell had promised that he and others in New York "intend to act in good faith notwithstanding the temptation to rebel."[36] When despite their efforts the Union Safety Committee eventually broke with the Whig ticket worked out by the Unity Conference, Bokee apol-

[34]Foote to Fillmore, July 24, 1851; E. Brooks to Fillmore, June 16, 1851; J. Brooks to Fillmore, July 1, 1851; Hall to Fillmore, July 22, 1851; Spencer to Fillmore, July 22, 1851; Remus to Fillmore, June 5, 1851; Campbell to Fillmore, April 9, 1851; Bush to Fillmore, April 20, 1851, Fillmore Collection. See also Stetson to Weed, May 10, 1851; Draper to Weed, June 16, July 5; Sherman to Weed, July 18, 1851, Weed Papers.

[35]Maxwell to Fillmore, October 31, 1851, Fillmore Collection.

[36]Maxwell to Fillmore, October 29, 1851, *ibid*.

ogized to Fillmore. "The action of the Union Safety Committee is to be regretted, but we did our best to prevent it."[37] Then when the Whigs lost the election because of New York City Whig defection to the nominees of the Committee, Fillmore instructed Bush and the Administration journal at Albany to spread the word that Fillmore had supported the whole Whig ticket, and not alone those Whigs favored by the Union Safety Committee.[38]

The success of the Union Safety Committee in stopping the election of hated Sewardites to state offices inspired further talk of amalgamating Fillmorites with Hunker Democrats. But Fillmore continued to deprecate the strategy.[39]

Though Fillmore preferred to keep the Whig party alive, he was aware that his own strategy for peace and prosperity might go astray. It was a notable trait in his character that he could acknowledge the errors of his own judgment. During October and November, Whigs suffered serious reverses in local and state elections, losing in every northern state. For the immediate cause of Compromise and Union, this was no blow, for Democrats were more solidly pledged to accept the Compromise than were Whigs. But Whig defeats further disheartened those who already thought Whiggery effete, and they renewed their call for a new party.

Doubts about the wisdom of continuing his party began to creep into Fillmore's mind. A question of momentous impor-

[37]Bokee to Fillmore, [n.d. rec'd by Fillmore October 30, 1851], *ibid.*
[38]Bush to Fillmore, November 7, 1851, *ibid.*
[39]Haven to Fillmore, January 1, 1851: "Your letter of the 22nd . . . has been of considerable service to me politically. I had entertained my own notions of things before, as to the probable result of all this talk about amalgamation and breaking up of parties. I have always regarded the idea as fallacious. I found you corresponded with me in sentiment, and being strengthened in that belief, I have thought best to lay still here, decline profers for a Union meeting, and having the political organization of the county in our hands, I think it best to treat the Hunkers kindly, but wait until they come to us which I am sure they will not do." Fillmore Collection. Fillmore likewise was trying to harmonize party factions in Pennsylvania after Gov. Johnson's defeat, instead of using Whig defection from Johnson (because of his veto of a bill to open jails for recovered slaves) to start a new party. See Harvey to Fillmore, October 23, 1851, *ibid.*

tance confronted him. He had two public objectives: to save the Union from dissolution, and to achieve the economic program of the original Whig party. As President and titular head of his party, how best could he achieve both goals? Follett and his ilk charged Fillmore with leadership in forming a new party dedicated to Union and business. Yet the President preferred the Whig party in that role.

He resolved his problems with his customary caution. In either case time and patience were the essence of success. If the Whigs were to be revitalized, time and patient care alone would heal the wounds of interparty strife. One poor move, and the intersectional truce that Fillmore had imposed would dissolve and with it would go party and cause. If the Whig party were not to be revitalized, and another organized around its old-guard core, time and patience were just as necessary. If Whigs dissolved their organization before the old guard had prepared the ground for a new party, the disintegrating pieces would gravitate to one or the other sectional parties, and the Whig causes and program would evaporate.

Fillmore reached no definite decision. He contented himself with letting his perception of the problem guide his personal actions. Since he was not going to run for office, no reason existed for him to solve the problem. As a retiring President he felt he could leave the way open for his successor to follow either alternative. Without realizing it, by failing to reach a decision, Fillmore was forcing himself into a position where he could not withdraw from the Presidential campaign. A gnawing sense of responsibility, moreover, bored into his conscience and whispered that his loyalty to Whig objectives required more of him than merely leaving the way clear for successors.

*   *   *   *   *

Now, in the President's study on December 7, Dr. Foote listened to Fillmore explaining that he had called his friend to Washington to discuss the election. He heard Fillmore reaffirm his intention of retiring at the end of his term, hopeful that the

Whig party could survive, and not at all certain that a new party might not be the best thing for the country. It was too conciliatory a mood in which to meet Dr. Foote, who was strong-willed and decided about the future of Fillmore. Again the President had called upon his editor-friend to make the announcement of his withdrawal, and again the doctor was prepared to fight off the announcement.

In the quiet of the winter night, before the fireplace, the two men talked over Fillmore's future course. Shrewdly, Foote played upon the very chord in Fillmore's make-up which was out of tune with his immediate desires — the self-sacrificing spirit that had sustained him in the Compromise.

The doctor painted a picture of hope. "No other president," he flattered Fillmore, "ever commenced his administration amid like storms; none other could look forward to a close more auspicious and serene." Yet, as Dr. Foote continued, he revealed that he, like the President, could see something other than a bright and shining future for the nation. If progress toward sectional peace were to continue, he noted, stealing a precept out of Fillmore's past reasoning, it would depend on the "integrity of the Whig Party. . . . The hopes of good men" rested upon Fillmore. Improvements could come, moralized the learned doctor, only "as the result of steady perseverance in well-doing." For Fillmore to withdraw at this point would demoralize all of the Administration's friends. It would leave them "without an acknowledged head and rallying point; it would . . . [be] proclaimed as a confession of weakness and submission to your opponents and revilers; and sectional, incendiary agitation would . . . [be] renewed with fresh fury and more disastrous effects than threatened before." Yield, he pleaded with Fillmore, "to the wishes . . . of your friends . . . and . . . as I know . . . the result [will] . . . justify the decision."[40]

---

[40]Drawn from the argument Foote used as he recounted it a few months later to justify himself in having placed Fillmore in a position where the public thought him a candidate. He began this letter: "I have never distrusted the soundness of the opinions I entertained last December advertise to withdrawing . . . . " Foote to Fillmore, April 19, 1852, *ibid*.

To this eloquent plea for more self-sacrifice, Fillmore yielded, and for the third time he postponed the announcement of his withdrawal. But he extracted from Foote, and all who Foote represented, a tacit acknowledgment of his right to withdraw at any time he felt that the use of his name could no longer be used profitably. Until that moment, the President promised to settle back once again in silence and let "National" Whigs use him as a rallying point.[41]

[41]*Ibid*.

Chapter 19

Webster and the Baltimore Convention

ARDLY had Fillmore agreed to remain silent on the Presidency than administration journals inadvertently pushed him into the race. "Many of his friends strongly importuned him," said the Buffalo *Commercial Advertiser*, "to continue to occupy his former position, reserving to himself . . . the right to say whether he would . . . be considered a candidate. He will not seek a nomination or election."[1] Not knowing his true sentiments, the nation accepted this announcement as Fillmore's decision to run.

The lid was off. Day by day, it became harder to withdraw. Protestations of support flooded the White House mail. "As certain as you live," wrote Leslie Coombs, after the Kentucky state convention endorsed Fillmore, "we can carry Kentucky for you and I do not know that we can do it for anyone else."[2] From New Orleans William Garland sounded the theme of Louisiana Whigs: "Your administration has been marked by such a just appreciation of the rights of every section of the country — by so high and lofty a tone in your intercourse with foreign nations and by such a fixed determination to see the Constitution and the laws faithfully executed . . . that [all] . . . acknowledge the correctness of your course. In Louisiana you are stronger than any other Whig."[3] John W. Ashmead, editor

[1]Buffalo *Commercial Advertiser*, February 11, 1852.
[2]to Fillmore, February 26, 1852, Fillmore Collection.
[3]to Fillmore, February 17, 1852, *ibid.*

of the Philadelphia *Daily Sun,* shouted: "The Native Americans are for you to a man,"[4] and he assured Fillmore that "Scott doesn't stand a hog's chance in Pennsylvania. . . ."[5] From the Deep South came the report that "President making is the all absorbing topic. Fillmore . . . [is] overwhelmingly popular in every section I have visited. I should judge he will receive the unanimous vote of the South in the convention."[6]

The high point of endorsements came when Clay broke his silence. Early in December he arrived in Washington fatigued by the journey. He was thinner and less buoyant and could not rally from his fatigue. He actually was slipping fast, and by the middle of the month, Fillmore, in defiance of etiquette, visited Clay at the National Hotel.[7] Twice in the next two months the President forgot all state matters to pay his respects to a dying founder of the Whig party.[8] Little except a common party had ever tied the two men together. Yet since Fillmore became President his almost sullen hostility to Clay had disappeared. A compromiser himself, he was coming to appreciate the forces that dictated Clay's actions. Then suddenly Clay recovered enough to make an announcement. Before leaving Kentucky he had expressed his preference for Fillmore, and he had frequently repeated it in private conversation. Now he made a deathbed appeal and asked his party to nominate Fillmore. "The foundation of my preference is, that Fillmore had administered the Executive Government with signal success and ability. He has been tried and found true, faithful, honest and conscientious. I wish to say nothing in derogation from his competitors. They have both rendered great services to their country — the one in the field, the other in the Cabinet. They might possibly administer the Government as well as Mr. Fillmore has done. But then neither of them has been tried. He has been tried in the elevated position he now holds, and I think that prudence and wisdom

[4] to Fillmore, February 27, 1852; see also Chalmer to Fillmore, March 4, 1852, *ibid.*
[5] Ashmead to Fillmore, March 25, 1852, *ibid.*
[6] Cassell of Macon, Georgia, quoted in Hall to Fillmore, March 31, 1853, *ibid.*
[7] *National Intelligencer,* December 6, 17, 20, 27, 1851.
[8] *Ibid.,* January 14, February 25, 1852.

had better restrain us from making any change without the necessity for it — the existence of which I do not perceive."[9]

The jacksnipes were at work, too. In no previous Presidential race had politicians turned with such malice on one of their own party's possible nominees as the Seward Whigs turned upon Fillmore. By half-truths and vicious misrepresentation, they wove a story of Fillmore's life that made Fillmore into a traitor to freedom, principle, and party. They charged that Fillmore was a blackguard who sullied every sense of self-respect to gratify an overweening ambition. Bit by the "Presidential Bug," ran this catechism of hate, Fillmore had turned on his old friends who for twenty years had wished him well. Fillmore had not only deserted old and cherished friends since he became President, but sacrificed older and even more cherished principles. Upon the slavery question, claimed the vilifiers, Fillmore had always been more pronounced and aggressive than even a man like Seward, and he had sympathized and acted with Giddings and J. P. Hale. Yet among the measures of the Compromise of 1850 was a fugitive slave bill, so revolting to every sentiment of justice and humanity that it was thought impossible to find approval with Fillmore. But the promise of reward for sacrificing all that was sacred, continued the indictment, was strong enough to command Fillmore's approval of the Fugitive Slave Law. Up to the time of his temptation, he had adhered so firmly to his political convictions that all Whigs had unbounded confidence in him. Now he even plots a new party as his vehicle to power and he might exclaim with Cardinal Wolsey:

> "Fling away ambition,
> By that sin fell the angels. How can man then,
> The image of his Maker, hope to win by it?"[10]

[9]*Ibid.*, January 7, February 25, March 17, 24, 1852; Bryant to Fillmore, March 18, 1852, Fillmore Collection.

[10]For the preceeding synthesis and illustrations see Barnard to Fillmore, June 15, 1852; Fish to Fillmore, May 14, 1852; Campbell to Fillmore, March 31, 1852; Palmer to Fillmore, March 4, 1852; P. Greeley to Fillmore, March 9, 1852, Fillmore Collection. *Buffalo Express*, February 13, 20, 1852, March 27, 29, April 3, 17, 20, 23, May 3, 25, 1852; Albany *Evening Journal* and New York *Tribune*, any day's issue from mid-February, 1852, onward.

The concentrated attack upon him, and the protestations of support for him, made it increasingly difficult to withdraw. He began to recognize his mistake. Instead of a substitute candidate appearing, the field narrowed to Scott and Fillmore. Webster was always an alternative to Fillmore, but he was running a poor third. By the day the Whig convention met, Scott and Fillmore had ceased to be real men and in the eyes of partisans had become factional symbols. So ossified had the Whig factions become that neither side had the flexibility to adjust to another candidate. Each would rather go down in defeat than see the other side win. Each side supported its candidate as much to stop the other from winning as to see its own victorious. The party's will to win had evaporated and with it was rapidly going the living spirit.

George R. Babcock, Fillmore's ears, eyes, and mouth, in Buffalo and Albany, perspicaciously analyzed the New York situation. ". . . Friends of Governor Seward neither expect nor desire Gen'l S[cott]'s success. They wish to nominate him to defeat you." Babcock further perceived that Sewardites actually desired the succession of "some out and out Southern man" to the Presidency, for they had their sights trained on the election of 1856. If a southern President were elected and showed himself hostile to manufacturers, rivers and harbors, northern interests, and northern antislavery feelings, then Sewardites could hope to unite the North on a sectional candidate in 1856. "Who," asked Babcock, would "so likely . . . be the man as Governor S[eward]?"[11]

Fillmore grew disquieted. If he withdrew, Sewardites would win their point. The confusion this would cause among "National" Whigs would leave the well-ordered supporters of Seward in control of the convention. They could make the platform obnoxious to Southerners and force them out. The sectionalizers would then control the party's machinery.[12]

---

[11]Babcock to Fillmore, March 8, 1852, Fillmore Collection.
[12]Washington *Republic*, December 3, 1851; *National Intelligencer*, December 3, 1851; *Congressional Globe*, 32 cong., 1 sess., 6-7; *National Intelligencer*, May 8, 1852.

This displeased Fillmore. It placed on him the final responsibility for foiling Seward's plans. He tried to disentangle himself by finding another candidate. "Is there any Whig who can win New York State?" he asked his friends. From his own careful calculations through six Presidential campaigns he realized that of New York, Pennsylvania, and Ohio, a successful Whig candidate had to carry two of them. The answers droned back. None of the queried could think beyond Fillmore, Scott, or Webster. "I deem Mr. Webster entirely out of the question in this state. . . . Nor do I see how Gen'l Scott can carry it," Babcock opined with unvarnished candor. "I deem your chances not desperate," he told Fillmore, only because it was "improbable" that the Democrats could forget their differences. But ". . . it cannot be shown that you can carry the state" against any Democratic candidate who received the cordial support of his entire party.[13]

James Kidd, dilettante in politics, replied to Fillmore's question: "doubtful." Only the divisions among the Democrats supposed that the Whigs had an equal chance.[14] Thomas Foote asserted the same thing. "Your chances for nomination," he told Fillmore, "are better than anyone else if the South will be nearly unanimous. But the defection of the South would be fatal. . . . But can you or any Whig be elected? I have great doubts. It depends on the Democrats. They are split, but as Calhoun said a 'cohesive bond' holds them together. . . . I fear the worst after careful study."[15]

When it was all added up, Fillmore knew that among the Whigs, only he had a chance of winning the election, and that chance rested only on the weakness of the Democrats. Soon even that possibility melted away as the breach within the Democratic party closed. By the time their convention ended in late May, Democrats presented a united front behind the dark horse, Franklin K. Pierce.

[13]Babcock to Fillmore, March 8, 1852, Fillmore Collection.
[14]Kidd to Fillmore, February 27, 1852, *ibid.*
[15]Foote to Fillmore, April 19, 1852, *ibid.*

Fillmore's five months of waiting for the leader to appear who would carry the torch of Whig victory were in vain, and the President was caught in a grave dilemma. If he stayed in the race and won the nomination, he would probably lose the election.[16] If he withdrew from the race before the nomination, instantly the convention would become the fulcrum for the Sewardites to boost the "Nationals," North and South, out of the party, and Seward would be given a prefabricated vehicle for the Presidential race in 1856. Fillmore had a choice between evils — loss of dignity or sectional discord. Thoroughly convinced of the rightness of Compromise and the danger of sectionalizing parties, Fillmore swallowed his pride and set about to foil the enemies of peace. Out of the debacle something could be saved. At least the engine of Sewardism could be dismantled and made useless.[17]

*   *   *   *   *

Baltimore, where the Whigs assembled for their last tilt, sweated in the humid atmosphere of June temperatures that ranged into the nineties. At the beginning of the week as the overheated delegates gathered and sought converts to their favorites, the town's temperature rose a few degrees. The heat seemed to case-harden their iron determination. Liquor flowed in the hotel rooms, but the jovial mood of a holiday was lacking. Here and there a delegate made himself conspicuous by lurching through the canopy of sullenness that covered the meeting. Most behaved with funereal sobriety as if they appreciated that they were attending their party's wake.

A few days before the convention opened, Seward arrived to direct the forces of Scott. Weed had conveniently hied himself off to Europe and had not scheduled his return until the convention would be over. To others he had left the responsibility of making something of the debacle he had helped to create. Delegates, friendly and hostile, funneled through Seward's Wash-

16 Hall to Fillmore, November 3, 1852, *ibid.*
17 *Whig Review*, May, 1852; Bokee to Fillmore, March 12, 1852; Fillmore Collection.

ington house and then his Baltimore hotel room, until he complained that he was being "badgered out of patience and almost out of his senses."[18] He even began to lose heart in the affair. He lacked the courage either to forbid surrender or enter into it frankly and thought to escape by going "to Auburn and be out of the affair."[19]

The omens were not propitious for Webster.[20] The Secretary of State stayed in Washington — a discreet distance from the convention. Correspondents of Boston newspapers announced fitfully that Webster's stock was rising, but with Fillmore's name still in the ring, Webster's chances were nil. His delegates flitted about, seeking support, making promises, bolstering their self-confidence with high resolve.[21] One observer said they were acting "like a parcel of school boys, waiting for the sky to fall, that they might catch larks. Such another collection of very respectable, out of place gentlemen, was never seen."[22]

Fillmore's friends arrived in Baltimore uninstructed by the President. Yet all, intuitively, knew what to do. They were very still, making no noise, as if their determination to see either Fillmore nominated or the party rendered useless to the enemies of sectional peace gave them strength and imperturbability. Some suspected that George Babcock, who had spent a few days with the President before the convention, was carrying special instructions. They could only guess that Babcock had been authorized to withdraw Fillmore's name at a propitious moment.[23] When he hinted at nothing, attention turned to N. K. Hall. But Hall was missing — held up in Princeton by cholera and diarrhea.[24] Haven, of the Buffalo triumvirate, could frankly deny that he had any knowledge of such a letter, and he painstakingly avoided asking Babcock if the rumor were true.[25]

[18]Seward, *Seward,* 2:185.
[19]*Ibid.,* 2:184.
[20]Hunter to Fillmore, May 30, 1852, Fillmore Collection.
[21]Haven to Fillmore, June 18, 1852, *ibid.*
[22]Granger to Fillmore, June 30, 1852, *ibid.*
[23]Babcock to Fillmore, June 3, 1852, *ibid.*
[24]Hall to Fillmore, June 17, 1852, *ibid.*
[25]Haven to Fillmore, June 18, 1852, *ibid.*

Vote-counting statisticians quickly drew conclusions. Except for New York City and Iowa, Fillmore's backing came from the South. Scott held the Middle West and the North; and Webster controlled New England except for Maine. It was clear that Scott and Fillmore would poll the largest votes on the first ballots, and some "outsiders," who wanted Fillmore, moaned that they had failed to secure a few more northern delegates. Soon it became clear that the uncertainty about Fillmore's candidacy, plus Fillmore's failure to use federal patronage, had lost him many northern delegates. Only a few extra would have given him the nomination.[26]

On Wednesday, June 16, the convention opened. During that morning and previous evening, an immense throng of delegates and visitors poured into the city. An hour and a half before the convention began, spectators filed into the hall — a full 3,000 of them. Tanbark had been spread on the streets outside the hall to reduce noises. Inside, the speaker's platform had been covered with carpeting, and over the platform in large transparency was a banner: "Liberty and Union Now and Forever, One and Inseparable." In front of the officers' stand was another: "The Union of the Whigs for the Sake of the Union." Delegates had spent the previous evening caucusing, and all were prepared to take up the first day's work of selecting permanent officers and appointing a platform committee. The southern delegates held a caucus in the morning and unanimously adopted a platform that embraced the Compromise as final. When the gavel descended at noon all was in readiness.

In a few minutes two committees of one delegate from each state were appointed; one to select permanent officers, the other to pass on credentials. The convention adjourned to evening, and by that action rid itself of any semblance of peace.[27]

For the next two days Baltimore rang with the skirmishes

---

[26]Foote to Fillmore, March 18, 1852; Thompson to Fillmore, March 29, 30, 1852; Campbell to Fillmore, April 24, 1852; Wetmore to Fillmore, May 13, 1852; P. Fuller to Fillmore, May 14, 1852; Gibbs to Fillmore, June 30, 1852; Newton to Fillmore, June 20, 1852, *ibid.*
[27]New York *Express*, June 17, 1852.

of the main political battle. Impatient to test its strength, each faction fought over every action — instructions to the committees, acceptance of their reports, appointment to the platform committee, and orders of procedure. At every turn motions of adjournment *sine die,* amendments to amendments, substitutes for resolutions, and motions to unseat delegates obstructed the progress of the conclave. Whenever the struggle subsided in the main hall, it continued in the back rooms. Then, it would adjourn to the streets. At regular intervals, manifestoes from caucusing Southerners challenged, dared, and implored the convention to write a "finality" platform. Finally, after two days, the convention framed a platform that unequivocally endorsed the Compromise measures. The Fillmorites had won the first line of battle.[28]

Fillmore now cared to go no further. He thought the moment propitious to withdraw. He asked that his delegates be transferred, if possible, to Webster.[29] The party had vindicated his administration. If Sewardites now got the Presidential nomination, it would put them in an extremely embarrassing spot. For the remainder of the campaign, their antislavery mutterings would be gagged. In all likelihood they would lose the election, and since Democrats had also pledged finality, Democrats could be trusted to prevent further agitation. On Sewardites would devolve the blame for Whig failure, and small politicians would retreat from the Seward camp. A victory for the old guard was there, though it had been achieved undramatically. But to his request to withdraw, Fillmore's friends again said no. They were politicians looking for victory.

Balloting began late Friday evening. One-hundred and forty-seven votes were necessary for a choice. When the first roll call ended, Fillmore led with 133 votes, closely trailed by Scott with 131, and Webster held the balance of 29. All except one of the South's 115 votes had gone to Fillmore. He also got one from Vermont, one from Rhode Island, one from Con-

[28]*Ibid.,* 18, 1852.   [29]Barney to Fillmore, June 19, 1852, Fillmore Collection.

necticut, seven from New York City, one from Pennsylvania, one from Ohio, four from Iowa, one from Wisconsin, and one from California. Again the roll was called. The results were the same. A third roll call brought no break. Four. Five. Six. Still only a slight shift of one or two votes was recorded. Together Fillmore and Webster had a clear majority over Scott if the followers of one could be transferred to the other. But there was a firm determination to hold the line.[30]

After the first ballot Babcock grew uneasy. He felt in his pocket and reread the letter he had from Fillmore. " . . . Present to the presiding officer of the convention . . . whenever you may deem it proper, the enclosed letter, withdrawing my name from . . . consideration . . . . " it read. "In determining the proper time . . . you will consider only the cause in which we are engaged. . . . I ask nothing for myself. . . . You will be careful to guard against any premature act or disclosure which might embarrass my friends . . . while . . . you will not suffer my name to be dragged into a contest for a nomination which I have never sought, [and] do not now seek. . . . "[31] As the balloting continued, Babcock made a survey and discovered that no substantial part of his friends would consent to unconditional abandonment of Fillmore. As Babcock "was unable to see that the Whig party would be harmed," he "allowed Fillmore's name to remain before the convention in the belief that such devotion . . . called for the sacrifices on Fillmore's part of all personal consideration."[32]

After the sixth ballot, the convention adjourned. During Friday evening, delegation leaders exhausted themselves in caucusing. To Choate, wizened crackpot at the head of Webster's group, John Barney proposed that he assume the responsibility of transferring Fillmore's votes to Webster. But nothing came of the proposal.[33]

[30] New York *Express,* June 20, 1852.
[31] Fillmore to Babcock, June 12, *Fillmore Papers,* 2:329-330.
[32] Babcock quoted in *Buffalo Express,* July 2, 1852.
[33] Barney to Fillmore, June 20, 1852, Fillmore Collection.

The next morning the balloting began again. The heat was intense, the hall was jammed, and the galleries swarmed with ladies. Each roll call passed. Seven. Eight. Nine. Ten . . . . Fifteen . . . . Twenty. Noon came, and still there was no break in the lines. Twenty-five . . . . Thirty. Thirty-one. It was already 2:00 p.m., and the delegates had been balloting for three and one-half hours. The convention decided to adjourn for two hours.[34]

When the assembly reconvened at four o'clock, a delegate from Florida moved that if no candidate had a majority on the fiftieth ballot, then the election would go to the highest. It was voted down. The roll call began. Thirty-two. Thirty-three. Thirty-four. Someone proposed adjournment to Monday, but this was defeated. Thirty-five. A motion to adjourn to evening was lost in great confusion. On another motion to adjourn *sine die,* the chairman refused to put the question. Cries for order rent the air. When quiet was restored, a Louisiana delegate read a dispatch from New York threatening that if Scott were not nominated, New York would not support the nominee. Near rioting broke out. More motions to adjourn *sine die* filled the air. Finally the billowing noise subsided.[35]

The roll call droned on. Thirty-six. Thirty-seven. Thirty-eight. Thirty-nine. Forty. Forty-one. A member arose to announce that if there was no selection by the fiftieth ballot, he would move a *sine die* adjournment and call for a new convention. Forty-two. Forty-three. Forty-four. Forty-five. Forty-six. Exhausted, the convention adjourned until Monday.[36]

The persistent token vote for Webster from the East had greatly surprised many southern delegates, and the stubbornness of Webster's small minority left Southerners with a mixed feeling of desperation and disgust. Private canvasses revealed the impossibility of transferring Fillmore's entire delegation to Webster. Some southern delegates were being reached by Scott workers who promised he would accept the platform. In morti-

[34]New York *Express,* June 22, 1852.   [35]*Ibid.*   [36]*Ibid.*

fication, John Barney abandoned Baltimore. He sought out Webster himself in Washington to impress him with his need for withdrawing. Barney found Webster overwhelmed with humiliation. After forty-two years of public service, he had received only 28 votes out of 296. Barney implored prompt action, but Webster begged off. " 'All I ask is a decent vote that I may retire without disgrace.' "

" 'It is a fearful responsibility you are about to assume of defeating the *true* Whig party by delaying action.' " replied Barney and left.[37]

Back in Baltimore, Fillmore's managers employed other tactics. After the adjournment on Saturday night, by special invitation friends of Fillmore met with Webster's agents. They proposed two distinct and fair courses of action. If Webster's managers could bring their favorite "to the Maryland line" after one or two more ballots, "with forty votes," Fillmore's managers would swing 107 votes they knew they could transfer to Webster. "If, however, Webster's friends couldn't get forty Northern votes, then his managers would transfer his votes to Fillmore. Choate, Childs, Grinnell, Webb and others readily accepted the first proposition." But they did not say that they would accept the second.[38]

During Sunday groups traveled down to Washington to see both Fillmore and Webster. During the entire week, these two candidates had not seen each other. When the delegations left Washington Sunday night and early Monday, those who stayed at the White House returned with definite instructions to attempt the transfer, irrespective of consequences. But Webster's retinue was still determined to stick by their favorite.

Early Monday morning, Webster had a change of heart. "I have sent a communication to Baltimore this morning to have an end put to the pending controversy," he wrote to Fillmore. "I think it most probable you will be nominated before

[37]Barney to Fillmore, June 25, 1852, Fillmore Collection.
[38]Cobb to Fillmore, June 28, 1852, *ibid.*

1 o'clock. . . . "[39] Dryly, but without bitterness, Fillmore replied: "I had intimated to my friends who left last evening . . . a strong desire to have my name withdrawn. . . . Your communication . . . I apprehend . . . may be too late to effect anything."[40]

It was too late. On Monday morning as the balloting began, Webster's friends had failed to gain the votes that he needed according to the Saturday agreement. Nor did his friends pay any attention to Webster's communication. Possibly they had not received it. The forty-seventh ballot took up where the convention left off. On the forty-eighth, two Fillmore votes from Missouri switched to Scott. It was now time for Webster's votes to be transferred to Fillmore. But as the Webster line began to break, instead of going to Fillmore, the votes went to Scott. Dismayed, perturbed, and angered by the combination of Webster's stubbornness and the faithlessness[41] of the Webster delegates who deserted to Scott, the solid phalanx of Fillmore votes who could have been transferred to Webster — seeing that such a transfer would be useless — refused to accord the Secretary of State any sign of respect.[42] On the fifty-third ballot, Scott passed the halfway mark and was nominated.[43]

*   *   *   *   *

The news of Scott's victory at Baltimore left Fillmore unperturbed. Nor did he hold any grudge against Webster. When the Secretary heard the result, his only comment was, "How will this look in history?" He was disconsolate and could not drive from his mind the idea that his life was a failure because he had missed the Presidency.[44] Yet after a few days, the effect of his action struck him with full force. He mourned in bitter-

[39]Webster to Fillmore, [June 21, 1852], Fillmore Collection, rec'd at White House at 9:30 a.m.

[40]Fillmore to Webster, June 21, 1852, not sent, but shown to Webster when he followed his letter to the White House, *ibid.*

[41]For evidence of faithlessness, see P. Greeley to Seward, May 27, 1852, Seward Papers.

[42]Cobb to Fillmore, June 28, 1852, Fillmore Collection.

[43]New York *Express*, June 23, 1852.

[44]Fuess, *Webster*, 2:289.

ness his fatal and irretrievable error, and the idea that Fillmore might have thought he deliberately gave preference to Scott goaded him to frenzy. Webster's thinking was cloudy, for Fillmore, devoid of malice, felt personally responsible for relieving Webster's distraught emotions. Webster thought of retiring from the cabinet. With kindness and sympathy that brought tears to the Old Lion's eyes, Fillmore insisted that he stay with the official family.[45]

If the President could take the nomination of Scott without a cry of anguish, and a magnanimity that was more than human, the party could not. In Buffalo, a ratification meeting turned into a respectable, cold affair. The crowds and enthusiasm which were promised a few weeks before in the event of Scott's selection were not visible. "Perhaps," surmised one observer, "the celebration which is to be on the 27th at Niagara Falls may develop the enthusiasm which is said to be latent. . . . Our friends here . . . do not profess any confidence of success."[46] Two days after the convention, a southern conference, held in Washington, resolved not to vote for Scott under any circumstances. Momentarily it even thought of condemning Graham, of Fillmore's cabinet, for accepting the Vice-Presidential nomination, but confined itself to an expression of grief that Graham's name was connected with Scott.[47] In New York City, Boston, and other quarters, the nomination was regarded as a needless sacrifice of the party. In Boston the news of Scott's nomination "fell like a funeral pall upon the spirit of the Whigs generally except a few of free-soil proclivities." Throughout New England the nomination hung over the political sky like a black, ponderous cloud. "National" Whigs generally, and in the Southern states universally, considered the party broken.[48] "The election will show," shouted one New York paper, "That the [Whig] party will no longer have a show of existence."[49]

[45]Barney to Fillmore, June 25, 1852, Fillmore Collection.
[46]Babcock to Fillmore, July 15, 1852, *ibid.*
[47]Barney to Fillmore, June 25, 1852, *ibid.*
[48]Wholey to Fillmore, June 24, 1852, *ibid.*
[49]Quoted in James K. McGuire, ed., *The Democratic Party of the State of New York* . . . . 1:288-289.

For himself, Fillmore hardly needed the protestations of irate editors and discouraged politicians to know that nothing could now save the party. For six months a dual purpose had dictated his conduct: prevent the creation of conditions that would make dissolution inevitable, and if that failed, leave the party dismantled and useless to the Seward wing. Fillmore appreciated that there was no recovery from this last blow, for he knew the character of the support behind himself and Webster and the distrust with which that support looked upon Seward's backing of Scott. That distrust now inevitably consigned the Whig party to death. Scott carried only four states (Massachusetts, Vermont, Kentucky, and Tennessee) while Franklin K. Pierce won the other twenty-seven with 54 per cent of the total vote. The fires of the campaign had consumed the life of the Whig party, but possibly from its ashes, like the ancient Phoenix, new life would spring.

Chapter 20

Retirement to Grief

OULD you be kind enough to look around
Buffalo for a suitable house for me?" asked Fillmore of his
friend, Nathan K. Hall. Such were the thoughts that occupied
the President's mind while the contenders for his post sparred
in open campaigning. Few could recall within the past decade
as serene and unruffled a Washington and as calm a White
House occupant as they beheld in the fall and winter of 1852.

Fillmore's last days in office passed without crisis or jarring
incident. When the lame-duck Congress convened, even the
slavery question appeared forgotten. The word "slavery" seldom
passed the lips of Representatives and Senators. A calm persisted, as if Congress and President were enjoying the beauty of
an Indian Summer after hard labor through a heated summer.

Fillmore's only official worry was his cabinet. It had remained loyally with him through the thick of the fight, but with
retirement imminent, it began to dissolve. He lost Nathan K.
Hall's services by appointing him to a district judgeship in western New York.[1] In these last days the President tried to reward
and secure the future of other intimate friends, but he ran into
the spiteful Senator Hamilton Fish, who gleefully went out of

[1]Hunt to Fillmore, August 10, 1852, Fillmore Collection.

his way to prevent confirmations.[2] Graham resigned from the cabinet because he was a candidate for Vice-President. After approaching several men as replacements,[3] Fillmore finally found in John P. Kennedy of Baltimore, a man sufficiently detached from politics to be more interested in the post of Secretary of Navy than in mending political fences. For many years, Kennedy's home in Baltimore had been a distinguished social and literary center. He himself had penned several popular political satires. Because he personally knew most of the country's literati, he brought a new note into the Fillmore household. Senator Pearce, Fillmore's staunch friend, and a man more interested in the Congressional Library than politics, had brought Fillmore and Kennedy together. Then, through Kennedy, Fillmore struck up a friendship with the lion of American letters, Washington Irving. Though the President was a bit gauche concerning things literary, Irving's genial idling, romanticizing, and fastidious pursuit of ease must have touched a kindred note. The two were destined to while away many an hour together.[4]

Webster's death in October further disrupted the cabinet. Again the Chief Executive bore the whole weight of the State Department. So frequently had Webster absented himself from Washington that Fillmore had made most of the major decisions. Nonetheless, the President kept the character of the State Department in harmony with the past when he appointed one of Webster's closest friends, Edward Everett. The addition of Samuel Hubbard in the Postmaster-General's post and of Kennedy and Everett, however, did not disturb the serenity or tranquility of the Indian Summer before retirement.[5]

*   *   *   *   *

2Fish to Weed, September 1, 1852, Weed Papers: "Hall . . . is confirmed . . . in spite of Seward & myself . . . . [But Jerome] Fuller was laid out . . . . Within five minutes the business was concluded and Jerome was a 'dead cock in the pit' — Now he & I are 'quits' until he may choose to try his hand again."

3Fillmore asked J. R. Ingersoll of Philadelphia, John Bell of Tennessee and E. P. Chambers of South Carolina.

4E. M. Gwathmey, *John P. Kennedy*, 192-193; *Fillmore Papers*, 2:iv.

5[Chamberlain], Fillmore, 192; Everett to Fillmore, October 16, 1852; Hubbard to Fillmore, October 18, 1852, Fillmore Collection.

Though Fillmore calmly bore his expected return to private life, he was painfully conscious that he was a retiring President. He had always insisted on correct social behavior. In a crisis this penchant gave him strength, and at all times it surrounded him with an aura of dignity. Now, however, it caused him mental discomfiture. He pictured himself as responsible for carrying Presidential dignity into private life. Little wonder then that he hesitated to return to his modest frame house in Buffalo. It was a proper residence for a New York assemblyman, which he had been when he bought it, but not for an ex-President. A neighbor's house added to his doubts. It was between his house and Hall's, and he considered it disreputable. He thought to escape the neighborhood and considered buying the Shearer house for twenty thousand dollars or the Efner house on Prospect Hill for eighteen thousand dollars. The house that appealed to him most, however, was the one owned by Bela D. Coe on the corner of Niagara and York, formerly the public square of the town of Black Rock. A merchant with rococo tastes, Coe valued his house at thirty thousand dollars, but would not sell at any price. Already the prosperity of the fifties was driving up the costs of homes. "I don't believe you can buy any house here, which will suit you, at any reasonable price." wrote Hall. "The expense of living here and the prices of houses & furniture have much increased since we left. I am not sure you could live cheaper and more satisfactorily if you . . . got a good situation four or five miles out of town and built a house to suit yourself." Possibly Hall's judgment was colored because he really wanted Fillmore to "stay in the neighborhood." Buy the house and lot next door and "get the nuisance out of the way" was his advice. Yet Fillmore could not make up his mind. March 4 came, and he was still looking for the "suitable" house.[6]

Another problem of propriety troubled Fillmore. All other Presidents before him had either returned to gentlemen's

<hr />

[6]Coe to Fillmore, August 6, 1852; [Mss. illegible] to Fillmore, August 20, 1852; Hall to Fillmore, October 3, 13, 1852; Marshall to Fillmore, November 2, 1852; Wm. Ketchum to Fillmore, January 18, 1853, Fillmore Collection.

estates or to the protection of family patrimonies. He had neither. Thus he had to find suitable employment. What he was going to do after March 4, he did not know. He was worth about 75 thousand dollars, enough to give him a comfortable living if wisely invested, but not enough to support him and his family in a manner befitting his position. He had to earn money but he insisted it be made in a genteel manner. Again he consulted Hall. Hall thought he should return to law, but confine his practice to the highest courts. "You can make as much as you will need by the practice of your profession in the highest courts & in important causes only, and . . . there is no impropriety in your practicing your profession to that extent. . . . All whose opinions are worth having would feel that under the circumstances . . . such a course was honorable and praiseworthy." Fillmore was uncertain and briefly considered a bank presidency that was to be a sinecure. After turning it over in his own mind for a month, however, he finally agreed with Hall that he should rely on his profession.[7]

* * * * *

During his Presidency Fillmore occasionally stopped to review the slavery question. He knew that the Compromise of 1850 had been a solution only of the immediate problems of slavery in the territories. At any moment agitation might flare out again with less fortunate results. Because of this fear, he had tried to deny agitators opportunities for action. Yet for all his suppression, he, himself, dreamed of a final answer to the entire slavery problem. Through the years he permitted this dream to recur and finally in the closing months of office he had set about to find the answer.

As was his habit before preparing the annual message, he requested each cabinet member to prepare the paragraphs relating to his department as he might wish to have it appear in the message. Matters relating to general policy he prepared him-

[7]Hall to Fillmore, October 15, November 3, 17, December 13, 1852, *ibid.*

self. In November the cabinet met to discuss the Administration's last state-of-the-union message, and to this meeting Fillmore brought his views on how to solve the problems slavery had created and would continue to create. He took the cabinet somewhat by surprise. But after his essay had been read, it won the cabinet's hearty approval.

With typically rational approach, Fillmore disclaimed any need to resolve the question of slavery into a question of conscience or the problem of right or wrong. "Let us," he invited the nation, "look at it as it is — see what has been its operation upon our social organization heretofore, and thence infer what are to be its effects hereafter." Here was an approach that would deny the casuist and economic determinist alike. Instead it played on the haunting theme of race warfare.

With the logic of a dismal scientist, Fillmore analyzed the growth of America's white and Negro population and concluded that if both races continued their rate of growth, in less than a century the human race would press upon the land for sustenance. "What will happen?" "It will give birth to a conflict of races with all the lamentable consequences which must characterize such a strife. . . . The terrific scenes of St. Domingo are sooner or later to be re-enacted here, unless something be done to avert it." Worse, continued Fillmore, even before a struggle for existence brought on the race war, it might be started by the agitation of abolitionists. He held out no hope that antislavery agitation would ever cease. "It is manifest from all our past history that . . . [agitation] is to be renewed with increasing violence as often as any new State shall apply for admission. . . . " This unsolicited interference would only aggravate the evil, he warned.

Nor would eliminating slavery alone avoid the evil of a civil war between the races, predicted Fillmore. Just as the South would never accept forcible emancipation, it would not voluntarily free its slaves, if such freedmen remained in the South. Nor would northern people welcome the freedmen. Free or slave, therefore, the presence of the Negro would eventually lead to civil war.

Fillmore was convinced that the only remedy was the long proposed recolonization of Negroes in Africa or the West Indies. To achieve this the colonist-to-be must first be freed. Congress, he thought, could not abolish slavery, but it could encourage the southern states to emancipate their slaves by offering to remove the free blacks to other areas. Then, "If emigration [of freed slaves] could take place at the rate of 100,000 per annum, that would not only prevent the increase of the slave population, but constantly diminish it, and at last . . . wipe it out entirely." The resulting problem of labor supply could be solved by immigration from Asia. The work of colonization, Fillmore recognized, would take years, not to say centuries, but its gradual accomplishment was the only "sure mode of relieving the country from the increasing evil without violence and bloodshed."[8]

Here was the thought of a rationalist as he approached a socio-economic problem. It was touched with both Ricardian gloom and philanthropic hope and cast on the stage of constitutionalism. After reading the lengthy essay, no rationalist could charge that Fillmore failed to see the pitfalls of abolition. But no humane man could be patient enough to await the fulfillment of this program. Here was a logical, forceful, practical mind applying itself to a problem. This mechanistic, administrative solution was the President's offering to his cabinet.

The cabinet took the paper and subjected it to careful reading and deliberate consideration. Along with the rest of the pieces of what was to be Fillmore's last message to Congress, it was printed on a private press in the Executive Mansion. Broad margins were left to these slips for amendments and annotations. Each member was furnished with a copy to take home for careful revision. At a subsequent meeting, it was again considered

---

[8]For the full text see "Mr. Fillmore's Views Relating to Slavery: The Suppressed Portion of the Third Annual Message to Congress, December 6, 1852," *Fillmore Papers*, 1:311-324.

and a few changes made. Finally the paper as agreed to was given to Everett for close inspection of every sentence and word.[9]

Yet in the time that elapsed from presentation to adoption, a feeling had grown among like-minded cabinet members that it would be imprudent to expose Fillmore's views to open discussion. Though the nation had ostensibly accepted the Compromise, little evidence existed that the public either understood or endorsed the political philosophy behind the Compromise. To reopen the question of slavery's ultimate destiny might reexcite the public mind. This certainly was not the President's objective, but his message, the cabinet "feared would prove an additional element of discord." Some thought "it would not be right to leave such a legacy of strife to our successors."[10]

By such arguments, the cabinet prevailed upon Fillmore to drop his views on slavery from the text of the annual message.[11] He consigned his essay to semi-oblivion. Hints of its reached the newspapers, but several years elapsed before it found its way to the voters in the form of a pamphlet.[12]

The peace of his last months remained unbroken.

※   ※   ※   ※   ※

If Fillmore weighed his birthright to action against the national good and found liberty lacking in the balance, others, more anxious to guarantee the future than protect the present, read the scales with a different idea.

Friends at every hand protested his retirement. With near-unanimity they looked toward 1856. "You are yet young and . . . the end of your career is not yet, I trust," confided Babcock. "For 1856 you will have, in the expected course of things, fewer years, more experience and greater capital than a majority of our Presidents. Duty to your country and yourself requires that you should do nothing to render it impracticable for you then to be a candidate. . . . Time will bring with it an entire change

[9]Stuart to Wilson, May 8, 1878, Fillmore Mss.
[10]*Ibid.*   [11]*Ibid.*   [12]Editor's note, *Fillmore Papers*, 1:311.

of views in certain sections and your course will be indicated not only by future but by co-temporaneous history."[13] After the convention, Babcock returned to the theme. "Your [action] . . . at the Convention, has increased, if possible, the attachment of your friends to your fortunes, and they one and all, do not consider your political course at an end with the Presidential term."[14] A Rochester editor asserted: "I say that President Fillmore never stood so high in the estimation of all good men as since the election."[15] Mechanics impatient for 1856 thought to put up a separate ticket in 1852 with Fillmore at its head.[16] "Fillmore is my choice," stated a Philadelphia Quaker. "I would support him with my whole Soul. . . . "[17] From Rhode Island still another friend had "a strong presentiment that in 1856, we shall require all your energies & services. The people will not forget the wisdom of your administration."[18] Speaking for the mercantile Whigs of New York City, George Davis asserted that "our Whigs say Fillmore's chances in the next election, i.e., after this, is almost sure. . . . "[19] H. M. Solomon urged the President to run on a separate ticket.[20]

Edward Everett, before his appointment to the cabinet, repented the bullheadedness of the Webster convention delegates and prophesied the future. "If you," he addressed Fillmore, "incline to continue in public life, I feel confident you will have no difficulty in rallying about yourself the great constitutional party of the state of New York — which certainly must at all times afford a most commanding position in the Union."[21] If the South's solid convention support had not demonstrated the trust that southern Whigs had in him, notes and meetings put into words and deeds their unbounded confidence.[22] One

13Babcock to Fillmore, March 8, 1852, Fillmore Collection.
14Babcock to Fillmore, July 15, 1852, *ibid.*
15Lee to Fillmore, November 15, 1852, *ibid.*
16Nevins to Fillmore, June 30, 1852, *ibid.*
17Newton to Fillmore, November 2, 1852, *ibid.*
18Gibbs to Fillmore, October 17, 1852, *ibid.*
19Davis to Fillmore, July 4, 1852, *ibid.*
20Solomon to Fillmore, June 18, 1852, *ibid.*
21Everett to Fillmore, June 23, 1852, *ibid.*
22See *Fillmore Papers*, 2:330-332 for example.

Georgia meeting extended a hearty invitation to him to visit the South.[23]

Along with other events, these affirmations of faith began to undermine Fillmore's complacent acceptance of retirement. He had striven for national peace, and in doing so, he had felt he was sacrificing himself. After the first months in the White House, he had concluded that the nation would never endorse his policy which called for self-restraint. Like a bitter draught, those policies would have to be forced upon the nation. In calling for repression of humane feelings, he had felt righteous, but his vanity longed for approval of that course. The belief that he could never win such acclaim had made him chary of a referendum.[24] Now, however, signs at every hand indicated a wholehearted endorsement. Not only his friends' plaudits, but his unsolicited convention strength, both parties' platform approval of his Compromise, and the victory of a candidate untouched by any heresy, made him less shy of public opinion. Just at election time he revealed to Hall that he had in mind a "political future."[25]

Whether because of Georgia's invitation, or the desire to seek out the nature of his "political future," or solely to enjoy the thrills of a traveler, Fillmore mapped out an extended tour through the South. As soon as his term was over, he, his wife, and several cabinet members planned to go south through a round of political dinners and sightseeing.

*   *   *   *   *

The fourth of March was ushered in with a raw, northeasterly wind bearing wet masses of snow that melted almost as quickly as it struck the ground. Fillmore rose to the roll of drums in honor of his successor. As he prepared for Franklin Pierce's inauguration, he cast his last glance around the disorderly room of the Executive Mansion: the library, which had once

[23]Resolutions of the Constitutional Union Party of Georgia at Milledgeville, Georgia, A. H. Chappell to Fillmore, July 26, 1852, Fillmore Collection.
[24]Ullman to Fillmore, September 29, 1850, *ibid.*
[25]Hall to Fillmore, November 3, 1852, *ibid.*

been the famous oval salon that Mrs. Fillmore had made over into a sitting room, and that Fillmore had persuaded Congress to fill with books, the other chambers of their seven-room family apartment on the second floor, and especially the bathroom, which boasted one of Washington's few bathtubs, albeit galvanized iron. On this wet March morning, dampness, caused by an inadequate heating system, made the Executive Mansion even less inviting. Fillmore had had all the family belongings moved to Buffalo, except the few possessions he and his wife needed for their southern trip. Those were at the Willard Hotel, where the Fillmores expected to stay a few days.

About noon, Fillmore climbed into an open barouche and, escorted by numerous military organizations and fraternal orders, called for the President-elect. They made their way down Pennsylvania Avenue. The throngs cheered, and the incoming magistrate rose in the carriage and lifted his hat again and again on the way to the capitol. They entered the capitol grounds, and the whole corps of officials gathered at the east front of the Senate chamber. Thousands of spectators milled about, undiscouraged by the snow and raw wind.[26]

Fillmore heard and saw Pierce take the oath of office and then saw him begin to peel off his coat before declaiming his inaugural. The March wind rose to a gust; Fillmore shuddered and drew his own coat about him more tightly. What he heard the speaker proclaim, however, warmed his soul. " . . . With the Union my best and dearest earthly hopes are entwined," announced Pierce. "I hold that the laws of 1850, commonly called the 'Compromise measures,' are strictly constitutional and to be unhesitatingly carried into effect. . . . " Occasionally the retiring President glanced behind him toward the group of dignitaries that shared the portico to see how his wife was faring. She was braving it all with a weak smile, but her face was drawn, her lips pinched and blue, her feet moving in the slush and water to keep warm.

[26]*National Intelligencer*, March 5, 1853.

"We have been carried in safety through a perilous crisis. Wise counsels, like those which gave us the Constitution prevailed to uphold it," continued Pierce. The words warmed Fillmore, for the new Administration was pronouncing benediction over his entire course. The picture of Mrs. Fillmore trying to repress the shudders of a chill, however, quickly dispelled the warmth. For many months she had been ailing, and this exposure was not kind to her.[27]

After the ovation, Fillmore escorted Pierce back to the White House and left the new President there with the muddy-footed throng pressing to greet their chief magistrate. Fillmore had no heart for this scene and was anxious to leave. He hurried back to his suite at the Willard to find his wife dispirited, but apparently well.[28]

The next morning told a different tale. Mrs. Fillmore had obviously contracted a severe cold. By night she was running a high temperature. Quickly it became serious and developed into pneumonia. All plans to leave Washington were abandoned, and hour after hour, day after day, Fillmore kept vigil at his wife's bedside. Occasionally there were signs of improvement, but slowly she slipped away, bearing "all of her sufferings with uncomplaining fortitude." Son and daughter kept close at hand, mirroring the father's grief in their uncontrolled features. At last, after three weeks of illness, on the thirtieth of March, she expired.[29]

The next day the grief-saddened family left with her remains for Buffalo and buried her the following day. All plans for trips and politics, all worries about employment and dignity, all thoughts of stately homes dissolved before the spectacle of death.

Retirement was to be a horrible loneliness.

[27]Irving to Winthrop, April 4, 1853, *Fillmore Papers*, 2:iv.
[28]*National Intelligencer*, March 9, 1853.
[29]Fillmore described it as "inflammation of the lungs arising from a severe cold . . . which soon terminated in dropsy of the lungs." To Charles Fillmore, April 3, 1853, Fillmore Mss.

Chapter 21

National Whigs Find a Host

MERICANS paused only momentarily in their activities to share the grief of their ex-President. A momentous development that would eventually reshape the nation's future absorbed their attention, and they had little time for Fillmore's tragic misfortune. Since the late forties, purposeful men had been restirring the potent brew of anti-Catholicism and it was now sending forth a heady vapor. Now, by 1853, the violent and emotional results of that intoxicant had the nation's attention.

Many Protestant-Americans hated Catholicism and dreamed of the day when it would cease to exist. In the past few years events in Europe had given them hope that its end was near. A revolution had caused the Pope to flee Rome in 1849; a liberal minority had appeared in the French Catholic church; and other evidences of dissatisfaction among Catholics in Europe encouraged the Protestant evangels to hope that they might yet "drive the devil," as they regarded Catholicism, from his traditional lands.[1]

Many other Americans were equally certain that Catholi-

[1] Theodore Dwight, *The Roman Republic of 1849; with Accounts of the Inquisition and the Siege of Rome*, 32-34; New York *Express*, April 10, 1847.

cism would never die and that its leaders were contriving to extend their authority throughout Christendom. A papal bull setting up an English hierarchy offered positive proof to many Protestants, already alarmed by Romeward drift of the Oxford group, that Pius IX was extending the spiritual arm of the church over that realm.[2] In the United States the steady flow of Catholic immigrants and the unprecedented growth of their church convinced others of the existence of a papal campaign of aggression. Americans had no doubt that the English could protect themselves, but outside aid would be helpful. They began to call for an antipapal mission which would help end Romanism in Europe. In turn this would purify the stream of immigration to America. Europe's conversion thus became a starting point in the revival of the American nativistic movement.[3]

The American and Foreign Christian Union, an alliance of three anti-Catholic societies, led the crusade. It employed all known methods to convert "corrupted" Christians: lectures, missions, propaganda, resolutions, and mass meetings. The Methodist general conference and the Old School Presbyterian General Assembly joined them with funds, journals, and preachments.[4]

The Union tried to arouse an American protest against the imprisonment of two Tuscan peasants, Francisco and Rosa Madiai. According to the word reaching America, these two peasants had been sentenced to long imprisonment for reading a Protestant Bible. By fomenting giant mass meetings, the American and Foreign Christian Union inspired resolutions expressing sympathy with the sufferers and collected funds to ease their suffering in their Tuscan dungeon. Swept away by the enthusiasm of the movement, even the New York legislature passed resolutions of sympathy. Pressure on the national govern-

---

[2]*Ibid.*, November 30, 1850; January 31, 1851; Philadelphia *Daily Sun,* November 25, 29, December 18, 1850.
[3]Nicholas Murray, *The Decline of Popery and its Causes. An Address Delivered at the Broadway Tabernacle January 15, 1851,* 20-21.
[4]American Protestant Society, *Sixth Annual Report,* 41, 44-45.

ment to intervene grew so great that at one time Fillmore considered a note requesting the release of the Madiai.[5]

If the missionary spirit were not enough to give anti-Catholicism a place in the hearts of American Protestants, the fear of Catholic striving for an American dominion did. Protestants were accustomed to seeing their Roman Catholic neighbors timid and retiring. But in recent years Archbishop John Hughes of New York, spiritual leader of the Catholic church in America, fostered an arrogant attitude among his followers that was new and alarming.

In November, 1850, at St. Patrick's Cathedral, Hughes spoke to his congregation on "The Decline of Protestantism and its Causes."[6] Protestant nations were crumbling before the force of Rome, Hughes said, and would continue to do so until all the world was under the spiritual rule of the holy mother church. "There is no secret about this. The object we hope to accomplish in time, is to convert all Pagan nations, and all Protestant nations, even England with her proud Parliament and imperial sovereign. There is no secrecy in all this. It is the commission of God to his church, and not a human project. . . . Protestantism pretends to have discovered a great secret. Protestantism startles our eastern borders occasionally on the intention of the Pope with regard to the Valley of the Mississippi, and dreams that it has made a wonderful discovery. Not at all. Everybody should know it. Everybody should know that we have for our mission to convert the world — including the inhabitants of the United States, — the people of the cities, and the people of the country, the officers of the navy and the marines, commanders of the army, the Legislatures, the Senate, the Cabinet, the President, and all!"

Protestants, who had for years disregarded the warning of Samuel F. B. Morse and his followers as the ravings of alarmists,

[5]New York *Express*, January 8, 22, 30, February 12, 14, March 4, 1853; A. C. Flick, ed., *History of the State of New York*, 5:322; American and Foreign Christian Union, *Fifth Annual Report*, 19-20.
[6]John Hughes, *The Decline of Protestantism and its Causes.*

now heard a Catholic church leader freely admit that Roman ambitions did exist. The Pope did intend to move to the Mississippi Valley; he did seek to "subjugate" free America!

Protestant reaction was violent,[7] and the alarm grew fiercer when the same archbishop reopened two ancient sources of rancor between the sects — Bible reading in the schools and trusteeship of Catholic church property. Protestants heaped vituperation upon the Roman Catholic church and abused Hughes as a "cloven-hoofed enemy of freedom."[8] Ossa was piled upon Pelion when the American and Foreign Christian Union imported a fiery denunciator of popery — an Italian ex-priest, Alessandro Gavazzi. His experience as a liberal in the Italian revolution had convinced him that popery and liberty were incompatible. Determined to devote his life to "stripping the Roman harlot of her garb," he had renounced the priesthood and fled to England.[9] He now brought to America a message of hate, and in his wake anti-Catholic street preachers became mob leaders, who, with success, urged their audiences to burn, kill, and destroy.[10]

In these attacks on Catholicism organized nativists had none of the previous decade's tolerance. There was only hysterical fear and fanatical hate. Admissions and blunders of the Catholic church brought the lower classes firmly within the nativistic fold. As a result the anti-Catholic forces were numerically stronger than at any time before in the country's history.

Americans, meanwhile, were also acquiring a fear of, and distaste for, the recent immigrants. In the last few years the rate of immigration had quadrupled. During the six years after

[7]New York *Express,* November 30, December 6, 8, 1850; *Buffalo Express,* December 1, 3; Philadelphia *Daily Sun,* December 4, 5, 8, 1850; Washington *Republic,* December 9, 1850.
[8]New York *Express,* September, 1852 through October, 1853, *passim.,* quotation from October 3, 1853.
[9]*Life of Father Gavazzi,* 1-64; American and Foreign Christian Union, *Third Annual Report.*
[10]Ray A. Billington, *The Protestant Crusade,* 305-312.

the Mexican War nearly two million Europeans had found their way across the ocean. One-half of New York City's and nearly one-third of Philadelphia's residents were foreign born. It was easy to magnify the effects of this alien invasion. The average American had only to look about him to find tangible evidences of the propagandists' worst fears. He could see the foreigners' touch transform quiet city streets into unsightly slums. He could see corrupt political machines thriving upon foreign votes and deadlocked political parties struggling for the support of inexperienced and unconditioned aliens. He could see the traditional policy of American isolation threatened by immigrant blocs seeking to embroil the United States in the affairs of their homelands. He could see intemperance, illiteracy, pauperism, and crime, all increase with the foreigners' coming. He could see alien labor, content with a low standard of living, taking over more and more of the work which American hands had formerly performed. And were he a conscientious Protestant, he could link the growth of Catholicism with this rise of immigration. Under the circumstances the desire to protect established values — identified as "American" — became vocal and active. No special talents were needed to divert this rising emotion of "Americanism" into politics, especially when the keynote of the day was the salvation of the Union.[11]

At first no prominent politicians embraced the new nativism; no political party appeared to capitalize on the excitement. By early 1852, however, in New York City's municipal elections, a mysterious influence made itself felt. A new political force was afoot in the land. All over the city men had been forming nativist clubs. One was the Order of the Star Spangled Banner, founded by Charles B. Allen in 1849. Like others, it was a secret fraternal order hostile to Catholics and foreigners. Measured in terms of recruitment, its success was no more notable than sixty other city clubs. But in the spring of 1852

---

[11]*Facts for the People. Truth is Mighty and Will Prevail* [n.p., n.d.]. Lewis C. Levin, *The Union Safe. The Contest between Fillmore and Buchanan;* Anna Ella Carroll, *The Great American Battle,* 27-40.

James W. Baker, a wholesale dry goods merchant with a genius
for organization, forced Allen to reliquish control.[12]

By carefully screening applicants for admission, Baker
turned the Order into a political balance wheel. "Are you," he
asked an applicant for the first degree in the Order, "willing to
use your influence and vote for native-born American citizens
for all officers of honor, trust or profit in the gift of the people,
the exclusion of all foreigners and Roman Catholics in particular, and without regard to party predilections?"[13] If an applicant
could subscribe to these objectives, he next swore to support
candidates for office dictated by the Order. Then having pledged
allegiance to the Order he was entrusted with the secrets which
lent so much charm — grips, passwords, signs, phrases of recognition, signals of distress, and other well-tested accessories of
secret orders. Such delightful secrets made many a member glad
that he had decided to cast his lot with the Order.

A holder of the second degree was eligible both for office
within the Order and to represent it as a nominee in regular
political contests. As he was admitted to the exalted level, he
was instructed "that, if it may be done legally, you will, when
elected or appointed to any official station conferring on you
the power to do so, remove all foreigners, aliens, or Roman
Catholics from office or place, and that you will in no case
appoint such to any office or place in your gift."[14]

Under Baker's direction the Order expanded rapidly. Within four months the New York City membership reached a
thousand. Soon its leaders established a state "wigwam" to encourage expansion and branching. Members migrated to other
states, and by the close of 1853 they had formed branches in
New Jersey, Maryland, Connecticut, Massachusetts, and Ohio.
Yet no real organizational bond held them all together.[15]

[12]Thomas R. Whitney, *A Defense of American Policy*, 280-284; New York *Herald*,
December 20, 1854; New York *Tribune*, June 4, 1855.
[13]N. W. Cluskey, *Political Text Book and Encyclopoedia*, 55.
[14]*Ibid.*, 57.
[15]Scisco, *Political Nativism in N. Y.*, 68-77.

Soon after the November election of 1853 the organization received another stimulus that mushroomed it to mammoth size. In December a knot of Whigs who had been closely associated with Fillmore's administration — Daniel Dewey Barnard, David Ullman, and James and Erastus Brooks — while keeping their hands concealed, created a schism in the Order's New York state wigwam. By the time that breach closed in May of 1854, the friends of this knot of "National" Whigs were guiding the Order. Though still dedicated to its proscription policy, the Order now had other political objectives that eclipsed its original antiforeign, anti-Catholic purpose.[16]

Quickly the new directors brought together the locals of thirteen states at a national convention. In June, 1854, in New York City, the conclave adopted a formal national constitution modelled upon established political machines. It created councils corresponding to county, state, and national central committees. Now the Order, acting as a political party, could advance national, state, and local tickets. Almost immediately it adopted the name "American Party." The public, however, referred to it as the "Know-Nothing Party" because in its former secret political activities its members had protected themselves and their group by claiming, when questioned: "I know nothing about it."

Wherever the American, or Know-Nothing, ticket appeared, its members were oath-bound to vote the party's choice. But this did not preclude the tactic, earlier employed, of secretly endorsing other candidates. In its own jurisdiction, each county and state organization was autonomous. It could sample the nominees of other parties or present its own slate. The way was open, therefore, to attract voters from other parties on other grounds besides the ostensible nativistic program.

By early 1854, then, politicians had taken full charge of the nativistic machine and converted it into an engine of politics

[16]*Ibid.*, 96-98; New York *Times*, March 8, 16, May 22, October 23, 1854; New York *Herald*, October 30, 1854; New York *Tribune*, March 1854; Barnard Letter Book, October 24-29, 1855, Barnard Papers.

capable of tremendous acceleration and power. Its fuel was nativism, and natives were at work manufacturing it. When, however, that fuel could not be used, the machine was so engineered that it could use other types, too. That changed the nature of its combustion.

*   *   *   *   *

After the election of 1852 a nationwide but illusory unity existed within the Whig party. Fillmore's and Seward's activity before and during the national convention had actually divided the party. Its major groups had either deserted or were ready to leave. Only the professional politicians hesitated to abandon their crumbling abode, principally because they had no place to go.

Those Whigs whose destiny lay with patronizing nationalism had to await the creation of a new party. Some hoped one could be made out of Whig wreckage. Others hoped it would be done by merging "National" elements from among Whigs and Democrats into a coalition if not an organic union. Still others hoped that a national party would appear and that they could use it as a host.

Those Whigs whose future lay with antislavery pinned their hopes, too, on one of the three alternatives — resurrection, coalition, or reincarnation. But in 1853 resurrection was impossible, coalition remained unattractive to the victorious Democrats, and no hosts existed for the reincarnate spirits to invest.

This the broken fragments of the Whig party lay undisturbed. Both Fillmorites and Sewardites pretended that the party was still a living organism, but they knew full well that the life it displayed was either the nerve twitch of the dying or the maggots of death. Only a major disturbance could arouse them to life and activity; otherwise they might well have lain there indefinitely, and a new "era of good feeling" might have ensued with the Democrats enjoying solitary rule.

On January 4, 1854, this seismic tremor began. Stephen A. Douglas started on its way through Congress a bill to open the Nebraska territory to white men. Whether he was motivated by personal ambition, Missouri politics, Presidential aspirations, railroad rivalries, or just playing the part of an innocent or naive fool, no one knew.

His measure carved two territories, Kansas and Nebraska, out of the unorganized part of the old Louisiana Purchase. It provided that the question of slavery in these territories should be left to the inhabitants themselves. This provision clashed directly with the Missouri Compromise of 1820, which had proscribed slavery forever in the area north of 36°30′. To prevent all doubt as to which should prevail, Senator Dixon added a clause declaring the 1820 compromise was superseded by that of 1850 and no longer in effect.

In the early morning hours of March 4, after an all-night debate, the Kansas-Nebraska bill passed the Senate. Instantly the nation was plunged into a morass from which no one had either the wit or the wisdom to extricate it. The healing virtues that Fillmore's administration spread after the 1850 adjustment were swept away. All of his work of three years was undone, and controversy flared anew. As the bill had made its way through Congress, its fateful consequences had become apparent. The Douglas who had been so helpful in the Compromise of 1850 had now opened a Pandora's Box of evils.

Antislavery men, long denied the nation's ear, now loosed their oratorical forces. Nothing in the past had convinced the North that an "aggressive slaveocracy" ruled the South; but the repeal of the Missouri Compromise accomplished this in a flash, and the new converts brought an angry spirit to a movement that had gone flat during Fillmore's administration. Chase, once before an apostate Democrat, again broke with his party and issued an appeal to others to join him in rebellion.

A tempest raged. Mobs hanged Douglas in effigy, and a new series of forcible rescues of runaway slaves plagued Pierce's administration. Emigrant aid societies were organized to save Kansas for "freedom." Whigs, more in the West than in the East, began to meet with rebellious Democrats. In Congressional elections that year, "anti-Nebraska" coalition tickets began to appear. In Wisconsin and in Michigan, and soon in Ohio and Iowa, the opponents of Douglas' bill began to organize a coalition party. On July 4, the famous Michigan "Republican" convention was held. The selection of the new name had at first no marked effect, for the politicians were not desirous of calling themselves Republicans before a corresponding organization existed in their own states; so they continued to be known as the "anti-Nebraska" men.

The Kansas-Nebraska bill's concussion jolted the pieces of the inert Whig party. Its fissures and cracks widened, the last cohesion between the factions dissolved, and Whig politicians picked up the loose pieces and carried them to new grounds to add to structures already in existence. Looked at through the years, the process seemed simple enough. Generally the old "Silver Greys" or "Nationals," including the mercantile, ocean-commerce Whigs of the North, and the southern Whigs who had made up the core of Fillmore's support in his own party, gravitated to the Know-Nothing party. These "Silver Greys" had had nothing to do with starting the nativist movement. They had little in common with the nativist program. They simply found the existing organization, in the summer of 1854, a convenient host from which to draw nourishment.

The Sewardites, or as they were also called, "Woolly-heads," or "Conscience" Whigs, generally gravitated to the anti-Nebraska coalitions, and then into the Republican party. But this new sectional party had not been organized by the time the Congressional elections of 1854 were held. It was a year behind the American party. Because "Silver Greys" were largely Easterners, as well as for the reason that the perturbation aroused by the emigrants were most felt in Atlantic port cities, it was in the East that the American party grew most substantially. And because the strength of the "Woolly-heads" was concentrated in the West, the nascent Republican party has its firmest materialization there.

But a closer analysis of the disposal of Whig factions revealed that the simple pattern of "Silver Greys" migrating to nativism and "Woolly-heads" to Republicanism was a complex movement in which the actors felt rather than saw their way clearly toward one party or the other. Elements of the broken Whig party, which had lain inert for eighteen months, spent another eighteen finding lodgement in the two new parties. During that time confusion reigned. There were both deviations from the pattern and circuitous routes of migration. Massachusetts and Indiana "Woolly-heads" went in large numbers into the Know-Nothing party before becoming Republicans. Connecticut "National" Whigs coalesced with anti-Nebraska Democrats; shrewd, calculating strategists like Thurlow Weed planted affiliates in both new parties. But during the year and one-half of confusion, when few had prophetic wisdom, politicians fought a Presidential campaign.

*   *   *   *   *

Mrs. Fillmore's death snapped the irresolute mood that troubled Fillmore while he was contemplating retirement. The unpretentious house on Franklin street proved to be a satisfactory residence for a grief-stricken man; the sudden cessation of social activities made his income adequate to a circumscribed life. And circumscribed it was as he daily slumped into his library chair to read, or sat at his expansive desk to write. It was an unhurried life, calmed by an imperturbability gained from experience and grief. There appeared to be no need to resume the practice of law. He would "have been glad to continue" his profession, but on this point he was to remain sensitive for the rest of his life. "My colleagues at the bar would say, and quite naturally, 'Here, you have been to the pinnacle and ought to be content.' "[17] Censure could still mar his serenity. Though he never faced the possibility, the thought of what might have happened had

[17]*Fillmore Papers*, 2:140.

he not had a modest independent income could make him indignant. He considered it a national disgrace that Presidents
"should be cast adrift" at the end of their terms.[18]

After inactivity had performed its therapy, retirement had
no attraction for him. He kept looking around for something
to do. His own concept of an ex-President's duties had closed
most of the avenues of employment, and he felt that he could
function only in the field of public affairs without degrading
the office he had just left. The Presidential years, moreover, had
intensified his sense of social responsibility.

In his eyes the preservation of the Union had become the
highest goal of statesmanship. Since disunity could come only
after the political parties had been sectionalized, his role for the
future was almost predetermined. The "new relation" that some
northern Whigs had been seeking ever since the mid-forties as
the touchstone to their success he did not reject. But he was
resolved, even before nativism boiled to the surface or the
Kansas-Nebraska bill had destroyed intersectional peace, that
his own wing of the Whig party must be preserved. Its cross-
sectional character had acted as a powerful deterrent to disunion,
and, were it preserved, it could certainly prevent the impending
disaster. His Presidency had been devoted in large part to this
goal, and now through the months of his retirement his thoughts
kept returning to the need for its retention.

Finally thought gave way to action. In the early spring of
1854, just as his former associates were taking hold of the Know-
Nothing movement and the Kansas-Nebraska bill's full impact
was about to be felt, Fillmore brought his retirement to an end.
For the Union's sake party politics must be kept revolving on a
North-South axis, and he could contribute to that important
task. He would tour the country, and while ostensibly sight-
seeing, he would visit the centers of "National" Whig sentiment
to try to keep the lines of communication open among them.
While traveling, moreover, he could test the nation's temper.

[18]*Ibid.*, 2:139-40

Judgment about future action would then rest on sounder ground.

As an excuse for travel Fillmore revived his plans for the southern trip which he and his wife had made a year earlier. Now with Nathan Hall he set out for Columbus, Ohio. There John P. Kennedy, his Secretary of the Navy after Graham's resignation, joined them. Washington Irving was to have been the fourth person on the tour, but seeing what its true purpose would be, he excused himself: "I have no inclination to travel with political notorieties, to be smothered by the clouds of party dust whirled up by their chariot wheels, and beset by the speech-makers and little great men and bores of every community. . . . Heaven preserve me from any tour of the kind. . . . I would as lief go campaigning with Hudibras or Don Quixote."[19]

The tour was everything that Washington Irving wished to avoid. At Columbus the ex-President's party visited the senate and house and "attracted much attention, both from their high position among the leading men of the nation and the fact that they ranked among the best-looking men of the country."[20] On the way to Cincinnati, they stopped off at Lebanon, Ohio, to see another colleague — Tom Corwin. At Cincinnati a large public reception awaited them. General demonstrations of friendship and admiration marked the tour through Kentucky. They visited Louisville and Lexington, and at Frankfort Fillmore visited the grave of Henry Clay.[21] They went on to Vicksburg, New Orleans, Mobile, abandoned a visit to Cuba, and passed on to Savannah. By early April, they were in Charleston, South Carolina, where the visit coincided with the session of the Southern Commercial Convention. They reached Montgomery, Alabama, on April 15 and made their way north by way of Augusta, Atlanta, Nashville, and Baltimore, where Kennedy left the party. Fillmore and Hall reached New York on May 18 and Buffalo the evening of May 20th.[22]

19*Ibid.*, 2:v.   20*Ohio State Journal*, March 12, 1854.
21See New York City speech, *Fillmore Papers*, 1:439.   22*Ibid.*, 1:xxviii.

Nine days later he accepted an invitation to travel over the new rail lines that formed a part of the Rock Island system out of Chicago to St. Louis. Hall was still with him. This time Fillmore's son, Millard Powers, George R. Babcock, his 1852 convention manager and heir to his political machine in Buffalo and Erie county, and a number of other Buffalonians as well as several merchants and politicians from New York, Philadelphia, and other principal cities, made up the body of excursionists.[23]

The program included a trip by steamboat up the Mississippi, with stops at Galena, Dubuque, and St. Paul. At St. Paul a grand ball was one feature of entertainment. Fillmore addressed the dancers and revealed the tie which drew him and others to this extended celebration. He likened the Mississippi River to a tree: the Ohio, the Missouri, the Arkansas and other tributaries to its branches, with New Orleans at its foot naturally receiving the fruit as it dropped from the tree. But now through the ingenuity and perseverance of commercial and railroad men, "in building the Chicago and Rock Island Railroad," they "have set up a great ladder with its base at New York, to bear the fruit safely and securely to another commercial point."[24]

The southern and western tours kept Fillmore on the road for nearly five months. Everywhere public dinners, private meetings, caucuses, or state occasions greeted him. Everywhere an audience was ready to hear him. Yet most of the time his remarks were casual — thanks for the "unexpected" display of friendship, admiration of the region or city he was visiting, or expansive compliments to the members of the fair sex. When he broached politics, publicly, it was always to justify his own administration and repeat, time after time, that he was dedicated, pledged, and oath-bound to live by the Constitution and the law of the land, not by divine revelation. What he said in private, Fillmore never recorded.[25]

---

[23]Buffalo *Commercial Advertiser*, June 1, 1854.
[24]*Fillmore Papers*, 1:441.   [25]*Ibid.*, 1:441-3.

Those five months coincided almost exactly with the introduction, debate, and passage of the Kansas-Nebraska bill. When Ohio's Chase issued his appeal to Independent Democrats, Fillmore was just preparing to go to Columbus. While Republicans met at Ripon, he was passing through Wisconsin. When an irate mob was hanging Douglas in effigy, the ex-President was in Chicago. Never once through it all did Fillmore make a public utterance about the measure, though he felt pangs of distress that it had destroyed his own hard-won sectional peace.

Likewise Fillmore left for his trip south just as the nativists' cauldron bubbled over. His own city produced one of the eruptive bubbles. For over two years the Buffalo congregation of St. Louis' Church had carried on a heated struggle against their own bishop over the control of parish property. The nativist press made this the occasion for a redolent exposure of the whole question of Catholic church property. Unfortunately for Catholics in America, the Pope in 1853 dispatched Gaetano Cardinal Bedini, as a fully accredited papal nuncio, to settle the conflict in Buffalo and a similar one in Philadelphia. Few moves were more impolitic. The nativist press heralded Cardinal Bedini's coming as a carefully planned mission to begin the subjugation of America. Bedini visited Buffalo, settled the conflict in favor of the bishop, and blundered again when he began a tour of the United States to visit prominent Catholics and bestow upon them the papal blessing.[26]

Aroused by messages of hate preached against Bedini, a nativist Boston crowd burned his effigy;[27] only several hundred aroused Irishmen saved him from assassination in Wheeling;[28] and at Baltimore, several bullets were fired into his room.[29] His worst reception was in Cincinnati. On the night Bedini arrived there, some 20,000 citizens marched through the streets carrying an effigy of the priest, a gallows, and banners which proclaimed:

[26]Felicity O'Driscoll, "Political Nativism in Buffalo, "*Records of the American Catholic Historical Society*, September, 1937.
[27]New York *Express*, December 12, 1853.
[28]Philadelphia *Daily Sun*, December 23, 1853.
[29]*Ibid.*, January 3, 1854.

"Down with Bedini," "No Priests, No Kings, No Popery," "The Gallows Bird Bedini," "Down with the Raven Butcher."[30] Special police broke up the procession and injured about twenty persons. The clash fired nativists with renewed vigor, and Cincinnati seethed with hatred.[31]

A little over a month after the riots, Fillmore appeared in Cincinnati. He had just left Buffalo, where Bedini had been pilloried more genteelly but just as passionately. On his return from the South, Fillmore stopped in New York City. There for months a rabble-rousing street preacher, Daniel Parsons, had been inciting audiences to minor riots every Sunday. One had occurred two days before Fillmore arrived to be feted by the Clay Festival Association.[32] When he returned to Buffalo, he found the St. Louis' trustees again at odds with their bishop. They had ignored his interdict and had suffered excommunication.[33] The native press was loud in denouncing popery and its minions.[34]

Yet, as in the case of the Kansas-Nebraska ruckus, not one word of censure or approval for either side escaped Fillmore's lips. He delivered over a score of addresses, but never once referred to the rising nativist movement, which his political friends — Ullman, Brooks, and Barnard — were transforming into a powerful political party.

Behind his silence, however, he was still striving for the original goal of his trips: a political device to preserve sectional peace and the Union. The need was urgent. While he was traveling, the dreaded coalescing of northern Democratic and Whig factions had begun, and it was proceeding swiftly. A political party entirely confined to the North was appearing. For the Union nothing portended greater evil. Keenly aware of the techniques of politicians, he discounted the humanitarian

[30]*Ohio State Journal,* January 12, 1854.
[31]*Ibid.,* January 14, 20, 22, 28, 1854.
[32]New York *Express,* May 17, 1854.
[33]O'Driscoll, "Political Nativism in Buffalo," 432-437.
[34]Billington, *Protestant Crusade,* 298-299.

pleas of the anti-Nebraska orators who were creating this northern party. He assumed, and not without reason, that most of them were trafficking in the movement to further their own political or economic interests. He could remember in 1846 when he had done the same. Nor did he fear that the Kansas-Nebraska bill had been devised by slaveholders conspiring to expand slavery. A great number of the larger slaveowners were still in his camp as "National" Whigs and were as hopeful as he that the nation's unity might be maintained.

The question was: could the "National" Whigs stop the sectionalizing process? Once before, in the similar crisis of 1850, they had joined hands with their counterparts in the Democratic party and had succeeded. This might be done again except that men who controlled the Democratic machinery were committed to the Kansas-Nebraska act, and since they already controlled the national government, they sought no "National" Whig help. Further, his travels had shown that his friends, though potent, were probably incapable of succeeding with their plea for moderation.

At this juncture it took no great imagination to see the possibilities of the Know-Nothing party as a vehicle for the "National" Whigs: its program would appeal to Northerners and thus deny the anti-Nebraska leaders a clear field against the Democrats; it was readily acceptable in a Protestant South; and it would divert attention from the slavery issue.

Thus as Fillmore returned to his home in Buffalo he was eyeing the nativist movement, not with horror, or with approval, but as a possible means to success. Until the Know-Nothing party proved its ability to carry elections, however, he would remain silent on that subject, too.

*　　*　　*　　*　　*

The fall elections of 1854 put the Know-Nothings to the test. During the campaigning Fillmore remained an observer,

trying to gauge the worth of this new political vehicle. Throughout the summer its membership rose phenomenally. Everyone
seemed anxious to support and popularize the organization.
Vendors sold "Know-Nothing Candy," "Know-Nothing Tea,"
and "Know-Nothing Toothpicks." A clipper ship launched in
New York in 1854 was christened the *Know-Nothing*. Omni-
buses and stage coaches bore this popular name. A poem was
widely sold under the title, and jackets of nativistic books carried
the large letters, "K-N." The Know-Nothings had become
the rage of the day, and nativists confidently looked forward to
the fall elections.[35]

The results justified their expectations. They carried Massachusetts and Delaware, and, through a combination with Whigs,
Pennsylvania. In other northern and border states, they revealed surprising strength and sent about seventeen Congressmen to Washington. In Massachusetts they won their greatest
victory: except for two representatives, Know-Nothings carried
every state office. Though they had delayed entering the South
until summer, they had organized that region so rapidly that
their party nearly carried Virginia, Georgia, Alabama, Mississippi, and Louisiana and elected minor officials in Texas. In
Louisiana and the southern states east of the Mississippi, the total
Know-Nothing vote was only 16,000 less than its opponents.
Only in the West were they weak.[36]

The ex-President paid special attention to the election in
his own state. His friends controlled New York's Know-
Nothing machinery. They were confident of their party's future
and felt no need for opposing Weed's domination of what
was left of the Whig party. Controlled by the Albany editor,

[35]*Ibid.*, 388-389; Scisco, *Political Nativism in N. Y.*, 108-118.
[36]*Ibid.*, 118-124; John P. Senning, "Know-Nothing Movement in Illinois, 1854-56,"
Illinois Historical Society Journal, 8:16-17; Lawrence F. Schmeckebier, *History of
the Know-Nothing Party in Maryland*, Johns Hopkins University, *Studies in History
and Political Science*, 132-94; A. C. Cole, "Nativism in the Lower Mississippi
Valley," Mississippi Valley Historical Association, *Proceedings*, 6:271 (1912-13);
Joseph Schafer, "Know-Nothingism in Wisconsin," *Wisconsin Magazine of History*,
8:14-20.

this Whig rump nominated Myron Clark for governor.[37] The Know-Nothings nominated Daniel Ullman. And Democrats, cleft along ancient lines, could not agree and offered Greene C. Bronson, a "Hard" Democrat, and Horatio Seymour, a "Soft" Democrat. The surprise of the campaign was the Know-Nothing vote. Prognosticators had estimated Ullman's greatest strength at 65,000.[38] Yet November's count gave him 122,000 while Clark had 156,000 and Seymour was close behind.[39]

New York Know-Nothings had done as well as most of their partymen in other states, and encouraged by these results, Fillmore determined to use them. Already Solomon G. Haven, of Fillmore's old firm, was in Washington where he had joined the Know-Nothings and was keeping Fillmore posted. It was always clear to the ex-President that the Know-Nothings could be guided into becoming the party of the Union. He had foreseen that its actions would "depend very much upon the character of those who constituted its members." He now urged his friends to join the movement. " . . . Give it proper direction," he enjoined them, and make it a "truly national party."[40]

[37]Buffalo *Commercial Advertiser,* August 24, 1854; New York *Tribune,* August 19, 31, September 24, 1854, May 22, 1855; New York *Times,* August 26, October 10, 23, November 2, 1854; New York *Herald,* September 27, October 21, 31, 1854.
[38]New York *Tribune,* September 21, New York *Herald,* September 27, 1854.
[39]*Civil List of N. Y.* (1887), 166.
[40]Fillmore to Stuart, January 15, 1855, photo-copy in Fillmore Mss.

Chapter 22

Candidate of the Know-Nothings

XACTLY when Fillmore decided to make himself available to the Americans as their Presidential candidate no one ever knew. Though the thought may have been with him as early as spring, probably his firm decision came shortly after the fall election of 1854.

The sudden death of his daughter at the end of July may have affected his decision. Mary Abigail had gone to East Aurora to visit her grandfather for a few days. Old Nat was past eighty and enjoyed these visits from his charming and warm-hearted granddaughter. She had been in perfect health and on the very evening before her death had been full of gay humor. Yet within a few hours of the first signs of illness she had died, only twenty-two years old.

Fillmore's grief was boundless. He loved his daughter almost to the point of dotage. In Washington she had been a great comfort and had frequently acted as his hostess when her mother was indisposed. Since her mother's death, she had taken on the task of running the household. Possibly to still his grief he turned to politics. It was something that could consume all his attention.

That he could now think of himself as being the leader of a party dedicated to nativism was in keeping with his whole course of action. He understood and approved of the movement's changing purpose. And being unemployed and touched slightly with the spirit of martyrdom he was capable of offering himself as a useful instrument to fulfill that program. The Kansas-Nebraska eruption had shown him the need for action that would prevent the sectionalization of political activity; his trips had revealed to him that the goal had wide-spread support; and the election results had made plain that nativism might become the rallying point for a strong and truly national party.

If the idea of using the disguise of an antiforeign movement to promote national unity troubled his conscience, he left no record of apprehension. In his lifetime, moreover, this type of politicking had been common. A generation earlier he, himself, had been initiated into politics in a protest party whose leaders had converted its original purpose into a vote-getting platform for John Quincy Adams.

Whatever soul-searching the ex-President may have done was complete by the end of the year. On New Year's Day, 1855, he made his announcement to the party managers. Isaac Newton — an old friend who was high in the leadership of Philadelphia's Native American party — had asked him for his views on nativism. If he accepted the open principles of Know-Nothingism, he knew that Newton would display his letter — eventually publish it — and he would then have an open road to the party's nomination. No other potential candidate had his qualifications.

The answer, that New Year's Day, came clear and unmistakedly. " . . . I have for a long time looked with dread and apprehension at the corrupting influence which the contest for the foreign vote is exciting upon our election." Both parties, he continued, have bargained for the foreigners' ballots, and this led to practices that were "corrupting the ballot box — that great palladium of our liberty — into an unmeaning mockery," and sacrificing the rights of the native born.[1]

[1]Fillmore to Newton, January 1, 1855, *Fillmore Papers*, 2:347-349.

"Where," he cried, recognizing that while writing privately to a friend, he was addressing the nation, "is the true-hearted American whose cheek does not tingle with shame . . . to see our highest and most courted foreign missions filled by men of foreign birth to the exclusion of the native-born?" Then, abandoning the manner of platform declaration, he soberly declared that Europe's oppressed should be given asylum and equal protection of the law. But constitutional liberty could be preserved only by restricting office holding to those who had been "reared in a free country." Washington, he added, had perceived the danger of foreign influences and had warned against them.

Here was Fillmore's endorsement of nativism. Only one more action was necessary to qualify him for the party's nomination: membership in the Order of the Star Spangled Banner. Early in 1855, in the library of his home, he received the Order's secret rites. Thereupon, Charles McComber, presiding over the initiation, turned to the new member and said:

"Mr. Fillmore, you have taken this step which will certainly land you in the presidential chair at Washington."

"Charles," replied Fillmore, "I trust so."[2]

*   *   *   *   *

The decision made, Fillmore again took up his travels. Instead of stumping the country as a sightseer, however, he boarded the steamer *Atlantic* and headed for Europe. If a nosy public inquired why, he had prepared an answer. "It is better to wear out than rust out, and as my political life has unfortunately deprived me of my profession, perhaps I can do nothing better than to diversify my pursuits by travelling. . . ."[3]

In reality, sagacious advice and political wisdom took him on his twelve-month tour to England, Ireland, France, Italy, Egypt, Turkey, and Prussia. To be off the scene while others

[2]T. G. White to Andrew Langdon, December 8, 1898, Fillmore Mss.
[3]Fillmore to Maxwell, March 10, 1855, *Fillmore Papers*, 2:351-354.

laid the groundwork for his nomination was shrewder than staying at home where the seething, swirling forces of two political storms — abolitionism and nativism — raged.[4]

Fillmore's trip was not a solitary ramble through Europe. For part of the journey he had the companionship of two editor friends, Jewett and Foote; for another part of the trip, W. W. Corcoran. Though traveling as a private citizen — and his correspondence abounded with the usual traveler's clichés — Fillmore was not an ordinary tourist. State receptions crowded his days and even interfered with his amusements. Yet before he left Europe, crowned heads, ambassadors, and ministers were duly impressed with his graceful bearing and composure. His poise dealt a blow to the impression in European courtly circles that all Americans were gauche and gross. He was in London during the height of the season, as one observer described it, and "no American . . . ever received more attention in the mother country than Mr. Fillmore. His noble presence, his mild and courtly manners, about which there was the beauty of repose . . . combined to charm the English people."

On one occasion, the ex-President sat down to one of George Peabody's famous Fourth of July dinners with some two hundred Americans and about fifty distinguished Englishmen. During the dinner, Fillmore proposed a toast: "The health of our generous host." With an intonation of voice, "that at once attracted the attention of his hearers," Fillmore proceeded to describe Mr. Peabody as a noble specimen of American enterprise, of whom his countrymen were justly proud. After delivering himself of these highly flattering remarks, he "sat down amidst the most enthusiastic cheering with the band playing 'Auld lang syne.'" Leslie, the eminent painter, turned to a guest: "What a noble-looking man! What an agreeable speaker! He reminds me of Sir Robert Peel. You must present me to your friend, and bring him to my house."[5]

[4]Friends advised him to leave this country where it would be less incumbent on him to be drawn into the "cauldron of politics." *ibid.*

[5]*Ibid.*, 1:444-445; *A Report of the Proceedings . . . on the 4th of July, 1855* . . . . , 4.

Martin Van Buren was in London at the same time, and
frequently the two ex-Presidents crossed trails. One day, both
appeared in the gallery of the House of Commons. It elicited
an extended remark from John Bright. " . . . On Tuesday night
a very remarkable circumstance occurred . . . two of the distinguished men being present listening to the debates . . . have
occupied the position of President of the United States . . . "
and he passed on to a eulogy of America.[6]

At the opening night of the opera season, Fillmore was the
guest of Peabody, who had taken two large boxes, the partition
having been removed for the occasion. A dozen other Americans were present, including several Boston beauties. Van Buren
had been invited, but declined because of his son's recent death.
The Queen, most of the royal family and nearly all the titled
people known in the highest society of London were there. Yet
"the lorgnettes were chiefly directed at Mr. Peabody's box to
see the American beauties and the ex-Presidents of the United
States."[7]

A visit to the London docks turned into a tour of the wine-
houses. For the first and only time in his life — for he was a
temperate man — Fillmore became "slightly fuddled by merely
moistening his lips with such a variety of liquids." Like all
tourists, he walked through Westminster Abbey; but at the
Bank of England, unlike other tourists, he had the guidance of
the bank's governor, who encouraged him to "heft" a million
pounds sterling. Fillmore left no account of his presentation at
the Court of St. James, though tradition developed in America
that Her Majesty Victoria pronounced him the handsomest
man she had ever seen.[8]

While in England, Fillmore declined to accept the degree
of D.C.L. offered by the chancellor of the University of Oxford.
"I had not the advantage of a classical education," Fillmore
excused himself, "and no man should, in my judgment,
accept a degree he cannot read." He was thinking of

[6]*Fillmore Papers*, 2:481.   [7]*Ibid.*   [8]*Ibid.*, 2:482.

Major Jack Downing's description of Jackson receiving a similar honor from Harvard University, on which occasion the old hero — according to the humorist — concluded his remarks by shouting in tones of thunder all the Latin he knew: *"E pluribus unum! Sine qua non! Multum in parvo! Quid pro quo! Ne plus ultra!"* Dread of the ridicule usually visited upon those receiving honorary degrees by the unruly students of Oxford influenced the ex-President's decision. "They would probably ask," Fillmore said, "Who's Fillmore? What's he done? Where did he come from? and then my name would, I fear, give them an excellent opportunity to make jokes at my expense."[9]

Leaving England in late fall, Fillmore journeyed to France and arrived in time to attend the International Exposition, after being duly presented to the Emperor Napoleon III. During his stay in Paris, he rescued Horace Greeley from jail. The irascible editor had fallen afoul of the law and was shut up in a French prison for debt. Greeley wrote an account of this episode, but failed to mention that it was his mortal enemy, Fillmore, who came to his relief. Fillmore visited him in prison and supplied the money that gained his release. The story filtered back to America, and the chuckles redounded to Fillmore's credit.[10]

In mid-November, he left Paris, leisurely tarrying "long enough to see the objects of interest" in numerous southern French and northern Italian cities. At the end of the year, he arrived in Rome. Before he had been there "long enough to have become . . . familiar with the topography of Rome, ancient and modern. . . . As in duty bound," he "was presented to his Holiness the Pope." It was an ordeal for Fillmore, as he weighed the advantages against the disadvantages for his publicity in the American press. The day he was presented, he heard that eti-

[9] *Ibid.*, 2:483; Charles Francis Adams, the only other American who ever refused a similar honor, did so solely because he was unwilling to be subjected to such treatment.

[10] The Hon. Andrew D. White wrote: "I was in Paris at the time, saw Mr. Greeley and remember the circumstances well; but I cannot state whether Mr. Fillmore supplied the funds for Mr. Greeley's release, or not. All that I heard was, as regards Mr. Fillmore, that he called on Mr. Greeley when the latter was in Clinchy prison." *ibid.*, 1:xxix, note.

quette required all "to kneel and kiss the hand of the Pope, if
not his foot." Fillmore stormed in consternation: " . . . . if this
was the case, I must decline the honor. . . . " Only the assurances
of another American persuaded him to go through with the
presentation. The Pope received him sitting and, to his relief,
"neither offering hand or foot for salutation."[11]

After Rome, Fillmore and his companions, Foote and
Jewett, went to Naples, Cairo, Jerusalem, Constantinople, and
returned to Trieste. Then he moved northward toward Berlin.
There Fillmore left a most agreeable impression. The king was
delighted with him and told the American minister, George
Ticknor, he would vote for Fillmore for President. Ticknor
replied that Buchanan would get the election, notwithstanding
his majesty's vote.

"Well," he answered, "never mind, I am glad we are of
the same party, and you may always count upon my vote, at
any rate."[12]

*   *   *   *   *

For a year Fillmore absented himself from America. While
he idled away his time talking to kings, tasting new cuisine, or
sunning himself under a blue Italian sky, his friends back home
busied themselves on his behalf. Within a month of his leaving,
they took the next-to-last step in making the Know-Nothing
party the handmaid of the old "Silver Greys."

Each step had been a tactic of penetration. Initially "Silver
Greys" penetrated the Order's councils. In 1854 the addition
of a third, or "Union Degree," which pledged members to support the Union made the whole organization their happy home.[13]

[11]Fillmore to Haven, January 22, 1856, *ibid.*, 2:354-357.
[12]G. T. Curtis, *Life of George Ticknor*, 2:33.
[13]One of the steps in the process of boring came in November, 1854. The National
Council at Cincinnati brought the ritual into final form, adding among other
things the third or "Union" degree, so-called because it pledged members upon
oath to support the Union and to oppose all who aimed to destroy or subvert it.
This degree was proposed and urged by Kenneth Rayner of North Carolina, a former
Whig, who aimed to arrest disunion sentiment in the South and abolitionism in the
North. Henry Wilson, *Rise and Fall of the Slave Power*, 2:420-22.

The Order's secrecy, however, had attracted more than Fillmorites. Temperance men, abolitionists, Democrats, and Free-Soilers had flocked to the banner. As voters, these elements were satisfactory, but their leaders were completely out of harmony with the "Silver Greys" and their southern confreres. Now with the Presidential election at hand, non-Fillmorites had to be robbed of influence.

In June of 1855, the purge came. At the national convention in Philadalphia, the antislavery wing was on hand to do mischief to the American cause and thereby promote the Republican party. On the floor of the assembly hall, the antislavery leader was Henry Wilson of Massachusetts. A confessed opponent of the American party, he was in it only to convert it to antislavery or destroy it. Thurlow Weed went to Philadelphia, too, to take part in the same scheme.

The showdown came on a resolution. The platform committee's majority thought it would be unwise for Congress "to legislate on the subject of slavery within the territories."[14] Here was a condemnation of the anti-Nebraska movement and a left-handed endorsement of the principle of the Kansas-Nebraska bill. Wilson's antislavery faction tried to reject the new clause and replace it with a declaration that Congress might vote slavery in or out of a territory. But a solid Fillmore phalanx held its ground. The Know-Nothing party was now a bed of thorns for antislavery men. They stormed out of the hall to warn their constituents that the American party was a disguised tool of the slaveocracy.[15]

The purge, if it had the harmful effect of alienating large segments of northern support, had the salutary effect of casting all doubt out of southern minds about the character of the

[14]The resolution was as follows: "Permitting any opinion upon the power of Congress to establish or prohibit slavery in the territories, it is the sense of this National Council that Congress ought not to legislate on the subject of slavery within the territories of the United States, and that any interference by Congress with slavery as it exists in the District of Columbia would be . . . a breach of National faith." Humphrey J. Desmond, *The Know-Nothing Party,* 81.

[15]New York *Tribune,* June 18, 1855.

Know-Nothing party. That it was a reincarnation of "Silver Grey"-"National" Whiggery could no longer be doubted. Southern Whigs who had timidly hesitated to join the natives now accepted Senator Bell's pronouncement that the American party was the successor of the defunct Whig organization.[16]

*   *   *   *   *

If the capture of the national council of the American party, the Union Degree, and the purge of the antislavery element in June, 1855, were three high points in converting the nativist movement to "Silver Grey" politics, the action of Thurlow Weed during the same time assured the success of "Conscience" Whiggery within the fold of the Republican party.

During these months only the persistence of the "Conscience" Whig organizations in New York and Massachusetts prevented the full fruition of the anti-Nebraska movement and the creation of a strong, sectional antislavery party. Of all northern leaders who stood athwart the path of this rising Republican machine, Weed was the most important. He had blessed anti-Nebraska sentiment with editorials, but not with his political force. He made the Kansas-Nebraska agitation await his personal interests, first obtaining Seward's re-election to the Senate through the rump of the Whig organization he controlled. "He knew the magic of the Whig wand and how to use it."[17]

Seeing the power of the Know-Nothing party, however, Weed ordered innumerable lieutenants to creep into the lodges and entrench themselves. Sharpness, rather than honesty, directed this move, but Weed had obtained his start in politics with the same kind of maneuver within the anti-Masonic movement. The implanted minions then put forward candidates for the assembly, and these "when necessary to dispel suspicion, signed written pledges to vote against Seward."[18] They were elected as Know-Nothings and faithfully carried out the farce.

---

[16]Nashville *Republican Banner* cited in Cole, *Whig Party in the South,* 321.
[17]Bancroft, *Seward,* 1:375.   [18]New York *Evening Post,* February 3, 1855.

When the New York legislature in February, 1855, moved to elect a Senator, Weed's masterful management was very much in evidence. D. D. Barnard was disgusted when he saw how much more closely than Fillmore's managers Weed had applied himself to detail. "The state crept all over like an old cheese," Barnard declared, "and swarms of maggots had hopped and skipped about all the avenues to the state capitol."[19] The hopping and skipping were the result of Weed's crafty wire-pulling as he marshaled enough of the spurious Know-Nothings to re-elect Seward to the United States Senate.

Having elected Seward, Weed now gave the signal for New York "Conscience" Whigs to become Republicans.[20] After a conference, calls were issued for two state conventions — Whig and Republican — to be held in Syracuse on September 26. When the conventions met, Weed managed the unification. "Conscience" Whigs marched over to the Republican hall. Each group ratified the other's platform, and all agreed to a joint ticket now entitled "Republican." Well might the antislavery press rejoice that "At last there is a Political North."[21]

And so the sands of the Whig party, which five years earlier had begun to trickle away at another famous Syracuse convention, ran out. The last grain fell almost simultaneously with the emergence of a "Silver Grey" American party and a "Woolly-headed" Republican party.

*   *   *   *   *

At their national convention, Know-Nothings tried to recover some voters with antislavery sentiment who might have been driven away the preceding June by the neutral stand on slavery in the territories. In place of June's "Congress ought not to legislate on the subject of slavery within the territories," they now substituted a demand that Congress refrain from inter-

[19]Barnard to Fish, January 30, 1855, Barnard Papers.
[20]New York *Evening Post*, July 20, 24, 1855.
[21]C. Clay to Seward, September 29, 1855, Seward Papers; Syracuse *Daily Star*, September 23, 27, 1855.

fering with all "domestic and social affairs" in the territories. Under this principle they now condemned Pierce's administration for repealing the Missouri Compromise. Here, indeed, was masterful fence-straddling.[22]

Though intended to attract moderate antislavery voters, the platform modification did not indicate a change in Know-Nothing leadership. The dissemblers had been purged and the controlling "National" Whigs kept the convention in nearly perfect harmony. Earlier they had settled on Fillmore as their Presidential candidate and now on the first ballot, with only a few votes in opposition, they nominated him. For Vice-President, they selected Andrew Donelson of Kentucky.

Even while the Americans met in Philadelphia, across the breadth of the state Republicans convened at Pittsburgh in a raucous preconvention caucus. What Weed heard and saw there induced him to postpone his greatest ambition — to make Seward President. Though Seward yearned for the office, and like Achilles, sulked in his tent when told he could not have it, Weed was convinced that Seward's nomination would be unwise. The many uncertain factors forewarned Weed to postpone to another day both his and Seward's ambitions. Instead, the Albany editor joined the Massachusetts movement of Nathaniel P. Banks and Henry Wilson to nominate the romantic, if politically guileless, Pathfinder of the West, John C. Fremont. Fremont's wife, Jessie, his politician father-in-law Thomas Hart Benton himself, and the potent Blair family gave Fremont political leverage with the western Democracy. The addition of these Democratic votes to the young Republican party was more than Seward could promise. After Banks introduced Fremont to John Bigelow and William Cullen Bryant, thus assuring the support of the *Evening Post* and the eastern, free-soil Democrats, Weed gave his support to Fremont.

Nothing now stood in the way of Fremont's nomination. At Philadelphia in June Republican convention delegates rubber-

[22]Carroll, *American Battle*, 85, 97.

stamped their caucus candidate. Then in ringing tones they pledged themselves to erase "those twin relics of barbarism, polygamy and slavery" from the territories. If Fillmore's party was on record with a policy of non-interference with slavery in the territories, the Republicans were emphatically asserting their own intent to eliminate it.

The Democrats, meanwhile, convened in Cincinnati, passed by their President, Pierce, and leading contender, Douglas, and nominated the dignified and available James Buchanan of Pennsylvania. On slavery in the territories, which was to become the leading issue of the campaign, only words differentiated Democrats from Americans.

*   *   *   *   *

Fillmore's managers timed his return to the United States for early June, 1856, and had arranged a gigantic demonstration for him in New York. As the *Atlantic* passed Sandy Hook about nine o'clock on Sunday evening of June 22, the telegraph flashed the signal to the waiting delegations. But the telegraph was unnecessary, for other signals had been set. At Sandy Hook the *Atlantic* fired a gun, and a number of beautiful rockets climbed high into the night sky. Waiting at the Battery for that display, a group of Know-Nothing enthusiasts discharged a fifty-gun salute. Delegations from all over the city, Brooklyn, and Jersey City who had been waiting for the sound of the cannon, converged on the wharf where the *Atlantic* was to drop anchor.[23]

As Fillmore's ship rounded the Battery, another display of rockets flooded the sky, and another salute, this time from the Jersey shore, answered. Between two and three thousand well-wishers milled about the wharf. As soon as the gangplank was down, Alderman Briggs, leading a committee of reception from the common council of New York, boarded the ship as hundreds of others followed. All tried to crowd into the after-cabin.

[23]New York *Express*, June 22, 23, 1856.

There his partisans handed Fillmore the keys to the city and called for his return to the Executive Mansion "to remove the vermin that have gathered there during . . . [his] unfortunate absence from the national helm."[24]

Fillmore replied with his first speech of the campaign. He promised "a faithful and impartial administration of the laws of the country. . . . If there be those either North or South who desire an administration for the North as against the South, or for the South as against the North, they are not the men who should give their suffrages to me. For my own part, I know only my country, my whole country, and nothing but my country."[25] Here he sounded the keynote of the coming American campaign — an imputation of their opponents as servants of special sectional interests accompanied with a flat appeal to patriotism and the Union. His small audience in the cabin took Fillmore's words as a severe indictment of both their opponents and cheered heartily.

The echoes of the cheer resounded from the dock and spread to the heart of Manhattan. For the next seven days the din of cheers and music and cannon salutes hovered over the ex-President's entourage as he slowly made his way westward to Buffalo.[26] Few candidates for the Presidency had ever had the opportunity now presented to Fillmore to address so many voters. Normally, campaign decorum required Presidential candidates to sit at home in high solitude and write letters to their friends and relatives, while the nation swirled in a political campaign. Eventually the correspondent would feel it his duty to reveal the thoughts of his candidate to the public through the columns of the party newspapers. From such a strait jacket Fillmore momentarily escaped. Without doing violence to tradition, as he made his way home he could stump the entire length of his native state by permitting insistent enthusiasts to entice him to rear platforms and improvised stages.

[24]*Ibid.*, June 23, 1856; *The Arrival, Reception and Speeches of Millard Fillmore, from New York to Buffalo*, 2.
[25]*Ibid.*   [26]*Ibid.*, 3-9.

In that triumphal procession, designed every mile of the way to appear to be spontaneous explosions of enthusiasm, Fillmore made twenty-seven public addresses. When not talking to an audience, he was huddled with delegations that rode with him from one town to the next.

During the entire time, one and only one message poured from his soul. The Union was in danger. Its enemies must be defeated. " . . . When I left the Presidential chair, the whole nation was prosperous and contented. . . . But where are we now?" he asked. "Alas! threatened at home with civil war. . . . " The bloody scenes in Kansas, he charged, were brought on by "selfish" men who "recklessly and wantonly" produced the Kansas-Nebraska bill "to aid in personal advancement." Yet the real danger, he continued, no longer lay in past greed, but in the election of a sectional Republican candidate. " . . . [O]ur Southern brethren," he warned would never "submit to be governed by such a Chief Magistrate. . . . Therefore, you must see that if this sectional party succeeds, it leads inevitably to the destruction of this beautiful fabric reared by our forefathers."[27]

His audiences strained almost in vain to catch a note of antiforeign or anti-Catholic sentiment. In only three of the twenty-seven speeches did he tend to identify himself with nativism. "As an American," he told the citizens of Newburgh, "I have no hostility to foreigners. . . . Having witnessed their deplorable condition in the old country, God forbid I should add to their sufferings by refusing them an asylum in this." He also asserted his tolerance of all creeds. Yet if any sect suffered itself "to be used for political objects" he "would meet it by political opposition. In my view, Church and State should be separate, not only in form, but fact — religion and politics should not be mingled."[28]

He repeated the pledge at Little Falls,[29] and only once did he use the word "Catholic." He told an audience at Rome,

[27]*Fillmore Papers*, 2:20-21.   [28]*Reception and Speeches*, 16.   [29]*Ibid.*, 11.

New York, that a short time ago he was at Rome, in Italy, and saw the Pope, but he "had not become a Roman Catholic — far from it." He had returned to his country, loving it all the more for having compared it with Europe. "You should be thankful," said he, "that you live in this free and happy land. Guard well your institutions, and be ever watchful against any attempt to divide or destroy your country."[30]

The lack of nativism in Fillmore's appeal, if other things did not already bear it out, proved to the satisfaction of his opponents that the American party was nothing more than a disguised "Silver Grey" organization. Even the Catholic hierarchy had grown to realize that the American party was no threat to the Catholic church. As early as September, 1855, Buffalo's Bishop Timon assured his colleague in Cincinnati that "we have little to fear now from them. They have on the whole done us much more good than harm." Rather, he feared the Republican party "[because] there seems to be an anti-catholic twang in much of what they write and say. A moderate and Catholic party with a concealed warfare would do us much more harm than the brutal force and open warfare of the K.N."[31]

As late as October, 1856, the same bishop recorded in his diary that one of his parishioners, rather than fearing Fillmore's candidacy, felt he "would be the man who would aid the Catholics" and "would most probably . . . [become] a Catholic himself. . . ." The same parishioner urged Bishop Timon to cast his influence on Fillmore's side. He replied that he "avoided politics . . . [but] personally . . . esteemed Fillmore. . . ."[32] Possibly the ex-President's contribution to the purchase of the bells of the St. Joseph Cathedral and to other Catholic churches, and his daughter's earlier enrollment in the Buffalo Academy for Young Ladies, operated by the Sisters of the Sacred Heart, had convinced the bishop that if Fillmore was the American

[30]*Ibid.*, 13.
[31]Bishop Timon to Bishop Purcell, September 17, 1855, Archives, Buffalo Chancellery.
[32]Bishop Timon, Diary, Archives, Buffalo Chancellery.

party's candidate it sought something other than the destruction of Catholicism.[33]

*　　*　　*　　*　　*

Fillmore's chances for victory, if they were ever bright, faded rapidly during the summer months. After whistle-stopping through New York, he fell into the traditional patterns of expected behavior, and his managers were unable to maintain the enthusiasm. For the most part those Whigs who had the ability to drum up popular support for their candidate — as they did in 1840 and again in 1848 — had moved into the Republican camp. The policies of the Know-Nothings, under the new political leadership, attracted staid, rational men who knew nothing of drama. They did not know how to guide men's actions through emotion. The single compelling appeal of their successful campaigns of 1854 and 1855 was to racial and religious prejudice; this they now softened to an inoffensive but also quite ineffective slogan: "Americans should govern America." The one thing they stood for — sectional peace — they knew not how to sell.

Against experienced, practiced masters of political appeal, the Fillmore managers had little chance. They had never learned fully the lessons that Jacksonian politics had taught men like Weed, and they had never trained editors away from the verbosity they confused with erudition. Against the bouncing enthusiasm and opportunism of Republicans and the unremitting resolution of Democrats, the old "Silver Greys" had no effective defense or attack. The tactics of restraint and silence that Fillmore had used so effectively while in power were ill-suited to the demands of a bitter campaign.

In contrast, calculating men in Republican ranks had earlier seized upon disorders in Kansas — growing for the most part out of the conflicts common in a frontier body politic devoted exclusively to land-grabbing — and had twisted them into op-

[33]Callan, *Society of the Sacred Heart of North America*, 434-448.

portunities for gain — both material and political. Soon every
act of violence in Kansas had its interpreters who pointed to it
with alarm as evidence of a proslavery attack on freedom. Lurid
tales about a slavery war brought hundreds to the new region.
As the surveys caught up to the squatters, disorders mounted
and hopes rose to desperation in the gamble for county seats
and railroad sites. Soon press, pulpit, and platform raised selfish
striving to the dignity of battles for principle.[34]

To many of those northern voters who might have doubted
that an organized "slaveocracy" was intent on subduing a free
territory to the slave master's lash, two events in the late spring
of 1856 brought conviction. Early in May, the proslavery
marshal of Kansas issued a proclamation calling for a "posse"
to help him execute certain writs in the free-soil town of
Lawrence. Hundreds of zealots and adventurers responded.
The townsmen decided not to offer resistance, yet the "posse"
ran riot — burned the hotel that was the free-soil headquarters,
the home of Dr. Charles Robinson, leader of the free-soil group,
destroyed the free-soil presses, and retired in drunken and jubilant disorder, leaving five men dead in the ruins. A few days
later, on midnight of May 24th, John Brown, a man of doubtful
honesty and uncertain sanity, with a handful of men raided the
camp of some aggressively proslavery men who had accused
him of stealing horses, and coldly murdered five men in "divine"
retribution for the sacking of Lawrence.

Only twenty-four hours earlier, a thousand miles to the
east, Preston S. Brooks, a Representative from South Carolina,
entered the Senate chamber in search of Senator Charles Sumner.
In the debates a few days before, Sumner had deliberately,
calculatingly, and continuously insulted every southern tradition.
He also heaped abuse upon some southern Senators. One of
these, Andrew Pickens Butler, of South Carolina, unlike others
of the maligned, was not there to reply. His nephew, Brooks,

[34]Ralph V. Harlow, "The Rise and Fall of the Kansas Aid Movement," *American
Historical Review*, 41:1-25; Paul W. Gates, "A Fragment of Kansas Land History,"
Kansas Historical Quarterly, 6:227-240.

resolved to whip Sumner like a cur. For two days he had lain in wait for Sumner. Now he found him alone in the Senate chamber, writing at his desk. Coming unawares upon his prey, Brooks beat him over the head with a gutta-percha cane until the Senator fell senseless to the floor.

The howl of indignation that greeted this affair from the Republican press echoed throughout the campaign months. It was proof positive of all that the antislavery stereotype had pictured the southern slaveholder to be — a maddened beast disguised as a gentleman. All the other charges, ergo, were just as true. John Brown, meanwhile, was elevated on a wave of acclaim and portrayed as a hero who was defending free institutions against a murderous "slaveocracy."[35]

Against this kind of emotional appeal to the North and its equally vituperative southern response,[36] the American party, hobbled by its own incapacities, was helpless. Not only did Natives fail to match the extravagance of Republicans, but fear of the Republicans drove many who wanted to vote for Fillmore into Democratic ranks. As the campaign progressed, the old line Whigs desperately struck out at Fremont. "We cannot divide our fire," shouted Hiram Ketchum. "We must defeat the Republicans. Better to sacrifice Fillmore by throwing our weight behind Buchanan who is safe on the sectional issue than by our division permit Fremont to win."[37]

This attitude was not unknown earlier. Before the nominations, Charles A. Davis indicated that "National" Whigs might support a Democrat rather than Fillmore. "The impression is — at least in 'our Back Parlor' — that Fillmore will be the next President unless the Democratic Party nominates a strong conservative name — so much stronger than Fillmore as to take a large share of Whigs and good folks who are now wandering among unknown islands. . . ."[38] By July a New York merchant

[35] Avery Craven, *The Coming of the Civil War*, 365.
[36] Cole, *Whig Party in the South*, 322.
[37] H. Ketchum to Barnard, September 21, 1856, Barnard Papers.
[38] Davis to Marcy, March 3, 1856 quoted in Foner, *Business and Slavery*, 120.

revealed that a growing panic among his friends over a possible Republican victory was working against Fillmore. "I have been and am for Mr. Fillmore. But I am first of all for defeating Col. Fremont. This should be the great measure and object of all true Whigs and honest men. If this can be best accomplished by voting for Mr. Buchanan would we, as Whigs be inconsistent in so doing? . . . . However much we may desire it, Mr. Fillmore cannot be elected."[39] In August other former Whigs published similar appeals. Rufus Choate announced that it was the "first duty" of all Whigs "to defeat and dissolve the new geographical party" and thus he would vote for Buchanan. Robert Winthrop, Caleb Cushing, and Amos A. Lawrence adopted the same position.[40] Fletcher Webster and James B. Clay, the sons of the former Whig leaders, joined in denouncing the Republican party.[41]

In the South the Americans tried to prevent desertions by arguing that no candidate would receive a majority of the nation's electoral vote. The election would be thrown into the House where it was thought that Fillmore's chances were better than those of his opponents. It was, therefore, incumbent on all his friends to remain with Fillmore. Yet as time passed, a strong feeling developed that Fillmore could not be elected under any circumstances and that a division of southern votes would elect Fremont. The argument caused many a Fillmore editor to wince, and many of Fillmore's friends abandoned him. It was a case of voting on the strongest side to guarantee the defeat of that "sectional, dangerous, and unprincipled combination called the Republican Party."[42]

Accordingly many old line Whigs, who had thus far been Americans, now made their way into the ranks of Buchanan's

[39]"Whig," July 1, 1856 in New York *Commercial Advertiser*, July 19, 1856.
[40]New York *Times*, August 15, 1856; see also pamphlet, *Old Line Whigs for Buchanan*; R. C. Winthrop, Jr., *A Memoir of Robert C. Winthrop*, 182: Fuess, *Cushing*, 2:192; W. S. Appleton, "The Whigs of Massachusetts," Mass. Historical Society, *Proceedings*, 3-7.
[41]*Journal of Commerce*, August 28, 1856.
[42]Cole, *Whig Party in the South*, 324-325.

party. Maryland's most prominent Whigs took this course — Senators Pratt and Pearce and two of their predecessors, Merrick and Reverdy Johnson. All over the South, a host of others made the same decision — Jones of Tennessee, Benjamin of Louisiana, Preston and James B. Clay of Kentucky, and Jenkins of Georgia. In vain certain Fillmore papers changed their tone and now declared that Fremont could not be elected in any contingency, that the contest was one between Buchanan and Fillmore.[43] Only Bell, Crittenden, Graham, Mangum and a few others of the old guard took to the southern stump for Fillmore and Donelson.

*　　*　　*　　*　　*

The alarmists who feared a Republican victory by default might have exaggerated their case, for when compiled the returns gave Buchanan an easy victory. He polled 500,000 more votes than Fremont and twice as many as Fillmore. Maryland alone stood in Fillmore's column. Buchanan carried the other fourteen slave states plus California, Illinois, Indiana, New Jersey, and Pennsylvania. Fremont captured the remaining eleven northern states, but 67 per cent of the voters had cast against the sectional party.[44]

[43]*Ibid.; National Intelligencer,* October 13, 1856.
[44]Analysis of vote:

	Buchanan	Fremont	Fillmore	Fillmore's % of Total
New England (Conn., Mass., R. I., Vt., N.H.)	163,353	307,657	28,208	5.65 %
Northern Middle States (N. Y., Pa., N. J.)	473,521	451,855	230,894	19.96%
West & Farwest (Ohio, Ill., Ind., Mich., Wisc., Iowa, Calif.)	589,416	388,997	135,540	12.16%
Total North	1,226,290	1,340,070	394,642	13.32%
Border States (Del., Ky., Md., Mo., Tenn.)	263,563	901	235,753	48.08 %
Deep South* (Va., N. C., Ga., Fla., Tex., La., Ala., Miss., Ark.)	358,316	291	244,139	40.54%
Total South	611,879	1,192	579,892	43.90%
Total Vote	1,838,169	1,341,264	874,534	28.63%

*S. C. not included. Its legislature selected electors.

As the statisticians delved deeper into the figures, however, they discovered that Buchanan's victory was none too sweeping. Fillmore's candidacy had almost thrown the election into the House of Representatives. A total change of approximately eight thousand votes from Buchanan to Fillmore in Kentucky, Tennessee, and Louisiana would have given those states to Fillmore, and no candidate would have had an electoral majority.[45]

Had the election gone to the House, no one could have predicted its outcome. The Congress that would have sat in judgment was elected in 1854 when politicians were experimenting with new loyalties. The House's political complexion was indeterminable, and no party controlled a majority of states. Had not a few voters transferred from Fillmore to Buchanan in the closing hours of the campaign the scenes of 1824 might have been repeated and the story of the coming of the Civil War been vastly altered.

[45]Following table illustrates:

	Electors	Buchanan	Fillmore	Fremont	Needed to give state to Fillmore	Percentage of change needed
Ky.	12	74,642	67,416	0	3,563	2.50%
Tenn.	12	73,638	66,178	0	3,730	2.66%
La.	6	22,164	20,709	0	723	1.68%
Total	30				8,016	

Spectator

HE ELECTION returns of 1856 were no shock to the ex-President. He was a "little mortified" at "being so unanimously rejected." Yet he had expected defeat, and if it now disturbed his composure, he concealed the fact. "Personally, I have nothing to regret in the results. . . . I envy not my successful rival; but sincerely hope that . . . [he] may so discharge the . . . duties of his exalted station as to restore peace and harmony. . . . If this be done, I can cheerfully forgive my enemies for the falsehoods which they have published against me. . . ."¹

Unfortunately for Fillmore, the finality of his defeat could not be gainsaid. "I consider my political career at an end," he confided to a friend, "and have nothing further to ask."² As he looked into the future, he did not know exactly what he would do. Years of inactivity seemingly stretched out before him. In 1853 out of consideration for his colleagues he had reluctantly avoided returning to the bar. Now his defeat eliminated the possibility of continuing in politics.

Relatively young, only 56, he was still uncertain that the modest fortune he had accumulated was adequate for permanent

¹Fillmore to [a party committee], November 24, 1856, *Fillmore Papers*, 2:368.
²*Ibid.*

retirement. Yet he felt that he had been denied the privilege of working. He had railed against this before, and on the eve of his death, he was still keenly sensitive to the matter. "It is a national disgrace that our Presidents . . . should be cast adrift, and perhaps be compelled to keep a corner grocery for subsistence. . . . We elect a man to the Presidency, expect him to be honest, to give up a lucrative profession, perhaps, and after we have done with him we let him go into seclusion and perhaps poverty." He thought the solution would have been a pension of about $12,000 annually for outgoing Presidents.[3]

If his household worries were more than academic, chance coupled with romance soon put them to rest. In February, 1858, he married the former Mrs. Caroline C. McIntosh. She was the fifty-two-year-old, childless widow of a Troy merchant. Fragile, with a tragic air about her — almost giving the appearance of a Mona Lisa grown old — she quickly won acceptance amid Fillmore's wide circle of friends and effortlessly became one of Buffalo's leading ladies. Her finishing-school training and her dilettante achievements enhanced a native graciousness.

To the union Mrs. Fillmore brought a handsome estate which, by a marriage contract, she turned over to Fillmore to administer. When news of this contract came to light, Buffalonians winked slyly. A later generation even suggested that Fillmore had been a clever fellow, indeed, and had somehow feathered his nest through this contract. Even though their knowledge about property rights of married women was dim, his contemporaries should have known that Fillmore's behavior would always be socially as well as legally correct. His consent to the marriage contract was an act of self-denial. By it his wife safely kept her property in her own name rather than submit it to the protection of the law of 1848, an insecure attempt to grant to married women the right to retain their property. Instead of acquiring a fortune, Fillmore became responsible for the investment of one and was strictly accountable to his wife for every

[3]*Ibid.*, 2:139.

penny except the income from 10,000 dollars — a modest fee for managing the estate.[4]

Mrs. Fillmore, of course, had no desire to hoard her money and willingly joined her husband in purchasing John Hollister's huge mansion on Niagara Square. Alone, Fillmore's savings were too small to undertake both purchase and maintenance. This mammoth structure became their home for the remainder of their lives. Its gothic style, with parapets, balustrades, and simulated towers, decorated in the elegant taste of the Victorian era, sharply contrasted with the "plain, white two-story house with green blinds, and a little yard in the front" at 180 Franklin Street that had been Fillmore's home for twenty-six years.

In another way the Niagara Square home differed from the old house. The new one was ideally suited to the kind of life that circumstances had created for the Fillmores. In the past both had paid punctilious attention to social requirements. And now, with little else to occupy their time, they turned their home on Niagara Square into one of society's most gracious centers. Hardly a distinguished person of America or other lands who

[4]Exactly how much money Fillmore and his wife had is impossible to determine. All except two figures are unknown. In December, 1847, Fillmore had property valued at approximately $30,000. The next sum total does not appear until 1889, fifteen years after Fillmore's death. At that time, Millard Powers Fillmore left an estate of $285,705.56. It was supposed at the time of Powers' death that most of his money was inherited from his father and step-mother. This conclusion was drawn by contemporaries who asserted Powers was not capable of accumulating that much property. And the conclusion is borne up by the fact that $174,570 were in United States, New York State, and New York Central Railroad bonds. Fillmore had directed in the second codicil to his will, on April 28, 1873, that his personal property be invested in those securities. Certain rationalizations help bear out this conclusion. Fillmore provided from his own property, exclusive of his wife's, for annuities to his brothers and sisters totaling $1,700 annually. To provide such payments, principal earning five per cent would have equalled $34,000. In an earlier will, 1865, he indicated that this was less than one-third of his estate. That would place his estate above a minimum of $102,000. Possibly it was as great as $174,000 since all domestic property, one farm, taxes, insurance, and a bequest for $1,000 to the Buffalo Orphan Asylum plus the annuities were part of the "one-third" of which he was writing.

Besides assigning the residual part of possibly $110,000 of Powers' estate as having come from his second wife, another way of judging the size of her property is seen in the marriage contract. That instrument permitted her to dispose of $10,000 when and as she pleased. It was implicit that that amount would not seriously affect the income producing capacity of the rest of her estate.

visited Buffalo failed to experience the Fillmores' hospitality. Besides a long list of political celebrities, they shared in entertaining a Japanese ambassador, Tomomi Iwakuar, and H. R. H. Prince Arthur of England.[5]

The Fillmores easily became models for other slowly ageing couples everywhere. Respect and admiration never seemed to have left their treatment of each other. To the second Mrs. Fillmore the ex-President paid the same marked attention and courtesy that had made the first wife the envy of her circle. For her part Mrs. Fillmore revealed her pride in her husband by the number of his portraits and busts she had scattered throughout the house. So seriously and persistently did she display these objects of art that her efforts became the butt of much amusement among the young people.[6]

*   *   *   *   *

Though Fillmore seemingly lost himself in social pleasantries, he could not break the habits of a generation. Events drew his attention toward politics. "I take no part in political affairs," he sadly confided to a correspondent. Yet he was an eager and critical spectator of all that transpired. Like the actor driven off the stage, he took a seat in the audience to see how the role should be interpreted. He stayed in the recesses of the theater, unwilling at first to let anyone know that the old actor stood critic of the new. He avoided public meeting places, the old haunts of his former colleagues. "I dare not go to Washington," he told his confidant, lest "I am publicly attacked for interfering."[7] The defeat of 1856 had shorn him of responsibility to speak out, and he shied away from publicity, but his focus was always on the national scene, and eventually some of his criticism came to light.

As he sat in judgment all considerations except the need to preserve the Union were cast aside. He constantly compared

[5]Buffalo *Commercial Advertiser,* 1854-74, passim.
[6]*Fillmore Papers,* 2:493, 516.
[7]Fillmore to W. W. Corcoran, October 12, 1858, Fillmore Mss.

his victorious rival's rule with his own dedicated efforts and found it wanting. That intricate weaving of patriotism, ambition, factious spirit, ineptness, and politicking that marked the byplay between Republicans and Democrats in Buchanan's administration left him convinced that he, rather than his successors, had chosen the right course.

With each passing month he grew more certain that he had been misjudged. In the face of impending destruction of the Union no other interpretation of the President's role, except his, was proper. As one by one events occurred that snapped the cords of the Union — growing Republican strength, continued trouble in Kansas, the Dred Scott decision, economic panic, John Brown's raid, the division of the Democratic party into two sectional parties — he despaired. " . . . At a time like this I should rejoice to meet my countrymen . . . and pledge . . . ourselves . . . to maintain this Government, and 'to frown indignantly upon the first dawning of any attempt to alienate any portion of our country from the rest, or to enfeeble the sacred ties which now link together the various parts.' "[8] Though the words were Washington's the sentiment was truly his.

" . . . If I had the power to speak," he remarked after the Harper's Ferry incident, "I would say to my brethren of the South: Be not alarmed . . . . We" of the North "are all anti-Slavery in sentiment, but we know that we have nothing to do with it in the several states, and we do not intend to interfere with it." And he would say to the North: ". . . Respect the rights of the South; assure them by your acts that you regard them as friends and brethren." He would "conjure all" to cease this agitation. "Let harmony be restored between the North and the South, and let every patriot rally around our national flag, and swear upon the altar of his country to sustain and defend it."[9]

Though each event challenged him to take to the platform

[8]Fillmore to [a committee], February 1, [1858], *Fillmore Papers*, 2:372.
[9]Fillmore to Hunt, Brooks, etc., December 16, 1859, *ibid.*, 2:377-378.

and plead again for the Union, Fillmore stayed faithful to his decision to be a private citizen. It was as if he regarded himself as a discredited officer in the cause of nationhood who, by returning to the public forum, would do more harm than good. Even when old friends — remnants of the "National" Whigs — made a last effort to revive their organization as the Constitutional Union party, he gave them his "most hearty approval" but refused to abandon his retirement.[10]

Friends of the Union were reluctant to let their ex-President's talents go unused. Within a week after the election of 1860, South Carolina began the process of secession, and a month later, she withdrew from the Union. During that month of trial, alarmed Unionists put forth scores of proposals to stay the action. One group called Fillmore to the cause. On December 15, 1860, New York City merchants met in a Pine Street office "to consult as to the best means . . . to avert the danger now threatening the Union, and to assure to the South sufficient protection to their constitutional rights within the Union." Ex-President Van Buren and numerous Democratic politicians were present. Its chief result was to ask Fillmore to travel to South Carolina "as commissioner from New York to exhort temperate action and delay."[11]

Fillmore refused the commission. This seemed strangely out of character in the light of the sacrifices he had already made for the Union. Yet the futility of any effort at conciliation drove him to his decision. It could not "do any good" he explained. No conciliation would succeed without the cooperation of Republicans. " . . . What I want, is some assurance from the Republican Party . . . that they, or at least the conservative portion of them, are ready and willing to come forward and repeal all unconstitutional state laws; live up to the compromises of the Constitution, and execute the laws of Congress honestly, and faithfully, and treat our Southern brethren as friends."[12]

[10]Fillmore to [a Philadelphia Committee], February 2, 1860, *ibid.*, 2:378-379; Buffalo *Morning Express*, February 8, 1860.
[11]Buffalo *Commercial Advertiser*, December 16, 1860.
[12]Fillmore to Dix, December 19, 1860, *Fillmore Papers*, 2:391.

He did not expect to get these assurances from the Republican party because he had a deep and abiding distrust of its leaders. For eight years, between 1848 and 1856, he had battled them either as Whigs, Democrats, or Republicans, and his close association convinced him that they were irresponsible to the core. Their overweening ambitions would stop at nothing — not even in the face of dismemberment of the Union. Well might he have exclaimed in 1860 as he did in 1869 of the Republicans: " . . . I shall regard it as a blessing to break the ranks of the corrupt proscription radical party, that now curses the country. Could moderate men of both parties unite in forming a new one . . . it would be well." But he saw that moderate men were "the inactive men, and move too slow for the corruptionists, who are wide awake in pursuit of plunder."[13] When James O. Putnam, in an effort to persuade Fillmore to go to South Carolina, suggested that all "men capable of statesmanship have learned that there is a wide difference between contesting for power and wielding it," Fillmore rejoined that if "the Republican Party should appreciate this sentiment in time and act upon it, they might save the Union, but I fear that a majority can not be brought to take so sensible a view."[14]

It quickened Fillmore's heart and healed some of the wounds of malignant politics when he saw Weed and Seward somersault into a program of conciliation that made them supporters of everything he had done in the sectional conflict. Weed now proposed to strengthen the Fugitive Slave Act, for which ten years earlier he had excoriated Fillmore unmercifully; he sought modification of the personal liberty laws, behind which he had fought Fillmore in 1851-1852; he called for an abandonment of the Wilmot Proviso (which the Compromise of 1850 had already done) although the Proviso had fathered the Republican party, thus repudiating his own invention.[15]

Weed's belated conversion did not make the Albany editor

13Fillmore to Stuart, November 4, 1869, copy in Fillmore Mss.
14Fillmore to Putnam, January 28, 1861, *Fillmore Papers*, 2:392.
15Van Deusen, *Weed*, 266-267.

into a shining example of responsible statesmanship in Fillmore's eyes. Rather he surmised that Weed might be behaving in a normal fashion: ready to repudiate the instrument by which he had campaigned to power, since that campaign had created confusion in the machinery he wanted to operate. Whatever Weed's motives, however, the ex-President was "grateful" to see "the head of his party" exhibit such "good sense" and a willingness "to sacrifice all false pride, and even party itself to save the country."[16] If Weed continued to pursue such a course, Fillmore was "ready to forgive him all his hostility to me and my administration."[17]

On the eve of war Fillmore's criticism was not confined to Republicans. When President Buchanan did not take quick military action to stop South Carolina's secession, Fillmore labeled it a "mistake." "That the general government is sovereign . . . admits of no doubt in my mind," he asserted. From that precept, he argued that no state could "set up its will against" the national government. "Secession and all such acts are absolutely void." Buchanan made his "mistake," Fillmore thought, when he said the national government has "no authority to 'coerce a state.' " In reality, those who passed the ordinance of secession, Fillmore thought, should have been "regarded as an unauthorized assembly of men conspiring to commit treason, and as such liable to be punished like any other unlawful assembly engaged in the same business."[18] In all probability, considering his action in 1850, had Fillmore been in Buchanan's place he would have strengthened the federal garrisons in the Deep South and would have been prepared, if conciliation failed, to use force against the secessionists.

Conciliation failed and the South took its course to rebellion. Meanwhile fate carried to Buffalo the successful candidate of the Republican party on his way to Washington, and it fell to Fillmore to play host to Abraham Lincoln.

[16]Fillmore to Dix, December 19, 1860, *Fillmore Papers*, 2:391.
[17]Fillmore to Putnam, January 28, 1861, *ibid.*, 2:392.
[18]Fillmore to Prince, September 6, 1867, Fillmore Mss.

No one knew definitely how Fillmore voted in 1860,[19] but his anti-Republicanism was well enough known to make his reception of the President-elect a subject of much gossip and speculation.[20] Lincoln arrived on Saturday, February 16. The next morning the Fillmores accompanied him to the First Unitarian Church. In the evening, the two men attended a public meeting at St. James Hall in behalf of "the poor Indians." During all this time the gossips had no occasion to acquire an anecdote about, or word play between, the ex-President and the President-elect. Fillmore harbored no personal hostility toward Lincoln for the character of the Republican party. Nothing stood in the way of a cordial weekend. He entertained Lincoln at his home and paid him every attention consistent with the simple, unostentatious hospitality that the guest preferred.[21] Yet exactly what his thoughts were as he gauged the Republican standard-bearer for the task that lay ahead, Fillmore judiciously withheld from public view and discreetly concealed forever.

*　*　*　*　*

With armed conflict at hand Fillmore made restoration of the Union his sole war aim. For nearly eleven years, in office and in retirement, he had opposed every public act that might have led to disunion, and now he supported a war to re-establish the nation. Unhesitatingly he gave his time, his money, and his heart to the effort.

One day after President Lincoln had called for volunteers, on April 16, 1861, and four days after Beauregard had fired on Fort Sumter, Fillmore rallied his fellow Buffalonians into a giant Union demonstration. By this action he became Buffalo's spiritual and civic war leader. " . . . My fellow-citizens," he said simply and earnestly as chairman of the rally, "it is no time for any man to shrink from the responsibility which events have cast upon him. We have reached a crisis . . . when no

19Buffalo *Commercial Advertiser,* June 1, 1861.
20*Ibid.,* January 30, February 9, 15, 1861.　　21*Ibid.,* February 18, 19, 23, 1861.

man . . . has a right to stand neutral. Civil War has been inaugurated, and we must meet it. Our Constitution is in danger,
and we must defend it. It is no time now," he added, brushing
aside his own misgivings, "to inquire by whose fault or folly
this state of things has been produced. . . . " Rather, "let every
man stand to his post, and . . . let posterity . . . find our skeleton
and armor on the spot where duty required us to stand."[22]

His hearers rose to their feet and "cheered for several
minutes swinging their hats and manifesting the wildest enthusiasm." Fillmore called for "three glorious cheers for the Union
and the Constitution." Again the din was deafening.[23]

The purpose of the rally had been to incite enthusiasm for
enlistment, and in a gesture that was not play-acting, Fillmore
punctuated his words and the cheers with a pledge of $500 for
the support of families of volunteers. In Buffalo his was the
first money paid for the cause.[24] Southward his address caused
the Richmond, Virginia *Examiner* to smear him as a "fair-
weather friend" who lacked "moral courage." It caused a New
Orleans school board to call him a "hypocrite" and a "fanatic"
and have his name chiseled off a school house and that of Jefferson Davis substituted.[25]

The rally was only a beginning. Fillmore's leadership did
not flag. Before April had passed he organized the "Union
Continentals." Legally it was a company in the home guard —
that portion of the New York militia composed of men too old
to be subject to call by the federal government but prepared to
act in a local emergency. Yet the military purpose played only
a small part in his decision to create this unit. Rather he sought
to heighten fervor for army enlistments, encourage civilian participation in the war effort, and bring social pressure to bear on
Buffalo's leaders to contribute freely to the charity funds that
would soon be needed. He made up the Union Continentals

[22]*Fillmore Papers*, 2:62-63.
[23]Buffalo *Commercial Advertiser*, Buffalo *Morning Express*, April 17, 1861.
[24]*Fillmore Papers*, 2:xxxiii.   [25]Buffalo *Morning Express*, May 13, 1861.

from retired officers of the militia. In practice this brought most of Buffalo's "solid men" into the group. Every one was over forty-five and most of them were "large portly grandfathers with grey heads." It was quickly recognized that raising the company among the fathers "had a mighty influence upon the military spirit and upon . . . recruiting" in the city.[26]

First as a major and then as its captain and commander, Fillmore used his group in a very simple but effective way. Each member outfitted himself in a colorful uniform and was drilled to act as an escort guard. Thereafter, whenever an affair needed a bright show of pomp and glory, or of honor and patriotism, the Union Continentals supplied it.[27]

Their initial public appearance came on May 3, 1861, the day Buffalo's first volunteers departed for war. "Of all the noble events that marked the history of" Buffalo, remarked one observer, "not one possessed so much . . . proud display, excitement and significance, or contained one half its touching pathos." The Union Continentals escorted four Buffalo companies to the station. At the head of the column, Major Fillmore "marched stately and erect wearing a sword and plume, and looking like an emperor." At the depot, Fillmore, uncovering his white locks, and raising himself to his full height, cried, "Old Guard, attention! Three cheers for the Buffalo Volunteers!" Every head in the ranks was bare, every arm lifted, and every voice shouted a stentorian hurrah, hurrah, hurrah! The soldiers hoarsely responded — all but a few who, with faces turned from the scene, were soothing the sorrowing females who clung to them.[28]

During the rest of the war the Union Continentals figured in many of the stirring scenes of those sad, excited days. They marched as funeral escorts for heroes and led Fourth of July parades. On Washington's birthday, 1862, Fillmore even led his company in full uniform to Dr. Lord's Central Presbyterian

[26]*Ibid.*, September 9, 1862.
[27]Buffalo *Commercial Advertiser*, April 17, 18, 19, 23, 1861.
[28]*Ibid.*, May 4, 1861.

Church where, after prayer by the chaplain, the ex-President read Washington's Farewell Address — probably the first President's most moving plea for the Union. The regular drills of the Union Continentals, bringing together Buffalo's men of property, facilitated the solicitation of funds for meritorious causes, and to these Fillmore gave generously. Then in November, 1862, having shown the organization its way, and seen it through its first year, Fillmore retired from its command.[29]

His war efforts did not abate. At still another level he hurried to promote the nation's defenses. The spark for action came in November 1861 when Captain Wilkes stopped the British merchantman, the *Trent,* and took from her two Confederate emissaries, Mason and Slidell. That action quickly brought on jingoistic calls for war. Neither government had any intentions of permitting the incident to develop that far, but Americans little appreciated these attitudes.

One alarmed American was Fillmore. Fearful of the consequences of a war with England, he headed an organization that badgered the President, Secretary of War, Congress, and the governor of New York for defense of Buffalo and its environs. He asked for munitions, artillery, and troops. His request grew out of a genuine concern for the consequences of British troops crossing the Niagara frontier. Even in this critical hour, his careful recitation of the number of ships and tonnage that cleared Buffalo each year and entered the canal traffic revealed where his sentiment lay. One well-placed demolition charge would efface the dam at Lockport and dry up the canal. Buffalo's prosperity would vanish, and the main east-west highway of commerce, vital to the war, would be seriously impaired. In his eyes the canal was so important to the war that he even tried to persuade the federal government that it should undertake enlarging the locks to permit the use of longer and wider barges. Since his proposals coincided exactly with the final settlement of the *Trent* affair, nothing came of them.[30]

[29]Buffalo *Morning Express,* November 19, 1862.   [30]*Fillmore Papers,* 2:379-416.

To this point Fillmore's zealous actions endeared him to the war party. But for all his support, he could not rid himself of the notion that the war was unnecessary and that the Republican party not only shared the onus of causation but was responsible for its undue continuation. Except for an occasional hint, he had kept his opinions to himself. The years of sickening failures on the war front, however, had gradually eroded his patience. Then suddenly, in a passionate outburst he unburdened his soul and stirred up about his head a hornet's nest of recrimination.

The occasion was a Great Central Fair sponsored by the Ladies Christian Commission for the benefit of the war's sick and wounded. The fair consisted of a number of booths where donated articles were sold. Both Fillmores threw themselves into their tasks and eventually the fair earned over $25,000 for the cause. The ex-President, moreover, had been selected to give the opening address. It was February, 1864, and the nation had heard almost no good news from the war front for six months.

"Three years of civil war," Fillmore informed his audience, "have desolated the fairest portion of our land, loaded the country with an enormous debt that the sweat of millions yet unborn must be taxed to pay; arrayed brother against brother, father against son in mortal combat; deluged our country with fraternal blood, whitened our battle-fields with the bones of the slain, and darkened the sky with the pall of mourning."[31] His audience was shocked. It had come to have its spirits uplifted and instead he spelled out a tale of woe in a manner that suggested that all could have been avoided.

Then he castigated the Washington administration and revealed his basic distrust of Republican leadership. "We cannot, in our humble capacity, control the events of this desolating war. . . . It is no time now to inquire whether it might have been avoided. . . . Nor are we now to criticise the conduct of

[31] *Ibid.*, 2:86.

those who control it. . . . " Let the "impartial historian" inquire into the "partisan prejudice, petty jealousies, malignant envy, and intriguing, selfish ambition" that have accompanied the war. One thing, however, was clear. Before "lasting peace" could be restored, "much must be forgiven, if not forgotten." When the North should have conquered the Confederate armies, "then let us show our magnanimity," he begged, "by winning back the deluded multitude who have been seduced into this rebellion, by extending to them every act of clemency and kindness in our power, and by restoring them to all their rights under the Constitution. This I conceive to be Christian forgiveness, and the best policy and the only one which can ever restore this Union."[32]

Here was an obvious condemnation of both the Republican party's conduct of the war and its war aims. In a Presidential year, Republican editors could not let the slur go unchallenged. "Shocking bad taste," cried the *Commercial Advertiser*, no longer in the hands of Fillmore's friends. "It is certainly not in the interest of the patriotic ladies who had inaugurated this great charitable work to make a political matter of it. . . . We . . . say that few public men would have taken advantage of their position . . . to deliver such a speech. . . . "[33]

Yet it was not the "bad taste" that alienated the Republican press. It was rather the anti-Republicanism in the speech which drove them to forget the ex-President's unselfish support of the Union's cause. Their partisanship would leave posterity a heritage of deliberate misrepresentation.

Long after the fair was over the arraignment continued. "Mr. Fillmore," sneered the editor of the *Commercial Advertiser*, belonged "amongst the bitterest opponents of the war" and should have found happy refuge with that "infamous circle made up of such men as Vallandigham, the Woods, the Seymours and the Brooks[es]."[34] He "had gone too far in his

[32]*Ibid.*, 2:87.
[33]Buffalo *Commercial Advertiser*, February 23, 1864.   [34]*Ibid.*

advance toward Copperheadism," charged the editor, finding the reason to be "insane craving after a lost political position." Until Fillmore identified himself with Copperheads, said his vilifier, "he was entitled to the consideration due to the dignity of his personal character, and to the remembrance of the high official station he once held." Now he, himself, had shattered "the idol thus reared in his home."[35]

The passion of these words only slowly subsided, for the nation was convulsed by a Presidential campaign, and Fillmore had condemned an administration when it could ill afford to take on another opponent. In the spring of 1864 prospects for Republican success appeared nearly hopeless. Grant seemed to be accomplishing nothing; Lee appeared invincible, Early almost seized Washington; Sherman was apparently lost; Lincoln was on the verge of breaking with his own party on war aims and reconstruction; the vindictive Wade-Davis bill was before Congress; a faction of the Republican party was preparing to bolt; another faction was calling for a more vigorous candidate than Lincoln; the government's credit was ebbing; further call for troops emphasized the futility of the administration's efforts; and two New York City newspapers were seized by military force and their publication suspended. Three years of war and hundreds of thousands of casualties had gone for naught. The administration risked repudiation at the polls. Little wonder that the Republican attack on Fillmore in his home town was vicious.

The charges, however, could not dissuade him. He shared the despair of the war-weary North and called for a change of national leadership. "I sincerely feel that the country is on the verge of ruin," he predicted in midsummer, and "unless the policy which governs our national affairs can be changed, we must soon end in national bankruptcy and military despotism. Perhaps the former cannot now be averted, but the latter may. . . . " To save the country from "military despotism" he proposed "a change of Administration."[36]

35*Ibid.*, March 7, 1864.
36Fillmore to Robinson, August 12 [?], 1864, *Fillmore Papers*, 2:431.

Although Fillmore's influence in forming public opinion was slight, he attitude was characteristic of old-line Whigs. They turned to the war faction of the Democratic party. Occasionally one of them would link Fillmore's name with the coming Democratic convention. But Fillmore was not interested.[37] Early in August he privately endorsed George B. McClellan, and when the Democratic convention made the General their candidate, Fillmore openly supported him.[38]

As a result in Buffalo Fillmore proved a convenient whipping boy for Republicans. Whenever it was necessary to have a local example of a Copperhead, Republicans pointed their fingers at him.[39] So frequently did they hurl the charge that the taint of treason, though wholly absurd, plagued Fillmore's private life.

Even after the fall of 1864, when the gloom of military defeat gave way to victory's brilliant colors and Lincoln was re-elected, the charge persisted. Though Republican editors put aside their rancor, all their readers did not. When the news of Lincoln's murder flashed across the nation, Fillmore was again the target of ill will. Everywhere evidences of mourning appeared. Householders adorned their doors with black drapes. But Fillmore's door remained naked and unmarked. A passerby, conditioned to hatred, quickly espied this oversight, saw in it another proof of treason, and smeared the house with black ink.[40] It made no difference that Fillmore, who had been out of town, appropriately draped his doorway as soon as he returned. It made no difference that a few days later it was Fillmore who headed the citizens' committee appointed to meet the Lincoln funeral train at Batavia and serve as an escort to Buffalo.[41] Poor reporting made it appear that a vast throng of respectable fellow townsmen had gathered in front of his home and vied with each other in insulting the ex-President.[42]

[37] Fillmore to H. Ketchum, August 17, 1864, *ibid.*, 2:432-433.
[38] *Ibid.*; Fillmore to Churchill and others, September 5, 28, 1864, *ibid.*, 2:433-434.
[39] See for example, Buffalo *Commercial Advertiser*, June 4, 22, July 1, August 2, 14, October 22, 1864.
[40] *Ibid.*, April 25, 1865.
[41] *Ibid.*, April 27, 1865.
[42] *Ibid.*, April 30, May 1, 3, 1865.

Chapter 24

First Citizen of Buffalo

OLITICS aside, his achievements during the years of retirement gave Fillmore rich satisfaction. They materially lessened the pain that Republican misrepresentation caused him. Though the "bloody-shirt" continued to wave, once war ended neighbors quickly put aside their anger and restored their ex-President to his old position. Again he became the city's patriarch.

Here was a role he thoroughly enjoyed. Civil war or no, he had always been public spirited, and he had devoted years to civic improvement. To the question: What should an ex-President do as a private citizen? his last eighteen years answered: Give his talents to his community. From 1856 onward his handsome figure stalked the town purposefully as he made his rounds from committee to committee in search of action to improve the city. Each year his hair grew whiter and his tread less resilient, but his enthusiasm never waned. A stubborn desire for accomplishment and its resulting glow of satisfaction kept him going. He worked on numerous committees without publicity while others enjoyed the applause; none could accuse him of seeking either gain or glory.

Few things were closer to his heart than the desire to see Buffalo prosper. Although not a businessman, business aroused his sympathy and sometimes even played on his credulity. Late in 1859 a local inventor, Rollin Germain, caused a flurry of excitement among Buffalo's lake shippers and investors. He had developed drawings for a thousand-foot, iron-hulled craft that could carry 3,000 tons of freight and 3,000 passengers at speeds up to fifty miles per hour. Possibly news of Isambard Brunel's construction of the seven-hundred foot *Great Easterner* in England made them credulous. In any event a public meeting to set up a company to build the ship found Fillmore chairman of the group. Three months later after a special investigating committee reported adversely, the project collapsed, and Fillmore felt the need to explain his role. He knew nothing about engineering, he told his neighbors, and had taken part "only . . . to assist in procuring . . . [a] careful investigation . . . and . . . to aid every undertaking which would enure to the interest of our city."[1]

This was his sentiment at all times. Because of it Buffalo's merchants — especially those dependent on the "Dock" and the canal — could always reach Fillmore's heart. On every appropriate occasion he did yeoman service for them. Even in wartime he sought enlargement of the canal and represented the Buffalo Board of Trade in Chicago at a National Canal Convention.[2] Yet he was drawn to this work more to promote the general welfare than special interests.

The hustling city merchants used Fillmore's talents constantly. They had been the first business group on the Great Lakes to organize for mutual promotion. In 1844 they had created the Board of Trade — eventually remade into the Chamber of Commerce — when only six other cities had similar institutions. In 1862, at the opening of its new Exchange Rooms on Central Wharf, Fillmore was among the guests. Unexpectedly called on for a few words, his unrehearsed response left no doubt of his affection for the group because of what it could

[1]Buffalo *Morning Express*, November 4, 1859, February 11, March 8, 1860; *Fillmore Papers*, 2:373-374.
[2]Buffalo *Morning Express*, May 25, 1863.

do for Buffalo. He gloried in the progress of "the princely merchants of Buffalo," he told the gathering, because he regarded them "as the life-blood" of Buffalo's "prosperity." When "trade prospers everything prospers, and when it languishes all feel its depressing influence." Because of her merchants, he predicted, "Buffalo . . . is destined by its position to be what Alexandria and Venice were" to their eras.[3]

On the role of commerce and manufacturing in promoting a community's progress, Fillmore could almost become eloquent. It at least tempted him to rhetoric. In Olean at the opening celebration of the Buffalo, New York and Philadelphia Railway, he again showed his hand. Though the road had drawn heavy investments from Buffalo promoters, he focused his remarks on the progress Olean had made through the years. Good-naturedly he jested about the time when men in Buffalo escaping their creditors took flight to Olean — when Olean had an unsavory name in business circles. But now, by way of contrast, he found a "beautiful village" giving forth evidences of "thrift and enterprise." He was "pleased that Buffalo and Olean were brought into such close and pleasant relationship" and for this he toasted the railroad officers.[4]

If any basic rivalry existed between commerce and industry for the nation's favor, he failed to reflect it. In almost his dying hour he pronounced his peroration on urban economic pursuits. "It is now more than fifty years since I first became an inhabitant of Buffalo," he recounted. "I remember well that about 1825, when the Erie Canal was completed, the commercial advantages which Buffalo possessed gave a great impulse to our growth and prosperity, and it seemed . . . as though Buffalo was to be chiefly a commercial city. Buffalo had little available water power and Rochester had it in abundance, and she turned it to a very good account." But now, after the introduction of cheap and abundant coal, the "busy hum of industry is heard on all sides, and the worshippers in this temple have laid upon its

[3]*Ibid.*, June 27, 1862; *Fillmore Papers*, 2:67-69.   [4]*Ibid.*, 2:129.

altars their choicest offerings for the admiration of the world.
. . . I see no reason why Buffalo should not become a great
manufacturing city."[5]

*   *   *   *   *

Fillmore used the years of his retirement to return to old
loves. His contemporaries never regarded him as a man of
great learning or cultural attainment. Yet they knew of his
steadfast encouragement of their city's intellectual life. No contradiction existed here. The teacher in him, rather than the
scholastic or artistic muses, called him to action. His youthful
experiences had made him a lifelong friend of learning, and
now, in retirement, the urge to help others release their talents
had full sway.

In these last years five educational groups drew on him for
ideas, energy, and money. With one, the Young Men's Association, his work had begun long before retirement. From its
founding in 1836, as the spiritual successor of the Buffalo Lyceum, he had concerned himself with its destiny. Founded in
an era of prosperity, it had been well supported and had almost
realized its great desire to create a superior lending and reference
library for its members. The severe depression that followed
soon, however, made its task difficult.

Libraries had held Fillmore's respect ever since his wool-
carding days in New Hope when he had joined a library group.
He had helped Buffalo's Y.M.A. survive the hard times, and when
it moved to new quarters in 1841, still fighting the depression,
he had boosted its chances with a life membership subscription.[6]

His absence in Washington, moreover, did not dull his
interest in books — he had created the first permanent library
in the Executive Mansion — and on retiring to Buffalo, he gave
liberally to the Y.M.A.'s book collection. By the mid-fifties the
association was well established and was distinctly at the forefront of the city's intellectual life. On the eve of the Civil War

[5]*Ibid.*, 2:143-144.   [6]*Ibid.*, 1:xxxiii.

it celebrated its twenty-fifth anniversary and was anxious to move into bigger and permanent quarters. It solicited a building fund with the view of bringing together into one cultural center the Grosvenor Library, the Fine Arts Academy, the Buffalo Historical Society, the Society of Natural Science, as well as the Y.M.A. With the destiny of several of these Fillmore was already tied and for him the Y.M.A.'s building program became a three-fold blessing.

Lars Gustaf Sellstedt, the town's arbiter of artistic taste, later discredited "Fillmore's art idea" as "not of a high order." True or not, this did not gainsay the ex-President's interest in art. In November of 1862 he was as active as Sellstedt in bringing into existence the Buffalo Fine Arts Academy. A few months later Sellstedt became the Academy's superintendent, and he was happy to have Fillmore as one of the lifetime members of the board. That position may have come to him as a contributor of at least five thousand dollars, but if his purse counted with the board, his judgment was not without value for the museum. Annually he was elected as one of its curators, and his pride was as great as Sellstedt's when the Academy's inaugural exhibition, on December 23, 1862, marked Buffalo as the third city in the country to establish a permanent art gallery. Only Boston and Philadelphia had preceded her. The vigorous Academy was soon, like the Y.M.A., looking for new quarters. Its rooms in the Arcade building were inadequate.[7]

Meanwhile, the ex-President's talents were given unstintingly to nurturing the Buffalo Historical Society. In March of 1862 Lewis F. Allen had suggested to Orsamus H. Marshall that "we ought to do something" about preserving "the records and relics" of Buffalo's history. That casual conversation prompted them to call upon others. They enlisted Fillmore's aid and within a month he presided over the meeting that brought the society into being. By unanimous election he became its first

7*Ibid.*, 2:494; Buffalo *Morning Express*, November 13, 1862 ff.; *Buffalo Commercial Advertiser*, December 28, 1863.

president, and for the next five years he guided the new organization's growth.[8]

Probably no other civic cause won his affection as thoroughly as the Historical Society. For weeks at a time it seemed to possess his life. At the inaugural ceremonies he proposed that "the object of this society" was "not to study history . . . or the formation of a library for that purpose; but its chief object is to collect and preserve materials of history relating to western New York, and especially to Buffalo, for future use. . . . Its object is not to teach, but to preserve history."[9]

During Fillmore's time the Society did not shirk its collecting function. To the monthly meetings its members came bearing books, pamphlets, photographs, holographs, newspapers, relics — whatever they could collect from others or part with themselves.[10] Some contributions, no doubt, were castoffs, but the members treasured enough of them to seek safe, fireproof quarters. Early in January, 1863, Fillmore leased several rooms from a fellow member, William Dorsheimer. The Society also needed an operating fund, and the president came forth with the suggestion that fifty gentlemen bind themselves to "pay $20.00 each year for five years." It was accepted, and the plan set the Society on the road to fundamental health.[11]

In spite of protestations Fillmore could not hold himself merely to collecting "records and relics." His soul would not permit him to give up teaching. During his installation, with an audience before him that needed enlightenment, he tried to explain the origin of Buffalo's name. Considerable research had gone into this study, and he felt compelled to share his findings.[12] With this gesture, however, went the narrower goal of collect-

[8]Frank H. Severance, "The New Home of the Historical Society," Buffalo Historical Society *Publications*, 5:386-387; Buffalo *Morning Express*, March 24, March 27, April 16, May 22, 1862.
[9]*Fillmore Papers*, 2:70.
[10]Buffalo *Commercial Advertiser*, January 14, 1863; Buffalo *Morning Express*, February 14, March 14, April 20, 1863.
[11]Buffalo *Commercial Advertiser*, January 14, 1863.
[12]*Fillmore Papers*, 2:388ff.

ing, and the Society launched itself on a program of both studying and teaching history.

The group was scheduled to meet monthly in their "Rooms"
at No. 7 Court Street but such infrequent gatherings satisfied
neither his nor his associates' enthusiasm. They wanted to learn
more about their area. As a result in winter months they met
each week in someone's home in an informal "social." The
gathering came to be called the History Club, and each week at
least one member read a paper of his own writing to the group.
Some were reminiscences, others research papers. By this procedure little by little they either inspired or created almost all
the early historical writings of their city's past. By 1867 they
were involved in preparing a history of Erie County. In the
final reckoning these amateurs put together the story of pioneer
Buffalo.[13]

Like the other organizations the Historical Society outgrew
its rooms rapidly. When asked, therefore, to support the
Y.M.A.'s building program by becoming tenants in a new cultural center, neither Fillmore nor the society hesitated.[14] By the
fall of 1864 over eighty thousand dollars were raised, and the
Y.M.A. purchased the St. James Hotel on Main, Eagle, and
Washington Streets. Remodeled, it provided for a number of
years ample room not only for its own library, but those of the
Grosvenor, the Historical Society, the Fine Arts Academy, and
the Society of Natural Sciences. Three of Fillmore's favorite
institutions were now housed under one roof, and his work with
each was made more convenient. He continued, however, to
give the Historical Society more attention than the rest, at least
until 1867 when he gave up its presidency.

The association in a common building, meanwhile, involved him in the fate of the Grosvenor Library and the science
group. A New York merchant, Seth Grosvenor, who had once

---

[13]Buffalo *Morning Express*, February 13, 1862, December 9, 1865; Buffalo *Commercial Advertiser*, November 21, 1863, December 17, 1864, December 24, 1866,
January 15, 1867.
[14]*Ibid.*, October 17, 25, 1864.

lived in Buffalo, had bequeathed forty thousand dollars to the people of the city for a reference library. The fund, however, could not be used until Buffalonians made provision for paying the current expenses of the library once it was established. Finding housing in the Y.M.A. building helped to comply with the terms, and in 1865 the trustees received the money.

Here, while attending to the affairs of his other organizations, Fillmore gradually became involved in the library's growth. Then in 1870, when its board decided to relocate in its own quarters, he helped in the decision. That same year he became president of the group and remained on the board until his death, helping thus to lay a firm foundation for what would become one of the great reference libraries of the United States.

The Natural Sciences Society's interests were more esoteric than those of the other groups in the Y.M.A. building, and as a result Fillmore became only a casual member. When, however, it found itself in financial straits in 1868, he headed a rescue committee. The technique he employed had wide use in fund drives and was destined to become even more popular. He staged the "Grand Ball for Science." A newspaper man reported it as "the most recherché and elegant affair ever given in this city. . . . " It served its purpose. It brought together the rich and the not so rich and let rivaling values of *noblesse oblige* solve the society's problems.[15]

Fillmore's promotion of education found still another outlet. Back in the thirties, Buffalonians had tried to start a university but the panic of 1836 and subsequent depression had stopped them.[16] Ten years later a number of men, mostly physicians, had renewed the idea. Among these new promoters had been Fillmore, his editor-doctor friend, Thomas M. Foote, his former law partner, Nathan K. Hall, and the inheritor of his political machine in Buffalo, George R. Babcock.

At the time they could not meet the Regents' qualifications for a charter and had turned to the state legislature for help.

[15]*Ibid.*, February 14, 1868.   [16]*Fillmore Papers*, 2:45.

There Nathan K. Hall, serving as an assemblyman, had guided a special bill through the legislature chartering the University of Buffalo. The founders obtained the privilege of beginning a true university and envisioned one with an arts and science college, a law school, a theological division, and a medical school. Unable to create such an institution overnight they had started with what had been their prime object, a medical school, and assigned the rest to the future.

From this founding in 1846 to his death, Fillmore served as the university's chancellor. Strictly an honorary position, the post gave him practically one duty: to confer degrees upon candidates at commencements. He participated, however, in fund raising for constructing a two-and-one-half story brownstone building on the corner of Virginia and Main Streets. For the next forty-five years this structure served as the university.[17]

Though the medical school made rapid progress the hope for a complete university only slowly materialized. Though chancelor, Fillmore had no unique obligation to prod the university into other areas of higher learning. He was, however, alert to the need. At the commencement of 1847 he voiced his hopes of seeing "the academic department [liberal arts college] organized, and at the earliest possible moment. . . . " Such an institution, he continued, was "indispensable to the wants . . . of our city." "Why," he asked, "should a father be compelled to send his son to some eastern village or distant city to give him a liberal education? Can it be that this proud Queen City of the Lakes, into whose lap is poured the commercial wealth of eight states, cannot maintain a single college! Are our crowded wharves and glutted warehouses mere mockeries of wealth? No," he answered, "our numerous and costly temples for religious worship . . . show what . . . Buffalo can accomplish when its sympathies . . . are enlisted in a good cause. Then let me appeal to you on behalf of the University of Buffalo. . . . Will you see it perish, or will you step forward . . . and minister

17Buffalo *Commercial Advertiser*, September 18, December 7, 1849; Julian Park, "A History of the University of Buffalo," Buffalo Historical Society *Publications*, 22:37.

to its wants, and raise it from dependency to hope, from weakness to power, from childhood to manhood? If you will, be assured that you will establish an institution eminently useful to yourselves, which will become the pride and ornament of our city, and for which you will receive the grateful thanks and fervent blessings of unborn millions."[18]

Frequently the chancellor returned to the same theme,[19] but Buffalo's citizens did not respond. When he died after twenty-eight years in the chancellorship, the university still lacked a liberal arts college. Indeed it was still only a medical school, albeit a superior one. Fillmore might have been comforted in this failure could he have forseen that until 1886 no one could persuade Buffalonians to support the university's expansion in any direction, and the desired liberal arts school had to await the twentieth century.

*   *   *   *   *

His work with the medical college took him into the related hospital field. At the time the college was established Buffalo possessed no hospital. A movement that year to supply the deficiency failed, and eight years later another effort came to nought. In 1848, meanwhile, the Sisters of Charity made a beginning but Buffalo's needs far outstripped the Sisters' facilities. Public-spirited men and women made a third try in 1855, created a General Hospital Association, and brought about a successful subscription campaign. It resulted in the fall of 1855 in the incorporation of the Buffalo General Hospital, and by July, 1858, its building was ready.[20]

Fillmore participated in this movement both as a worker and a contributor. Of the many institutions with which he served, none had greater value to the city than the General Hospital. During the Civil War alone it ministered to over 1,200 sick and wounded soldiers. Fillmore's active support of the

18*Fillmore Papers*, 2:49.
19See Buffalo *Morning Express*, February 26, 1862, for example of another appeal.
20Larned, *Buffalo*, 2:109.

hospital culminated in 1870 in his election as president of its board of trustees.[21]

Meanwhile, his public affairs were not confined solely to bettering living conditions and promoting higher levels of thinking. As the city's "great public man" everyone with a worthwhile cause called upon him for help, needing his prestige. Sometimes they also asked for money; at other times they required his administrative or organizational ability. In 1862 he served on a committee to plan a festival to raise money for the relief of the "Starving People of the Emerald Isle."[22] The next year, in connection with the Sanitary Commission's Great Central Fair, he helped plan the "Old Settlers' Festival." Its success and appeal — bringing together old acquaintances — caused it to be continued for years thereafter as a means of raising money for other worthy causes. The Buffalo Orphan Asylum, to which Fillmore left a bequest, and the General Hospital were two of the many beneficiaries.[23] The 1867 "Old Settlers' Festival" brought back memories for Fillmore that cheered him. Part of the program was a reunion dinner of five of fourteen surviving pupils who attended the district school in East Aurora that he taught in the winters of 1821 and 1822.[24] In the same vein the promoters of a boys' school, knowing of his attachment for learning, had no trouble persuading him to accept a position on the board of trustees.[25]

Buffalo expected their ex-President to welcome all important visitors or delegations. When General William Tecumseh Sherman arrived in Buffalo in July 1866, Fillmore was on the welcoming committee. The next month the American Association for the Advancement of Science held its annual meeting in Buffalo, and the ex-President served on the local arrangement committee and made his home available to visitors. President Andrew Johnson came through Buffalo on his way west in the

[21] *Fillmore Papers*, 1:xxxiii.
[22] Buffalo *Morning Express*, January 18, February 18, 1862.
[23] Buffalo *Commercial Advertiser*, December 28, 1864, February 2, 1866, February 8, 1867.
[24] *Ibid.*, January 25, 1867.   [25] *Ibid.*, December 14, 1863.

summer of 1866. He was engaged in his famous "swing around the circle" to help elect Congressmen who shared his opinion about reconstruction goals. Though he favored Johnson's policy, Fillmore avoided the politics of that year's Congressional race. He nonetheless served as chairman of a welcoming committee to the President and his party.[26]

Several other Buffalo institutions were touched by his hand — one unsuccessfully. At a meeting sponsored by the Historical Society, in July of 1867, he became the chairman of an association formed to erect "a suitable monument to the heroic dead of Erie County" who had fallen in the Civil War. The group could not raise the needed five thousand dollars. Years later the Historical Society revived the idea, and in 1882 Buffalo finally got its Soldiers and Sailors Monument.[27] During 1867 he helped found the Buffalo Club and served as the first president. It limited its membership to 200 and was Buffalo's first purely social club to own its club house.[28]

Even the welfare of Erie County's animals received Fillmore's compassion. The local Society for the Prevention of Cruelty to Animals, organized in 1867, was the second of its kind in the United States. Fillmore readily admitted that Mrs. John C. Lord was the person "who had done more towards establishing the Society than all the rest together. . . . "[29] But he was an eager supporter of her work. Serving as chairman of a series of organizational meetings, he spoke out passionately for enforcing laws, long in existence, against mistreating animals. After incorporation he gladly accepted a vice-presidential post in the society, in order to have the names "of prominent citizens who . . . will give weight and influence to the organization." This was no passing sentiment. To his last days he was still aiding the group's work.[30]

*   *   *   *   *

[26]*Ibid.*, May 21, August 7, 15, 28, 29, 30, September 3, 1866.
[27]*Ibid.*, July 8, 1867; *Fillmore Papers*, 1:xxxiv-v.
[28]Buffalo *Commercial Advertiser*, January 5, 1867.
[29]*Ibid.*, April 5, 1867.
[30]*Ibid.*, March 6, 21, 22, 29, April 5, 1867; March 4, 1873.

As a man of leisure with a strong desire to spend his time in civic efforts Fillmore passed his remaining years. Month after month he made the rounds of his organizations. On their behalf he moved constantly through the streets, lobbies, offices, and homes of Buffalo, and wherever he went his shock of white hair and kindly bearing contributed to the atmosphere of calm dignity that always surrounded him. His townsmen treated him with respect, and occasionally a note of envy touched the glances that turned his way. It was a long cry from his youth when he spent his waking hours at the plow or in the wool-dyeing factory. He talked about those days freely and even wondered how it could all have happened to him.

Upon his personal world he could smile benignly. It had been kind to him and generous with its material and spiritual wealth. The years passed in unhurried, comfortable living. Even the long political struggle with Thurlow Weed that had turned to estrangement had a near-happy ending.

In the summer of 1869 at a Saratoga hotel he accidentally met Weed's daughter at the dinner table. Taking the initiative he suggested to Miss Weed that if he were sure it would be agreeable to her father he would call upon him in his rooms. On hearing this, Weed sought out Fillmore, and with scarcely a momentary reference to bygones, peace was restored after twenty years of hostile silence.[31] In all likelihood its was superficial, for Weed soon included in his own autobiography a malicious appraisal of his old rival.[32] Yet Fillmore would never see this account, and the pleasantness was not marred.

The working of time never bent his figure or fettered his steady step. Years before, when he was still a young Congressman, a legend had begun to grow among his neighbors that "Lady Luck" shadowed his steps through life. As he entered his seventies, the legend added his robust health to its list of proofs. "I have taken but one dose of medicine in thirty years,"

---

[31] *Weed, Autobiography,* 2:462.   [32] *Ibid.,* 1:585-588.

he told a friend, "and that was forced upon me unnecessarily."[33] Rather than "Lady Luck" probably the physical constitution of the men in the Fillmore family explained his good fortune. His father lived until 92, hearty except for the infirmity of age, and his uncle, Calvin, who had been Nathaniel's partner in their migration out of Vermont, passed on at 90 years of age.[34]

In these late years Mrs. Fillmore became a chronic invalid, and in 1866 she and Fillmore went to Europe for a few months for her health.[35] But as late as January 7, 1874 Fillmore could brag, with an old man's attention to health, " . . . My health is perfect, I eat, drink and sleep as well as ever, and take a deep but silent interest in public affairs, and if Mrs. F's health can be restored, I should feel that I was in the enjoyment of an earthly paradise."[36]

The heavenly paradise, however, was not far away. Five weeks later, on the morning of February 13, as he was shaving, his left hand suddenly fell powerless. The paralysis soon extended to the left side of his face. Two weeks later he had a second attack, and on March 8, the end came.

Two days later his body was taken from the mansion on Niagara Square. Hundreds of city notables, representing every organization he had nurtured in his half century of public service, followed the funeral procession out stately Delaware Avenue to Forest Lawn Cemetery. A tombstone — a stark obelisk of classic propositions — would eventually mark the grave and state simply:

Millard Fillmore
Born
January 7, 1800
Died
March 8, 1874

[33]*Fillmore Papers*, 1:xxxvi.
[34]Buffalo *Commercial Advertiser*, March 28, 1863, October 22, 1865.
[35]*Ibid.*, May 26, 1866.
[36]Fillmore to Corcoran, January 7, 1874, Fillmore Mss.

A later generation, better able to evaluate Fillmore's work when the passions of the era of sectional conflict had passed, erected a statue of their first citizen before the City Hall on Niagara Square. Beneficently it looked out over the community which he helped create and which shaped his destiny. Eloquently it spoke out part of the story of his life. In its stony coldness, however, it could not reveal the warmth and wisdom with which he had defended the Union.

Bibliography

Most of the materials intimately concerned with Fillmore are located at the Buffalo Historical Society. These consist of three separate collections. The major one is made up of approximately 8,500 pieces covering the years of his presidency and is identified in this book as the Fillmore Collection. The second most numerous group is made up of the materials published in two volumes as the *Millard Fillmore Papers* (F. H. Severance, ed.,) by the Buffalo Historical Society. Citations have been made to the published material wherever possible. The third group, which is identified here as the Fillmore Manuscripts, is a small collection of approximately 200 pieces collected since the *Papers* were published.

I. MANUSCRIPTS

Archives. (Buffalo Chancellory of the Roman Catholic Church)

Daniel D. Barnard Papers. (Albany State Library)

Luther Bradish Papers. (New York Historical Society)

Clayton Papers. (Library of Congress)

Thomas Corwin Papers. (Library of Congress)

Crittenden Papers. (Library of Congress)

Millard Fillmore Collection. (Buffalo Historical Society)

Fillmore Manuscripts. (Buffalo Historical Society)

Fillmore, Haven and Hall Letterbook. (Buffalo. Held privately by James Babcock.)

Hamilton Fish Letterbook. (University of Rochester Library)

Oran Follett Papers. (Ohio Archaeological and Historical Society)

Francis Granger Papers. (New York Historical Society)

Francis Granger Papers. (University of Rochester Library)

Grinnell, Minturn and Company Letterbook. (University of Rochester Library)

Gerrit Smith Miller Papers. (Syracuse University Library)

Edwin D. Morgan Papers. (Albany State Library)

Edwin D. Morgan Letterbook. (University of Rochester Library)

Peter B. Porter Papers. (Buffalo Historical Society)

William H. Seward Papers. (Formerly held by William H. Seward at Auburn, N. Y. Now housed at University of Rochester Library.)

Alexander H. H. Stuart Papers. (Library of Congress)

Thurlow Weed Papers. (University of Rochester Library)

II. GOVERNMENT DOCUMENTS

Civil List of the State of New York. Albany, 1887.

Congressional Globe. Washington, 1833-35, 1837-43, 1849-53.

New York State. Annual Report of the Comptroller. Albany, 1849.

New York State. Annual Report of the Canal Commissioners. Albany, 1827-1831.

New York State. Assembly Journal, 1829-31, 1848-49.

New York State. Senate Journal, 1829-31, 1848-49.

United States. House Documents. 61 cong., 2 sess., no. 671.

United States. Senate Documents. 32 cong., 2 sess., no. 13; 62 cong., 1 sess., nos. 21, 71, 72.

United States. Senate Executive Documents. 52 cong., 2 sess., no. 77.

III. NEWSPAPERS

Albany Argus, 1827-34, 1837, 1843-56.

Albany Evening Journal, 1830-1856.

Albany Daily Advertiser, 1828-31.

Albany National Observer, 1830.

Albany New York State Register, 1850-54.

Boston Christian Register, 1829.

Buffalo Commercial Advertiser, 1834-1874.

Buffalo Daily Courier, 1852.

Buffalo Express, 1829-30, 1846-74, 1882.

Buffalo Journal, 1828-34.

Buffalo Patriot, 1828-33.

Buffalo Republican, 1828-33.

Chicago Democrat, 1846-47, 1852.

De Bow's Review, 1849-53.

Louisville Journal, 1854.

448

Lowell Daily Courier, 1846.

New York Commercial Advertiser, 1856.

New York Courier and Inquirer, 1832-36, 1841-55.

New York Daily Advertiser, 1833.

New York Express, 1843-56.

New York Herald, 1848-56, 1873.

New York Journal of Commerce, 1844, 1850-56.

New York Post, 1835, 1848-49.

New York Times, 1854-56.

New York Tribune, 1841-56.

Niles Register, 1826-48.

Ohio State Journal, 1846, 1854-56.

Ohio Statesman, 1846, 1850-53.

Philadelphia Daily Sun, 1850-53.

Philadelphia North American, 1846.

Rochester Antimasonic Enquirer, 1828-33.

Rochester American, 1850.

Rochester Daily Advertiser, 1826-34.

Syracuse Daily Star, 1850-55.

Washington Madisonian, 1839-43.

Washington National Intelligencer, 1833-36, 1837-53.

Washington Republic, 1849-51.

Whig Review, 1848-52.

IV. BOOKS, PAMPHLETS, AND ARTICLES

Abernethy, Thomas P. "The Origin of the Whig Party in Tennessee." Mississippi Valley Historical Review, 12(1926):504-522.

Adams, Charles F., ed. Memoirs of John Quincy Adams: Comprising Portions of His Diary from 1795 to 1848. 12 vols. Philadelphia, 1877.

Adams, Charles F. Jr. Charles Francis Adams. Boston, 1900.

The Agitation of Slavery. Who Commenced and Who Can End It? Buchanan and Fillmore Compared from the Record. Washington, [1856].

Albion, R. G., The Rise of the Port of New York, 1815-1860, New York, 1939.

Alexander, De Alva S. Political History of the State of New York. 4 vols. New York, 1906.

Allen, Lewis F., "The Cholera in Buffalo in 1832," Buffalo Historical Society, Publications, 4(1896):245-256.

American and Foreign Christian Union. Fifth Annual Report. New York, 1855.

American Party. U. S. Senatorial Question. [Albany], 1855.

American Protestant Society. Sixth Annual Report. New York, 1849.

[Anon.] "The Influence of Manufacturing upon Political Sentiments in the United States from 1820-1860." American Historical Review, 22(1935): 58-64.

[Anon.] Life of Father Gavazzi. London, 1851.

[Anspach, Frederick, R.] The Sons of the Sires. Philadelphia, 1855.

Appleton, Nathan. Introduction of the Power Loom and the Origin of Lowell. Lowell, 1858.

---------- Labor, Its Relations in Europe and the U. S. Compared. Boston, 1844.

---------- "Memoir of Abbott Lawrence." Massachusetts Historical Society, Collections, sr. 4, 4(1858): 495-507.

---------- Remarks on Currency and Banking Having Reference to Present Derangement of Circulating Medium. Boston, 1841.

---------- Slavery and the Union, Letter from Hon. Nathan Appleton, of Boston to Hon. Wm. C. Rives of Virginia. Boston, [1860].

---------- What is a Revenue Standard? And a Review of Secretary Walker's Report on the Tariff. Boston, 1846.

---------- and Palfrey, John G. Correspondence between Nathan Appleton and John G. Palfrey Intended as a Supplement to Mr. Palfrey's Pamphlet on the Slave Power. Boston, 1846.

Appleton, William S. "The Whigs of Massachusetts." Massachusetts Historical Society, Proceedings, 39(1897): 3-7.

The Arrival, Reception and Speeches of Millard Fillmore from New York to Buffalo. New York, [1856].

Avary, Myrta Lockett, ed. Recollections of Alexander H. Stephens. New York, 1910.

Baker, George E., ed. Works of William H. Seward. 5 vols. Boston, 1884.

Bancroft, Frederick. Life of William H. Seward. 2 vols. New York, 1900.

Barnard, Daniel D. *Letters from the, addressed to James A. Hamilton, Esq., on the . . . state of parties, and in favor of Millard Fillmore for President.* Albany, 1856.

Barre, W. L. *The Life and Public Services of Millard Fillmore.* Buffalo, 1856.

Batchelder, Samuel. *Introduction and Early Progress of Cotton Manufacturing in the United States.* Boston, 1863.

Beeler, Dale. "The Election of 1852 in Indiana." *Indiana Magazine of History,* 11(1914):301-23, 12(1915): 34-52.

Benton, T. H. *Thirty Years' View.* 2 vols. New York, 1856.

Bigelow, Samuel A. "The Harbor-Makers of Buffalo: Reminiscences of Judge Samuel Wilkeson." Buffalo Historical Society, *Publications,* 4(1896):225-40.

Billington, Ray Allen. *The Protestant Crusade, 1800-1860.* New York, 1938.

Binkley, N. C. "The Question of Texan Jurisdiction in New Mexico under the United States, 1848-1850." *Southwestern Historical Quarterly,* 24(1920): 1-38.

Birney, William. *James G. Birney and His Times.* New York, 1890.

Boston Herald. *Commercial and Financial New England.* Boston, 1906.

Boucher, Chauncy S. "In Re that Aggressive Slaveocracy." *Mississippi Valley Historical Review,* 8(1922):27-108.

---------- "The Secession and Cooperative Movements in South Carolina, 1848-1852." *Washington University Studies,* 5(1928): no. 2.

Bradey, H. W. "The Hawaiian Islands and the Pacific Fur Trade. 1785-1813." *Pacific Northwest Quarterly.* 30(1939):275-99.

Bradlee, Rev. C. D. *Death and Resurrection.* Boston, 1874.

Branch, Douglas E. *The Sentimental Years, 1836-50.* New York, 1934.

Brand, Carl F. "The History of the Know-Nothing Party in Indiana." *Indiana Magazine of History,* 18(1922): 47-81, 177-206, 266-306.

Bretz, Julian P. "The Economic Background of the Liberty Party." *American Historical Review,* 34(1928): 250-64.

Brooks, Erastus. *Speech of, at Hartford, Conn., July 8, 1856. Mr. Fillmore's Claims on Northern Men and Union Men for the Presidency.* [n.p.], 1856.

Brooks, James. *Defense of Mr. Fillmore by Hon. James Brooks (of New York), before a Meeting of the American Party, Held at Cincinnati, Friday Evening, May 30, 1856.* New York, 1856.

Brown, Samuel G. *Life of Rufus Choate.* Boston, 1870.

Buckingham, J. S. *America, Historical, Statistical, and Descriptive.* London, 1841.

Bungay, George W. *Off-Hand Takings: or, Crayon Sketches of Noticeable Men of our Age.* New York, 1854.

Butler, William Allen. *A Retrospect of Forty Years, 1825-1865.* Edited by Harriet Allen Butler. New York, 1911.

Brummer, Sidney Davis. *Political History of New York During the Period of the Civil War,* (Columbia University Studies in History, Economics, and Public Law, vol. 39). New York, 1911.

Carlton, F. T. "The Workingmen's Party of New York." *Political Science Quarterly,* 22(1907):401-415.

Carroll, Anna Ella. *The Great American Battle.* New York, 1856.

Carroll, E. Malcolm. *Origins of the Whig Party.* Durham, 1925.

Catterall, R. C. H. *The Second Bank of the United States.* Chicago, 1903.

[Chamberlain, Ivory]. *Biography of Fillmore.* Buffalo, 1856.

Chapelle, H. I. *History of American Sailing Ships.* New York, 1935.

Chapman, Sydney J. *The Cotton Industry and Trade.* London, 1905.

Chase, Salmon P. *Diary and Correspondence of Salmon P. Chase,* (Annual Report of the American Historical Association, 1902, vol. 2). Washington, 1903.

Chitwood, Oliver P. *John Tyler: Champion of the Old South.* New York, 1939.

450

Church, Charles. *History of the Republican Party in Illinois, 1854-1912: with a Review of the Aggression of the Slave-power.* Rockford, Ill., 1912.

Claiborne, J. F. H. *Life and Correspondence of John A. Quitman.* 2 vols. New York, 1860.

Cluskey, N. W. *Political Text Book and Encyclopoedia.* Washington, 1857.

Cole, Arthur C. *Era of the Civil War, 1848-1870, (Centennial History of Illinois,* edited by Clarence W. Alvord, vol. 3) Chicago, 1922.

---------- "Nativism in the Lower Mississippi Valley." *Mississippi Valley Historical Association, Proceedings,* 6(1913):258-275.

---------- "The South and the Right of Secession in the Early Fifties." *Mississippi Valley Historical Review,* 1(1915)375-99.

--------- *Whig Party in the South.* Washington, 1913.

Coleman, Mrs. Chapman, ed. *The Life of John J. Crittenden.* 2 vols. Philadelphia, 1873.

Colton, Calvin, ed. *Works of Henry Clay: Comprising His Life, Correspondence and Speeches.* Federal Edition, 10 vols. New York, 1904.

Comegys, Joseph P. *Memoir of John M. Clayton, (Publications of the Historical Society of Delaware,* vol. 1). Wilmington, 1882.

Commons, John R. "Horace Greeley and the Working Class Origins of the Republican Party." *Political Science Quarterly,* 24(1909):468-488.

Constitutional Union Party. Boston, [n.d.].

C[ooke], J[oshua]. *Reminiscences of the Buffalo Bar of Sixty Years Ago.* Buffalo, 1907.

Copeland, Melvin Thomas. *The Cotton Manufacturing Industry of the United States, (Harvard Economic Studies,* vol. 7): Cambridge, 1923.

Coulter, E. Merton. "The Downfall of the Whig Party." *Kentucky Historical Society Register,* 22(1924):162-174.

Cralle, Richard K., ed. *Works of John C. Calhoun.* 6 vols. New York, 1854-1855.

Cross, Ira. "Origin, Principles, and History of the American Party." *Iowa Journal of History and Politics,* 6(1906):526-53.

Curtis, George Ticknor. *Life of Daniel Webster.* Boston, 1870.

Cutler, Carl C. *Greyhounds of the Sea.* New York, 1937.

Darling, Arthur B. *Political Changes in Massachusetts, 1824-48, A Study of Liberal Movements in Politics.* New Haven, 1925.

"A Davidson County Political Circular, 1843." *Tennessee History Magazine,* 5(1919):195-196.

Davis, Harold. *Economic Basis of the Whig Party in Ohio.* An unpublished doctoral dissertation, dated 1938, in the library of Western Reserve University.

Denman, Clarence P. *The Secession Movement in Alabama.* Montgomery, 1933.

Dennett, Tyler. *Americans in Eastern Asia.* New York, 1922.

Desmond, Humphrey J. *The Know-Nothing Party.* Washington, 1904.

Dodd, Dorothy. "The Secession Movement in Florida." *Florida History Society Quarterly,* 12(1919):3-19.

Dodd, William E. "A Fight for the Northwest, 1860." *American Historical Review,* 16(1910):774-788.

Donovan, Herbert D. A. *The Barnburners.* New York, 1925.

Dorgan, Maurice B. *History of Lawrence, Massachusetts, with War Records.* Cambridge, 1924.

Doty, Lockwood L. *A History of Livingston County, New York.* Geneseo, N. Y., 1876.

Duane, W. J. *Narrative and Correspondence Concerning the Removal of Deposits.* Philadelphia, 1838.

Dumond, Dwight L., ed. *Letters of James Gillespie Birney, 1831-1857.* 2 vols. New York, 1938.

Dyer, Oliver. *Great Senators of the United States Forty Years Ago.* New York, 1889.

Dwight, Theodore. *The Roman Republic of 1849; with Accounts of the Inquisition and the Siege of Rome.* New York, 1857.

Eiselen, Malcolm R. *The Rise of Pennsylvania Protectionism.* Philadelphia, 1932.

Evans, Paul D. *The Holland Land Company,* (Buffalo Historical Society, *Publications,* vol. 28). Buffalo, 1924.

Everett, Edward. *Orations and Speeches,* 4 vols., Boston, 1870-1878.

Facts for the People. Truth is Mighty and Will Prevail. [n.p., n.d.].

Faulkner, Harold. "Political History of Massachusetts, 1829-1851." *Commonwealth History of Massachusetts,* edited by A. B. Hart, 4:74-102. New York, 1930.

Fillmore, Millard. *Address and Suppressed Report of the Minority of the Committee on Elections in the New Jersey Case. . . .* Washington, 1840.

The Fillmore and Donelson Songster. New York, [1856].

Mr. Fillmore at Home; His Reception at New York and Brooklyn and Progress through the State, etc. Buffalo, 1856.

Fite, Emerson David. *The Presidential Campaign of 1860.* New York, 1911.

Flick, Alexander C., ed. *History of the State of New York.* 10 vols. New York, 1934.

Foner, Philip Sheldon. *Business and Slavery: The New York Merchants and the Irrepressible Conflict.* Chapel Hill, 1941.

Foik, Paul J. "Anti-Catholic Parties in American Politics, 1776-1860." American Catholic Historical Society, *Records.* 36(1925):41-69.

Franklin, Gladys. "The Know-Nothing Party in Connecticut." Clark University, *Abstracts of Dissertations and Theses.* Worcester, Mass., 1933.

Freedley, Edwin T. *Leading Pursuits and Leading Men: A Treatise on the Trades and Manufactures of the United States.* Philadelphia, 1856.

French, J. H. *Gazetteer of the State of New York.* Syracuse, 1860.

Fox, Dixon Ryan. "The Economic Status of the New York Whigs." *Political Science Quarterly,* 33(1918):501-518.

Frothingham, Paul R. *Edward Everett, Orator and Statesman.* Boston, 1925.

Fuess, C. M. *The Life of Caleb Cushing.* 2 vols. New York, 1923.

---------- *Daniel Webster.* 2 vols. Boston, 1930.

---------- *Rufus Choate, Wizard of the Law.* New York, 1928.

Fuller, John Douglas Pitts. *The Movement for the Acquisition of All Mexico, 1846-48,* (Johns Hopkins University Studies, sr. 54, no. 1). Baltimore, 1936.

Ferguson, Russell J., ed. "Minutes of the Young Men's Whig Association of Pittsburgh, 1834." *Western Pennsylvania Historical Magazine,* 19(1936):213-220.

Gammon, S. R. *The Presidential Campaign of 1832,* (Johns Hopkins University Studies). Baltimore, 1922.

Garrison, Wendell P. and Francis Jackson. *William Lloyd Garrison.* 4 vols. Boston, 1885.

Garrison, William L. *Fillmore and Sumner. A Letter from the Boston Journal,* Mar. 19, 1847. [n.p., n.d.].

Gates, Paul W. "A Fragment of Kansas Land History." *Kansas Historical Quarterly,* 6(1936):227-240.

Geiser, Karl F. "The Western Reserve in the Anti-slavery Movement, 1840-1850." Mississippi Valley Historical Association, *Proceedings,* 5(1912):73-98.

Goodwin, Daniel. *In Memory of Robert C. Winthrop.* Chicago, 1894.

Greeley, Horace. *Recollections of a Busy Life.* New York, 1868.

Green, Samuel A. *Memoir of Abbott Lawrence.* Boston, 1908.

Greer, James Kimmino. *Louisiana Politics, 1845-60.* Baton Rouge, 1929.

Griffis, William E. *Millard Fillmore.* Ithaca, 1915.

---------- "Millard Fillmore and his part in the Opening of Japan," Buffalo Historical Society, *Publications,* 9(1906):53-80.

Gwathmey, E. M. *John P. Kennedy.* New York, 1931.

Hale, Edward Everett. *William H. Seward.* Philadelphia, 1910.

Halstead, Murat. *Caucuses of 1860.* Columbus, 1860.

Hamilton, Holman, *Zachary Taylor,* 2 vols. Indianapolis, 1951.

452

Hamilton, James A. *Reminiscences.* New York, 1869.

Hamilton, Milton W. "Anti-Masonic Newspapers, 1826-34." Bibliographical Society of America, *Papers,* 32(1938): 71-86.

Hamilton, Thomas. *Men and Manners in America.* Edinburgh and London, 1843.

Hamlin, L. Belle, ed. "Selections from the Follett Papers." *Quarterly Publication of the Historical and Philosophical Society of Ohio,* 9(1914):69-100; 10(1915):1-33; 11(1916):1-35.

---------- "Selections from the William Greene Papers." *Quarterly Publication of the Historical and Philosophical Society of Ohio,* 13(1918):1-38; 14(1919):1-26.

Hammond, Jabez D. *History of the Political Parties in the State of New York.* 3 vols. Syracuse, 1852.

Harlow, Ralph V. "The Rise and Fall of the Kansas Aid Movement." *American Historical Review,* 41(1935): 1-25.

---------- *Gerrit Smith: Philanthropist and Reformer.* New York, 1939.

Hawks, F. L. *Narrative of the Expedition of an American Squadron to the China Seas and Japan.* New York, 1856.

Haymond, W. S. *Illustrated History of the State of Indiana.* Indianapolis, 1879.

Haynes, George H. "The Causes of Know-Nothing Success." *American Historical Review,* 3:67-82.

Hearon, Cleo. "Mississippi and the Compromise of 1850." Mississippi History Society, *Publications,* 16(1931).

Hewitt, Warren F. "Know-Nothing Party in Pennsylvania." *Pennsylvania History,* 2(1935):69-85.

Hill, Hamilton A. *Memoir of Abbott Lawrence.* Boston, 1884.

Hilliard, H. W. *Politics and Pen Pictures.* New York, 1892.

Holt, Edgar A. *Party Politics in Ohio, 1840-1850,* (Archeological and Historical Society of Ohio, *Publications,* vol. 1). Columbus, 1930.

Hone, Philip. *The Diary of Philip Hone, 1828-1851.* Edited by Bayard Tuckerman. New York, 1910.

Horton, John T., Williamson, Edward, Douglas, Harry S., *A History of Northwestern New York,* 3 vols. New York, 1943.

Howe, Daniel W. *Political History of Secession to the Beginning of the American Civil War.* New York, 1914.

Hughes, John. *The Complete Works of the Most Rev. John Hughes, D.D., Archbishop of New York.* 2 vols. New York, 1866.

Hughes, Sarah Forbes, ed. *Letters and Recollections of John Murray Forbes.* 2 vols. Boston, 1900.

Hunt, Washington. "Letter of W. Hunt to George Dawson." Massachusetts Historical Society, *Proceedings,* 53 (1897)57-58.

Hurt, Peyton. "Rise and Fall of the Know-Nothings in California." California History Society, *Quarterly,* 9(1930):16-49, 99-128.

Jackson, Andrew. *Correspondence.* 5 vols. Edited by J. J. Bassett. Washington, 1926-33.

Jackson, Samuel M., comp. "A Bibliography of American Church History, 1820-1893." *The American Church History Series,* 13 vols., 12:441-513.

Jameson, J. Franklin, ed. *Correspondence of John C. Calhoun,* (Annual Report of the American Historical Association of 1899, vol. 2). Washington, 1900.

Julian, George W. *Life of Joshua R. Giddings.* Chicago, 1892.

---------- *Political Recollections, 1840-1872.* Chicago, 1884.

Jenkins, John S. *History of Political Parties in New York to 1849.* Auburn, 1849.

---------- *Life of Silas Wright.* Auburn, 1874.

Johnson, Crisfield. *Centennial History of Erie County, New York. . . .* Buffalo, 1876.

Johnson, R. M. and Brown, W. H. *Life of Alexander H. Stephens.* Philadelphia, 1878.

Kendall, Amos. *Autobiography.* Boston, 1872.

Kennedy, John P. *Life of William Wirt.* 2 vols. Baltimore: 1834.

King, Ameda R. "Last Years of the Whig Party in Illinois, 1847 to 1856." Illinois State Historical Society. *Transactions,* 32(1925):108-54.

Knight, Thomas Arthur. *The Strange Disappearance of William Morgan.* Brecksville, O., 1932.

Kuykendall, R. S. *The Hawaiian Kingdom, 1778-1854.* Honolulu, 1935.

Lambert, Oscar D. *Presidential Politics in the United States, 1841-1844.* Durham, 1936.

Lance, William. *American Railroads; Their Origin, Progress and Value as Investments.* London, 1864.

Langford, Laura. *Ladies of the White House.* New York, 1881.

Larned, J. N. *A History of Buffalo,* 2 vols. New York, 1911.

----------, "Historical Sketch of the Buffalo Public Library," in Buffalo Historical Society, *Publications,* 5(1902): 361-376.

Latourette, K. S. *The History of Early Relations between the United States and China, 1784-1844.* New Haven, 1917.

Leonard, L. O. "The Know-Nothing Party in Des Moines County." *Annals of Iowa,* 3rd Ser., 19(1927):187-88.

Letters to the People, from Washington Hunt, Daniel D. Barnard, and Sam. Houston. Buffalo, [1856].

Levin, Lewis C. *The Union Safe. The Contest between Fillmore and Buchanan.* Philadelphia, 1856.

Lockey, J. B. "A Neglected Aspect of Isthmian Diplomacy." *American Historical Review,* 41(1936):305.

Lord, John C. "Samuel Wilkeson." Buffalo Historical Society, *Publications,* 4(1896):71-84.

Lynch, William O. "Anti-Slavery Tendencies of the Democratic Party in the North West, 1848-50." *Mississippi Valley Historical Review,* 11(1925): 319-331.

Mabee, Carleton. *The American Leonardo, A Life of Samuel F. B. Morse.* New York, 1943.

McCarthy, Charles. *The Antimasonic Party: A Study of Political Antimasonry in the United States, 1827-1840, (Annual Report of the American Historical Association, 1902).* Washington, 1903.

McCormac, Eugene I. *James K. Polk, Political Biography.* Berkeley, 1922.

McGehee, Montford. *Life and Character of the Hon. William A. Graham.* Raleigh, 1877.

McGrane, R. C., ed. *Correspondence of Nicholas Biddle, dealing with National Affairs, 1807-1844.* Boston, 1919.

McGuire, James K., ed. *The Democratic Party of the State of New York.* New York, 1905.

March, C. W. *Reminiscences of Congress.* New York, 1850.

Marrow, R. L. "The Liberty Party in Vermont." *New England Quarterly,* 2(1929):234-248.

Marryat, Frederick. *A Diary of America.* 2 vols. Philadelphia, 1839.

Martin, Thomas P. "The Upper Mississippi Valley in Anglo-American Anti-Slavery and Free Trade Relations: 1837-1842." *Mississippi Valley Historical Review,* 15(1929):204-220.

Martineau, Harriet. *Retrospect of Western Travel.* 2 vols. London, 1838.

Miller, David Hunter, ed. *Treaties and Other International Acts of the United States of America.* Washington, 1931-43.

Miller, Thomas Southworth. *The American Cotton System Historically Treated.* Austin, Tex., 1909.

Minnigerode, Meade. *The Fabulous Forties.* New York, 1924.

Morrow, Josiah, ed. *Life and Speeches of Thomas Corwin.* Cincinnati, 1896.

Morse, H. B., and MacNair, H. F. *Far Eastern International Relations.* Boston, 1931.

Morse, Samuel F. B. *Foreign Conspiracy.* New York, 1835.

---------- *Imminent Dangers,* New York, 1835.

Mueller, Henry R. *Whig Party in Pennsylvania, (Columbia University Studies,* vol. 10). New York, 1922.

Murray, Nicholas. *The Decline of Popery and Its Causes. An Address Delivered at the Broadway Tabernacle, January 15, 1851.* New York, 1851.

Myers, William Starr. *The Republican Party: A History.* New York, 1928.

Noonan, Carroll John. *Nativism in Connecticut, 1829-1860.* Washington, 1938.

Nevins, Allan. *Grover Cleveland, A Study in Courage.* New York, 1933.

Newhard, Leota. "The Beginning of the Whig Party in Missouri, 1824-40." *Missouri Historical Review,* 25 (1939): 254-280.

O'Driscoll, Sister M. Felicity. "Political Nativism in Buffalo, 1830-1860." American Catholic Historical Society of Philadelphia, *Records,* 48 (1937): no. 3.

Overdyke, W. Darrell. "History of the American Party in Louisiana." *Louisiana Historical Quarterly,* 15-16 (1932-33): 84-91, 256-277, 409-426. 581-588.

Palfrey, John G. *Papers on the Slave Power.* Boston, [1846].

Park, Julian. "History of the University of Buffalo." Buffalo Historical Society, *Publications,* 22 (1918): 1-88.

Pelzer, Louis. "The Disintegration and Organization of Political Parties in Iowa, 1852-1860." Mississippi Valley Historical Association, *Proceedings,* 5 (1912): 158-166.

---------- "History of Political Parties in Iowa, from 1852 to 1860." *Iowa Journal of History,* 7 (1908): 179-229.

---------- "The History and Principles of the Whigs of the Territory of Iowa." *Iowa Journal of History,* 5 (1906): 493-533.

Phillips, Ulrich B., ed. *Correspondence of Robert Toombs, Alexander H. Stephens, and Howell Cobb, (Annual Report of the American Historical Association,* vol. 2, 1911), Washington, 1913.

---------- *The Southern Whigs, 1834-1854.* New York, 1910.

Pierce, Edward L. *Memoir and Letters of Charles Sumner.* 4 vols. Boston, 1894.

Plunkett, Margaret L. "A History of the Liberty Party with Emphasis upon its Activities in the New England States." Cornell University, *Abstracts of Ph.D. Thesis.* Ithaca, 1930.

Poage, George. *Henry Clay and the Whig Party.* Chapel Hill, 1936.

Poole, Martha E. "Social Life of Buffalo in the '30's and '40's." Buffalo Historical Society, *Publications,* 8 (1905): 439-494.

Poore, Benjamin Perley. *Perley's Reminiscences of Sixty Years in the National Metropolis.* 2 vols. Washington, 1886.

Porter, George Henry. *Ohio Politics during the Civil War Period.* New York, 1911.

Principles and Objectives of the American Party. New York, 1855.

Proceedings and Debates of the Virginia Convention of 1829-1830. Richmond, 1830.

Proceedings at Celebration of the Fiftieth Anniversary of the Birth of the Republican Party, at Jackson, Michigan, July 6, 1904: together with a History of the Republican Party in Michigan. Detroit, 1904.

Proceedings of Anti-Masonic Republican Convention of the County of Cayuga, held at Auburn, Jan. 1, 1830. Auburn, 1830.

Proceedings of the Genesee Synod, September 30, 1829. [n.p.], 1829.

Proceedings of the Oneida Synod of February, 1820. [n.p.], 1831.

Proceedings of the Whig State Convention Held at Springfield, Massachusetts, September 10, 1851. [Springfield, 1851].

Putnam, James O. "Nathan Kelsey Hall." Buffalo Historical Society, *Publications,* 4 (1896): 285-298.

Quaife, Milo M. ed. *Diary of James K. Polk, during his Presidency, 1845-1848,* 4 vols. New York, 1910.

Quincy, Josiah. *Whig Policy Analyzed and Illustrated.* Boston, 1856.

Rapp, Marvin A., *The Port of Buffalo, 1825-1880,* unpublished doctoral dissertation, dated 1939, in the library of Duke University.

Raum, Green Berry. *History of Illinois Republicanism.* Chicago, 1900.

Rayback, Joseph G. *Presidential Politics, 1845-1848.* Unpublished doctoral dissertation, dated 1939, in the library of Western Reserve University.

Reeves, Jesse S., ed. "Letters of Gideon J. Pillow to James K. Polk, 1844." *American Historical Review,* 11(1905): 832-43.

Read! Digest! Act! A few facts or reasons why or for whom I may vote!!! by a New York Merchant. . . . [New York, 1856].

A Report of the Proceedings at an Entertainment . . . by . . . George Peabody. . . . [London, 1855].

Richardson, James D., comp. *A Compilation of the Messages and Papers of the Presidents.* 10 vols. Washington, 1903.

Rose, James A. "The Regulators and Flatheads in Southern Illinois." Illinois History Library, *Publications,* 11(1907):108-21.

Russel, Robert R., *Improvement of Communications with the Pacific Coast as an Issue in American Politics, 1783-1864,* Cedar Rapids, Iowa, 1948.

---------- "The Pacific Railroad Issue in Politics Prior to the Civil War." *Mississippi Valley Historical Review,* 12(1926):187-200.

Salisbury, Guy H. "The Speculative Craze of 1836." Buffalo Historical Society, *Publications,* 4(1896):398.

Sargent, Nathan. *Public Men and Events.* 2 vols. Philadelphia, 1875.

Schafer, Joseph. "Know-Nothingism in Wisconsin." *Wisconsin Magazine of History,* 8(1924):3-21.

Schmeckebier, Lawrence F. *History of Know-Nothing Party in Maryland,* (Johns Hopkins University Studies in History and Political Science, vol. 17). Baltimore, 1899.

Schouler, James. "Whig Party in Massachusetts." Massachusetts Historical Society, *Proceedings,* 50(1916):39-53.

Scisco, Louis D. *Political Nativism in New York State,* (Columbia University Studies in History, Economics, and Public Law, vol. 13). New York, 1901.

Selby, Paul. "Genesis of the Republican Party in Illinois." Illinois History Library, *Publications,* 11(1907):270-283.

Severance, Frank H., ed. *Millard Fillmore Papers.* 2 vols. (Buffalo Historical Society, *Publications,* vols. 10, 11). Buffalo, 1907.

---------- "Historical Sketch of the Board of Trade." Buffalo Historical Society, *Publications,* 13(1909):237-331.

---------- "Notes on the Earlier Years." Buffalo Historical Society, *Publications,* 5(1902):385-389.

Seward, Frederick W., ed. *William H. Seward: An Autobiography.* New York, 1891.

Sharp, Walter R. "Henry S. Lane and the Formation of the Republican Party in Indiana." *Mississippi Valley Historical Review,* 7(1921):43-112.

Shepperman, Alfred B. *Cotton Facts, a Compilation from Official and Reliable Sources.* . . . New York, 1890.

Shryock, Richard. *Georgia and the Union in 1850.* Durham, 1926.

Simms, Henry Harrison. *The Rise of the Whigs in Virginia, 1824-1840.* Richmond, 1929.

Siterson, J. C. *The Secession Movement in North Carolina.* Chapel Hill, 1939.

Sketch of the lives and public service of General Zachary Taylor and Millard Fillmore. [n.d., n.p.].

Smith, H. Perry. *History of the City of Buffalo and Erie County.* 2 vols. Syracuse, 1884.

Smith, Joseph P., ed. *History of the Republican Party in Ohio.* 2 vols. Chicago, 1898.

Smith, T. C. *The Liberty and Free-Soil Party in the Northwest.* New York, 1897.

---------- *Parties and Slavery, 1850-1859.* New York, 1906.

The Speeches of Philip A. Bolling in the House of Delegates of Virginia on the Policy of the State in Relation to her Colored Population. . . . Richmond, 1832.

The Speeches of Thomas Marshall . . . in the House of Delegates. . . . Richmond, 1832.

Stanwood, Edward. *History of the Presidency.* Boston and New York, 1898.

Steiner, Bernard. "Some Letters from the Correspondence of James Alfred Pearce." *Maryland Historical Magazine*, 16(1921):150-178.

Stephens, Alexander H. *A Constitutional View of the Late War Between the States*. 2 vols. Chicago, 1868-70.

Stickney, Charles. "Know-Nothingism in Rhode Island." *Rhode Island Historical Society, Publications*, 1(1894): 243-257.

Stocking, William. *History of the Republican Party in Michigan*. Detroit, 1904.

Stoddard, William. *Zachary Taylor, Millard Fillmore, Franklin Pierce, James Buchanan*. New York, 1888.

Stone, W. L. *History of Masonry and Anti-Masonry*. New York, 1832.

Stovall, P. A. *Robert Toombs: Statesman, Speaker, Soldier, Sage*. New York, 1892.

Streeter, Floyd B. *Political Parties in Michigan, 1837-1860*. Lansing, 1918.

Strohm, Isaac, ed. *Speeches of Thomas Corwin, with a Sketch of His Life*. Dayton, Ohio, 1859.

Sumner, Charles. *Works of Charles Sumner*. 15 vols. Boston, 1875.

Swisher, C. B. *Roger B. Taney*. New York, 1935.

Tappan Correspondence, Journal of Negro History, 12(1927).

Taylor, William A. *Hundred Year Book and Ohio Statesman, from 1788 to 1892 Inclusive*. Columbus, 1892.

Thompson, Charles Manfred. *The Illinois Whigs Before 1846, (University of Illinois Studies in the Social Sciences)*. Urbana, 1915.

Thompson, Richard W. "Letter of a Conservative Indiana Whig of 1848." *Indiana Magazine of History*, 31 (1935):251-254.

Treat, Payson J. *Diplomatic Relations Between the United States and Japan, 1853-1895*. 2 vols. Stanford U., 1932.

Tribute to the Memory of the Hon. R. C. Winthrop by the Trustees of the Peabody Education Fund. [n.p., 1895].

Tuska, Benjamin. "Know-Nothingism in Baltimore, 1854-1860." *Catholic Historical Researches*, n.s. 5(1909):217-251.

Tyler, Lyon G. *Letters and Times of the Tylers*. 3 vols. Richmond and Williamsburgh, 1884-1896.

Van Alstyne, R. W. "Central American Policy of Lord Palmerston, 1846-1848." *Hispanic American Review*, 16(1936):352-57.

---------- "British Diplomacy and the Clayton-Bulwer Treaty, 1850-56." *Journal of Modern History*, 9(1939): 157-164.

---------- "Great Britain and the United States and Hawaiian Independence." *Pacific Historical Review*, 4(1935): 15-25.

Van Buren, Martin. *Autobiography*. Edited by J. C. Fitzpatrick. *(Annual Report of the American Historical Association, 1918)*. Washington, 1919.

---------- and Bancroft, George. "The Van Buren-Bancroft Correspondence, 1830-1845." *Massachusetts Historical Society, Proceedings*, 3rd sr., 2:381-442.

Van Deusen, Glyndon G. *Henry Clay*. New York, 1935.

---------- "Thurlow Weed in Rochester." *Rochester History*, April, 1940.

---------- *Thurlow Weed, Wizard of the Lobby*. Boston, 1947.

Van Tyne, Claude H., ed., *Letters of Daniel Webster*. New York, 1902.

Walker's Statesman's Manual. *Life of Ex-president Fillmore*. New York, 1856.

Webster, Daniel. "Letters of Daniel Webster, 1844-1851." *Massachusetts Historical Society, Proceedings*, 45: 159-165.

---------- *Writings and Speeches of Daniel Webster*. National Edition, 18 vols. Boston, 1903.

Weed, Thurlow. *Life of Thurlow Weed including his Autobiography and a Memoir*. 2 vols. Boston, 1883-4.

Whitney, Thomas R. *A Defense of the American Party*. New York, 1856.

Williams, M. W. *Anglo-American Isthmian Diplomacy, 1815-1915*. Washington, 1911.

Willis, N. P. *Hurry-Graphs: or, Sketches of Scenery, Celebrities and Society.* Detroit, 1851.

Wilson, Henry. *History of the Rise and Fall of the Slave Power in America.* 3 vols. Boston and New York, 1874.

Wilson, James Grant. *Presidents of the United States.* [n.p.], 1902.

---------- "Traits of Mr. Fillmore." *The Home Journal.* June, 1874.

Winden, Julius. *The Influence of the Erie Canal upon the Population along Its Course.* Unpublished Ph.D. thesis in library of the University of Wisconsin, 1900.

Winston, James E. "The Mississippi Whigs and the Tariff, 1834-44." *Mississippi Valley Historical Review,* 22 (1936):505-524.

---------- "The Mississippi Whigs and the Annexation of Texas." *South West Historical Quarterly,* 29(1935): 161-180.

Winthrop, Robert C. *Addresses and Speeches on Various Occasions.* 4 vols. Boston, 1852-1886.

---------- *Memoir of the Hon. Nathan Appleton.* Boston, 1861.

Winthrop, Robert C. jr. *A Memoir of Robert C. Winthrop.* Boston, 1897.

---------- *A Short Account of the Winthrop Family.* Cambridge, 1887.

---------- "Tribute to the Memory of Robert C. Winthrop." Massachusetts Historical Society, *Proceedings,* Boston, 1894.

Wise, Henry A. *Seven Decades of the Union.* Philadelphia, 1876.

Wyeth, Newton. *Republican Principles and Politics.* Chicago, 1916.

Zimmerman, Charles. "The Origin and Rise of the Republican Party in Indiana from 1854-1860." *Indiana Magazine of History,* 13(1917):211-69, 349-410.

Index

A

Abolition, *see* Slavery

Adams, John Quincy, 62, 128, 395; up for re-election, 20, 21-24; no electoral votes, 58; leader of Antimasons in Massachusetts, 81; chairs committee charging Tyler with "executive usurpation," 132; defends right of petition, 153; "conscience" Whig, 174; quoted on Fillmore, 147

Albany *Evening Journal*, 36, 63, 109, 153, 211, 255, 279, 280, 281, 285

Albany Regency, 28-29, 35, 73, 74, 77, 90, 102, 103, 106

Albany *Register*, 21; *see also* New York State *Register*

Allen, Charles, 184; founded Order of the Star Spangled Banner, 343, 379

Allen, Lewis F., 92

Allen, Levi, 204, 213, 257

Allison, J. S., 191

American Anti-Slavery Society, 141

American Party, *see* Native American Party

American and Foreign Christian Union, 343, 376, 378

American Republican Party, 139

Anticlericalism and conflict of church and state, *see* Religion

Antimasonic Party, 5; origins, 16-19, 22; growth, 23, 27-28, 29, 31, 33; decline 58-68 *passim*, 66, 80-81, 82, 88, 106, 257, 402

Anti-Rent Party, 166, 167

Antislavery, *see* Slavery

Appleton, Nathan, 129, 164, 174; quoted on trade, 181

Arista, President of Mexico, 308

Ashburton, Lord, 144, 146

Ashmead, John W., 349-350

Ashmun, George, 341

Aulick, Commodore, 314-315

B

Babcock, George, 168; special emissary for Fillmore, 283, 285, 286; quoted on Scott's chance for nomination, 352; campaign manager for Fillmore, 355, 358; quoted on Fillmore's political future, 370-371; Buffalo politician, early interest in University of Buffalo, 438

Baker, James W., 380

Bank of the United States, 69, 71-73, 75, 83n, 123; bill for Third or "Fiscal" Bank, 119-121

Banks, Nathaniel P., 404

Barnard, Daniel Dewey, 61, 258; connection with nativists, 390; quoted on politics in New York State, 403

Barnburners, radical wing of New York Democrats; control of state canal board, 278

Barney, John, 358, 360

Barstow, Gamaliel, 30

Barton, James L., 164

Bates, Edward, 245

Bates, William, 340

Bedini, Cardinal, 389-390

Beekman, James W., 283, 284

Bell, John, Whig Senator from Tennessee, 120, 236, 365n, 413; compromise scheme, 223, 232

Bell, John, Governor of Texas, 249, 250; vowed to uphold Texas' claim, 234; *see also* Texas

Bennett, Philander, 15

Benjamin, Judah P., 306-309

Benson, A. G., 318, 320

Benton, Thomas Hart, 219, 404

Berrien, John M., 121, 128

Biddle, Nicholas, 71, 72, 74, 75, 77, 81, 82-83, 83n, 95; *see also* Bank of the United States

Bigelow, John, 404

Birney, James J., 142, 152

Bokee, D. A., 182, 320, 325, 342, 344

Botts, John Minor, 121, 128, 132

Boycott, southern against New York market, 225, 262

Bradish, Luther, 98, 99, 148, 150

Branch, Judge, 241

Brooks, Erastus, 342, 381, 390

Brooks, James, 182, 320, 381

Brooks, Preston S., 410-411

Brown, John, 410, 411

Bryant, William Cullen, 404

Buchanan, James, 419; candidate for President 411-413; election victory, 414; criticized by Fillmore for failure to stop recession, 422

Buel, Jesse, 30

Buffalo, in 1818, 11; in 1822, 11-12; booming village, 41-43; cholera, 47; incorporated as a city, 48; free schools, 54-55; Bank of United States in, 73; financial panic, 91, 93; gun runners, 107-108; importance as a lake and canal port, 163, 172; University, 161, 438-440; Board of Trade, 432; Fine Arts Academy, 435; Society of Natural Science, 435, 438; Historical Society, 435-437, 442; libraries, 434-435, 437-438; Young Men's Association, 434-435, 437; General Hospital Association, 440-441; commercial advantages extolled by Fillmore, 433-434

Buffalo *Commercial Advertiser*, 87, 113, 333, 349, 428

Buffalo *Journal*, 61, 87

Buffalo *Patriot*, 67; became *Commercial Advertiser*, 87

Bush, John T., 211-212, 284, 285, 333, 345

Butler, Andrew Pickens, 239, 410

C

Calhoun, John C., quoted on Southern disunionists, 217; quoted on Democratic unity, 353

California, 193, 200, 205, 207, 208, 214, 215, 218-223 *passim*, 231, 233-235, 250, 252, 275, 276, 296, 321

Canada, nationalist revolt, 107-108

Canal fund, *see* New York State, canal system

Caroline affair, 144

Cass, Lewis, 191, 239

Castle Garden Meeting, *see* Union Committee

Catholic politics, *see* Religion

Chambers, E. P., 365n

Charleston, 274-275

Charleston *Mercury*, 135

Chase, Salmon P., 153, 383, 389

China Trade, *see* Trade, foreign

Choate, Rufus, 358, 360

Church and state, conflict of, *see* Religion

Clark, Myron, 393

Clary, Joseph, 12, 13, 40, 48n, 50, 51, 92

Clay, Henry, 98, 239; Masonic affiliation, 59; nomination for presidency (1824, 1828) 62, 63; presidential race of 1836, 86, 90; presidential race of 1839, 105-110; struggle for Whig party leadership, 116-118; efforts to break Tyler, 118-122; sought nomination in 1844, 129, 148, 151; final effort to obtain nomination, 176, 177, 183, 185; program for compromise, 219-221, 223, 226, 230-233, 235, 248; quoted on annexation of Texas, 152; quoted on compromise resolutions, 220; quoted on Fillmore, 350-351.

Clay, James B., 412, 413

Clayton, John N., 175, 199; sought self-perpetuation in office, 194; strategy with regard to territories, 200; New York patronage, 201-202; Secretary of State, 297-298

Clayton-Bulwer Treaty, 298, 302, 304

Cleveland, Grover, 55

Clinton, Dewitt, 21-22, 30, 31

Clipper ships, 298-299, 312

Cobb, Howell, 209-210, 222, 276

"Coffeehouse letter," 121

Collier, John A., 190; candidate for governor, 148-149, 150, 151-152, 154, 182; nominated Fillmore Vice-President, 185-186; sought senatorship, 186, 195; recommended by Fillmore, 204

Collins, Robert, 272-273

Committee of Safety, *see* Union Committee

Committee of Seventy, *see* National Republican Party

Compromise proposals, 219-221, 222-223; *see also* Omnibus Bill, Compromise of 1850

Compromise of 1850, 254, 255, 259-264 *passim*, 273-274, 276-278, 280-282, 284, 285, 289, 290, 334, 345, 351, 356-357, 367, 370, 372, 383, 421

Conrad, Charles Magill, 235; Secretary of War in Fillmore's cabinet, 245, 316, 324

Conkling, Roscoe, 309

Cook, Bates, 104

Coombs, Leslie, 349

Copperheads, 429

Corwin, Thomas, 176; Secretary of the Treasury in Fillmore's cabinet, 244, 279, 335, 387

Costa Rica, 303-304

Crary, John, 63

Crawford, William H., 205

Crittenden, John J., Governor of Kentucky and southern Whig, 175-176; Attorney General in Fillmore's cabinet, 236, 244, 252, 270; quoted on Fillmore, 335; campaigned for Fillmore in 1856, 413

Crittenden, Thomas, 176

Crofts, William and Ellen, 272-273

Cuba, 321-325

Cushing, Caleb, 135n, 295, 412

D

Dallas, George, 196

Davis, Charles A., 411

Davis, George, quoted on Fillmore's chances for re-election, 371

Davis, Matthew, 30

Dawson Proviso, 249-250

Day, Hiram C., 57

De Bow's Review, 314

Debt, imprisonment for, 37; law taxing payment to nonresident creditors, 88-89

Deflation of 1833, 77-78

Democratic Party, 25, 70, 101, 111, 115, 130, 132, 152, 156, 157, 221-222, 337, 341, 342, 345, 353, 357, 384-385, 389, 390, 391, 393, 401, 404, 405, 409, 411, 419, 421, 430; Barnburners, 278; Hunker, 345, 345n; Locofocos,

28; "Nationals," 215, 216-218, 382; New York City, 76, 80, 157, *see also* Tammany Hall; New York State, 25, 28-29, 70, 73-74, 97-98, 145, 169, 278, *see also* Albany Regency; southern, 178, 207-208, 215, 216-217, 218

Devins, Marshal, 272-273

Dickinson, Daniel S., 281, 283

Distribution, 94, 96, 125, 129, 131, 132

Dix, John A., 195

Dixon, Archibald, 383

Donelson, Andrew, 404, 413

Dorsheimer, William, 436

Doty, James, 221, 222

Douglas, Stephen A., personal qualities, 221; compromise plan, 221-222, 232, 233, 246; leader of Democratic "Nationals," 248; renewed efforts for compromise, 250; federal land grants for railroads, 294; Kansas-Nebraska bill, 383-384, 389

Dow, Neal, 291

Dred Scott decision, 419

Dudley, Charles E., 77

Duer, William, statement of Whig position on Compromise, 259

E

East Aurora, N. Y., 10, 13, 14, 15, 20, 34

England, *see* Great Britain

Erie Canal, *see* New York State, canal system

Erie County, 1, 12, 23, 24, 25, 31, 35, 81-82, 104, 166, 388, 437

Erie Railroad, 289

Ewing, Thomas, 120, 199, 244

Everett, Edward, lead Antimasons, 81; in Congress, 129; Secretary of State, 316, 328, 365, 370; quoted on Cuba, 326; supported Fillmore for re-election, 338, 371

F

Field, Cyrus W., 225

Fillmore, Abigail Powers, 7, 14, 43-44, 160, 254, 373-374

Fillmore, Calvin, 3, 444

462

Fillmore, Caroline C. McIntosh, 416-418

Fillmore, Mary Abigail, 47, 160, 171, 254, 394

Fillmore, Millard, parentage and birth, 2-3; boyhood on a frontier farm, 4; apprenticeship, 5-6; struggle for an education, 6; opportunity to study law, 7-10; obtained needed funds teaching school, 9, 10, 12; clerkship in Buffalo law firm, 12; early law practice in East Aurora 13-15; marriage, 14; personal qualities, 36, 38, 53; success as a lawyer 50-53, 55-57, 69, 92-93; moved into Antimasonic politics, 23-24, 33; New York state assemblyman, 1, 25, 33-35; headed for party leadership, 35-36; sponsored state bankruptcy law and law abolishing imprisonment for debt, 37-39; moved family to Buffalo, 40; joined Unitarian Church, 45-46; active in life and growth of Buffalo, 43-44, 47-49, 50; first term in Congress, 50, 64, 69, 71, 73-76, 81-82, 85; sponsored bill to eliminate test oaths from court, 66-67; position on separation of church and state, 66; worked toward building a new party, 65-68, 70-71, 75-76, 85-89; condemned New York state bank practices, 74; position on Biddle and the Bank of the United States, 75, 96n; speech against the general appropriation bill, 76; Antimason turned Whig, 82; supported Harrison for President, 87, 90; effort to strengthen Whig party in western New York, 87-88, 89; interest in western New York lands, 85, 88-89; accepted Whig nomination for Congress, 89; second term in Congress, 94-97; attitude toward antislavery, 101; campaign and re-election to Congress, 100-102; declined state comptrollership, 103; reluctance to support Clay, 106; weighed possible Whig candidates, 106, 110; urged defense measures against Great Britain, 108; member of Committee on Elections in New Jersey election case, 110-114; chairman of Ways and Means Committee, 122-136; efforts for Tariff of 1842, 130-136; decision to retire from Congress, 136; concern for condition of Whig party in New York state,

142-143; returned to law practice, 146-147; declined nomination to Congress, 146; sought Vice-Presidential nomination 147-151; stand on abolition, 152-153, 155; nominated for governor of New York, 154; gubernatorial campaign, 157-158; defeated, 158-159; position on nativism, 156; failure to obtain the foreign vote, 158; home life in Buffalo, 160-161; effort for Whig party unity, 166-168; elected state comptroller, 168-170; terminated law practice, 170-171; efforts for Erie Canal enlargement and improvement of the Buffalo basin, 172; administrative ability, 177; effort in national campaign of 1848, 186-187, 189; saved unity of Whig party in New York state, 189-191; nominated for Vice-President, 185-186; lack of contact with Taylor, 196-197; inaugurated Vice-President, 197-199; political prestige undermined by Weed and Seward, 201-205; obliged to fight for his political life against Weed, 210-213, 224-225, 227-228; Vice-Presidential problems, 232, 235, 236-237; political relationship with Taylor, 213-214, 237.

Became President 238-240; faced a critical national situation, 241; cabinet appointments, 242-246; his solution of the compromise issue, 247-253; signed the Fugitive Slave Act, 252; resolved that the nation must be freed from sectional discord, 256; pursued a policy of restraint and magnanimity toward political enemies, 255-259, 263, 335, 335n, 336n; political policy to protect the Compromise of 1850, 263-267; further efforts to promote sectional peace, 268, 270-277, 289; struggled with problem of enforcing the Compromise, 270-286; success of policy for sectional peace, 286-288; effort to divert national attention to other channels, 289-290; policy for sectional peace resulted in national prosperity, 290-292; his foreign policy based on honorable promotion of American interests abroad, 293-299, 300-309, 318n; policy with respect to the Hawaiian Islands, 310-312; policy with respect to the Japanese Islands, 312-317; policy with respect to commercial interests in the Lobos Islands, 317-321; non-expansionist policy with respect to Cuba, 321, 323-327; policy on the problem of Louis Kossuth and Hungarian freedom, 329-332; summary of his administration policies and objectives, 332, 346; decision to withdraw from Presidential race of 1852, 334, 337, 341, 346; effort to aid Webster's campaign for nomination, 341; attempt to keep Whig party alive, 344-346; faced major difficulties in withdrawing his candidacy, 346-348, 349-350; reluctant decision to seek nomination in order to prevent discord, 354, 357-361, *passim;* unperturbed by failure to gain nomination, 361-362; convinced that nothing can now save the Whig party, 363; last days in office, 364; made cabinet changes, 364-365; faced the problems of retirement, 366-367, 372; his last state-of-the-union message, 367-370; his retirement from political life protested, 370-372; participation in inauguration of Franklin Pierce, 372-374.

Death of Mrs. Fillmore, 374; his return to private life, 385-386; his southern trip, 386-387, 388, 389; his western trip, 388-389, 390; foresaw political possibilities of nativism, 391-393; returned to public life, sought Presidential nomination, 394-396; death of his daughter, 394; journeyed abroad, 396-400; welcomed enthusiastically on his return from Europe, 405-406; his campaign of 1856, 406-409, 411-413; defeated by Buchanan, 413-414; considered his political career at an end, 415-416; second marriage, 416-418; his concern for the Union, 418-422, 423-424; host to President-elect Lincoln, 423; organized Union Continentals, 424-426; concern for the safety of Buffalo and the Niagara frontier, 426; his anti-Republicanism, 423, 427-430; first citizen of Buffalo, 423, 431-445.

Quoted on Henry Clay, 73, 86-87; on state appropriation bill, 76; on Daniel Webster, 87; on Hugh Lawson White, 87; on "political banks," 95, 96; on proposed free banking system, 103; on political appointments, 103, 105; on the problem of selecting candidates, 106-107, 108; on protection of industry, 126-127; on John Tyler, 143; on his reluctance to run for governor, 150-151, 154; on the annexation of Texas, 153; on the constitution in respect to legislation for the Great Lakes, 162; on the Polk administration, 162; on the veto of the river and harbors bill, 164; on slavery and states rights, 187; on the Omnibus Bill, 235, 237; on putting national loyalty above regional loyalty, 241; on the Texas boundary dispute, 251; on nullification, 270; on slavery 271; on safeguarding the liberty of free Negroes, 277; on national expansion of trade and transportation, 293-294, 300; on extending means of intercourse with foreign countries, 300; on the importance of the Hawaiian Islands, 310; on the problem of Cuba, 326-327; on the great responsibility to keep sectional peace, 334; on the effects of slavery, 368; on proposals for the solution of the slavery problem, 369; on the foreign vote, 395; on nativism, 396; on sectionalism, 406, 407; on the separation of church and state, 407; on the Kansas-Nebraska bill, 407; on the plight of retired Presidents, 416; on the Civil War, 427-428; on the Republican party and the Union, 421; on the sovereignty of the general government, 422; on Buffalo's future, 423-424.

Political relationship with Henry Clay, 106, 117, 121-122, 185-186, 350-351.

Political relationship with William H. Seward, 98-100, 100-101, 102, 104-105, 160, 199, 201-202, 339-340.

Political relationship with Thurlow Weed, 85-87, 98, 102-105, 108, 109, 146, 148-154, 160, 165-168, 177-178, 180-181, 189-191, 201-203, 210-213, 224-225, 227-228, 255-259, 263, 278, 339, 443.

Fillmore, Millard Powers, 46, 57, 160, 171, 254, 388, 417n

Fillmore, Nathaniel, 2, 3, 5, 7, 10, 394, 444

Fillmore, Phoebe, 2, 3

Fillmore, Hall and Haven, law firm, 55-56

Fire-eaters, 254, 270, 274-275, 276, 287, 289, 290, 337

Fish, Hamilton, Weed's nominee for governor, 189; a possible senator, 195; governor of New York, 203, 236; Senator, 281-285, 364-365

Flagg, Azariah C., 169

"Fiscal bank," see Bank of United States

Follett, Oran, political principles, 61; Committee of Seventy, 67; move to Sandusky, 87; quoted on Fillmore's withdrawal, 341-342; looking toward a new party, 343, 346

Foote, Henry S., 219, 232

Foote, Thomas M., relationship with Fillmore, 88, 333-334, 337, 346-347; quoted on Fillmore's moral obligation to run for office, 347; accompanied Fillmore to Europe, 397; University of Buffalo, 438

Fonseca, Gulf of, 297

France, 310-312, 324, 326

Free Masonry, see Masons, Order of

Free Soil party, 183-184, 189, 216, 401; see also Liberty party, "Conscience" Whigs

Free-Soilers, 193-194, 209, 216, 231, 254, 257, 258, 259, 400, 404

Frelinghuysen, Theodore, 151, 153

Fremont, John C., 404, 411-413

Fugitive Slave Act, 252, 265, 268-273, 277, 280, 281, 287, 338, 351, 421

Fuller, Jerome, relationship with Fillmore, 212, 226-227, 258, 261, 284, 285; quoted on the use of patronage, 335n; appointment blocked by Fish, 365n

G

Garay, Don Jose de, 305-307, 308

Garland, William, quoted on Fillmore's administration, 349

Garnett, Muscoe R. H., 226

Garrison, William Lloyd, 141

Germain, Rollin, 432

Giddings, Josuah, 351

Globe, see Washington Globe

Great Britain, Canadian revolt, 107-108; China trade, 295; Cuba, 324-326; Fillmore's visit in England, 397-399; Hawaii, 310, 312; Panama Canal interests, 297, 300, 302-305; Panama railroad, 301; trade rivalry, 301; Trent affair, 426

Great Lakes, 12, 161-164, 293

Greytown, see San Juan

Graham, William Alexander, Secretary of the Navy in Fillmore's cabinet, 244, 319-320; Vice-Presidential nominee, 362, 365; campaigned for Fillmore in 1856, 413

Granger, Francis, 150; early career, 32-33; defeated for governor, 63; failed to win nomination, 98-99; estimated abolitionist strength, 101; and Weed, 102; Postmaster-General, 117; conflict with Clay, 120; resigned cabinet post, 121, 122n; Congress, 128; chairman Whig convention at Syracuse, 259; led convention revolt, 260; "Silver Grey," 264, 283

Granville, Lord, 304

Greeley, Horace, endorsed Fillmore for Vice-President, 149; quoted on Silas Wright, 155; and Weed, 165, 179; favored Taylor over Clay, 189; rescued from Paris jail, 399

Greeley, Phillip, Jr., 336

Grinnell, Moses H., 279, 360

Gross, Ezra, 30

Grosvenor, Seth, 437

H

Hale, John P., 174

Hall, Nathan K., early life and education, 51-52; Fillmore's law partner, 51; qualities as a lawyer, 53; office holder and public servant, 54; efforts to improve schools, 54; master in chancery, 55; and western New York lands, 85; fought for river and harbor bill, 164; nominated for Congress, 166; quoted on Weed's dictatorship, 213, 224; Postmaster-General, 245, 279, 335; absent from convention, 355; district judgeship, 364, 365n; advised Fillmore, 367; accompanied Fillmore on southern tour, 387-388; a founder University of Buffalo, 438-439

Hall, Willis, 148, 149, 150

Hamilton, Alexander, 125

Hamilton, General James, 288

Hammond, J. H., 207

Hargous, Peter A., 306, 309

Harper, James, 156

Harris, Ira, 166, 167

Harrison, William Henry, nomination, 71, 86, 90; candidacy, 105, 107, 110; president, 116-117; death, 118

Haven, Solomon G., member of law firm with Fillmore and Hall, 52, 170-171, 279; qualities as a lawyer, 53; public servant and office holder, 54; mayor, 166; attended Whig convention 1852, 355; and Know Nothings, 393

Hawaii, 295, 310-312, 318

Heacock, Reuben B., 61

Herrera, President of Mexico, 307

Holland Purchase, 89

Holley, Myron, 143

Home League, 127-128; see also Tariff

Hone, Philip, 30, 60, 78-79, 204, 230

Houston, Sam, 234

Hoxie, Joseph, 30, 60, 321-325

Hubbard, Samuel, 365

Hughes, Bishop John, 137, 139, 204, 377-378

Hulsemann, J. G., 327-328

Hunt, Washington, 152, 153, 195; anti-slavery, 178; nominated for governor of New York, 259, 261n, 263, 264-265, 266; governor-elect, 279; governor, 286

Hunter, William, 328

I

Immigration, 290, 376, 378-379

Independent Treasury, 94-97

Industrialization, 125, 126, 229, 290

Ingersoll, J. R., 365n

Intelligencer, see National Intelligencer

Irving, Washington, 365, 387

J

Jackson, Andrew, 25, 62, 79, 86, 118, 399; popular appeal, 59, 61; and Webster, 69, 71-72; opposition to Bank of United States, 72-73, 77-78, 92, 95; "executive usurpation," 83n

Japanese Islands, 313-317

Jenkins, Charles J., 276, 413

Jewett, Elam, R., 397

Johnson, Andrew, 441-442

Johnson, Reverdy, 236, 413

Jones, James C., 413

"Juridicus" (Fillmore), 67

K

Kansas-Nebraska Bill, 383, 386, 389, 391, 401

Kellogg, P. V., 202

Kennedy, John P., 128, 365

Ketchum, Hiram, 30, 60, 319

Ketchum, Morris, 226, 264

Ketchum, William, 204, 257n

Kettel, Thomas Prentice, 226

King, T. Butler, 128, 200

Know Nothings, see Native American party

Knower, Benjamin, 73, 77

Kossuth, Louis, 327-332

L

Labor, 29, 35, 37, 128, 339, 391

Lane, Henry Smith, 128

Law, George, 324-325

Lawrence, riots in, 410

Lawrence, Abbott, and merchant interests, 164, 180-181; and Cotton Whigs, 174; Vice-Presidential nominee, 181-182, 185; Minister to Great Britain, 302-303

Lawrence, Amos A., 412

Lawrence, C. W., 79

Lawrence, J. L., 30

Lawrence, W. B., 60

Leopold Society, 138

Le Roy, Jacob, 88-89, 98
Levin, Lewis, 343
Lewis, William D., 336
Letcher, Robert, 307
Liberty party, 142, 143, 152, 174
Lincoln, Abraham, 422-423, 429-430
Lobos Islands, 318-320
"Locofocos," see Democratic party
Lopez, Narciso, 322-324
Lord, Mrs. John C., 442
Love, Thomas C., 92
Lyman, Samuel P., 279-280

M

Madisonian, 114, 121
Mangum, Willie P., 90, 175, 413
Mann, A. Dudley, 327
Marcy, William L., 18, 28; governor of New York, 84, 97
Mason and Slidell incident, 426
Masons, Order of, 17-19, 24, 34, 59, 87
Marshall, Humphrey, 235
Maxwell, Hugh, 182, 202, 258, 261, 325; instigates meeting of New York merchants, 264-265; opposition to Weed, 278, 279, 280, 283, 286, 335n; Union Safety Committee, 282, 342, 344
McClellan, George B., 429
McClernand, John A., 222-223
McComber, Charles, 396
McKennon, Thomas M. T., 246
McLean, John, 62, 70-71, 86, 90, 176, 179
McLeod, Alexander, 144
Meredith, William M., and Taylor administration, 194, 199, 200, 201 202, 204; Secretary of the Treasury, 213, 229, 236, 246
Mexican War, 162, 174, 175, 321, 322
Mexico, 296, 305, 307-309
Military Tract, 2, 3
Minturn, Robert B. 279
Missouri Compromise of 1820, 383, 404
Mitchell, Charles Francis, 110
Monroe, Col., 233-234, 240, 250

Morgan, William, 17-18, 32, 34-35
Morse, Samuel F. B., 138, 377-378
Mosquito Indians, 297, 304
Mower, J. B., 338

N

Nashville Convention, see Southern Convention
"Nationals," 215-219, 220, 223, 231, 235, 247-248, 287, 382; see also Whig party
National Banking Act, 172
National Intelligencer, 114, 236
National Republican party, 5, 59-60, 61, 62-64, 67; Committee of Seventy, 67; alliance with Antimasonic party, 75, 89; in Erie County, 23-24, 25, 81; in New York City, 76, 78-79; in New York state, 30-31; remnants of, 106
Native American party, 138-140, 187; changed name to American Democratic party, 385; convention of 1855, 401-402, 408; Know Nothings, 384-385, 391-392, 395, 400, 401, 402-403, 409; see also Nativism
Nativism, early movement, 138-139, 142, 155, 156-157; later movement, 343, 378-379, 381-382, 385, 389-390, 391, 394, 396, 402, 408
Nelson, Samuel, 18
New Granada, Treaty of, 296, 302
New Mexico, 215-217, 219, 220, 231, 233, 234-236, 240, 249, 252, 259, 260, 274
New York *American*, 60
New York City Public School Society, 139
New York *Commercial Advertiser*, 60
New York *Courier and Inquirer*, 63, 79
New York *Express*, 320
New York Protestant Association, 138
New York State: banking in, 73-74, 77-78, 82-83, 95-96; safety fund system, 74, 92, 172; canal system, 11, 35, 41, 49-50, 74, 96, 165, 168, 169, 172, 278, 293, 426, 432, 433; comptroller, powers of, 168-169; constitution of 1846, 168; schools, 96-97; school law, 139n

New York *State Register*, 212, 333

New York *Tribune*, 149

Newton, Isaac, 395

Nicaragua, 296, 297, 302-305

Nullification, 69, 118, 127, 270

O

Ogden, David B., 30, 60

Omnibus Bill, 232-233, 235, 247-250

"Open door" policy, 310-311

Oregon, 152, 295, 296

Order of the Star Spangled Banner, 343, 379-381, 396, 400

Oswego Canal Company, 140

P

Palmerston, Lord, 298, 303-304, 320

Panama Canal, 296-298, 300, 302-305, 318

"Panic Session," 71, 76; *see also* Bank of United States

Patronage, 102, 201, 203, 255, 264, 335, 335n, 336n

Pearce, James A., and bill for "Fiscal Bank," 120; refused cabinet post, 245; and Omnibus Bill, 249-250; and Texas boundary bill, 250-251; interest in Congressional Library, 245, 365; supported Buchanan for President, 413

Perry, Commodore Matthew C., 312-313, 315-317

"Pet" Bank System, 72, 92, 94, 95; *see also* Bank of United States

Petigru, James L., 274

Philadelphia *Daily Sun*, 339, 343, 350

Pierce, Franklin, candidate for President, 353, 363; inauguration, 372-374; and Conkling Treaty, 309; administration, 383, 404; passed by for renomination, 405; quoted on Compromise of 1850, 373

Polk, James K., administration policies, 161-162, 296; vetoed river and harbor bill, 164, 178; attempt to purchase Cuba, 321-322

Porter, Peter B., 23, 30, 36, 61, 67, 109

Poughkeepsie *Eagle*, 147

Powers, Abigail, *see* Fillmore, Abigail Powers

Preston, William B., 194, 199, 200, 201, 205, 236

Pratt, Hiram, 92, 93

Protectionism, *see* Tariff

Public lands, federal income from the sale of, 124, 129

Putnam, James O., 264, 421

R

Railroads: federal aid to, 124, 294; Erie, 289; New England, 290; proposed Central America Isthmus, 296, 301-302, 305-309, 318; Chicago and Rock Island, 388; Buffalo, New York and Philadelphia, 433

Rathbun, Benjamin, 91-92

Raymond, Henry J., 211, 281

Redfield, Herman J., 88-89, 98

Regency, *see* Albany Regency

Religion, and Antimasonry, 66; Anti-Catholic movements, 139, 375-381; church property, struggle over, 389; Fillmore's position on religion and politics, 407-408; in New York politics, 137-140, 143; in national politics, 408-409; riots over Cardinal Bedini, 389-390

Rice, Asa, 12

Robinson, Dr. Charles, 410

Rochester *Antimasonic Enquirer*, 20, 22

Rochester *Telegraph*, 21, 22

Rogers, Bowen and Rogers, law firm of, 55

Rough and Ready Clubs, 187, 339

S

Safety Fund System, *see* New York State banking

Salas, General Mariano de, 306-307

Salisbury, Hezekiah A., 67, 87

Saltonstall, James S., 128

San Juan (Greytown), 297-298, 299, 302, 303, 304

Sandwich Islands, *see* Hawaii

Santa Anna, President of Mexico, 305-306

Sargent, Nathan, 121

Savannah *Republican*, 127, 176, 183

Scott, Winfield, and Canadian revolt, 107-108; Whig "Stalking horse," 108-109; advised strengthening fortifications at Charleston, 275; Whig presidential candidate, 336, 339, 350, 352, 353, 356-362 *passim*

Sellstedt, Lars Gustaf, 435

Secession, agitation for, 274-277, 287; South Carolina trend toward, 420, 422; *see also* Fire-eaters

Severance, Luther, 311-312

Seward, Alexander, 212

Seward, William Henry, Antimason, 83-84; defeated for governor, 84; Whig candidate for governor, 97-100; elected, 101-102; turns patronage over to Weed, 102; relationship with Clay, 109; relationship with Weed, 117, 149, 182, 404; governor, 138-139, 143-145; loses gubernatorial election 1842, 148; unsuccessful in obtaining Vice-Presidential nomination, 186; struggle for seat in Senate, 195, 196; and Taylor administration, 199-205, 214; political war with Fillmore, 255-257, 259-260, 351; stand on Compromise of 1850, 257-258, 278; and Louis Kossuth, 330-331; supported Scott for President, 339, 352, 354, 357; re-election to Senate, 402-403; reversal of policy, 421

Seymour, Horatio, 393

Sherman, William Tecumseh, 441

Silver Greys, 258-260, 261, 262-265, 278, 282-283, 344, 384-385, 400-402, 403, 408

Slavery, 100, 106, 128, 141, 162, 208, 215, 216, 219-220, 222-223, 224, 225, 226, 229-230, 233, 240, 241, 247, 259, 260, 262, 263, 271, 277, 286-287, 321-322, 338, 364, 367, 366-370, 383, 391, 403, 405, 410

Sloo, A. G., 309

Smith, Gerritt, 140-141

Smith, Shelden, 61

Society of St. Tammany, *see* Tammany Hall

Solomon, H. M., 371

Southern Convention: planned, 207, 218, 226; first convention at Nashville, 234, 240; second convention at Nashville, 274, 275, 276

Spain, *see* Cuba

Specie Circular, 92

Spencer, Ambrose, 30

Spencer, John C., 38, 102, 103, 104, 144

Spoils system, *see* patronage

Stability of the Union, (Kettel) 226

Stanley, Edward, 236

Steamships, 299-300, 315

Stephens, Alexander H., southern Whig leader, 175, 205; strategy against Taylor, 208-210, 214, 218, 222-223, 236, 246; for Omnibus, 232, 233; quoted on Texas, 240; supported Compromise of 1850, 276

Stevens, Samuel, 35

Stevens, Thaddeus, 81

Stewart, Andrew, 246

Stockton, Robert F., 300

Stuart, Alexander H. H., 120, 128, 246, 274, 290; quoted on Fillmore, 334-335

Sub-treasury system, *see* Independent Treasury

Sumner, Charles, 174, 410-411

T

Tammany Hall, 28, 60, 137, 138, 139

Tallmadge, Nathaniel P., 97-98

Tappan, Lewis, 141, 230

Tariff, Compromise of 1833, 115, 123, 127, 132-133

Tariff of 1842, 132-136, 146, 161, 178, 185, 214

Tariff policies, 123, 125-130

Taylor, Zachary, nominated by Whigs for President, 176, 180, 181, 184, 188, 189, 339; also nominee of Charleston Democrats, 188; advisors, 194; inauguration, 197-199; message to Congress, 215-216; territories, issue of administration, 200, 205, 207-209, 214,

215-223, 231-237, 240, 246; foreign policy, 322, 327; relationship with Fillmore, 213; relationship with Weed, 203, 224, 236, 237; death, 238-239

Tehuantepec Isthmus, 296, 305, 307, 309

Ten Nights in a Bar Room (Arthur), 291

Territories, *see* Taylor, California, New Mexico, Texas, Utah

Texas, 152, 153, 216, 217, 219, 220, 223, 231, 233-236, 240, 248, 250-252, 274, 321

Thompson, Smith, 30

Throop, Enos, 32

Ticknor, George, 400

Tigre Island, 297

Timon, Bishop, 408

Toombs, Robert, conversion from nullification, 127-128; southern Whig leader, 175, 205; strategy against Taylor, 208-210, 214, 218, 222-223; 246; for Omnibus Bill, 232; remonstrated with Taylor over New Mexico, 235-236; supported Compromise of 1850, quoted on Taylor administration, 217

Tracy, Albert H., early career, 31; nominated for New York state senate, 32, 35, 68n; did not favor Seward, 100, 102; sought comptrollership, 103-104

Trade, foreign, 6, 135n, 295, 298-299, 310, 313-314, 318

Tyler, John, principles, 118; fight over bank bill, 119-122; fight over Tariff, 130-132; accused of "executive usurpation," 132; cabinet resigned, 121, 144; repudiated by Whig party, 122

U

Ullman, Daniel, 258, 390, 393

"Underground railroad," 271-272

Union Association, *see* Union Committee

Union Committee, 78-79, 80, 83, 266, 282, 283, 335n, 342-345 *passim*

Union Safety Committee, *see* Union Committee

Union, Past, Present and *Future, How It Works and How to Save It* (Garrett), 226

Union and Southern Rights Party, 276

Unity Conference, 344

Utica *Gazette,* 212

Utah, 222, 250, 259, 260, 274

V

Van Buren, Martin, 25, 31, 70, 73, 90, 107, 148, 155, 398, 420; resigns as governor for cabinet post 28; political talent, 30; Vice-President, 85, 86; President, 94; bank policy, 94-97; depression measures, 115-116, 119, 123; no-annexation policy, 152

Varnum, J. B., 280, 282-283, 284

Verplanck, Gulian, C., 60, 79, 80, 83, 84, 117

Vinton, Samuel Finley, 244

W

Wade-Davis bill, 429

Walker, William, 305

Washington *Globe,* 96n, 114

Webb, James Watson, 63, 79, 182, 211, 342, 360

Webster, Daniel, 239, 270, 279; interested in Fillmore, 69; made national bank a campaign issue, 71; appeared at Castle Garden celebration, 79-80; abandoned bank issue, 83, 83n; an unlikely presidential candidate for 1836, 86, 87, 90, 105, 106; struggle with Clay for Whig party leadership, 116-118; sought commercial privileges with China, 135n; asked dismissal of case against McLeod, 144; supported Cotton Whigs, 174; famous speech for the Union, 229-230; supported Omnibus Bill, 232, 248; Secretary of State, Fillmore's administration, 242-243; aided Fillmore in making cabinet appointments, 243-244, 246; active in Texas boundary dispute, 250; ill health while in office, 301, 319; policy in Central America, 303-304, 307; opposed annexation of Hawaiian Islands, 310-311; favored seeking commerce with Japan, 315; promised United States protection to New York merchants trading with Lobos Islands, 319-320; policy with relation to Cuba,

321, 325; policy in the matter of Louis Kossuth, 328-331; sought presidential nomination in 1852, 338-341, 353; sought to form a national Union Party, 342-343; failure to obtain nomination, 355-363; death, 365; quoted on Japan, 315; quoted on the office of President, 340

Webster, Fletcher, 135n, 412

Weed, Thurlow, attempt to re-elect J. Q. Adams 20-21; personal qualities, 31, 60, 178; education in printing and politics, 21-22; Antimason, 24, 66; created Albany *Evening Journal*, 36; effort to convert Clay to Antimasonry, 63n; helped to establish Whig party 63, 80, 80n; espoused political future of Seward, 83-84, 98-99, 117, 148-149, 168, 179; patronage policy, 102, 143, 195, 278; maneuvered against Clay, 109; opposed Whig-American Republican alliance, 139; early political relationship with Fillmore, 85, 108, 165-166, 180, 182, 189-190; effort to undermine Fillmore's influence in Taylor administration, 194-196, 201-205, 236-237; sponsored Ira Harris, 166; foresaw antislavery issue, 178; struggled for party control in 1848, 179-183, 189-191; pushed for endorsement of Wilmot Proviso, 224-225; challenged Compromise settlement, 256-258, 278; determined to keep New York Whigs committed to free soil ideology, 257; continued political war against Fillmore, 255, 259-261, 267, 279-286; called bolting Whigs "Silver Greys," 261; blamed New York merchants for southern boycott, 262; political relationship with Hamilton Fish, 189, 203, 236, 281-282, 283, 284-285; disregard for sectional peace, 335; trip to Europe, 339, 354; activity in the coalescing of new parties, 385, 401-404; policy of conciliation, 421-422

Wheaton, Henry, 30

Whig party: 77, 79-90, 97, 99-100, 101, 105, 114, 116-119, 122, 126, 130-132, 151, 158, 161, 167-168, 173-176, 183-186, 189, 243, 257, 259, 263, 264-265, 278-279, 340, 341-342, 344, 345-347, 349, 350, 352,

354-361, 363, 382, 384-385, 38,6 392-393, 411, 412-413, 421; and American Republican party, 139; and antislavery issue, beginning of, 174, 175, 178, 186; and Bank of United States, 77, 82-83; "Conscience" Whigs, 174, 181, 384-385, 402-403; "Cotton" Whigs, 174; economic program, 118-119, 122-123, 183, 342, 346; and "Know Nothings," *see* Native American party; and Nativism, 138-139, 157n; *see also* Native American party; "National" Whigs, 215-218, 222, 232, 342, 343, 348, 352, 354, 362, 381, 382, 384-385, 386, 391, 402, 404, 411, 420; in New York City, 83-84, 138, 139, 145, 156-158, 165, 280-281, 342, 343, 345, *see also* Tammany Hall; in New York state, 157-158, 157n, 165, 189-191, 257-260, 283-285, 352-353, 371; "Silver Greys" bolt Whig party, 258-260, *see also* Silver Greys; in southern States, 175-176, 178-179, 183, 193, 205, 208-210, 218, 276, 287-288, 337, 371; "Young Indians," 176, *see also* Whigs in southern States; "Woolly Heads," *see* "Conscience" Whigs

White, Hugh Lawson, 86, 87, 90

White, John, 118

Whittlesey, Frederick, 104

Wilkins, Samuel J., 155

Williams, Elisha, 30

Wilmot, David, 175

Wilmot Proviso, 175, 178, 200, 205, 224, 421

Wilson, Henry, 401, 404

Winthrop, Robert, 174, 209, 242-243, 412

Wirt, William, 62-63

Wood, Walter, 7-9

Woodbury, Levi, 115

Working Men's Party, *see* Labor

Wright, Silas, 28, 155, 158, 167

Y

Young, John, 61, elected governor, 166-168; opposed to Weed, 182, 202, 258, 278, 279, 280, 283, 335n; and Union Safety Committee, 282, 342, 344